# Getting Jesus Right

*James A. Beverley and Craig A. Evans*

"The authors deal with every topic, from ancient manuscripts to terrorism, from Jesus to Muhammad, from the Crusades to colonialism, with accuracy, originality and courage. *Getting Jesus Right* is a provocative and powerful work."

— David Cook
Associate professor of Religion, Rice University, and author of
*Understanding Jihad*

"Reza Aslan has won renown for telling the mainstream media what it wants to hear, while his media sycophants never challenge his statements, no matter how wildly false and inaccurate they are. But now he has definitively been exposed. This book is a scholarly and devastating critique of Aslan's views on Jesus and Islam."

— Robert Spencer
*New York Times* bestselling author of *The Politically Incorrect Guide to Islam (and the Crusades)* and *The Truth About Muhammad*

"Essential reading for anybody who wishes to understand and respond to the Islamic argument about Jesus and Christianity. We are far too quiet and ill-informed; it is time to be equipped and to be able to proclaim truth to all and not just some people. A vital book."

— Michael Coren
Columnist, author, public speaker, and radio and television talk show host

"As a former Muslim, I know how easy it is to get Jesus wrong, which is why *Getting Jesus Right* is so important. Scholarly yet readable, Evans and Beverley respectfully challenge us to take an unflinching look at history. And they especially shine when bringing the real Jesus of history into focus. For Christians and non-Christians alike, I enthusiastically recommend *Getting Jesus Right*."

— Abdu Murray
Author of *Grand Central Question—Answering the Critical Concerns of the Major Worldviews*

"The squaring of faith with historical research is at least as much of a challenge for Muslims as it has long been for Christians; James Beverley and Craig Evans, in this learned and wide-ranging book, demonstrate exactly why."

— Tom Holland
Author of *In the Shadow of the Sword*

# GETTING
# J E S U S
## RIGHT

HOW MUSLIMS GET JESUS AND ISLAM WRONG

JAMES A. BEVERLEY AND CRAIG A. EVANS

INCLUDES A CRITIQUE OF REZA ASLAN'S *ZEALOT* AND *NO GOD BUT GOD*

CASTLE QUAY BOOKS

# GETTING JESUS RIGHT: HOW MUSLIMS GET JESUS AND ISLAM WRONG

Copyright © 2015 James A. Beverley & Craig A. Evans
All rights reserved
Printed in Canada
International Standard Book Number 978-1-927355-45-9 soft cover
ISBN 978-1-927355-47-3 Hard Cover
ISBN 978-1-927355-46-6 EPUB

Published by:
Castle Quay Books
Lagoon City, Brechin, Ontario
Tel: (416) 573-3249
E-mail: info@castlequaybooks.com   www.castlequaybooks.com

Edited by Marina Hofman Willard, and Lori Mackay
Cover design by Burst Impressions
Printed at Essence Printing, Belleville, Ontario

**Library and Archives Canada Cataloguing in Publication**

**Beverley, James A., Evans, Craig A., authors**
      **Getting Jesus Right : How Muslims Get Jesus**
**and Islam Wrong / Craig A. Evans, James A. Beverley.**

**Includes bibliographical references.**
**Issued in print and electronic formats.**
**ISBN 978-1-927355-45-9 (pbk.).--ISBN 978-1-927355-46-6 (epub)**

      **1. Jesus Christ. 2. Islam. 3. Aslan, Reza--Criticism and**
**interpretation. I. Beverley, James A. II. Title.**

BT301.3.E93 2013          232.9'01          C2013-906619-5
                                              C2013-906620-9

CASTLE QUAY BOOKS

In memory of Jennifer Susan Keirstead
Daughter of David and Darlene Keirstead
March 3, 1993–September 6, 2014
Memories of fun times, your loving spirit,
your amazing creativity and your fabulous smile
will hold us
Until we meet in that place where God will wipe away all tears from our eyes

(Revelation 21:4)

*Was Jesus a muslim? pg 166-167
No, and neither were His followers

# Table of Contents

# Introduction

P eace on planet Earth depends on Christians and Muslims. It is quite simple. There are over 2 billion Christians on planet Earth and 1.6 billion Muslims. If demographic trends continue, followers of these two world religions will make up more than 50 percent of humanity. As Hans Küng has stated eloquently, if these two groups don't learn to live with each other and with other religions or philosophies, we are doomed as God's creatures to lives of discord, hatred, bloodshed and terror.

Given numbers alone, understanding Islam and Christianity is an imperative.

The necessity is made more acute by the tensions of our current world, particularly given the failure of the Arab Spring and the rise in 2014 of the Islamic State and its brutal takeover of large areas of Iraq and Syria. For the first time in recent history an Islamic caliphate has been announced and a new caliph is now celebrated by radical Muslims from all over the world. The familiar questions are back: What is jihad? Is Islam a religion of peace? Does Islam liberate women? Is shariah law the right path for humanity?

Behind these issues lie fundamental matters about the nature of God, how Christian and Muslim Scripture should be evaluated, what a proper assessment of Muhammad is and how one gets accurate information about Jesus. In spite of common ground between Christians and Muslims, their respective religions offer largely different views on these four general matters and the related subtopics noted previously. At one level, one must choose Christianity or Islam, the Bible or the Qur'an, Muhammad or Jesus. While binary options are not always necessary and nuance is usually crucial, in this case a choice must be made. Both Islam and Christianity demand either a yes or a no: one cannot choose both together. They are largely irreconcilable religions and worldviews.

*Getting Jesus Right* is an extended argument that humanity should choose Christian faith for spiritual truth, not Islam. We argue that Islam makes major errors in its understanding of God, teachings on Jesus, views on salvation, attitudes about Muhammad, stress on the Qur'an, downplaying of the Bible and ethical guidelines for humanity. These flaws in Islam have real-life, negative consequences for the Muslim world, for Muslim families, for Muslim men, women and children and for those who do not follow Islam. Our book, then, is an invitation for the Muslim world and everyone else to consider the Christian gospel of Jesus Christ as the true and better alternative to Islam.

We are not naïve. We know that the vast majority of Muslims reject our fundamental beliefs and our arguments. For Muslims, Islam is the one true religion, Muhammad is the final prophet, the Qur'an is the eternal, perfect Word of God, Jesus is not the Son of God, and true liberation is achieved only through following the will of Allah. We recognize that Muslims believe we should abandon Christianity, submit to Allah as the one true God, follow Muhammad as the prophet of God and believe and obey the teachings of the Qur'an. We respectfully disagree, and our book tells why.

In defending Christian faith and offering our critique of Islam, we decided to use the work of a very popular Muslim writer as our way to examine key issues. In the summer of 2013, Reza Aslan, a former evangelical Christian, became a publishing sensation courtesy of a Fox News interview with him that went viral. Aslan was grilled over his new book, *Zealot,* which was his study of Jesus of Nazareth. Both of us wrote articles on Aslan and *Zealot* shortly after his interview. We decided quite quickly to expand our work into a book but with the added element of analyzing Aslan's popular apologetic for Islam called *No god but God* (now in a revised edition and published in several languages). While we deal with the basic subjects at the core of the Christian-Islam divide, there are some complicated topics left for future analysis (like the Israel-Palestinian conflict and the contours of Sufi Islam).

We chose Reza Aslan not because of his accuracy but because his ideas express well what so many believe and repeat about both Islam and Christianity. To be clear, in spite of his popularity with Muslims and with mainstream media, Reza Aslan is not the source to seek for careful, accurate, truthful information on Jesus. His book on Jesus is an academic failure, proof that distinguished publishers sometimes place sales above scholarship. Likewise, Reza Aslan's apologia for Islam is a failure. It is based on misleading argument, special pleadings, avoidance of crucial issues, misrepresentation of others, twisting of issues and hollow, unsupported assertions about Muhammad, the Qur'an, jihad and the treatment of women. Of course, it is hard to be totally wrong, so we celebrate his choice of moderate rather than radical Islam. We share his dislike for many Islamic traditions and shariah law, but in the end we believe Aslan should give up his inconsistent, mangled defense of Islam and return to the worship of Jesus of Nazareth as Savior and Lord. He owes the world an apology for his reckless views on Jesus and his weak arguments for Muhammad as prophet and the Qur'an as God's word. The same holds for his distorted understandings of jihad and his strained reasoning that Islam is the best path to liberate women.

We do not expect the assertions of our introduction to convince anyone. This is simply laying out our general positions. The rest of the book provides the evidence that clearly supports our views. Did we say clearly? Yes. On the matters we address, we believe that the evidence is overwhelming that Reza Aslan and the vast majority of Muslims do not get Jesus or Islam right. In terms of specifics, the New Testament is the place to turn for accurate information about Jesus (see chapters 1–5), not the Qur'an or Islamic tradition (chapters 11–13). The historical worth of the New Testament is excellent, and the manuscript tradition supporting the New Testament is superb. In contrast, in spite of the highest regard for Muhammad in Islam (chapter 6), the historical reliability of Muhammad is doubtful (chapter 7). Likewise, the traditional Muslim portrait of the prophet is morally questionable (chapter 8). The Qur'an is not divine, as Muslims believe (chapter 9), but is a flawed human product that contains mistaken teaching about Jesus, huge distortions of the Bible and unethical guidelines, and all in a confusing, disorderly and often nasty text (chapter 10).

When the traditional Islamic view of Muhammad gets combined with traditional Islamic interpretations of shariah law and morality, we often get the consequent mistreatment of women (chapter 14) and the emphasis on jihad in terms of military conquest, dominion over non-Muslims and the harsh binary division of humanity into the Abode of Islam and the Abode of War (chapter 15). This goes a long way to explain the military expansion of Islam after the prophet gained power in Medina, the Arab conquests after the death of the prophet and the reality of Islamic imperialism ever since.

Three caveats are in order here. First, we ask readers not to use the bare assertions of this introduction as grounds for aligning us with extreme and ill-informed critiques of Islam. For example, we do not share the view of some right-wing critics that radical Islam (aka jihadist Islam) is obviously the true understanding of Islam. Does this mean we believe Islam is a religion of peace? We will save that question for later. For now, we gladly acknowledge that most Muslims today are deeply disturbed by Abu Bakr al-Baghdadi and his Islamic State (aka ISIS, ISIL). From another angle, while we do not believe that Islam offers women true liberation, we do not think that every Muslim woman who veils herself is a slave. The veil can be a liberating reality for Muslim women in our sex-saturated cultures, West and East. Likewise, our hatred of Islamic jihad interpreted as conquest and terrorism should not be taken to mean that we have a Pollyanna view of Western societies or of British, German, French, Dutch, Russian, American or other non-Muslim imperialisms.

Second, our strong critique of Islam and our confidence in Christian faith does not mean that there are no serious problems in the Bible or in under-standing the Christian view of God, the nature of humanity, the extent of sal-vation, the problem of pain and evil and so on. Nevertheless, in spite of ambiguities and problems, we assert that Christian faith in Jesus of Nazareth offers true liberation and salvation to all humans.

Third, we ask readers to pay special attention to the fact that the concerns of our book in relation to Muhammad are directed to the traditional interpreta-tion of him and not to Muhammad directly. We do not believe that anyone can credibly describe or reach the historical Muhammad. We do argue, however, that the traditionalist perspective creates many of the moral complications about the prophet and, consequently, that Muslims like Reza Aslan need to learn how to better handle these serious issues for the survival of a healthy Islam.

In our respective disciplines we are used to debate and polemic, but we have written this book to inform, not inflame, even when we offer blunt ver-dicts about Reza Aslan's numerous errors in scholarship on both Jesus and Islam. The same applies to our critique of Islam. Our concerns about the tra-ditional view of Muhammad and the standard Islamic view of the Qur'an are raised because of our serious, lengthy academic study of the historical Jesus, Christian tradition and Islamic faith. Given this, our book invites rational examination. We remain open to correction of any errors of fact or interpre-tation. And we are eager to engage in debate on the matters we address. Since there is a rich philosophical tradition in Islamic thought, we hope that Muslims will meet our perspectives and evidence with reasoned argument.

As the authors of the book we alone are responsible for its content. But we have many people to thank, some of whom are listed. Foremost among all, we thank our respective wives (Gloria Beverley and Ginny Evans) for enduring another book project. We also express our appreciation to Tyndale Seminary and Acadia Divinity College for consistently supporting our research in general and this project in particular. We remain appreciative to Brett Potter and Dwight Crowell for helping on various research tasks. It has been a pleasure to work with our publisher, Larry Willard, and his wife, Marina, on all the details that go into getting a book into print.

Lastly, readers will note the dedication page in memory of Jennifer Keirstead, Professor Beverley's niece, who died unexpectedly on September 6, 2014, at the age of 21. A month before her death she sat beside him at a baby dedication and sang with others "Jesus loves me, this I know, for the Bible tells me so." We offer this book in the unwavering conviction of the truth of that simple affirmation.

*James A. Beverley*
*Craig A. Evans*

Note: For spelling alternatives, we usually adopt the spelling *Muhammad* for the prophet and *Qur'an* for Islamic Scripture. We use different translations of the Qur'an but highly recommend Arthur Droge's new annotated version (Equinox, 2014). Generally, we avoid diacritical marks. To contact authors write professorjamesbeverley@gettingjesusright.com and professorcraigevans@gettingjesusright.com.

## A Thank-You to Colleagues, Friends and Fellow Scholars

We express our appreciation to Tyndale Seminary (President Gary Nelson, Vice-President Janet Clark, and Vice-President Randy Henderson) for funding three research trips for Professor Beverley over the last several years in relation to his ongoing research on Islam. We also thank Dave Collison, a close friend of Professor Beverley, who helped cover costs on one research trip in February and March 2014. These forays have sometimes included interviews or contact by phone and email (Robert Hoyland, Kevin Van Bladel, Herbert Berg, David Cook and Dan Brubaker, for example) and also face-to-face contact with other great scholars of Islam and related fields, including Hans Küng (Germany), Patricia Crone (USA), Lutz Richter-Bernburg (Germany), Frank Peters (USA), Efraim Karsh (England), Josef van Ess (Germany), Christopher Tyerman (England), Michael Cook (USA), Andrew Rippin (Canada), Gerald Hawting (England) and Angelika Neuwirth (Germany), among others.

Professor Neuwirth initiated a visit for Professor Beverley to her Corpus Coranicum project at the Free University of Berlin. The Corpus Coranicum is probably the most significant academic project on the Qur'an in history. Thanks to Professor Neuwirth and to three researchers at the Coranicum (Yousef Kouriyhe, Tobias Jocham and Laura Hinrichsen) for their assistance.

Professor Beverley is grateful to informed friends who helped him on various debatable issues in Islamic studies and the study of religion. Among them are Jay Smith, Wafik Wahba, Sam Solomon, Andy Bannister, Eileen Barker, Bob Morris, Gordon Nickel, Tom Holland, Tony Costa, Keith Small, Rick Love, Don Wiebe, Chad Hillier, Robert Spencer, J. Gordon Melton, Daveed Gartenstein-Ross, Keith Small and Massimo Introvigne. Professor Beverley is also grateful to two Muslim friends, Muhammad Iqbal Al-Nadvi and Mohammed Atieque (leaders in Canada's Islamic community), for many hours of conversation.

We also thank President Harry Gardner and the Divinity College of Acadia University for its generous support of Professor Evans' research, which has made possible travel to scholarly conferences as well as to archaeological excavations in Israel. Professor Evans is grateful to several scholars who over the years have served as dialogue partners and collaborators in various scholarly projects. These include Dale Allison of Princeton Theological Seminary, Bruce Chilton of Bard College, John and Adela Collins of Yale Divinity School, Jimmy Dunn of Durham University, Shimon Gibson of the University of North Carolina at Charlotte, Helmut Koester of Harvard Divinity School, Joel Marcus of Duke University, Scot McKnight of Northern Seminary and Armand Puig i Tàrrech of the Faculty of Theology of Catalonia in Barcelona. Heartfelt gratitude is also extended to wonderful colleagues of Professor Evans who in recent years have passed from this life. This includes Martin Hengel of Tübingen University, Bruce Metzger of Princeton Theological Seminary, Ben Meyer of McMaster University, and Graham Stanton of Cambridge University. The world of biblical studies and scholarship concerned with the historical Jesus and Christian origins is challenging and rewarding, but above all it is collegial.

# Chapter 1

# Are the New Testament Gospels Reliable?

*Jesus and His Followers*

A ll competent study of the historical Jesus begins with the four New Testament Gospels (Matthew, Mark, Luke and John). This is because they are the oldest sources and exhibit the features that historians expect of sources that are likely to provide reliable information. Of course, from time to time someone expresses skepticism about the New Testament Gospels. Sometimes Muslims express skepticism, especially when the Gospels and the Qur'an disagree. Therefore we begin our book by addressing the question of the reliability of the Gospels. Do these Gospels tell us the truth about Jesus, about what he taught, what he did, and what really happened to him?

One of the reasons it is good to begin with the Gospels is because they are biographies, based in part on eyewitness testimony. They were written 30 to 40 years after the time of Jesus, while some of his original followers were still living. The sources the Gospel writers drew upon circulated during this period, when the apostles of Jesus were active, teaching and giving leadership to the new movement. The Gospels are not biographies in the modern sense, but they are biographies as written in antiquity.[1] We have good reasons for believing that these Gospel biographies in fact provide us with a great deal of useful, reliable material.

We do not begin with the Qur'an, not only because it was written almost 600 years later than the New Testament Gospels, but because it really is not a historical narrative or a biography. There may well be historical and biographical data within it, the kind of data that historians can utilize, but the Qur'an as a whole is obviously not a historical work. Later in our book we shall look at what the Qur'an and other early Islamic sources have to say about Jesus.

In this chapter, we will treat two important questions that relate to the Gospels as potentially accurate and useful biographical histories concerning the life, teaching and activities of Jesus. The first question asks how close the New Testament Gospels are to the time of Jesus. The second question asks if the information in the Gospels is based on the testimony of eyewitnesses.

## How Close Are the New Testament Gospels to the Time of Jesus?

When it comes to comparing the Qur'an and the New Testament Gospels as potential historical sources, chronology and temporal proximity are very important. By temporal proximity we mean how close the written record is to the persons and events that the written record describes. Most historians agree that an account written within the lifetime of the participants and eyewitnesses is to be preferred to an account written centuries later. This is how historians think. They know, of course, that proximity is not the only criterion for evaluating the potential value a document has for historical research, but it is a very important criterion.

So when was the Qur'an written and when were the New Testament Gospels written? Muslims believe that Muhammad received the revelations that are in the Qur'an over a period of about 23 years, from AD 610 to 632, the year that he died. After Muhammad's death, written materials were gathered, and memorized material was committed to writing.[2] Within 20 to 70 years or so from the death of Muhammad, something pretty close to today's Qur'an ("recitation") had emerged. Most of the variant versions were gathered up and destroyed.[3] Given the close proximity of the Qur'an to the lifetime of Muhammad, it is reasonable to assume that this book contains some of what Muhammad taught, or at least something pretty close, though there are difficult historical issues involved.

Jesus of Nazareth was born shortly before the death of Herod the Great, the Idumean prince whom Rome appointed as king over the Jewish people in 39 or 40 BC. After defeating the last native Jewish ruler, in 36 or 37, Herod became king in fact. He died in either 4 BC or 1 BC, which means Jesus was born in either 4/5 BC or 2 BC.[4] Jesus began his public preaching and activities when he was about 30 (Luke 3:23). On the assumption that the death of Jesus took place in AD 30, it is likely that his ministry began in AD 28/29 and ran for about two years.[5]

Jesus was confessed by his followers as Israel's Messiah and as God's Son (e.g., Mark 8:29; Matt 16:16; Luke 9:20; John 1:49; 6:68–69). They and others regularly called Jesus *rabbi* and *teacher*. His closest followers were called *disciples*, which in Hebrew and in Greek means "learners." This is important to remember: Jesus was known as a *teacher* (which is also what "rabbi" more or less meant in the first century; see John 1:38) and his closest followers were *learners*. And what did they learn? They *learned* Jesus' teaching.

Judging by the length of the Gospels, the body of Jesus' teaching was not extensive, especially when we remember that there is a great deal of overlap among the first three Gospels: Matthew, Mark and Luke. It was not difficult for a devoted follower to commit to memory most or all of Jesus' teaching.[6] It is also believed that much of this teaching was committed to writing and would later be drawn upon by the authors of Matthew and Luke.[7]

Most scholars think Mark was the first Gospel to be written and circulated. According to Papias (c. AD 125)[8] the Gospel of Mark was composed by John Mark (Acts 12:12), who in the 50s and 60s AD assisted Peter, the lead disciple and apostle. Whereas the Gospel of Mark itself may have been penned in the mid- to late-60s, near the end of Nero's rule (AD 54–68), the reminiscences of Peter may well have circulated for many years earlier. Of course, Peter himself would have preached and taught everywhere he went until he was imprisoned and executed c. AD 65. We have reason to believe that a collection of Jesus' teachings also circulated perhaps as early as the 30s or 40s. Not too many years after the publication of Mark, the Gospels of Matthew and Luke were published and began to circulate. Later still, perhaps in the 90s (though some scholars argue for an earlier date), the Gospel of John was published.

## Oldest Synoptic Gospels Papyri

That the teaching of Jesus circulated and was known well before the Gospels were written is demonstrated by the appearance of his teaching and aspects of his life and death in earlier writings, such as the letters of Paul, the earliest of which were penned in the late 40s. Paul often alludes to Jesus' teaching, though sometimes he explicitly cites a "word" from the "Lord." We see an example of the latter when Paul charges the people in the church at Corinth not to seek divorce: "To the married I give charge, not I but the Lord, that the wife should not separate from her husband…and that the husband should not divorce his wife" (1 Cor 7:10–11). It is the *Lord*, Paul says, who has given command that divorce should be avoided. Paul has appealed to Jesus' teaching, which he gave in response to a question put to him concerning the divorce regulations in the Law of Moses (Matt 19:3–9; Mark 10:2–9). After quoting parts of Genesis 1:27 ("male and female he created them") and 2:24 ("they become one flesh"), Jesus asserts, "What therefore God has joined together, let not man put asunder" (Mark 10:6–9).

Another obvious Jesus tradition in one of Paul's letters is the citation of the Words of Institution, that is, the words Jesus spoke at the Last Supper (Matt 26:26–29 = Mark 14:22–25 = Luke 22:17–20). Paul finds it necessary to instruct the church at Corinth, reminding them of what Jesus did and said on that solemn occasion:

> For I received from the Lord what I also delivered to you, that the Lord Jesus on the night when he was betrayed took bread, and when he had given thanks, he broke it, and said, "This is my body which is for you. Do this in remembrance of me." In the same way also the cup, after supper, saying, "This cup is the new covenant in my blood. Do this, as often as you drink it, in remembrance of me." (1 Cor 11:23–25)

Paul's wording matches the form of the story in Luke very closely, which probably should not occasion surprise, for Luke the physician traveled with Paul on some of his missionary journeys.[9]

Of even greater significance is the appearance in Paul's letters of allusions to Jesus' teaching. When the apostle commands, "Bless those who persecute you; bless and do not curse them" (Rom 12:14), he has echoed the words of Jesus: "Love your enemies…bless those who curse you" (Luke 6:27–28); "Love your enemies and pray for those who persecute you" (Matt 5:44). When Paul speaks of mountain-moving faith, saying "if I have all faith, so as to remove mountains" (1 Cor 13:2), he has alluded to Jesus' famous teaching: "if you have faith…you will say to this mountain, 'Move from here to there,' and it will move" (Matt 17:20). When Paul warns the Christians of Thessalonica that "the day of the Lord will come like a thief in the night" (1 Thess 5:2), he has alluded to the warning Jesus gave his disciples: "if the householder had known in what part of the night the thief was coming, he would have watched" (Matt 24:43). Paul's admonition that the Thessalonian Christians "be at peace among" themselves (1 Thess 5:13) echoes Jesus' word to his disciples that they "be at peace with one another" (Mark 9:50).[10]

Paul is not the only New Testament writer to show familiarity with the teaching and stories of Jesus; the letter of James is filled with allusions to the teaching of Jesus.[11] There are important allusions in Hebrews and 1 and 2 Peter also. All of this shows that the teaching of Jesus was in circulation long before the Gospels were written, and even when the three early Gospels (Matthew, Mark, and Luke) were written, many of Jesus' original followers were still living and active in the Church.

What all of this means is that the four New Testament Gospels were written early enough to contain accurate data relating to the teaching and activities of Jesus. Three of the four Gospels were written within the lifespan of many of Jesus' original disciples. The Gospels were not written hundreds of years after the ministry of Jesus and the birth of the Church; they were written toward the end of the first generation. And the New Testament Gospels are not the oldest documents in the New Testament. Older writings, such as the letters of Paul (and probably James as well), contain quotations, allusions and echoes of the same material.

But what about the Jesus stories and teachings in the Qur'an that are distinctive to the Qur'an? Should we accept these materials as authentic and therefore historically reliable? And if the Qur'an's version of the Jesus tradition contradicts the tradition of the New Testament Gospels, should the Qur'an's version be preferred?

The first and most obvious problem with the Qur'an as a source for new stories and teachings that supposedly go back to Jesus is that the Qur'an was written 600 years after the ministry of Jesus. We don't doubt that the Qur'an might give us some authentic thoughts and teachings of Muhammad. Several friends and supporters who had heard his teaching were still living after he died and were able to assemble his teaching and write out the Qur'an. The Qur'an was written in its final form only about one generation after the death of Muhammad (though the process of editing may have continued for another generation or two), just as the New Testament writings were written only about one generation after the death and resurrection of Jesus.[12]

But does this mean that the Qur'an is a reliable source for the historical Jesus, especially if in places it contradicts what is said in the first-century Christian Gospels? No, it does not. The problem is that the Qur'an was written *more than half a millennium after* the time of Jesus, some 550 years after the writing of the New Testament Gospels. No properly trained historian will opt for a source that that was written more than five hundred years after several older written sources.

We face the same problem with distinctive Jesus traditions in the rabbinic literature. Jesus appears in the Tosefta, which cannot be dated earlier than AD 300, or about 225 years after the New Testament Gospels were written. More traditions about Jesus appear in the two recensions of the Talmud. The Palestinian recension dates to about 450 AD, while the Babylonian dates to about AD 550. Historians and serious scholars find this material colorful, even entertaining, but they view it with suspicion as regards trustworthiness about Jesus. And why shouldn't they? These compendia of Jewish law and lore were compiled hundreds of years after the time of Jesus and the New Testament Gospels. They are almost as far removed in time as the Qur'an. Historians make little use of rabbinic literature as historical sources in writing about the historical Jesus.

As we will see in a later chapter, almost all of the Qur'an's distinctive Jesus tradition seems to have been derived from later times and places, such as Syria in the second and third centuries. The Jesus of the Qur'an seems to be very much colored by the type of asceticism that was taught in second- and third-century Syrian Christian circles, such as the Encratites. Some of the sources on which Muhammad relied are quite dubious, such as the Infancy Gospel stories (where, for example, Jesus gives life to birds made of mud) or the strange idea of Basilides (who said it was not Jesus who was crucified but some poor fellow who looked like Jesus). Some of Jesus' alleged pronouncements in the Qur'an (e.g., where Jesus denies his divinity) reflect the debates and polemics that were part of Muhammad's context in Arabia in the late sixth and early seventh centuries, not the context of Jesus and his contemporaries in first-century Israel. Indeed, the Jesus of the Qur'an is largely an imagination of a mid-seventh century religious community.[13]

For all of these reasons, very, very few historians make use of the Qur'an as a source for finding out what the historical Jesus said and did. We suspect this is why Muslim writer Reza Aslan in his recent book on Jesus makes no use of the Qur'an and early Islamic tradition.[14] Having had some graduate education in a setting where he would have learned something about the work involved in doing historical Jesus research, Aslan would know that the Qur'an and rabbinic literature are not useful sources for such a purpose.

Although their assessments may differ, historians agree that our best sources for understanding what Jesus really said and did are the New Testament Gospels and some other early Christian and non-Christian writings. In the balance of the present chapter, we address three important questions that must be faced in the study of the New Testament Gospels. The first question asks if the Gospels are based on eyewitness testimony, the second asks if the ancient manuscripts of the Gospels are reliable, and the third question asks if the Gospel manuscript record compares to that of the great classics from late antiquity.

## Are the New Testament Gospels Based on Eyewitness Testimony?

Historians always want to know if the sources they have are based on eyewitness testimony. Also, especially in societies in which teaching tended to be preserved in oral form years before being written down, they want to know about customs relating to memorization, education, and expectations and practices relating to remembering, editing and passing on someone's teaching. All of this is relevant for the Gospels.

In his recent book, popular writer Reza Aslan declares that not only are the Gospels not based on eyewitness testimony, they really are not historical documents. He says,

> The [G]ospels are not, nor were they ever meant to be, historical documentation of Jesus' life. They are not eyewitness accounts of Jesus' words and deeds, recorded by people who knew him. They are testimonies of faith composed by communities of faith and written many years after the events they describe. Simply put, the [G]ospels tell us about Jesus the Christ, not Jesus the man.[15]

This statement is highly dubious in almost everything it asserts. The Gospels certainly *are* historical documentation. If they were not, no one—including Aslan—would be in any position to say anything about the Jesus of history. The statement that the Gospels were "not eyewitness accounts...recorded by people who knew him" requires qualification. First of all, the Gospels of Matthew and John may well have been written by eyewitnesses or by persons acquainted with eyewitnesses. Secondly, although the apostle Peter did not himself compose the Gospel of Mark, early, credible tradition says the evangelist Mark made use of Peter's reminiscences. Finally, almost all critics agree that the Gospels, especially the three Synoptic Gospels, heavily rely on very early material (such as Q), much of which likely originated with eyewitnesses.

Aslan's final statement, that the "[G]ospels tell us about Jesus the Christ, not Jesus the man," is little more than a gratuitous assertion. Some critics may agree with it, but many will not. Aslan's book shows no acquaintance with the ablest and most recent scholarship concerned with the historiography of the New Testament Gospels. And in any event, if Aslan actually believed that the Gospels do not tell us about "Jesus the man," how was he able to write a book about the historical Jesus?[16]

In recent years, there has been a considerable amount of work done in the fields of orality, memory, pedagogy and historiography in late antiquity. All of these fields are relevant when we consider the nature of the portraits of Jesus that the New Testament Gospels have given us. We can only touch on a few of the most significant contributions.

In 2003, James Dunn, Lightfoot Professor of Divinity at the University of Durham, published his monumental *Jesus Remembered*,[17] in which he argued that although the Jesus tradition in the early Christian community was a living tradition that could be adapted as the need and occasion required, the tradition as a whole was early, stable and reliable.

Dunn's findings complemented Samuel Byrskog's work, which focused on pedagogy (teaching youth) and the protocols for the transmission of a master's teaching. Byrskog shows that within the Gospel of Mark, the first of the three Synoptic Gospels to be published, is evidence of the pedagogical practices of the time, by which a master's teaching was carefully preserved and accurately taught, and not free-wheeling invention of tradition, as at one time imagined by some critics.[18]

Building on the work of Byrskog and others, Richard Bauckham, longtime Bishop Wardlaw Professor of New Testament at the University of St. Andrews in Scotland, has made a compelling case for the presence of extensive and accurate eyewitness testimony in all four New Testament Gospels[19] and that this eyewitness tradition remained available until the time when the Gospels were composed.[20]

One of the important indications of an ancient document's veracity is something historians call verisimilitude.[21] That is, do the contents of the document match with what we know of the place, people and period described in the document? Do the contents of the document cohere with what is known through other written sources and through archaeological finds? Do the contents of the document give evidence of acquaintance with the topography and geography of the region that forms the backdrop to the story? Does the author of the document exhibit knowledge of the culture and customs of the people described? Historians ask these questions and others like them of a document they think may contain historical information.[22] If the document lacks verisimilitude, historians will make little or no use of it.

The New Testament Gospels and Acts exhibit a great deal of verisimilitude.[23] They speak of real people (e.g., Pontius Pilate, Herod Antipas, Annas, Caiaphas, Herod Agrippa I and II, Felix, Festus) and real events (e.g., death of John the Baptist, death of Agrippa I). They speak of real places (e.g., villages, cities, roads, lakes, mountains, political boundaries) that are clarified and corroborated by other historical sources and by archaeology. They speak of real customs (e.g., Passover, purity, Sabbath, divorce law), institutions (e.g., synagogue, temple), offices/officers (e.g., priests, tax collectors, Roman governors, Roman centurions) and beliefs (e.g., the beliefs of Pharisees and Sadducees; interpretation of Scripture). Jesus' engagement with his contemporaries, both supporters and opponents, reflects an understanding of Scripture and theology we now know, thanks to the Dead Sea Scrolls and related literature, was current in pre-70 Jewish Palestine.

The first-century New Testament Gospels and Acts exhibit the kind of verisimilitude we should expect of writings written within a generation of their principal figure, that is, writings significantly informed by eyewitness tradition. We find linguistic verisimilitude, and by this we mean Hebrew and Aramaic traces in what are otherwise Greek writings. We find geographic and topographical verisimilitude, cultural and archaeological verisimilitude, and religious, economic and social verisimilitude.

The verisimilitude of the New Testament Gospels and Acts is such that historians and archaeologists regularly make use of them. We can illustrate this claim by directing readers to a recently published book entitled *Jesus and Archaeology*,[24] a book that grew out of a conference in Israel that included the usual learned papers but also included onsite visits and examinations of archaeological excavations. The volume includes 31 essays. One-third of the contributors are Jewish, and about one-third are trained archaeologists. The remaining are historians and biblical scholars. If one turns to the index in the back of the book one will find more than one thousand references to the New

Testament Gospels and Acts. This simply would not happen if the New Testament Gospels did not contain accurate and informative information.

In contrast to the verisimilitude of the New Testament Gospels and Acts stand the apocryphal Gospels and Gospel-like writings of the second century, such as the Gnostic Gospels and Syria's *Gospel of Thomas*. These writings do not exhibit verisimilitude, at least not verisimilitude with early first-century Jewish Palestine. On the basis of *Gospel of Thomas* alone, would we know that Jesus was Jewish? Would we have any sense of his message? Any sense of his travels, of his itinerary? Would we know anything of Jesus' death? Would we have any sense of life in first-century Jewish Palestine? The answer to all of these questions is no.

We may raise the same questions with respect to the Qur'an and other early Islamic traditions. The historian will find in these writings even less verisimilitude than he will find in the second-century *Gospel of Thomas*. Despite its great length, if everything we could know about Jesus was limited to the Qur'an, we would know very, very little about this significant figure. For this reason, archaeologists and historians make no more use of the Qur'an in doing research into the history and culture of first-century Jewish Palestine than they make use of the apocryphal Gospels from the second century and later.

## Summary

Historians and archaeologists make use of the New Testament Gospels and book of Acts because they exhibit verisimilitude, a verisimilitude that is often confirmed through the discovery of new data. Further, historians believe they can recover a realistic and reliable portrait of Jesus from the New Testament Gospels because many of the events and sayings they record are found in two or more early, independent sources. Historians by and large trust the Gospels because they were written early enough to overlap with the lifetime of eye-witnesses—the people who knew Jesus and his original followers.

In the next chapter, we look at the oldest manuscripts of the Gospels and ask if they have been copied faithfully and accurately. After all, if the copies of the Gospels were poorly executed and if scribes made major changes, omitting stories and sayings and adding new stories and sayings, the copies might not say what the originals said. This important question must be addressed if we are to have full confidence in the Gospels as reliable witnesses of the historical Jesus.

Chapter 2

---

# Are the Manuscripts of the New Testament Gospels Reliable?

## *Jesus and the Copyists*

In the previous chapter, we found we have good reason to believe that the New Testament Gospels were written early enough to access living eyewitnesses and they were written in order to convey accurate information as well as the early Church's beliefs about the significance and achievement of Jesus. It was argued that we may have confidence in the New Testament Gospels because they exhibit the kind of verisimilitude—realism and confirmable information—that historians look for in doing their research and archaeologists look for in order to know where to dig and how to interpret what they find. This important feature is lacking in the Qur'an and other early Islamic traditions about Jesus. The Qur'an simply does not provide us with reliable, confirmable data with respect to the time and place of Jesus.

Most may agree with our assessment to this point. They may have confidence with respect to the Gospels as written and first circulated in the first century. But we no longer have the originals. What we have are later copies, copies produced in the second and third centuries and beyond. We must ask if these later copies were accurate and true to the originals. Or were their contents changed? Were new stories and new sayings added, things that Jesus never did and never said?

These are fair questions, and they should be addressed. In this chapter we examine the manuscript evidence of the New Testament—the age, quantity and quality of the copies of the New Testament—and then we compare it to the age, quantity and quality of manuscripts of other books from antiquity with which historians and textual critics normally work and in which they usually have confidence.

## Are the NT Manuscripts Reliable?

Even if one concludes that the New Testament Gospels, written in the first century and written in times when many of Jesus' original followers and eye-witnesses were still living, accurately recorded the things that Jesus said and did, one may still wonder if the later copies of these copies were faithful to the originals. This question can be answered if we have enough manuscripts, from different times and places, and at least a reasonable sample written within a century or two of the time when the original Gospel manuscripts were written and had begun to circulate. Of course, there is a bit more to it than that, but for our purposes it should be sufficient.

When Erasmus of Rotterdam (1466–1536) produced the first critical edition of the Greek New Testament in 1516, he had at his disposal only seven manuscripts, not one complete, and none older than the twelfth century.[1] As he published new editions over the next 20 years he acquired several more manuscripts. His work of comparison and collation laid the groundwork for the discipline now known as textual criticism.

Today we have approximately 5,800 Greek New Testament manuscripts, representing some 2.6 million pages of text. Most of these manuscripts are medieval, but several are much older. We now have Codex Vaticanus, which dates to AD 330–340 and preserves most of the Old Testament (in Greek) and the New Testament. We have Codex Sinaiticus (housed in the British Museum), which dates to the same period and also preserves most of the two Testaments (though several pages at the beginning of this codex are lost). Scholars suspect that Vaticanus and Sinaiticus are two of the fifty copies of Scripture that Emperor Constantine (AD 272–337) commissioned. We also have Codex Alexandrinus, Codex Beza and Codex Ephraemi Rescriptus, all of which date to the fifth century. We also have several more fifth- and sixth-century codices, often containing only parts of the New Testament. One of these is the very significant Codex Washington, which contains the four Gospels.

We also have a number of papyri, many of which are older, sometimes much older, than the codices that have been mentioned. The oldest of these ranges in date from the late second century to the late third century. They provide us with most of the text of the Gospels and virtually all of the text of Paul's letters, as well as fragments, sometimes large fragments, of the other New Testament writings. To date we have some 127 Greek New Testament papyri. More will be said about these papyri.

We have many "miniscules"—manuscripts written in smaller, longhand style. Most of these date to the ninth century or later. Among them, manuscript 33, known as the "queen of the miniscules," is a gem, for it is carefully copied and based on old text of good quality.

## Bart Ehrman and Text Criticism

In the last ten years or so Bart Ehrman (1955–), professor of religious studies at the University of North Carolina at Chapel Hill, has gained notoriety as a former-Christian-turned-agnostic and author of several books casting doubt on the reliability of the text of the Bible, the authorship of most of the books that make up the Bible and the reliability of the New Testament Gospels.

As a teenager Ehrman became a fundamentalist Christian. He attended Moody Bible Institute in Chicago and nearby Wheaton College and later received a PhD from Princeton Theological Seminary under the supervision of well-known textual critic Bruce Metzger (1914–2007). Critical study of the Bible led Ehrman to abandon his fundamentalism. Increasing doubts about the Bible, as well as his inability to explain suffering and evil in the world, led him to abandon his faith in God altogether.

Ehrman has published several books espousing his skeptical views. These books include *Misquoting Jesus, Jesus Interrupted, God's Problem* and *Forged*. Many scholars, including non-conservative Christians, have criticized Ehrman for misrepresenting the data or at least presenting the data in ways that misled many readers. Muslims have translated some of Ehrman's work into Arabic and Indonesian for purposes of showing that the Bible—in contrast to the Qur'an—is not inspired and cannot be trusted. What is usually not pointed out in these books is that Ehrman does not think the Qur'an is inspired or free from errors. But what really is Ehrman's position? In the second edition of *Misquoting Jesus* (252) he states that he actually agrees with Metzger in that "essential Christian beliefs are not affected by textual variants in the manuscript tradition."

We also have approximately 10,000 Latin translations of the New Testament. Again, most of these date to the medieval period, but some are earlier. We also have several thousand lectionaries, in Greek and in Latin, in which passages of Scripture are quoted. We also have countless tens of thousands of quotations of Scripture in the writings of the Church Fathers. From these alone we could reconstruct almost the entire New Testament. We also have thousands of manuscripts in Coptic, Ethiopic, Syriac and other languages from the Byzantine and Medieval periods.[2]

The value of this vast inventory of manuscripts is that scholars are able to compare the readings, so that in cases where there are variant readings or obvious mistakes in the text, it is possible to determine what the original reading was. Although there is some disagreement, textual critics believe that the text of the New Testament was quite stable in its first two centuries (for which, admittedly, we have only small samples of evidence) and that we have restored the text to within 98 percent or 99 percent of the original.[3]

There simply are no legitimate grounds for thinking that we do not know how the original manuscripts read. There are no grounds for thinking that the Jesus of the New Testament Gospels that we have today is different from the Jesus of the New Testament Gospels when they were first written and circulated in the first century.

## Oldest Greek Codices

The remarkable stability of the text of the New Testament sharply contrasts with the lack of textual stability in other writings, especially the apocryphal works, like the *Infancy Gospel of Thomas*, whose manuscripts and recensions vary considerably. We see this also in the Gnostic writings, most of which date to the second century. The codices that have been recovered—all from Egypt—date to the fourth century AD. The textual variations and discrepancies are such that it is not possible to determine how the original text read.

All in all, the evidence strongly suggests that the text of the New Testament that we possess today is very, very close to the original—in stark contrast to what we typically see in apocryphal writings. Modern textual criticism, aided by the discovery of thousands of manuscripts and the development of remarkable technologies that help us recover text, has been very successful.

# How Well Established Is the Arabic Text of the Qur'an?

In a later chapter we shall discuss significant discrepancies in Qur'anic manuscripts. But it will be helpful at this point to say something about textual study of the Qur'an, to see how it compares to New Testament textual criticism. The first thing we observe is that Qur'anic textual criticism is only in its infancy. Qur'anic textual critic Keith Small informs us,

> It is widely acknowledged that *there has never been a critical text produced for the Qur'an* based on extant manuscripts, as has been done with other sacred books and bodies of ancient literature. The current printed texts of the Qur'an are based on medieval Islamic tradition instead of collation and analysis of extant manuscripts. In other literary disciplines it is almost taken for granted that scholarly study of a text must start with a text based on the collation and analysis of the oldest and best manuscripts available for that text. Qur'anic studies operates with an open knowledge of this lack concerning the Qur'an, and as such methods and their results have had to be adapted to this fundamental deficiency.[4]

What Small has said here will come, we suspect, as a surprise to Christians and Muslims alike. We have had Muslims say to us that because the Qur'an is inspired it is without errors or textual variants ("unlike the Christian Bible," it is often implied!). Small adds, "There is a widespread and long held belief among Muslims that the text of the Bible was corrupted so much that a new revelation, the Qur'an, had to be sent" and "the text of the Qur'an has been preserved perfectly."[5] But this is plainly not true. We have read Small's studies, and the Qur'anic textual variants are plain to see. There seems to be a wide gap between Qur'anic textual reality and popular Muslim beliefs. Indeed, according to Qur'anic scholar Efim Rezvan,

> It is today evident that the real history of the fixation of the Qur'anic text attested in early manuscripts differs in extremely serious fashion from the history preserved in the Muslim tradition. Only an analysis of manuscripts will allow us to reconstruct the true history of the canon's establishment.[6]

Most Muslims know nothing of what Rezvan is saying. Muslim scholars usually maintain publicly the fiction that there are few variants and they are only minor and unintentional.[7] He and a number of Qur'anic scholars know full well that variants exist among the manuscripts of the Qur'an, despite the attempt in the seventh century to destroy all variant manuscripts. In the last fifty years, a number of projects have attempted to put the Qur'anic text on a firmer footing, but for one reason or another these projects have not been brought to completion. Sometimes the reason is resistance, motivated by religious ideology, perhaps out of fear that serious problems with the text will come to light.[8]

For his part, Keith Small is optimistic that by diligent study of Qur'anic manuscripts, through collation and comparison (as is done in New Testament scholarship), a critical text that closely approximates the original, or at least one of the early forms of the text, can be achieved. He states,

> The methods of textual criticism which have been developed over the last three centuries for sacred texts, the Greek and Latin classics, and other ancient literary traditions have proven that they can substantiate the historical authenticity of ancient texts, as well as document stages and changes in textual transmission of these bodies of literature. As a rule, manuscripts of the Qur'an have not been submitted to this kind of study.[9]

When it comes to textual criticism, New Testament scholarship is miles ahead of Qur'anic scholarship.[10] Christian scholars who have plunged into the world of manuscripts have openly acknowledged the presence of variants and, in places, uncertainties. The result has been the restoration of the text that closely approximates the original. The work is ongoing and optimistic.

Qur'anic scholars face a much greater challenge, for the formation of the Qur'an was nothing like that of the individual books of the New Testament. The New Testament books were written as discrete literary units by one author and then distributed and copied. The Qur'an did not come about this way. Muhammad did not write it. He may have dictated portions of it. Some of his followers may have written portions of it during Muhammad's lifetime. Others had memorized it. But exactly how the Qur'an as a whole came together in the aftermath of Muhammad's death is not clear. The manuscript evidence suggests "it cannot be demonstrated that there was one version going back to Muhammad" and that "there never was one original text of the Qur'an."[11] Notwithstanding the nature of the evidence, the belief in such a text is "a mainstay of popular Islamic discourse."[12] It is akin to Christian fundamentalists who think the Textus Receptus, which underlies the King James Version, goes back to the apostles.

## How Does the New Testament Manuscript Record Compare to that of the Classics?

One way of measuring the historical worth of the New Testament Gospels is to compare them to other writings from antiquity, writings on which modern historians rely. Allow us to mention a number of these writings, beginning with the oldest. Most of our examples are historical works, which makes for a more appropriate comparison with the New Testament Gospels, though we will look at a few examples of the writings of philosophers and poets.

The Greek historian Herodotus, who lived c. 488–428 BC, wrote a work called *The Histories*. The oldest major manuscript dates to AD 800, some 1,200 years later than the original. Thucydides of Athens, who lived c. 460–400 BC, wrote a work called *History of the War*, that is, the Peloponnesian War between Athens and Sparta (431–404 BC). Our oldest major manuscript dates to AD 900. Greek statesman and historian Xenophon, who lived c. 430–354 BC, wrote the *Anabasis*, the famous account of the march of the 10,000 Greek warriors. This classic was written in 394 BC and published c. 370 BC. We have six manuscripts of the work, the oldest dating to AD 1320, the others dating to the fifteenth century AD.

Most of our oldest manuscripts of the works of the great philosopher Plato, who lived c. 429–347 BC, date to AD 950. Our best manuscript of *Histories* by Polybius, who lived c. 200–118 BC, dates to the eleventh century AD. Lucretius, the Epicurean poet who lived c. 94–55 BC, wrote a work called *On the Nature of Things*. We have two manuscripts. The oldest dates to the eleventh century AD.

Julius Caesar (100–44 BC) wrote his *Gallic War* during the years 58–50 BC. We possess some ten fairly well preserved manuscripts, of which the oldest date to about AD 850. Titus Livius, or simply Livy, lived from 59 BC to AD 17. He authored *Roman History*. Of the original 142 books, only Books 1–10 and 21–45 survive. Our oldest manuscript, containing parts of Books 3–6, dates to about AD 350. Our largest manuscript, containing most of what is extant, dates to the fifth century.

Cornelius Tacitus, born, we believe, in AD 56, wrote *Histories* sometime around AD 110 and *Annals* sometime around AD 115. The latter may never have been completed. Portions of both are lost. Our oldest manuscripts date to the ninth and eleventh centuries AD. His minor works *Agricola* and *Germania* are preserved in a tenth-century codex.

The writings of Josephus (c. AD 37–100) are of great importance for New Testament studies. All seven books of his *Jewish War* (c. AD 75) survive in nine complete manuscripts, of which the oldest dates to the fifth century. His twenty-volume *Jewish Antiquities* (c. 93) is extant in six Greek manuscripts, the three most reliable of which date to the thirteenth, fourteenth, and fifteenth centuries. Despite this distance between the original work and the extant copies, no scholar seriously questions the integrity of the text.

---

## Josephus on Jesus of Nazareth

At this time there appeared Jesus, a wise man, *if indeed one ought to call him a man.* For he was a doer of amazing deeds, a teacher of persons who receive truth with pleasure. He won over many Jews and many of the Greeks. *He was the Messiah.* And when Pilate condemned him to the cross, the leading men among us having accused him, those who loved him from the first did not cease to do so. *For he appeared to them the third day alive again, the divine prophets having spoken these things and a myriad of other marvels concerning him.* And to the present the tribe of Christians, named after this person, has not disappeared. (*Ant.* 18.63–64)

The words placed in italics were not written by Josephus but are later Christian insertions.

---

Arrian, who lived c. AD 86–160, wrote the *Anabasis of Alexander*, some 450 years after the brief reign of the famous conqueror. Our earliest extant copy of Arrian's work, which is damaged and in places illegible, dates to AD 1200.

Against the backdrop of these classical works the New Testament Gospels compare quite favorably. Large portions of the four Gospels are preserved in $\beta^{45}$, a papyrus codex that dates to the early third century or perhaps the late second century, as some contend. Late second-century $\beta^{66}$ preserves most of the Gospel of John. Late second-century $\beta^{75}$ preserves large chunks of Luke and John. A number of small fragments are candidates for a second-century date. These include $\beta^{64,67}$, $\beta^{77}$, $\beta^{103}$ and $\beta^{104}$, which preserve fragments of Matthew; $\beta^4$, which may have been part of $\beta^{64,67}$, preserves a fragment of Luke; and $\beta^5$, $\beta^{52}$, $\beta^{90}$, $\beta^{108}$ and $\beta^{109}$ preserve small fragments of the Gospel of John. The prize for being the oldest fragment of a New Testament writing goes to $\beta^{52}$, which contains small portions of John 18 and is dated by most papyrologists to shortly before AD 150, or about 50 or 60 years after John was composed and first circulated.

There are a number of other papyri fragments dating to the third century. In all, some 60 manuscripts date before AD 300. Recall, too, that large portions of the Gospels are quoted in second- and third-century Church Fathers. And, of course, we have the great codices Sinaiticus and Vaticanus, which contain the four Gospels. These codices are dated to about AD 340. This means that we have the complete text of the four New Testament Gospels preserved in documents about 270–280 years removed from the autographs, that we have substantial portions of the text of the Gospels preserved in documents about 130–200 years removed from the autographs, and that we have tiny portions of the text in perhaps as many as one dozen documents about 70–120 years removed from the autographs. All in all, not a bad record. Compared to many of the classical writings and histories, where in most cases there are gaps of 800 to 1,000 years or more between the time of the author and our oldest surviving copy of his manuscript, it is an excellent record indeed.

With regard to the New Testament Gospels, the temporal distance between an event of history or a historical personage and its record is also impressive. The Synoptic Gospels were written about 30–40 years or so after the death of Jesus. Q, the source Matthew and Luke utilized, may have been written in part within a decade of Jesus' death. The fourth Gospel was written 60–70 years after the death of Jesus. In the case of some of the classical writers, the temporal distance is comparable. Indeed, some classical writers were eyewitnesses of at least some of the events they described; others claimed acquaintance with eyewitnesses. But this is not always the case. Livy and Tacitus wrote greatly removed in time from most of the events they describe in their respective accounts of Roman history.[13] Even with respect to the famous conqueror Alexander the Great, there is a surprising distance between the man and the sources that tell us about him.[14]

This list could be extended, but we think enough examples have been provided to make our point. Most of our literature from late antiquity that has survived is extant in small numbers of manuscripts, which in most cases are greatly removed in time from their authors. Some of the authors of these works were greatly removed in time from the events they narrate. Despite these disadvantages, historians of ancient Greece and Rome believe their sources are sufficient for the task.[15]

As historical sources the New Testament Gospels are very promising. Three of the four Gospels were written before the end of the generation that knew Jesus or heard stories and teachings from those who knew Jesus. This fact leaves open the possibility that their accounts can give us reliable and fair portraits of the life and teaching of Jesus. This possibility is strengthened by the observation that the Jesus tradition in the Pauline letters coheres with what is preserved in the Synoptic Gospels. Indeed, this coherence militates against the idea that the Jesus tradition of the Synoptic Gospels is the product of imagination and invented stories. After all, Paul was personally acquainted with several early Christian leaders who had been personally acquainted with and instructed by Jesus (Gal 1:18–2:14).[16] The coherence of the Jesus tradition in Paul with what we find in the Synoptic Gospels constitutes important evidence of the antiquity and authenticity of the Synoptic tradition.

## Greco-Roman Writers on Jesus

Cornelius Tacitus (c. AD 56–118) was proconsul of Asia (AD 112–113), friend of Pliny the Younger and author of *Annals* and the *Histories*. Only portions of these works are extant. In *Annals* 15.44 he provides a passing reference to Jesus:

> Therefore, to squelch the rumor [that the burning of Rome had taken place by order], Nero supplied (as culprits) and punished in the most extraordinary fashion those hated for their vice, whom the crowd called "Christians." Christus, the author of their name, had suffered the death penalty during the reign of Tiberius, by sentence of the procurator [sic] Pontius Pilate. The pernicious superstition was checked for a time, only to break out once more, not merely in Judea, the origin of the evil, but in the capital itself, where all things horrible and shameful collect and are practiced.

In his fifth volume of *De Vita Caesarum* (c. 120) the Roman historian Suetonius refers to the expulsion of the Jews from Rome in AD 49 during the reign of Claudius (*Divus Claudius* 25.4; cf. Acts 18:2). In his description he refers to one "Chrestus": "(Claudius) expelled the Jews from Rome who, instigated by Chrestus [sic], continuously caused unrest."

Pliny the Younger (or Gaius Plinius Caecilius Secundus, c. 61–113), who in AD 111–113 was the governor of Bithynia in Asia Minor, wrote to Emperor Trajan for advice in how to deal with Christians. The passage that is of interest is found in his *Epistles* Book 10, Letter 96:

> They [the Christians] assured me that the sum total of their error consisted in the fact that they regularly assembled on a certain day before daybreak. They recited a hymn antiphonally to Christus as to a god and bound themselves with an oath not to commit any crime, but to abstain from theft, robbery, adultery, breach of faith, and embezzlement of property entrusted to them. After this it was their custom to separate, and then to come together again to partake of a meal, but an ordinary and innocent one.

## Summary

The text of the New Testament Gospels is fully extant in manuscripts 250 years or so removed in time from the originals, and it is partially extant in several manuscripts much closer in time. It is widely agreed that the text we have today is very close to the original, so close that no major teaching is in doubt. This fact calls for a presumption that we have something pretty close to the original text of the Gospels.

How reliable is the text of the Qur'an? It is hard to say, because proper collation and comparison have not yet taken place. The work of Francois Deroche, Keith Small, and Dan Brubaker, among others, suggests that a lot of work needs to be done with Qur'anic manuscripts before we know if the text of the Qur'an has been as well preserved as the text of the New Testament.[17]

In chapter 1 we were able to show that there are good reasons to conclude that the Greek New Testament Gospels provide us with early, reliable historical information about Jesus. In the present chapter we have seen that the manuscripts of the Greek New Testament are old, numerous, and accurate. In the next chapter we will address the important question of how Jesus understood himself and his mission.

# Chapter 3

---

# How Did Jesus Understand Himself and His Mission?

*Messiah and Son of God*

P robably the biggest debate relating to Christian origins and theology centers on the question of who Jesus really was (and is). This debate centers on the question of how Jesus understood himself. Did Jesus understand himself as the Messiah? Did he think of himself in divine terms?

The first question can be answered by appeal to the crucifixion of Jesus as "king of the Jews," which is acknowledged by all four New Testament Gospels (Matt 27:37; Mark 15:26; Luke 23:38; John 19:19) and in an indirect way by Paul (Rom 1:3–4, NKJV: "born of the seed of David"; cf. 2 Tim 2:8). The execution of Jesus as Israel's king almost certainly implies that Jesus had allowed, even encouraged, his followers to regard him as Israel's anointed king. In Roman eyes, of course, the Jewish Messiah is the equivalent of what Rome preferred to call "king of the Jews." Accordingly, the first question is not especially difficult. We'll pursue it further in chapter 12.

The second question is much more difficult to answer: Did Jesus think of himself in divine terms? Part of the problem stems from the Jewish religious culture, in which modesty is expected: "Are you he who is to come?" "Go and tell John what you hear and see." "Are you the Messiah?" "You have said so." These questions and their respective answers are examples of this modesty. As a rule, Jesus does not provide an explicit answer. He does not tell his disciples that he is the Messiah; he asks them their opinion (Mark 8:27–29). He does not say "yes" to the messengers of John; rather, he tells them to go back and report to John what they have observed (Matt 11:2–6).[1]

The second question is especially difficult in reference to Jesus, because he and his disciples were devout Jews and as such were strict monotheists. But if they were monotheists, in what sense could they have viewed Jesus as divine? Before we can answer that question we need to look at Jewish monotheism.[2]

## Jewish Monotheism

The major distinctive of the religion of ancient Israel was its commitment to monotheism, the belief in one God. The people of Israel did not always live up to that ideal, and without doubt many were *henotheists* (those who believe in one particular deity) as opposed to genuine *monotheists* (those who believe that there is only one God).[3]

In any event, Israelite monotheism was quite remarkable in light of the fact that, with rare exception, the ancient Near East was a polytheistic world. Most peoples worshipped many gods, even if one or two of their deities were held in especially high regard (such as Baal by the Philistines or Marduk by the Babylonians). The temptation faced by the ancient kings of Israel was to compromise their monotheistic faith by agreeing to treaties with other nations in which the gods of these nations would be respected, perhaps even worshipped. Sometimes this meant placing an image (or idol) of a foreign deity in the city of Jerusalem, perhaps in the temple sanctuary itself. It was against this sort of thing that the Old Testament prophets spoke so harshly, calling Israel a harlot for chasing after other lovers, as it were (e.g., Isa 1:21; Jer 3:1; Ezek 16:26).

In the aftermath of destruction and exile at the hands of the Babylonians (586 BC), the people of Israel had learned their lesson. The nation was now committed to the ancient command of Moses:

> "Hear, O Israel: The LORD our God is one LORD; and you shall love the LORD your God with all your heart, and with all your soul, and with all your might. And these words which I command you this day shall be upon your heart; and you shall teach them diligently to your children, and shall talk of them when you sit in your house, and when you walk by the way, and when you lie down, and when you rise. And you shall bind them as a sign upon your hand, and they shall be as frontlets between your eyes. And you shall write them on the doorposts of your house and on your gates." (Deut 6:4–9)

This is the famous passage known as the Shema' ("Hear"). In Deuteronomy, the fifth and final book of Moses, in which the Law is given a second time (for the benefit of the generation of Israelites about to cross the Jordan River and enter the Promised Land), Israel is commanded to love the Lord their God. But even here it would be possible to hold to henotheism, loyally holding to only one God (Yahweh), but at the same time, at least in principle, acknowledging the existence of other gods.

It is against this possibility that Isaiah speaks, giving voice to the word of Yahweh:

> "You are my witnesses," says the LORD, "and my servant whom I have chosen, that you may know and believe me and understand that I am He. Before me no god was formed, nor shall there be any after me." (Isa 43:10)

> "Fear not, nor be afraid; have I not told you from of old and declared it? And you are my witnesses! Is there a God besides me? There is no Rock; I know not any." (Isa 44:8)

These prophetic utterances give clear expression to what we would today call strict monotheism. Isaiah asserts that there simply is no other God than Yahweh (or "the LORD"). He and he alone is God. No god existed before Yahweh and no god will exist after him. There is no god besides Yahweh. Moses and the prophets were not only monotheists; they were Yahwists. That is to say, the God they believed in was Yahweh, the God of the patriarchs Abraham, Isaac and Jacob. The people of Israel are commanded to embrace monotheism and not merely henotheism.

Jewish monotheism only intensified in the struggle against Antiochus IV Epiphanes, the Syrian Greek ruler who in 167 BC attempted to coerce the Jewish people into giving up their ancestral faith and embracing that of the Greeks. The attempt failed, resulting in an independent Jewish state and a deeply entrenched commitment to Yahweh as Israel's only God. Those who suffered and died for their faith in Yahweh (the "Maccabean martyrs") were regarded as heroes and exemplary models. Polytheism or belief in another god was simply not an option for anyone at the turn of the era who claimed to be a true Jew.

It has sometimes been suggested that Jews worshipped angelic figures, in addition to God. But the evidence does not support this proposal. Angels and various powers were shown great respect, perhaps even venerated on occasion, but there really is no evidence that Jews who were committed to their ancestral faith worshipped angels.[4] Jews in the time of Jesus never offered sacrifices to an angel—only to God. Jewish mystics may have attempted, or even experienced, a form of soul-ascent, whereby they entered heaven and partook in angelic liturgies, but they did not worship angels. They, along with the angels, worshipped God.

The divinity of Jesus—however it arose in the thinking of the followers of Jesus—must be interpreted against the backdrop of Jewish monotheism, belief in one supreme, absolute God, maker of all things, to whom everyone is accountable. How belief in Jesus as "God in the flesh" arose in what in its first decades was predominantly Jewish is the big question we must ponder.

## Jewish Ideas Regarding the Awaited Messiah

At the beginning of the first century, in which Jesus and his future disciples and followers were raised, a number of Jews held to messianic ideas and hopes. It is quite likely that at least two of the persons who attempted to gain control of Israel when Herod the Great died (4 or 1 BC) saw themselves as Israel's anointed kings. During the revolt against Rome (AD 66–73), it is probable that another one or two men claimed to be Israel's divinely anointed king.

A survey of the literature that was produced in the intertestamental period (i.e., between the Old and New Testaments, or from about 400 BC to the beginning of the first century AD) shows that Jews held to a variety of messianic ideas and expectations.[5] Much of this expectation was anchored in a few specific Old Testament texts, such as Genesis 49:8–12, Numbers 24:17 and Isaiah 11:1–16. The idea that Israel's anointed king would in some sense be God's son is expressed in 2 Samuel 7:12–16 and Psalm 2:2, 7; 89:26–29. The latter texts provide much of the inspiration for the prophecy found in a first-century BC Aramaic text recovered from among the Dead Sea Scrolls:

> [His son] will be called "The Great," and be designated by his name. He will be called the "Son of God," they will call him the "Son of the Most High." But like the meteors that you saw in your vision, so will be their kingdom. They will reign only a few years over the land, while people tramples people and nation tramples nation. Until the people of God arise; then all will have rest from warfare. Their kingdom will be an eternal kingdom, and all their paths will be righteous. They will judge the land justly, and all nations will make peace. Warfare will cease from the land, and all the nations shall do

obeisance to them. The great God will be their help, he himself will fight for them, putting peoples into their power, overthrowing them all before them. God's rule will be an eternal rule. (4Q246 1:9–2:9)[6]

The expected figure in this prophetic vision will be called "The Great," "Son of God," and "Son of the Most High." He and the people of God will experience an "eternal kingdom." Those who know the Gospels well will immediately be reminded of Gabriel's announcement to Mary regarding the conception and birth of her son Jesus:

"He will be great, and will be called the Son of the Most High; and the Lord God will give to him the throne of his father David, and he will reign over the house of Jacob for ever; and of his kingdom there will be no end...the child to be born will be called holy, the Son of God." (Luke 1:32–33, 35)

Here we find the same titles and concepts: Jesus will be "great," he will be called the "Son of the Most High" and the "Son of God," and he will reign forever (or eternally).

Another fragmentary scroll from Qumran, this one written in Hebrew and also dating to the first century BC, describes what will take place when God's Messiah makes his appearance:

The heavens and the earth shall obey his Messiah and all which is in them shall not turn away from the commandments of the holy ones. Strengthen yourselves, O you who seek the Lord, in his service. Will you not find the Lord in this, all those who hope in their heart? For the Lord attends to the pious and calls the righteous by name. Over the humble his spirit hovers, and he renews the faithful in his strength. For he will honor the pious upon the throne of his eternal kingdom, setting prisoners free, opening the eyes of the blind, raising up those who are bowed down (Ps 146:7–8). And forever I shall hold fast to those who hope and in his faithfulness shall [...] and the fruit of good deeds shall not be delayed for anyone and the Lord shall do glorious things which have not been done, just as he said. For he shall heal the critically wounded, he shall revive the dead (Isa 26:19), he shall send good news to the afflicted (Isa 61:1), he shall satisfy the poor, he shall guide the uprooted, he shall make the hungry rich. (4Q521 frag. 2, col. ii, lines 1–13)[7]

Once again we hear echoes in the New Testament Gospels. On one occasion, Jesus is asked if he is the "Coming One" (Matt 11:3, NKJV). He replies that the "blind receive their sight and the lame walk, lepers are cleansed and the deaf hear, and the dead are raised up, and the poor have good news preached to them" (Matt 11:5 = Luke 22:7). The implication is that, yes, Jesus is the Coming One, the Messiah (cf. Matt 11:2). When Jesus stills the storm, the disciples ask, "Who then is this, that even wind and sea obey him?" (Mark 4:41), which is consistent with the Qumran scroll's declaration that the "heavens and earth shall obey (God's) Messiah."[8]

Several other Jewish texts from the intertestamental period speak of the expected Messiah. According to the *Psalms of Solomon* (mid-first century BC), Israel's messianic king (twice called "Lord Messiah") "will gather a holy people who he will lead in righteousness; and he will judge the tribes of the people that have been made holy by the Lord their God" (17:26) and "he will be a righteous king over them, taught by God" (17:32; cf. 17:4, 21, 28, 30, 36–37, 40, 42). According to *4 Ezra* (first century AD), "the Messiah whom the Most High has kept until the end of days, who will arise from the posterity of David" will come and will judge the wicked and deliver the righteous (12:32–34).

In *Enoch* 37–71 (a major section called the *Parables of Enoch*) we find several references to the "Son of Man," the "Chosen One," and even two references to "Messiah" (*1 Enoch* 48:10; 52:4). The Son of Man references are clearly based on the vision of Daniel 7 (cf. *1 Enoch* 46:1–6). The Son of Man becomes the "Chosen One" (48:6) and probably should be identified with the "Messiah." The Messiah will sit on a throne and judge the kings of the earth. The Messiah envisioned in *Enoch* is reminiscent of the king in Jesus' parable of the sheep and the goats (Matt 25:31–46). Referring to himself, Jesus begins his parable by saying "when the Son of Man comes in his glory, and all the angels with him, then he will sit on his glorious throne" (Matt 25:31). This language alludes to the description of the Son of Man in Daniel 7, which speaks of "thrones" (v. 9), a "son of man" (v. 13), "myriads" (i.e., angels, v. 10, NASB), and "glory" (v. 14). Just as the Son of Man/King in Jesus' parable will gather all the nations and judge them (Matt 25:32), so the messianic Son of Man of *1 Enoch* will judge the kings of the earth (e.g., *1 Enoch* 46:5). The Son of Man will even sit on God's throne (*1 Enoch* 51:3; cf. 1 Chr 29:23).

There is no question that many Jews expected the appearance of the Messiah, though not everyone defined this figure or his mission the same way. That the Messiah would be an exalted figure seems clear, but whether he was expected to be in some sense *divine* is doubtful.[9] How did Jesus understand himself? Did he think of himself as in some sense divine?

## The Implicit Claims of Jesus

Earlier in this chapter we briefly described the Jewish tendency and expectation of "messianic modesty" when it came to identifying oneself as an agent of God. As an illustration, we may cite the oft-quoted declaration of the prophet Amos: "I am no prophet, nor a prophet's son" (Amos 7:14). The modesty of Amos almost borders on lack of candor, given what he says next: "The LORD took me from following the flock, and the LORD said to me, 'Go, prophesy to my people Israel'" (Amos 7:15). Amos was indeed a prophet; he simply did not presume to call himself a prophet.

We find a similar tendency in Jesus. What he says about himself tended to be indirect and allusive. For this reason, scholars speak of an "implicit Christology," in which Jesus' exalted identity is implied, not declared, and so must be inferred from actions and sayings. For example, Jesus frequently refers to himself as "Son of Man." This epithet reflects Aramaic idiom and apart from any special context simply means a man, a mere mortal. Yet every time Jesus uses this idiom, it is definite: *the* son of man. In fact, if the text is translated literally, it could be rendered *the* son of *the* man (Greek: *ho huios tou anthropou*). The appearance of this self-reference in the definite form every time leads interpreters to wonder if a *specific* son of man figure or passage of Scripture was in the mind of Jesus. Because the Son of Man is sometimes linked with "clouds of heaven" (Mark 14:62) or "glorious throne" (Matt 19:28), many scholars suspect that Jesus was alluding to the mysterious heavenly figure of Daniel 7 who approaches God and receives authority and kingdom.[10] If so, then this is a very powerful example of implicit Christology (and in a couple of cases it becomes a rather explicit Christology).

Let's pursue the Son of Man self-reference a little further. On one occasion, Jesus tells a man that his sins are forgiven. When some of the scholars who are present object, saying that *only God* can forgive sins, Jesus replies, "the Son of Man has authority on earth to forgive sins" and proves it by healing the man—on the spot and in front of everyone (Mark 2:10). Most readers and hearers of this story will assume that Jesus has acted with divine authority by forgiving someone's sin (and not merely, as a priest might, declaring that God has forgiven the man's sin). But there's more. The odd qualifying phrase, "on earth," appears because the Son of Man obtained divine authority from God *in heaven* (Dan 7:9–14) and now *on earth* he exercises that authority. So although Jesus makes no explicit claim to divinity or to exalted status, his claim that he possesses the authority to forgive sin implies divine authority or authorization. Moreover, to claim to be *the* Son of Man who has this authority *on earth* clearly implies that Jesus understands himself as the heavenly Son of Man figure who stands before God described in Daniel's vision (and this is why Son of Man is capitalized).

In another context, Jesus is accused of being in league with Beelzebul (Mark 3 = Matt 12 = Luke 11), which is another name for Satan. This accusation is leveled against Jesus because of his remarkable success in healing and exorcism. What I find quite amazing is the comparison Jesus makes between himself and Satan, who is described in a parable as a "strong man": "But no one can enter a strong man's house and plunder his goods, unless he first binds the strong man; then indeed he may plunder his house" (Mark 3:27). Here Jesus has implied that he has bound the strong man, that is, Satan. In doing this, Jesus is now able to cast out Satan and thus set free people under Satan's control. The claim is quite astonishing, for the power of Satan rivals that of God's most powerful angels (see Dan 10:13).

The debate between Jesus and his critics also appears in a longer, fuller context in Matthew 12, where some Jewish scholars request a sign from Jesus (Matt 12:38). Jesus tells them that the only sign they will be given will be the sign of Jonah (Matt 12:39). Reference to Jonah leads Jesus to declare,

> "The men of Nineveh will arise at the judgment with this generation and condemn it; for they repented at the preaching of Jonah, and behold, something greater than Jonah is here. The queen of the South will arise at the judgment with this generation and condemn it; for she came from the ends of the earth to hear the wisdom of Solomon, and behold, something greater than Solomon is here." (Matt 12:41–42)

What Jesus implies by these comparisons is quite remarkable. He claims that his preaching is such that one must conclude that "something greater than Jonah is here" and that his wisdom, which includes the power to heal and cast out evil spirits, is such that one must conclude "something greater than Solomon is here." Jonah's preaching and his call to repentance saved Nineveh, a great city, from certain destruction. Yet, the preaching of Jesus is much greater, in that it has the power to save a much greater number. The wisdom of Solomon was such that the Queen of the South travelled a great distance to hear it. Yet, the wisdom of Jesus is much greater. Remember, the prophetic power of Jonah and the wisdom of Solomon were themselves divine empowerments. What is present in Jesus is even greater. These claims may only be implicit, but they are highly suggestive of an exalted self-understanding.

The reactions of people to what they see or sense in the presence of Jesus sometimes imply an exalted status. When Jesus heals the paralyzed man, people "were all amazed and glorified God, saying, 'We never saw anything like this!'" (Mark 2:12). When the disciples witness the transfiguration of Jesus on the mountain, they are frightened, and Peter wants to build shelters to commemorate the event (Mark 9:5). His reaction strongly implies that he has witnessed a divine event. Even more dramatic is Peter's reaction to the catch of fish. He cries out to Jesus, "Depart from me, for I am a sinful man, O Lord" (Luke 5:8). The entire scene is in some ways reminiscent of the reaction of Isaiah the prophet when he suddenly comes into the presence of God: "Woe is me! For I am lost; for I am a man of unclean lips, and I dwell in the midst of a people of unclean lips; for my eyes have seen the King, the LORD of hosts!" (Isa 6:5; cf. v. 7, "Behold...your guilt is taken away, and your sin forgiven").

## The Explicit Claims of Jesus

In the fourth Gospel (the Gospel of John) Jesus makes a number of rather exalted claims: "I and the Father are one" (John 10:30), "He who has seen me has seen the Father" (14:9), "Before Abraham was, I am" (8:58), just to cite three clear examples. The explicit Christology is made quite clear at the outset, when the author of this Gospel states, "In the beginning was the Word, and the Word was with God" (1:1) and "the Word became flesh and dwelt among us" (1:14).

Because the fourth Gospel is so different from the Synoptic Gospels and its Christology is often explicit (in contrast to the implicit Christology typical of the Synoptics), many scholars are not sure what to make of it. Some think that this work is highly confessional and symbolic and that what it says of Jesus, therefore, is not historical or biographical in the conventional sense. Of course, not everyone agrees with this perspective. Some maintain that the historical Jesus is portrayed in this Gospel and that it is in fact based on eyewitness testimony.[11]

Whatever position one takes with respect to the fourth Gospel, the Synoptic Gospels also bear witness to a high Christology that, taken with the implicit materials previously briefly considered, suggest that Jesus held a rather exalted self-understanding. The first indication of this is Jesus' frequent "I have come" statements. These statements are not in reference to arriving at a particular village, but rather refer to entering the human sphere. Indeed, this is the very language used of angels who exit heaven and enter the mundane world, in order to deliver a message or otherwise accomplish some task. Let's look at some examples.

The angel of the Lord warns Balaam, "*I have come* forth to withstand you" (Num 22:32, with emphasis added here and following). The angel Gabriel says to Daniel, "O Daniel, *I have* now *come* out to give you wisdom and understanding. At the beginning of your supplications a word went forth, and *I have come* to tell it to you, for you are greatly beloved" (Daniel 9:22–23). Another angel says to Daniel, "*I have come* because of your words" (10:12), "*I have come* to reveal to you what will happen" (10:14) and "*I have come* to reveal the truth to you" (11:2, in the Greek version, not the Hebrew). In an apocryphal work, the angel Raziel says to Adam, "*I have come* to make known to you pure words and great wisdom" (*Soda Raza*, or *Book of Noah*). In another apocryphal work, the angel Michael says to Jeremiah, "*I have come* to redeem this people" (*Jeremiah Apocryphon* 35, Coptic version), or "*I have come* to you today to save your people" (ibid., Arabic version). The angel Uriel says to Ezra, "*I have come* to show you these things" (*4 Ezra* 6:30) and "Rise, Ezra, and listen to the words which *I have come* to speak to you" (7:2). The angel Michael says to the aged patriarch Isaac, "Be courageous in your spirit, for *I have come* to you from the presence of God in order to bring you up into heaven" (*T. Isaac* 2:2). There are many more examples.[12]

It is in this light that Jesus' "I have come" statements should be understood. He has not come *as an angel*, of course; rather, he has come from heaven to accomplish his saving work among humanity, even as God himself came down to deliver Israel from Egypt: "*I have come* down to deliver them out of the hand of the Egyptians" (Exod 3:8); "You cannot see my face since you are mortal, but my words you are allowed to hear, those which *I have come* to speak...*I have come* to save my people, the Hebrews" (*Ezekiel the Tragedian* 103, 107). We note too what the pagans say in reference to Paul and Barnabas, in reaction to the healing of the crippled man: "The gods *have come* down to us in the likeness of men!" (Acts 14:11).

Jesus uses the same language in the Synoptic Gospels to describe the purpose of his ministry. He tells his disciples, "Let us go on to the next towns, that I may preach there also; for that is why *I came* out" (Mark 1:38). When criticized for associating with sinners, Jesus replies, "Those who are well have no need of a physician, but those who are sick; *I came* not to call the righteous, but sinners" (Mark 2:17). Elsewhere he states that, as the Son of Man, he "*came* not to be served but to serve" (Mark 10:45) and "*came* to *seek* and to *save the lost*" (Luke 19:10). The latter passage is quite significant, for it recalls the promise of God to act as Israel's true shepherd: "*I will seek the lost*, and I will bring back the strayed, and I will bind up the crippled, and I will strengthen the weak" (Ezek 34:16).[13]

That this manner of speaking implies coming from heaven to earth to accomplish a saving work is made explicit in the Gospel of John. Jesus declares, "*I have come* in my Father's name" (John 5:43); "*I have come* down from heaven, not to do my own will, but the will of him who sent me" (6:38, 42); "I know whence *I have come* and whither I am going" (8:14); "for this purpose *I have come* to this hour" (12:27); "*I have come* as light into the world" (12:46); and "For this I was born, and for this *I have come* into the world, to bear witness to the truth" (18:37). These explicit statements are consistent with the more transparent Christology in the Gospel of John, but they also clarify the rather exalted Christology implied by the "I have come" statements in the Synoptic Gospels.

We find additional evidence of the exalted meaning of the "have come" language in how evil spirits react to encounters with Jesus. In the synagogue at Capernaum, a demonized man says to Jesus, "What have you to do with us, Jesus of Nazareth? *Have you come* to destroy us? I know who you are, the Holy One of God" (Mark 1:24). When Jesus speaks of having come, it is in reference to redeeming humanity. But from the point of view of the evil spirit, the coming of Jesus means destruction. We see this again in the encounter of the demonized man in the vicinity of Gerasa, on the east side of the Sea of Galilee: "What have you to do with me, Jesus, Son of the Most High God? I adjure you by God, do not torment me" (Mark 5:7).

The people at Capernaum are astounded by what they have witnessed, declaring, "What is this? A new teaching! With authority he commands even the unclean spirits, and they obey him" (Mark 1:27). Jesus has made use of no incantations or charms. He has not invoked any holy names or made use of any paraphernalia (as exorcists typically did). He has commanded the evil spirit to depart, and he did so by his own authority. The power of Jesus is such that when he encounters evil spirits, they are terrified and cry out, "You are the Son of God" (Mark 3:11). The implication is that they know perfectly well that Jesus' origin and authority are not those of an ordinary human. This is because they know where he *has come* from.

Jesus' divine origin is clearly implied in the parable of the vineyard (Matt 21:33–46 = Mark 12:1–12 = Luke 20:9–19). The parable tells the story of an absentee landlord who leases his vineyard to tenants. When the time comes to collect the profits, the landlord sends his servant. The tenants refuse payment and rough up the servant. The landlord sends more servants. They too are treated violently. Finally, the landlord sends his "beloved son." The tenants see their chance and so murder the son.

The parable is an allegory. Jesus has drawn on Isaiah's song of the vineyard, which is itself an allegory that describes Israel's utter fruitlessness despite God's loving and sufficient care (Isa 5:1–7). Jesus employs the general setting of Isaiah's song, but he introduces new characters (tenants, servants and the son) and shifts the blame from the vineyard itself to the tenants. The meaning of the allegory is quite clear: God is the owner of the vineyard, the vineyard is Israel, the tenants are the religious leaders, the servants are the prophets, and the son of the vineyard owner is Jesus.[14] The parable of the vineyard clarifies just who this Jesus is who *has come*.

The most explicit Christological expression in the Synoptic Gospels is found in the hearing before the Jewish high priest and council (Sanhedrin). Jesus is asked by the high priest, "Are you the Christ, the Son of the Blessed?" (Mark 14:61, i.e., "Are you the Messiah, the Son of God?"). Jesus replies, "I am; and you will see the Son of Man seated at the right hand of Power, and coming with the clouds of heaven" (14:62). The high priest is shocked. He regards Jesus' answer as blasphemy and as deserving of death (14:63–64).

The high priest is shocked because Jesus has not only answered in the affirmative (yes, he is the Messiah, Son of God), he has declared that as the Son of Man who comes with the clouds (a clear allusion to Dan 7:13) he will sit at God's right hand (an allusion to Ps 110:1: "Sit at my right hand, till I make your enemies your footstool"). The statement is shocking indeed, for Jesus has implied that he will sit at God's right (a place of honor) on God's throne, sharing in God's authority, which includes judging the enemies of God. This is a rather exalted self-understanding, and its claim to authenticity is very strong.

It is in the light of material such as this that distinguished Princeton New Testament professor Dale Allison Jr. can say, "We should hold a funeral for the view that Jesus entertained no exalted thoughts about himself."[15] As we have ourselves, Allison mostly focuses on the Synoptic Gospels, dealing with materials that almost all critical scholars accept as authentically reflecting Jesus' teachings.

## What Paul and Other New Testament Writers Say

Before concluding this chapter we should ask what other first-century writers had to say about Jesus. We are especially intrigued by the testimony of Paul, whose letters predate the Synoptic Gospels by a couple of decades and so reflect very early beliefs about Jesus. What was it about Jesus that so moved the Pharisee, Saul of Tarsus, "Hebrew of Hebrews"?

There can be no doubt that before his conversion to the Jesus movement, Saul was a devout Jewish monotheist. There was nothing pagan about him. There would have been no openness to the idea that God could somehow have taken up residence in a human being. What Christology, or messianic hope, Saul may have entertained would likely have been the hope that God would some day raise up a gifted man from the line of David, a man who would restore Israel's fortunes, drive the Romans from the Holy Land and bring about peace and justice for all. But I doubt very much that Saul the Pharisee would have understood such a Messiah as in some sense God in the flesh.

Yet, several times in his letters Saul—who adopts his Roman name *Paul*—applies to Jesus texts that refer to Yahweh. Let us explain. When in his letter to the Christians of Rome, Paul says, "For, *every one who calls upon the name of the Lord will be saved*" (Rom 10:13), he has quoted Joel 2:32 (noted in italics). In the context of Paul's argument, "Lord" refers to Jesus (as is clear in Rom 10:14–17). Humans cannot call on the name of the Lord (Jesus) unless the good news is proclaimed, that is, the "preaching of Christ" (v. 17). What is important to note is that the Lord of whom Joel the prophet speaks is Yahweh, the God of Israel. Paul's knowledge of the Hebrew Scriptures, as well as the Greek translation, assures us that he knows full well what he has done.

In his letter to the Christians of Philippi (in Macedonia) Paul says that though Jesus "was in the form of God," he "humbled himself and became obedient unto death, even death on a cross" (Phil 2:6, 8). Therefore, "God has highly exalted him and bestowed on him the name which is above every name, that at the name of Jesus *every knee should bow*, in heaven and on earth and under the earth, and *every tongue confess* that Jesus Christ is Lord, to the glory of God the Father" (2:9–11). What is remarkable is that the words found in italics are taken from Isaiah, where Yahweh, the God of Israel, says of himself, "By myself I have sworn, from my mouth has gone forth in righteousness a word that shall not return [void]: 'To me every knee shall bow, every tongue shall swear'" (Isa 45:23). The passage from Isaiah reappears in Paul, this time quoted fully in Romans 14:11. Here again the context suggests that Paul understands the Lord, to whom every knee will bow, once again to be none other than Jesus, who "died and lived again, that he might be Lord both of the dead and of the living" (Rom 14:9).

Other Yahweh texts cited in Paul's letters appear to be applied to Jesus, some quoted (e.g., Num 16:5 in 2 Tim 2:19; Isa 40:13 in 1 Cor 2:16; Jer 9:24 in 1 Cor 1:31 and 2 Cor 10:17; Ps 24:1 in 1 Cor 10:26), others alluded to (e.g., Deut 32:21 in 1 Cor 10:22; Mal 1:7, 12 in 1 Cor 10:21; Ps 47:6 in 1 Thess 4:16). In an important and learned study of these passages and others, David Capes wonders how Paul could have held to a higher Christology than to apply to Jesus Old Testament passages that refer to God himself.[16] The implication is that Paul—a strict Jewish monotheist—believed that Jesus was in some sense God.

The author of Hebrews, who is thoroughly Jewish in perspective and tradition, begins his letter by saying, "In many and various ways God spoke of old to our fathers by the prophets; but in these last days he has spoken to us by a Son, whom he appointed the heir of all things, through whom also he created the world" (Heb 1:1–2). This Jewish author places Jesus in a category of his own. God has in the past spoken to his people "by the prophets," but in the last days he has spoken to his people "by a Son." This clearly implies that Jesus is no ordinary prophet. Far from it; Jesus is the "heir of all things" and it is through Jesus that God "created the world." This is an astounding claim.

Has the author of Hebrews implied that Jesus is perhaps an angel of some sort? Not at all. The author of Hebrews asserts that Jesus is "much superior to angels" (Heb 1:4). He demonstrates this claim by asking,

> For to what angel did God ever say, "Thou art my Son, today I have begotten thee"? Or again, "I will be to him a father, and he shall be to me a son" [cf. Ps 2:7]? And again, when he brings the first-born into the world, he says, "Let all God's angels worship him" [cf. Deut 32:43, according to the Greek version]. (Heb 1:5–6)

The angels are God's messengers and servants ("winds" and "flames of fire"), but of his Son God says, "Thy throne, O God, is for ever and ever, the righteous scepter is the scepter of thy kingdom. Thou hast loved righteousness and hated lawlessness; therefore God, thy God, has anointed thee with the oil of gladness beyond thy comrades" (Heb 1:7–9, quoting Ps 45:6–7). As does Paul in his letters, so the author of Hebrews has applied to Jesus an Old Testament text that speaks of God.

## Summary

All four Gospel writers give us essentially the same Jesus: an extraordinary, divine figure who makes extraordinary claims of authority, whose purpose is not to serve himself but to serve—indeed, save—all of humanity. Could such an idea arise from nothing more than a theologically-driven legend? And, if so, who gave it this shape?

The Jesus movement grew out of Jewish soil, a soil that was committed to monotheism and rejected pagan notions of divine men. Exalted Christology—both implicit and explicit—is deeply rooted in the tradition; it won't do to say that exalted ideas about Jesus, placed on his lips, entered the tradition from non-Jewish sources at a very early stage. Paul is himself a guarantor against such a theory, the man who was a Hebrew of Hebrews, a Pharisee, a zealot for the Law of Moses and a persecutor of the Church. But when he encountered the risen Jesus he began to speak of him in very exalted terms, even applying to him Old Testament texts that in their original context spoke of Yahweh, the God of Israel. None of this came from pagan ideas, which he would never have accepted. It came from his experience of Jesus, reinforced by the Jesus tradition itself, with which he became familiar as he matured in his new faith.

The exalted view of Jesus, or what is usually called high Christology, originated in the sayings and deeds of Jesus himself. It did not originate in some post-Easter gradual development, perhaps under the influence of Greco-Roman paganism. Such a proposed scenario strikes us as highly doubtful. Is it credible that four first-century Gospel writers, of whom at least two, if not three, were Jewish, arrived at such an understanding of Jesus—if he were nothing more than a Galilean holy man, prophet and teacher? Jews would hardly invent a story about a divine man, and a friend of sinners and tax collectors at that. Greeks and Romans would hardly invent a story about a suffering savior, especially if he is supposed to be divine. A crucified Son of God? Nonsense! The antiquity, coherence and—we might say—implausibility of the tradition compel us to conclude that it was Jesus himself who entertained exalted thoughts, not later followers.

Chapter 4

# Did James and Paul Preach a Different Gospel?

*Unity and Diversity in the Early Church*

In the previous chapter, it is argued that the belief that Jesus was divine originated in what Jesus said and did. His resurrection provided confirmation. The Jesus movement concurred on this vital point, but the movement did disagree over some matters, especially when it came to aspects of Jewish Law and custom, and expectations with regard to Gentile converts.[1] Some differences of opinion had the potential of being very divisive. Other differences may largely reside in the imagination of modern writers.

Some critics have claimed that James and Paul did not see eye to eye, that in fact they held to two very different understandings of the Christian message, the gospel (or "good news"). For this reason, some even go so far as to claim that Paul is the true founder of the Christian Church, since his theology was markedly different from the theology of Jesus and that of his brother James.[2] This idea comes to vivid expression in Reza Aslan's recent book, when he asserts that "Paul's Christ had long obliterated any last trace of the Jewish Messiah in Jesus…[Paul's] conception of Jesus as Christ would have been shocking and plainly heretical, which is why…James and the apostles demand that Paul come to Jerusalem to answer for his deviant teachings."[3] Contrary to this remarkable assertion, we shall see that when their respective arguments are fully understood, Paul and James are not at odds with one another in any significant way.

## The Message of James: "Without Works, Faith Is Dead"

Tradition holds that the New Testament letter of James was penned by James the brother of Jesus (see Mark 6:3, where the names of the brothers of Jesus are mentioned). The letter doesn't actually make this claim explicitly; it simply begins, "James, a servant of God and of the Lord Jesus Christ" (James 1:1). Not all Church Fathers believed the letter was written by James, but in the end most did, and so it was included in the canon of Scripture. Today a number of scholars, including some who have written major commentaries on James, have concluded that the letter probably was written by the brother of Jesus.[4] One reason for concluding this is the letter's rather modest claim to be written by "a servant of God and of the Lord Jesus Christ." In apocryphal and pseudepigraphal writings, claims of prominent authorship typically are more explicit. In this case, if the author is claiming to be the brother of Jesus, then why not say so? Why not make more of such a distinguished connection? The failure to exploit fully this potential is in favor of the traditional identification of the author.

James first appears in the book of Acts in the context of King Agrippa I's violence against the leaders of the Church. In Acts 12:1–5 we have an account of these actions:

> About that time Herod the king laid violent hands upon some who belonged to the church. He killed James the brother of John with the sword; and when he saw that it pleased the Jews, he proceeded to arrest Peter also. This was during the days of Unleavened Bread. And when he had seized him, he put him in prison, and delivered him to four squads of soldiers to guard him, intending after the Passover to bring him out to the people. So Peter was kept in prison; but earnest prayer for him was made to God by the church.

Agrippa I was the son of Aristobulus IV and Bernice I and the brother of Herodias (cf. Mark 6:15–28). Only the New Testament refers to Agrippa I as "Herod," a name that more or less functioned as a dynastic name since the time of Agrippa's famous grandfather Herod the Great. (Agrippa I is called Herod several more times, in Acts 12:6, 11, 19–21.)

In the passage cited from the book of Acts we are not told specifically why Agrippa arrested some of the Christians. Whatever his motive, he executed James son of Zebedee, the brother of John, and then, seeing that it pleased certain people, he proceeded to arrest Peter also. The church prayed for Peter, Peter then enjoyed a miraculous escape and safely reached the house of a woman named Mary, the mother of John Mark (Acts 12:6–16), who later accompanied Paul on his first missionary journey. It is in the conclusion of this remarkable story that James the brother of Jesus is mentioned.

After Peter describes his escape (Acts 12:17), he says, "Tell this to James and to the brethren" (12:17). The narrator then remarks abruptly and with little detail, "Then he departed and went to another place" (12:17). From this cryptic remark it is assumed that Peter has quit Jerusalem and that James the brother of Jesus has assumed the leadership. Not long after leaving Jerusalem, Peter visits Antioch and eventually takes up residence in Rome.

Peter's instructions "Tell this to James and to the brethren" implies that James is "second in command," as it were. But it also implies that James was not expected to quit Jerusalem, as Peter and others found it necessary. Why is this? Judging by the advice that James will later give (in Acts 15) and by the tradition of his piety and devotion in the precincts of the Jerusalem temple, along with no evidence that James either condemned the temple priesthood or threatened the temple with its destruction (at least not until shortly before his martyrdom), we may infer that James's commitment to Jewish faith and practice was such that the religious and political authorities saw no reason to take action against him. Evidently, the religious devotion of James was such that temple authorities saw no reason to persecute this particular leader of the Jesus movement.

What we learn from Acts 12:17, which records Peter's abrupt words "Tell this to James and to the brethren," is that, in the absence of Peter, James has become the leader of the Jesus movement. When the Church grapples with the vexatious question of whether Gentiles who become believers must also become Jewish proselytes and then turns to James (and not to Peter or Paul) for guidance, we begin to appreciate the gravity of his leadership and the respect with which James is treated by the Church.

If the author of the letter of James was in fact the brother of Jesus, which is the position taken here, then a disagreement with Paul would be a serious matter indeed. But was there really a disagreement? Some think so. Many will recall Martin Luther's famous dismissal of James as a "strawy epistle" whose character lacked the marks of the gospel. Luther said this because his critics claimed that James contradicted the great reformer's emphasis on Paul's doctrine of salvation by God's grace, received through faith alone, not by works.

James was held to be at odds with Paul because of the letter's declaration that "faith by itself, if it has no works, is dead" (James 2:17) and that a person "is justified by works and not by faith alone" (2:24). These categorical statements are not isolated; they reflect the tenor of the letter's thought throughout. James exhorts his readers to accept trials and testing with joy and to let it have its "perfect work [*ergon teleion*]" (1:3–4, NKJV). He urges his readers to become "doers of the word [*poiētai logou*], and not hearers only" (1:22). He speaks of the "perfect law [*nomon teleion*]" (1:25). He urges his readers not to be forgetful hearers but to be "a doer of the work [*poiētēs ergou*]" (NKJV), who "shall be blessed" (1:25).

The spirit of this teaching, as well as some of the vocabulary, brings to mind the teaching of Jesus, especially as we find it assembled in the Sermon on the Mount. According to Jesus, the person who "does them and teaches [*poiēsē kai didaxē*] them [the commandments] shall be called great in the kingdom of heaven" (Matt 5:19). The righteousness (*dikaiosynē*) of the disciples must exceed that of the scribes and Pharisees. How this can be accomplished is spelled out in the five antitheses that follow (5:21–47). At the conclusion of the antitheses, Jesus sums up his teaching: "You, therefore, must be perfect [*teleioi*], as your heavenly Father is perfect [*teleios*]" (5:48).[5] Perfection cannot be achieved without doing the commandments, as Jesus has taught. The conclusion of the Sermon on the Mount drives home this point (emphasis added):

> "Not every one who says to me, 'Lord, Lord,' shall enter the kingdom of heaven, but he who *does* the will of my Father who is in heaven." (7:21)
> "Every one then who hears these words [*tous logous*] of mine and *does* them will be like a wise man who built his house upon the rock." (7:24)
> "And every one who hears these words of mine and *does not do* them will be like a foolish man who built his house upon the sand." (7:26)

Elsewhere in Jesus' sayings in Matthew, we find similar teaching (emphasis added):

> "For whoever *does* the will of my Father in heaven is my brother, and sister, and mother." (12:50)
> "Which of the two *did* the will of his father?" (21:31)
> "*[Do] and observe* whatever they tell you, but not what they do; for they preach, but do not [do]." (23:3, RSV, modified)
> "They *do* all their deeds to be seen by others." (23:5, NRSV)

We may well hear echoes of this teaching in James's exhortations to be "doers of the word" and a "doer of work"—works that exemplify the "perfect work," "perfect law," and the "royal law."

Verse 27 sums up the point of the first chapter of James: "Religion that is pure and undefiled before God and the Father is this: to visit orphans and widows in their affliction, and to keep oneself unstained from the world."

This brings us to James 2. The second chapter is chiefly concerned to explicate the second commandment of the famous Great (or Double) Commandment (Mark 12:28–34; Luke 10:25–29), whereby one is to love God with all that one is and all that one has (Deut 6:4–5) and to love one's neighbor as one's self (Lev 19:18). The partiality described in James 2:1–13 fails to fulfill the second commandment, which is quoted in James 2:8. Although the remainder of the chapter (vv. 14–26) defines genuine faith, the focus remains on what it means to fulfill the second commandment. To fulfill "the royal law" (James 2:8) is to fulfill Leviticus 19:18, a commandment that lay behind much of what Jesus taught, either explicitly or implicitly.[6]

Failure to fulfill the second commandment has implications for the first commandment, to which allusion is made in 2:19: "You believe that God is one; you do well. Even the demons believe—and shudder." The mere belief, or faith, that God is one hardly fulfills the obligations to love one's neighbor and, harking back to James 1:27, hardly fulfills the command to "visit orphans and widows in their affliction."

To support his argument, James appeals to the example of Abraham, who was "justified by [his] works [ex ergōn edikaiōthē], when he offered his son Isaac upon the altar" (2:21). His willingness to obey God demonstrated that his faith was genuine. His "work" in Genesis 22 (where he showed that he was willing to sacrifice Isaac) fulfilled the statement of Scripture in Genesis 15:6 (James 2:23). We suspect that James had in mind Abraham's example of faith early on. We may hear an allusion to it in 1:3, where James declares that "the testing of your faith produces steadfastness," which in turn will lead to perfection (1:4).

James's understanding of Abraham's faith was not unique. A similar argument is found in 1 Maccabees, a book (composed c. 100 BC) that narrates the Jewish revolt against Antiochus IV Epiphanes in 167 BC. Abraham, his faith and his righteousness are cited by the leader of the Maccabean revolt. On his deathbed the priest Mattathias exhorts his sons,

> Now, my children, show zeal for the law, and give your lives for the covenant of our fathers. Remember the deeds of the fathers, which they did in their generations; and receive great honor and an ever-lasting name. Was not Abraham found faithful when tested, and it was reckoned to him as righteousness? (1 Macc 2:50–52)

According to Mattathias, Abraham was found "faithful" when he was "tested" by God's command to offer up his son Isaac (Gen 22). Abraham's faithful-ness (i.e., his faith in God) "was reckoned to him as righteousness." This last part of v. 52 is an unmistakable allusion to Genesis 15:6, which both James and Paul quote in their respective arguments. The argument of James, how-ever, parallels some of the argument in 1 Maccabees 2 more closely than does Paul's argument. In James and 1 Maccabees, the claim is made that Abraham's faith in God was witnessed *in his willingness to offer up his son.* It was this faith that was reckoned to him as righteousness. The overlap in the scriptural appeal of 1 Maccabees and James helps us understand more clearly the differences in the respective arguments of James and Paul.

Both James and 1 Maccabees argue that genuine faith takes action, or, to put it the other way, action demonstrates the reality of faith. For Mattathias, true faith was demonstrated by zeal for the Law of Moses. For James, true faith was demonstrated by fulfilling the "royal law," that is, loving one's neighbor as one's self (2:8–20). A faith that does not produce "works," that is, works of mercy toward those in need, is a dead faith (James 2:24–26). In the section that follows we shall see that this teaching does not contradict Paul's teaching about justification apart from works of the Law.

## The Message of Paul: "No One Is Justified by Works of the Law"

Before examining Paul's teaching, it will be helpful to review his relation-ship to James, as Paul himself describes it and as it is described by the author of the book of Acts. The evidence suggests that although Paul respected James, the brother of Jesus, there were some tensions.

In Galatians 2:9, Paul refers to James as one of the "pillars" of the Church. "Pillar" here may carry temple connotations, as when the word occurs in ref-erence to the pillars, or upright frames, in the wilderness tabernacle (e.g., Exod 26:15–37; 27:10–17; 35:11, 17; 36:36, 38; 38:10–19; 39:33, 40; 40:18). Some scholars suspect that the early Church viewed James, Peter (or Cephas) and John as pillars of the new temple. Richard Bauckham has argued that the leaders of the Jesus movement were called pillars as part of the "early Church's understanding of itself as the eschatological Temple," on analogy with the Qumran community, which also saw itself as a spiritual temple.[7]

In Christian tradition, Peter is the rock on which Jesus will build his Church (Matt 16:18), Jesus himself is the foundation (1 Cor 3:11) or cornerstone (Eph 2:20; 1 Pet 2:4, 6–7), and Christian believers are themselves the building blocks of a living temple (1 Pet 2:5; Hermas, *Visions* 3; and *Similitudes* 9). Some of this imagery is itself based on the temple imagery found in the Old Testament Scriptures, especially in reference to the promised and awaited eschatological temple: stones and foundations (Isa 54:11), cornerstone (Isa 28:16; Ps. 118:22; both quoted in 1 Pet 2:6–7) and pillars (Prov 9:1). In post-New Testament traditions, James is himself called the "Rampart of the People" (according to Eusebius, *Hist. Eccl.* 2.23.7), a title probably based on Isaiah 54:11–12 and likely also part of the imagery of the eschatological temple.

Being regarded as one of the "pillars" of the early Church testifies to the esteem in which James was held. The book of Acts also testifies to the esteem of James, as well as to his leadership. We see this when James directs Paul to purify himself and pay the expenses of four men who are under a Nazirite vow. Not only do we catch an important glimpse of James's continuing leadership and authority, we may also discover how it is that James was able to reside in Jerusalem while others, like Peter and the original apostles, found it necessary to relocate.

---

## James Meets the Risen Jesus

And when the Lord [Jesus] had given the linen cloth to the servant of the priest, he went to James and appeared to him. For James had sworn that he would not eat bread from that hour in which he had drunk the cup of the Lord until he should see him risen from among them that sleep. And shortly thereafter the Lord said: "Bring table and bread!" And immediately it is added: "He took the bread, blessed it and broke it and gave it to James the Just and said to him: 'My brother, eat your bread, for the Son of Man is risen from among them that sleep.'" (Jerome, *Vir. ill.* 2)

Jerome says he found this passage in the *Gospel of the Hebrews*, which scholars think was written c. AD 140.

---

When Paul returned to Jerusalem in 58 AD, in time for the Feast of Pentecost, he visited James and "all the elders" (Acts 21:18). Paul related to them what he had experienced in his recent travels and missionary activities, for which James and his colleagues expressed joy (21:19–20). But then James had advice for Paul on how to conduct himself (21:20–25). James told Paul that by doing what had been suggested, "all will know that there is nothing in what they have been told about you but that you yourself live in observance of the law" (21:24).

The author of the book of Acts has labored to show that Paul and James held to essentially the same view with respect to the crucial question of circumcision and law. Fair and careful reading of Paul's letters suggests that the portrait in Acts is accurate, even if vague and incomplete in places. But one important point of comparison remains to be considered. Did Paul and James differ over the place of "works of law" in the life of the believer? It is time now to turn once again to the letter of James.

In his polemical and at times heated letter to the churches of Galatia, Paul emphatically gives expression to his view that no one can be justified by works of the Law:

> We ourselves, who are Jews by birth and not Gentile sinners, yet who know that a man is not justified by works of the law but through faith in Jesus Christ, even we have believed in Christ Jesus, in order to be justified by faith in Christ, and not by works of the law, because by works of the law shall no one be justified. (Gal 2:15–16)

> Thus Abraham "believed God, and it was reckoned to him as righteousness." So you see that it is men of faith who are the sons of Abraham. (Gal 3:6–7)

> Now it is evident that no man is justified before God by the law; for "He who through faith is righteous shall live"; but the law does not rest on faith, for "He who does them shall live by them." (Gal 3:11–12)

One hardly needs to be a theologian or Bible scholar to hear what Paul is saying in these passages: "No one is justified by works of the Law." Paul bases his argument for the most part on the well-known passage in Genesis where Abraham, in response to God's promise of land, seed and blessing, "believed the LORD; and he reckoned it to him as righteousness" (Gen 15:6). He also appeals to Habakkuk 2:4 (in Gal 3:11). That the law requires "works" (or "doing") is seen in Leviticus 18:5, which Paul also quotes (in Gal 3:12).

In a less polemical tone, Paul restates his argument in his letter to the Christians in Rome. Here Paul has given careful thought to this interpretation of Scripture and how it sheds light on the question the law and justification. Paul says,

> But now the righteousness of God has been manifested apart from law, although the law and the prophets bear witness to it, the righteousness of God through faith in Jesus Christ for all who believe. For there is no distinction; since all have sinned and fall short of the glory of God, they are justified by his grace as a gift, through the redemption which is in Christ Jesus, whom God put forward as an expiation by his blood, to be received by faith...For we hold that a man is justified by faith apart from works of law. (Rom 3:21–28)

For Paul, salvation cannot be earned. If righteousness before God—and therefore salvation—could be earned, then there would have been no need for the Messiah, God's Son, to die on the cross. Rather, salvation is a gift of God, received through faith, not through works. This is seen in the great patriarch Abraham, who believed God's promise—understood to include the saving work of the Messiah—and was therefore reckoned righteous. Abraham's faith transformed him from a Gentile, as it were, to the father of the Jewish people. It was his faith, not his obedience to law or his later circumcision, that effected this transformation. So goes Paul's thinking.

For Martin Luther, the great German reformer of the sixteenth century, Paul's emphasis on God's grace and the demand for faith was just what was needed to challenge what he perceived to be an unhealthy and unbiblical emphasis on legalism and works in the Church of his day. The only problem was that the letter of James appeared to contradict Paul's teaching. Near the end of a major teaching section, James concludes, "You see that a man is justified by works and not by faith alone" (2:24). No wonder, then, that Luther showed little regard for James, referring to it dismissively as a "strawy epistle" (German: *strohern Epistel*) and, in comparison to the works of Paul, Peter and the Gospel of John, which "show thee Christ," saw it as containing little of the gospel.[8]

The problem for Luther was that he did not interpret James correctly. James's references to "works" have nothing to do with "works of the law," which Paul saw as antithetical to a gospel of grace, freely received through faith. Study of the whole of James 2 shows that the brother of Jesus offered an exposition of Jesus' principal teaching, his so-called

Great Commandment, that one is to love God with all that one is and has, and one is to love one's neighbor as one's self (Mark 12:28–34; cf. Luke 10:25–28).

Earlier in this chapter we noted that James insists that true faith fulfills the "royal law," the law based on Leviticus 19:18 (love your neighbor as yourself), to which Jesus made appeal. Feeding the hungry and caring for the poor is evidence of genuine faith. These are the "works" that demonstrate the reality of one's faith. Apart from such works, one's faith is "dead" (James 2:26). This is why James states categorically that one "is justified by works and not by faith alone" (2:24).

The works of which Paul speaks in Romans and Galatians are "works of law," works by which one establishes his righteousness. These are not works of the "royal law," works of mercy and loving-kindness. In Galatians, Paul angrily criticized Peter for withdrawing from Gentile Christians. In Antioch, Peter was willing to eat with Gentiles, but when emissaries from James came to Antioch, Peter withdrew from these Gentiles. Peter did not want the men from Jerusalem to think he was eating non-kosher food. Eating kosher food, observing the Sabbath, keeping oneself ritually pure—all of these things are what Paul calls "works of the law." These are not the works to which James makes reference in his letter.

We have a much better understanding of this important distinction thanks to the survival of six copies of a legal letter from Qumran's cave 4.[9] Although in fragments, the overlapping copies allow us to reconstruct almost the entire original letter. The letter defines and discusses some two dozen works of the law that one must do to maintain purity and righteousness. These works include not mixing the holy with the profane and avoiding Gentile food. Separation from things that defile is strongly urged. The letter concludes, "We have written to you some of the works of the Law, those which we determined would be beneficial to you and your people…[If you do these works] you shall rejoice at the end time…and it will be reckoned to you as righteousness, in that you have done what is right and good."[10] These are the works of the Law that Paul criticizes, not the works mentioned in the letter of James. The works of Law that calls for separation from Gentiles, only eating kosher food and the like are not what justifies one in the sight of God. But works of love and mercy—which is what James was talking about—Paul fully supports.

In a later letter, written either by Paul himself or by one of Paul's students writing in his name, we find similar thinking, where grace and faith, on the one hand, go hand in hand with good works, on the other:

> For by grace you have been saved through faith; and this is not your own doing, it is the gift of God—not because of works, lest any man should boast. For we are his workmanship, created in Christ Jesus for good works, which God prepared beforehand, that we should walk in them. (Eph 2:8–10)

## Summary

James and Paul agreed with respect to the essence of the gospel message. But their respective ministries were directed to two very different constituencies ethnically, culturally and geographically. It is not a surprise that their language is not always easy to reconcile.

The letter of James was addressed to the "twelve tribes in the Dispersion," that is, to Jewish Christians.[11] The letter was not addressed to Gentiles, unlike Paul's letters. Rather, the letter of James reinforced aspects of Jesus' teaching especially as it related to "doing righteousness" with respect to other human beings. The genuine faith that Jesus called for and James insisted upon was not pious platitudes but an active faith that manifested itself in substantial acts of compassion. A non-active faith runs the risk of being nothing more than a form of Pharisaism in which one doesn't lift a finger to help one in need (see Matt 23:4, where Jesus says of the Pharisees, "They bind heavy burdens, hard to bear, and lay them on men's shoulders; but they themselves will not move them with their finger").

Paul too is reacting against a Pharisaic understanding of works of Law, whereby through works that emphasize purity (and often that means separation from Gentiles) one believes that one has established a righteousness that will be pleasing to God. It is this "works" that Paul says cannot save and will not result in righteousness before God. James does not contradict this idea. He never addresses it.

There were differences between Paul and James, to be sure. But the differences largely centered on their very different constituencies. Paul's constituency was primarily a Gentile one, while the constituency of James was primarily, perhaps exclusively, Jewish. But on the matter of works they did not differ. Both embraced the good news of God's gracious provision in

Jesus, a provision received in faith, and both urged Christians to practice their faith as Jesus himself taught.

But very importantly, there is no evidence that Paul invented Christianity or altered the early Church's understanding of the person and work of Jesus. Paul stood in continuity with the original apostles, who after meeting Paul and hearing him out extended to him the "right hand of fellowship" (Gal 2:9).

# Chapter 5

# Was Jesus a Zealot?

*The Real Aims of Jesus*

When historians consider Jesus, they try to classify him. They do this with all historical figures. Here are a few examples: Aristotle was a philosopher, but his famous student Alexander the Great was a military commander and empire-builder. The first-century Jewish aristocrat Josephus was an apologist and historian. The early second-century Simon ben Kosibah, who became known as Bar Kokhba (Aramaic, meaning "Son of the Star"), was a charismatic messianic claimant who gave leadership to Israel's last great rebellion against Rome. Defining, or classifying, these figures helps us to interpret their activities more accurately.

Classifying figures of history is part of the historian's attempt to place them in the appropriate context. This is very true in the case of Jesus of Nazareth. Because of his multi-faceted activities and teachings, classifying Jesus has not been easy. Emphasizing his role as teacher, some see Jesus as a rabbi. Others think he was more of a prophet or a martyr. Others see him as a political leader, perhaps a king of sorts. More eccentric proposals include Jesus as a Pharisee, an Essene, a magician, or even an Eastern mystic. Another proposal made from time to time argues that Jesus was a zealot.

In this chapter we shall consider the zealot classification, which in one form or another has been proposed from time to time. To understand why it has been proposed, it will be necessary to review not only the evidence that has been offered for it but also the history and biblical background to zealotry. The topic is an important one, to be sure, but it is not always understood.

## Jesus as Zealot

One of the earliest and most influential expressions of the idea that Jesus was a zealot appeared in the posthumous publication of parts of a manuscript by Hermann Samuel Reimarus (1694–1768). This work is often given credit for launching what became known as the "quest of the historical Jesus." In the seventh installment, entitled *On the Aim of Jesus and His Disciples* and published in 1778,[1] Reimarus suggested that Jesus and his disciples attempted to seize control of the temple precincts in Jerusalem and establish a new government. Jesus was defeated and executed; his disciples were initially scattered but later regrouped and invented the story of the resurrection in order to re-energize the movement. Almost no one followed Reimarus.

In 1929–30, German scholar Robert Eisler revived the zealot theory, relying heavily on Josephus and the dubious Old Slavonic version of Josephus's *Jewish Wars*, in which are found a number of references to Jesus and his disciples.[2] No scholars today think these references were part of Josephus's original work. Rather, they are regarded as later insertions into the text in the early medieval period. As for Eisler's work itself, it is regarded as eccentric at best. Some have described it as perverse.

In the 1950s and 1960s, the zealot hypothesis was reformulated, this time with a bit more nuance, by comparative religions scholar and World War II veteran S. G. F. Brandon of the University of Manchester in the United Kingdom.[3] Like Eisler, Brandon argued that Jesus attempted to seize control of Jerusalem by force of arms. But his views gained no scholarly following.

In 1970, Martin Hengel, a well-known and respected professor of Christian origins at Tübingen University in Germany, published a brief but devastating critique of the zealot hypothesis.[4] Today this hypothesis is advanced by no scholar with expertise in the field. When in 1985 E. P. Sanders published his highly regarded *Jesus and Judaism*, he could say, "Brandon's view...will get no airing at all, since I consider that it has been sufficiently refuted," and then in a footnote cites Hengel's incisive study.[5] No one objected to what Sanders said.

The point of all of this is that the zealot hypothesis has been laid to rest. Scholars may talk about political unrest and banditry in Israel in the time of Jesus and how that potentially clarifies some of the dynamics and dangers that Jesus and his followers faced,[6] but they rightly recognize that Jesus himself was no zealot. This is why Reza Aslan's recently published

*Zealot: The Life and Times of Jesus of Nazareth,*[7] which resurrects the zealot hypothesis, strikes us as odd and strangely dated.

Aslan's version of the zealot hypothesis contains little that is new. Part of his interpretation rests upon the idea that the world of Jesus was one of zealotry, understood as a fervent nationalism that strongly desired an end of Roman and Herodian rule and the restoration of the Davidic royal dynasty. Aslan assumes that Jesus fits right into this picture, as one of dozens of wandering prophets and would-be Messiahs proclaiming the kingdom of God. To justify his classification of Jesus as a zealot, Aslan focuses on Jesus' entry into Jerusalem and his demonstration in the temple precincts. Jesus' actions were such that his disciples recalled the words of Psalm 69:9: "Zeal for thy house will consume me" (John 2:17). Aslan brushes aside learned scholarship that interprets this event very differently from the way he does as "centuries of exegetical acrobatics."[8] He does the same with the ancient sources themselves, dismissing the many passages in the Gospels that contradict the zealot hypothesis as "fanciful," "absurd," "fictional," "ridiculous," and "preposterous." The closed-minded bias is hard to miss.

In the balance of this chapter, we shall briefly explore Jewish zealotry in the time of Jesus and then inquire into the aims and goals of Jesus and his disciples. Our purpose is to define the zeal of Jesus and interpret it in context. We shall see that at points Jesus is similar to some of his predecessors and contemporaries, but at many points Jesus is quite different. We begin with a review of the history of zealotry in Israel.

## Jewish Zealotry in Old Testament Times and in the Time of Jesus

The Old Testament zealot par excellence is Phinehas. He makes his first appearance in Exodus 6, where he is identified as Aaron's grandson (Exod 6:25; 1 Chr 6:4, 50; 9:20; Ezra 7:5). He next appears in Numbers 25, in the episode where many Israelites join Moabites and Midianites in worshipping the god (or "Baal," presumably Chemosh; cf. Num 21:29) of Peor while they are encamped on the plain within sight of Mount Peor (cf. Num 23:28; 24:2; 31:16; Deut 3:29; 4:3; Ps 106:28). These activities, which involve sexual promiscuity and feasting in honor of the god of Peor, result in a plague. While Moses and others are weeping before the entrance of the Tent of Meeting, an Israelite man brings a Midianite woman into the camp. He does this in the very sight of the grieving Moses. The reader should infer that this man has no regard whatsoever for Moses or for Israel's sacred covenant with God.

When Phinehas sees this outrage, he takes a spear, kills both the man and the woman, and so brings the plague to an end. The reader learns why when God tells Moses,

> "Phinehas the son of Eleazar, son of Aaron the priest, has turned back my wrath from the people of Israel, in that he was jealous with my jealousy among them, so that I did not consume the people of Israel in my jealousy. Therefore say, 'Behold, I give to him my covenant of peace; and it shall be to him, and to his descendants after him, the covenant of a perpetual priesthood, because he was jealous for his God, and made atonement for the people of Israel.'" (Num 25:11–13)

What is translated "He was jealous with my jealousy" could also be translated "He was zealous with my zeal." So also in verse 13, "jealous for his God" could be translated "zealous for his God." On account of this episode, Phinehas is remembered for his zeal. God gives this priest a "covenant of peace" and his descendants a "covenant of a perpetual priesthood."

Phinehas reappears in the war with Midian (Num 31:1–12). He joins the army and is entrusted with the holy vessels and the trumpets (v. 6). Israel routs the kings of Midian, taking spoils and captives (vv. 7–12). Again Phinehas appears in Joshua 22, in which he is sent as an emissary of sorts to rebuke the tribes of Reuben, Gad and Manasseh (vv. 13–20). When the leaders of these tribes convince the priest of their fidelity, Phinehas is pleased and is able to give the rest of Israel a favorable report (vv. 30–34). Phinehas is mentioned later, in Judges 20, when readers are reminded that he used to stand before the ark of the covenant and minister (vv. 27–28). In his recounting of the principal priests in Israel's early history, the Chronicler mentions Phinehas, saying, "Phinehas the son of Eleazar was the ruler over them in time past; the LORD was with him" (1 Chr 9:20).

Phinehas makes his final appearance in Hebrew Scripture in Psalm 106, a psalm of repentance that recalls and confesses the many instances of Israel's sin and rebellion, including the aforementioned apostasy at Peor:

Then they attached themselves to the Baal of Peor,
  and ate sacrifices offered to the dead;
they provoked the LORD to anger with their doings,
  and a plague broke out among them.
Then Phinehas stood up and interposed,
  and the plague was stayed.
And that has been reckoned to him as righteousness
  from generation to generation for ever. (Ps 106:28–31)

Phinehas reappears in intertestamental literature and later Jewish writers. More will be said about him in the following section.

There are other acts of zeal recorded in the Old Testament. Out of his "zeal for the people of Israel and Judah" King Saul slaughtered the Gibeonites (2 Sam 21:2, harking back to Josh 9:3–15, where Israel had been deceived by the Gibeonites). Elijah recalls his zeal for God (1 Kings 19:10, 14), which among other things includes the defeat and destruction of the prophets of Baal (1 Kings 18:20–40). Jehu, newly crowned king of the northern kingdom of Israel, says to a companion, "Come with me, and see my zeal for the LORD" (2 Kings 10:16). He then kills every member of the family of Ahab, a king who earlier had ruled over Israel.

We cite these examples because the language of "zeal" and "zealous" appears. It is likely, however, that the violent deeds of a number of other figures would have been viewed in later times as acts of zeal for God and his Law. One thinks of Joshua and Caleb in the book of Joshua, many of the judges in the book of Judges, and the daring deeds of David and other righteous kings in the books of Samuel and Kings.

What is interesting is that most instances of zeal resulted in killing people. In other words, the writers of Israel's ancient narratives that chronicle the history of the patriarchs, leaders and kings tend to reserve high praise for men and women of very bold action, even violent action. In short, to be zealous for God or for God's Law often meant a willingness to die for it and, if necessary, to kill for it. This thinking takes a more definitive form in the intertestamental period and, not surprisingly, focuses on Phinehas the zealous priest.

## Examples of Zeal in the Intertestamental Period

The zeal of Phinehas, dramatically witnessed in the incident near Peor during Israel's wanderings in the wilderness, resulted in an almost iconic status for this priest. One of the oldest post-Old Testament testimonies is found in Sirach, who lauds Phinehas in his Praise for Famous Men (Sir 44–51). In his praise of Phinehas, one hears echoes of Numbers 25 and Psalm 106:

> Phinehas the son of Eleazar is the third in glory,
>> for he was zealous in the fear of the Lord,
>> and stood fast, when the people turned away,
>> in the ready goodness of his soul, and made atonement for Israel.
> Therefore a covenant of peace was established with him,
>> that he should be leader of the sanctuary and of his people,
>> that he and his descendants should have
>> the dignity of the priesthood for ever. (Sir 45:23–24)

Joshua ben Sira (Greek: "Jesus the son of Sirach") composed his work in Hebrew sometime around 180 BC. About 50 years later, his grandson prefaced it and translated it into Greek. Phinehas appears in exalted company indeed, preceded by Moses (vv. 1–5) and Aaron (vv. 6–22) and followed by David (vv. 25–26). The appearance of David is chronologically out of sequence, for Joshua the son of Nun, successor to Moses, will make his appearance in Sir 46:1–12. Mention of David is brought forward because he too was honored with a covenant. A covenant of peace and priesthood was established with Phinehas, and a covenant of kingship was established with David. The coupling of Phinehas with David, each blessed with a covenant, one priestly and the other kingly, is highly significant, testifying to the dyarchic nature of Israel's ordained leadership.

In 1 Maccabees the zealous actions of Mattathias, father of Judas Maccabeus and his brothers, are compared to the zeal and violence of Phinehas:

> When Mattathias saw it, he burned with zeal and his heart was stirred. He gave vent to righteous anger; he ran and killed him upon the altar. At the same time he killed the king's officer who was forcing them to sacrifice, and he tore down the altar. Thus he burned with zeal for the law, as Phinehas did against Zimri the son of Salu. Then Mattathias cried out in the city with a loud voice, saying: "Let every one who is zealous for the law and supports the covenant come out with me!" (1 Macc 2:24–27)

Phinehas is again mentioned by name in Mattathias's farewell to his sons, a farewell modeled after Jacob's farewell to his sons in Genesis 49, which gave rise to a genre that became very popular in the intertestamental and New Testament periods. Here is part of Mattathias's farewell:

| Maccabean Zealots/Leaders |
| --- |
| Mattathias (167–166 BC) |
| Judas Maccabeus (166–160 BC) |
| Jonathan Apphus (160–142 BC) |
| Eleazar Abaran (d. 163) |
| Simon Thassi (142–134 BC) |
| John Gaddi (d. 159) |

> Now, my children, show zeal for the law, and give your lives for the covenant of our fathers. Remember the deeds of the fathers, which they did in their generations; and receive great honor and an everlasting name...Phinehas our father, because he was deeply zealous, received the covenant of everlasting priesthood...Elijah because of great zeal for the law was taken up into heaven. (1 Macc 2:50–51, 54, 58)

Zeal for the Law is the theme that runs throughout this farewell testament. Once again we find Phinehas in illustrious company. The author of 1 Maccabees, a book composed sometime around 100 BC, cites the examples of Abraham, Joseph, Joshua, Caleb, David, Elijah, Daniel and the three faithful young men in Daniel 3 (1 Macc 2:52–60). Mattathias is a priest (1 Macc 2:1) and can find no better example of priestly zeal than that of Phinehas, grandson of Aaron.

Philo of Alexandria (c. 20 BC—AD 50) speaks approvingly of the zeal of Phinehas. In one place he says, "But Phineas the priest, who was zealous with a great zeal for God's service, did not provide for his own safety by flight" (*Allegorical Interpretation* 3.242). No, the priest did not flee; he struck down the wicked. In another place Philo says that "warlike reason" is called *Phinehas*, the priest who had "received a zeal for virtue" (*Confusion* 57). In recounting Israel's history, Josephus mentions Phinehas, stating that the priest "surpassed his contemporaries in the dignity of his father," the son of Aaron, brother of Moses (*Antiquities* 4.152; see also 5.104, where Phinehas is numbered among the men held "in esteem among the Hebrews").

In summary, we have four major texts in which the zeal of Phinehas is underscored: two in the Old Testament and two in important intertestamental literature. In Numbers 25, we hear of the priest's zeal, a promised covenant of peace and an eternal priesthood. In Psalm 106, we hear of his zeal, his action being reckoned to him as righteousness, and "from generation to generation," which may allude to the promise of perpetual priesthood. In Sirach 45, we hear of zeal, the covenant of peace and an eternal priesthood. And in 1 Maccabees 2, we read of zeal and everlasting priesthood.

For Mattathias, father of Judas Maccabeus, Jonathan and Simon, the men who gave leadership to the Jewish revolt against Antiochus IV Epiphanes, the zeal of the priest Phinehas was the inspiration for their own zeal. The sons of Mattathias heeded their father's exhortation and fought bravely against the Greeks. Each died, though not before gaining important victories and restoring Israel's independence and Israel's religious practices.

There were other zealots, though because they were seized, tortured and murdered, they were usually referred to as martyrs. But these people were every bit as zealous as those who were willing to kill those they regarded as wicked. We have graphic accounts of their martyrdoms in 2 Maccabees 6–7 and related literature.

What is important to remember is that to be "zealous" does not necessarily mean one who is ready and willing to kill for one's faith and convictions. It can equally apply to one who is ready and willing to lay down one's life for one's faith and convictions. Philo also speaks of this dimension of zeal, explaining in his statement to Roman emperor Gaius Caligula that Jewish "zeal for their holy Temple is the most predominant, and vehement, and universal feeling throughout the whole nation" (*To Gaius* 212). Philo further says, "our zeal and earnestness is displayed not in the cause of gain, but in that of religion; though indeed we speak foolishly in using such an expression as that, for what can be a more real and beneficial gain to them than holiness?" (*To Gaius* 242). Philo penned these words c. AD 40, only a few years after Jesus of Nazareth was seized by the Jewish ruling priests and was handed over to the Roman governor. Philo was speaking of zeal for the temple and zeal for holiness, not taking up arms against the Romans or other rulers.

## Jerusalem Temple Warning

A 19-inch high limestone fragment contains a warning to Gentiles to stay out of the temple. The fragment was found in 1935 outside the wall around Jerusalem's Old City. A complete version of the same inscription is in the Archaeological Museum in Istanbul, Turkey. The inscription reads,

Let no Gentile enter
within the partition and barrier
surrounding the Temple; whosoever
is caught shall be responsible
for his subsequent
death.

This is probably the warning described by Josephus: "upon [the partition wall of the temple court] stood pillars, at equal distances from one another, declaring the law of purity, some in Greek, and some in Roman letters, that 'no foreigner should go within that sanctuary'" (*J. W.* 5.193–94).

## Zealots in the Time of Jesus

In the approximate time of Jesus, there were a number of men who were in various ways zealous for the Law of Moses and were willing to kill or be martyred for their faith. These would include Hezekiah (called "Ezekias the brigand" by Josephus), who fought Herod the Great for control of Israel in the 30s BC. They would include various men who fought Herod's son Archelaus and the Romans following Herod's death and would also include others who led uprisings leading up to and including the great revolt in 66–73. Josephus described the whole lot of them as the "Zealots" and even claimed that they represented a "fourth philosophy" among the various Jewish sects. (The other three sects are Pharisees, Sadducees and Essenes.) Most scholars recognize that there really was no fourth philosophy as such. The *zealots* were various individuals and groups, including some who in fact were Pharisees, who were willing to take action against Romans, Gentiles and Jewish collaborators.

> ## Would-Be Messiahs and Deliverers
>
> Judas, son of Hezekiah ...........................................................4 BC
>
> Simon ......................................................................................4 BC
>
> Athronges ...............................................................................4 BC
>
> Menahem, son of Judas ........................................................AD 66
>
> Simon bar Giora ............................................................AD 68–70
>
> Simon bar Kohba ........................................................AD 132–135

With reference to the last of the rebels who died at Masada in AD 73, Josephus grudgingly acknowledges their zeal (*Jewish Wars* 7.270: "they gave themselves that name from their zeal for what was good"), though he could hardly approve of the direction it took. That they were zealous for God and his Law, there can be no doubt. They had hoped to defeat the Romans and liberate Israel. Unable to achieve this, they were willing to die.

There were also zealous men who publicly demonstrated but did not take up arms against Herod or the Romans. One of the most notable examples of this were two teachers and their students who in the temple precincts damaged a golden eagle that Herod had mounted over one of the gates in honor of Rome (*Jewish Wars* 1.648–55; *Antiquities* 17.149–67). They did this out of "zeal for the Law" (*Jewish Wars* 1.654) and were more than willing to die for the sake of piety (1.653).[9] Die they did; Herod executed the two teachers and 40 of their students. Some of them were burned alive.

## The Zeal of Jesus

In what sense, if any, was Jesus a zealot? In what sense did he have zeal? When he demonstrated in the temple precincts (Matt 21:12–13 = Mark 11:15–19 = Luke 19:45–48; cf. John 2:13–22), the fourth evangelist says, "His disciples remembered that it was written, 'Zeal for thy house will consume me'" (John 2:17). Reza Aslan sees in this incident compelling evidence for classifying Jesus as a zealot.[10]

The problem with such a bland description is that it is not particularly helpful and it may very well be misleading, taking unwary readers back to the theories of Eisler, Brandon and others. In fairness to Aslan, he ends his primary discussion of the zeal of Jesus by rightly stating that "Jesus was not a member of the Zealot Party that launched the war with Rome...Nor was Jesus a violent revolutionary bent on armed rebellion."[11] True on both counts. Aslan adds, "Jesus was crucified by Rome because his messianic aspirations threatened the occupation of Palestine, and his zealotry endangered the Temple authorities."[12] Again, accurate enough. But how exactly are we to understand this "zealotry" of Jesus?

Aslan himself is not clear where he stands. His chapter devoted to the zeal of Jesus seems to waver from saying Jesus was not a revolutionary to implying that perhaps he was. With regard to the latter option, Aslan notes that Jesus was ostensibly arrested as a "bandit" and that he was executed along with two other "bandits." In the middle of this section, Aslan briefly and without nuance discusses Jesus' symbolic saying about the need to "buy a sword," in view of what his disciples will face (Luke 22:36–38).[13] Jesus uses many symbols, metaphors and hyperbolic examples, none of which is to be taken in a literal sense.

Jesus had zeal for God and for all that the temple (God's house) stood for, but this zeal was not a call to arms, not a call to violence, and not a call for human beings to overthrow either the Jewish regime in Jerusalem or the Roman authority over Judea and Samaria. Jesus proclaimed the rule of God and called upon all to repent and receive it. The repentance and conversion of people will inevitably lead to changes in society. The *sword* of Jesus is his message.

## The Proclamation of Jesus

The ministry of Jesus is first and foremost grounded in his proclamation of the "good news" of the reign of God, or in more literalistic parlance, the "kingdom of God." The Markan evangelist contextualizes and summarizes Jesus' proclamation thus:

> Now after John was arrested, Jesus came into Galilee, preaching the gospel of God, and saying, "The time is fulfilled, and the kingdom of God is at hand; repent, and believe in the gospel." (Mark 1:14–15)

In material shared by the Matthean and Lukan evangelists, Jesus says,

"The blind receive their sight and the lame walk, lepers are cleansed and the deaf hear, and the dead are raised up, and the poor have good news preached to them." (Matt 11:5; cf. Luke 7:22)

And in the Lukan form of the Nazareth sermon (Luke 4:16–30; cf. Mark 6:1–6), Jesus declares that the words of Isa 61:1–2 are "fulfilled" in the ears of those in the synagogue:

"The Spirit of the Lord is upon me, because he has anointed me to preach good news to the poor. He has sent me to proclaim release to the captives and recovering of sight to the blind, to set at liberty those who are oppressed, to proclaim the acceptable year of the Lord." (Luke 4:18–19)

From this material it is evident that Jesus' proclamation of the kingdom of God is fundamentally indebted to the language and vision of Isaiah, especially as we hear it in 40:9 and 61:1–2. It is most probable that Jesus' "gospel" or "good news" (*besora* in Hebrew and Aramaic; *euangelion* in Greek) directly derives from these passages. According to Isaiah 40:9,

Get you up to a high mountain, O Zion, herald of good tidings; lift up your voice with strength, O Jerusalem, herald of good tidings, lift it up, fear not; say to the cities of Judah, "Behold your God!"

However, in the Aramaic tradition, which has ancient roots, some of which reach back to the time of Jesus, the prophet is to declare "The kingdom of your God is revealed!" The verbal coherence is not to be missed: The good news of which Isaiah speaks is the announcement of the revelation of God's kingdom. Although this is not the place to belabor the point, it is urged that the most probable meaning of "kingdom of God" is the "reign of God" or the powerful presence of God. This seems to be the underlying assumption in Jesus' rebuttal to the charge that his exorcisms were empowered by Satan rather than God: "But if it is by the finger of God that I cast out demons, then the kingdom of God has come upon you" (Luke 11:20; cf. Matt 12:28).

The "good news" of Jesus is the inbreaking reign of God. His powerful presence is at hand to redeem, save and restore. This proclamation in itself would have been understood by his contemporaries as the single most important part of his ministry. The joy of receiving such good news is captured, once again, in the vision of Isaiah:

How beautiful upon the mountains are the feet of him who brings good tidings, who publishes peace, who brings good tidings of good, who publishes salvation, who says to Zion, "Your God reigns." (Isa 52:7)

And once again, that significant paraphrase, "the kingdom of your God is revealed," appears in the Aramaic version of this passage.

Isaiah not only defines the essence of the "good news," that is, the revelation of God's reign, but the prophet also delineates several blessings of this reign, blessings that are witnessed in Jesus' ministry. To these blessings we now turn.

*Jesus as healer and exorcist.* The linkage of the ministry of healing and exorcism to the proclamation of the kingdom of God is attested by Luke 11:20, already cited, where the casting out of Satan is evidence of being overtaken by God's reign. 4Q521, a much celebrated text from Qumran, demonstrates the linkage of healing and the proclamation of the "good news." The relevant portion of this important scroll reads, "Heaven and earth shall obey his Messiah...He will honor the pious upon the throne of his eternal kingdom, setting prisoners free, opening the eyes of the blind, raising up those who are bowed down...He shall heal the critically wounded, he shall revive the dead, he shall send good news to the afflicted" (4Q521 frag. 2, col. ii, lines 1, 7–8, 12, alluding to Isa 61:1–2).

When asked if he was the "Coming One," Jesus offered as evidence what was happening in his ministry: "the blind receive their sight and the lame walk, lepers are cleansed and the deaf hear, and the dead are raised up, and the poor have good news preached to them" (Matt 11:5; Luke 7:22, alluding to Isa 61:1–2). The messianic task of Jesus involved healing and restoration.

*Jesus as provider of forgiveness and fellowship.* Jesus' healings were seen not only as evidence of the powerful presence of God but also as proof of the forgiveness of sins. The linkage between healing and forgiveness is seen clearly in the story of the paralyzed man, let down through the roof by his friends (Mark 12:1–12). Impressed by their act of faith, Jesus says to the paralyzed man, "My son, your sins are forgiven" (Mark 2:5; cf. Matt 9:2; Luke 5:20).

In response to the scribes who are offended by this assertion, Jesus heals the man "that [they] may know that the Son of man has authority on earth to forgive sins" (Mark 2:10; cf. Matt 9:6; Luke 5:24). Jesus' self-understanding as the Son of Man who has authority on earth derives from the vision of Daniel 7, where "one who looked like a son of man" approaches the divine throne and receives "authority…and a kingdom" (Dan 7:13–14 NIRV). This heaven-given authority is what authorizes Jesus to proclaim the kingdom of God and to demonstrate its presence through healing, as we see in the case of the healing of the paralyzed man, and through exorcism, as we saw earlier.

Forgiveness is also linked to fellowship and the acceptance of the impure as pure. This aspect of Jesus' ministry is illustrated beautifully in the moving story of the woman who anointed Jesus' feet (Luke 7:36–50). Simon the Pharisee assumes that Jesus would not allow this woman to touch him if he knew who and what sort of woman she is, that she is a sinner (Luke 7:37, 39). Because he evidently does not know, he must not be a true prophet. But Jesus turns the tables on Simon, challenging his assumptions. He indeed does know the history of this woman, that she has been a sinner (7:47). However, her thanksgiving and love for the proclaimer of the good news is evidence of her experience of grace. Before all, Jesus assures the weeping woman, "Your sins are forgiven" (7:48) and "Your faith has saved you; go in peace" (7:50).

Jesus defends his understanding of God's will with the parable of the two debtors (Luke 7:41–42). Commentators have pointed out that the Aramaic word *hoba'* means both "sin" and "debt," thus tying the parable very closely to the issues of sin, forgiveness and thanksgiving. Recognition of this nuance brings us back again to the proclamation of the good news, especially in the tones of Isaiah 61:1–2 and 58:6 (in Luke 4:18–19, cited previously): the "letting go" (or "forgiveness") of prisoners and the oppressed. Jesus has assured the woman that she has been released from the debts of her sin, which have burdened her and have led to her estrangement from the God of Israel. Recognizing this release, this forgiveness, she expresses her love and gratitude to Jesus. Her behavior sharply contrast with that of the ungracious Simon.

This aspect of Jesus' ministry frequently provoked criticism. Torah-observant Jews, often depicted in the Gospels as Pharisees and scribes, objected to Jesus' intimate association with "sinners," that is, with those who did not observe the laws of purity as their critics understood them. The tradition of this criticism leveled against Jesus is ancient and attested in Mark (e.g., 2:15–17) and the source used by Matthew and Luke (e.g., Matt 11:19 = Luke 7:34).

This tradition also makes it clear that Jesus regarded the people to whom he ministered as "sinners" in need of redemption. He acknowledged that the sins of the woman who washed his feet were "many" (Luke 7:47) and that she was a "debtor." By characterizing himself as a physician, ministering to the "sick," and as one who came "not to call the righteous, but sinners" (Matt 9:13), Jesus unequivocally identified those to whom he ministered and with whom he fellowshipped as sinners. On this question he was in agreement with the scribes and Pharisees. The issue had to do with what to do about the sinners. Were they to be shunned and condemned, or were they to be ministered unto? Herein lies a major difference between Jesus and many of the religious teachers of his time. It was also a major difference between Jesus and the zealots of his time.

The "zealots" of Jesus' time were not known for extending grace to "sinners." They were not willing to eat with them, fellowship with them or heal them. Rather, they judged them. Jesus criticized the ruling elite, for their oppressive tactics and depraved indifference. The zealots killed them. Jesus was willing to heal Gentiles, even the servant of a Roman centurion (Matt 8:5–13 = Luke 7:1–10). Zealots regarded Gentiles, especially Romans, as sworn enemies. The teaching and actions of Jesus reflect nothing of these zealot tendencies.

No, Jesus was no zealot, at least nothing like those described by Josephus. Jesus called for repentance and change, but he did not call for violence. He warned his disciples that he and they would suffer. Martyrdom was possible, perhaps even probable. He urged his disciples to remember his suffering (the Words of Institution, spoken during the Last Supper). He did not exhort his disciples to exact revenge against their enemies.

For us the most compelling argument against viewing Jesus as a zealot who called for the overthrow of the political regime is that there was very little violence against his following in the aftermath of his own death. If Jesus and his movement were anything like the movements of zealots, then it is impossible to see how his disciples and members of his family (e.g., James, who eventually gave leadership to the Church in Jerusalem) could have continued in Jerusalem and Judea. They suffered persecution, to be sure, but not a full-scale military assault.[14] Jewish Christians in Jerusalem, under the leadership of Peter and then under the leadership of James, lived in goodly numbers in Jerusalem right up until the Roman siege and capture of the city. James himself did not suffer martyrdom until the year 62.

## Summary

Jesus was no political zealot who hoped to seize control of the government and drive out the Romans and their Jewish collaborators. Jesus' ministry was inaugurated by and defined by the proclamation of the good news of the kingdom of God. Apart from this message, there could not have been any meaningful ministry. The good news entailed the restoration and redemption of Israel, the renewal of the covenant and the reclamation of the lost. The essence of this message guided all other aspects of ministry. The reality and power of the good news was demonstrated in healing and exorcism, the freeing of hostages, as it were, from the bondage of Satan and his allies. This freeing also entailed forgiveness of sin, which made renewed fellowship possible. The freely bestowed forgiveness of God made possible, and indeed required, freely bestowed forgiveness of one human being by another. Such forgiveness then made it possible to worship God freely and humanely and made contemplation of personal sacrifice, suffering and death imaginable, even acceptable.

Jesus' ministry not only established the paradigm upon which the Church's ministry would be founded, it also put in place the principal components of which Christian theology would be developed. For Christians past and present, Jesus' ministry remains normative, as well as inspirational. His was a zeal for God, a zeal that was summed up in the two great commandments: to love God and to love one's neighbor as one's self.

Chapter 6

# How Do Muslims View Muhammad?

*The Standard Islamic View of the Prophet*

A ll views of Muhammad, including those of Reza Aslan, must be framed in the context of the traditional Islamic understanding of the prophet. What follows is the standard outline of Muhammad's life from the perspective of Islamic orthodoxy. After looking at the traditional biography, we will examine Aslan's interpretation of the prophet and then assess the credibility of both the traditional view and Aslan's perspective. The standard Islamic view is derived from the Qur'an, early biographies of the prophet (sira), oral reports about him (hadith), military histories (maghazi) and early commentaries by Muslims (tafsir).

Most Muslims believe that Muhammad was born about AD 570 in the so-called "year of the elephant."[1] Muhammad's father (Abdullah) died before he was born, and his mother (Amina) died shortly after his birth. She claimed that when she was pregnant "she saw a light come forth from her by which she could see the castles of Busra in Syria."[2] According to traditional commentaries on the Qur'an, the death of his parents is the context for the question in surah 93:6: "Did He not find thee an orphan and give thee shelter (and care)?"[3] In his early years, Muhammad was cared for by his grandfather and then by an uncle (Abu Talib), who was his guardian until Muhammad reached his teen years.

The standard Muslim histories of the prophet mention that he went twice to Syria on trading missions with his uncle. These reports provided an apologetic motif not only for evidence of Muhammad's acumen in business but for early witness to his future greatness. It is said that Muhammad's prophetic status was foretold by Christian monks, on the first trip by Bahira (in some accounts an unnamed head of the convent gives the prophecy) and on the second journey by a monk named Nastur. The account of Bahira mentions a special physical mark on Muhammad's body (between his shoulders), and the monk tells Alu Talib, "Take your nephew back to his country and guard him carefully against the Jews, for by Allah if they see him and know about him what I know, they will do him evil; a great future lies before this nephew of yours, so take him home quickly."[4]

Muhammad was married in about 595 to a woman merchant named Khadijah. The Muslim histories state she was either 28 or 40 at the time and had been married twice before.[5] It is claimed that she married Muhammad after he had completed successful trade for her in Syria. Muslim sources also state that Khadijah's slave Maysara, who joined Muhammad on the trip to Syria, saw two angels protecting Muhammad. After Khadijah married Muhammad, they had four daughters and some sons, but the boys died early. Khadijah is famous for her affirmation of Muhammad's prophetic status, assuring him that he was not being influenced by demonic spirits.

## Traditional Muslim Dating of Muhammad's Life

| | |
|---|---|
| 570 | Birth in Mecca. |
| 575 | After death of parents, Muhammad was raised by his grandfather and uncle, Abu Talib. |
| 595 | Married Khadijah, a travel merchant. |
| 610 | Mystical experience of divine revelations that would form the basis of the Qur'an. |
| 613 | Began to preach monotheistic message, which led to his persecution. |
| 619 | Death of Khadijah and his uncle. |
| 619 | After the death of Khadijah, Muhammad married Sawdah, the first of many other wives. |
| 619 | Alleged incident over Satanic verses. |

619  Marriage to Aisha.

620  Muhammad was taken by the angel Gabriel to Jerusalem and ascended to the seventh heaven on a ladder. This is known as the *miraj*.

622  Escaped to Medina to avoid persecution in Mecca. This *hijra* is the start of the Muslim calendar.

623  Consummation of marriage to Aisha.

623  Raid on Nakhla.

624  Muhammad defeated Meccan enemies at the Battle of Badr.

624  Jewish Qaynuqa tribe exiled from Medina.

625  Meccans defeat Muslims at Uhud.

625  Jewish Nadir tribe exiled.

627  Married Zaynab, his cousin, who was previously married to the Prophet's adopted son Zayd.

627  Raided the Jewish clan of Qurayzah and ordered the death of hundreds of Jewish men.

628  Signed a treaty with Meccan leaders at Hudaybiyyah.

628  Siege of the Khaybar oasis.

630  Conquered his enemies at Mecca and removed idols from the city.

631  Overthrow of Ta'if.

631  Expedition to Tabuk.

631  Death of Ibrahim, infant son of Muhammad.

632  Death on June 8 after a period of ill health.

Muslims believe that Allah's call to Muhammad occurred on the 17th night of the Arabic month Ramadan in AD 610. According to both the *sira* and the traditional commentaries on the Qur'an, the archangel Gabriel (Djibril) is said to have visited him on Mount Hira, near Mecca. Surah 2:97 says of Gabriel that "he brings down the (revelation) to thy heart by Allah's will." Surah 96 is viewed by most Muslims as the first revelation from Allah, while other Muslims argue that surah 74 forms the earliest message from God.

It is customary for Muslims to argue that Muhammad was illiterate (*ummi*), a position used to advance the divine inspiration of the Qur'an. This is also a convenient way to rebut charges that Muhammad copied ideas from Jewish and Christian Scriptures. Most Muslims use surah 29:48 to support the notion that the prophet was illiterate. "And thou wast not (able) to recite a Book before this (Book came), nor art thou (able) to transcribe it with thy right hand: In that case, indeed, would the talkers of vanities have doubted." A minority of Muslims note that surah 25:4–6 mentions that the prophet's opponents said that Muhammad had "written down" stories.[6]

There has been much speculation about the episode of "the satanic verses," which formed the basis for the title of Salman Rushdie's controversial novel. The episode is reported in some early Muslim writings but is a rather disputed tradition (though one accepted by Watt and Guillaume, two famous Western scholars) that Muhammad at one time included a positive reference in surah 53 to the worship of three pagan goddesses (al-Lat, al-Uzza, and Manat). Gabriel is said to have excised the false teaching about these deities in a later revelation to the prophet.[7] The story is used by critics of Islam as proof that the Qur'an was not always an infallible text.

Most traditional biographers claim that there was a pause (*fatra*) of three years before Muhammad began to preach to his fellow Meccans in AD 613. His message was largely ignored, though there were some converts (notably Abu Bakr). Muhammad's early focus on social reform appealed most to the poorer clans. His preaching allowed focus on the Ka'ba and accommodated certain pagan elements in pre-Islamic pilgrimage rituals. Surah 2:158 gives permission for Muslims to trace a spiritual route between Safa and Marwa, two hills that once had stone idols on them. Muslims to this day follow the same pilgrimage during the Hajj.

As Muhammad turned his prophetic voice against idolatry and polytheism, he incurred the anger and insult of powerful tribal leaders. One of his uncles also resisted Muhammad, earning the uncle and his wife eternal damnation, according to the *tafsir* (commentary) on surah 111. The persecution of the prophet led him to try to gain support in Ta'if, 60 miles southeast of Mecca. The journey failed. Both there and in Mecca, support for polytheism had to do with vested commercial interests in supporting traditional Arab religious views and customs. It is no wonder that various surahs attempt to allay fears of financial loss for those who follow the path of Allah.

Overall, Muhammad was derided as a magician (*sahir*) and soothsayer (*kahin*) and said to be possessed by *jinn* (ghostlike beings often viewed as evil in both traditional Islamic theology and Muslim folklore).[8] These accusations suggest something about the manner in which Muhammad received the alleged revelations from Gabriel. He must have exhibited some behavior that led to such interpretations, right or wrong, conduct that would later provide rationale for a skeptical European audience to dismiss his so-called inspiration as epileptic seizures.[9]

Muslims believe that in 620, one year after the death of Khadijah, the angel Gabriel brought Muhammad by night to Jerusalem on the back of a heavenly winged creature named Buruq. Traditional biographers claim that surah 17:1 refers to this supernatural journey. "Glory to (Allah) Who did take His servant for a Journey by night from the Sacred Mosque to the farthest Mosque, whose precincts We did bless."

According to Islamic orthodoxy, while in Jerusalem the prophet was offered a choice of wine or milk. He chose the latter, earning commendation by Gabriel. Muhammad and his angel companion then ascended to the seventh heaven, conversing with various saints (Jesus, Moses, Abraham, etc.) at each level. Muslims believe that the Dome of the Rock in Jerusalem is built on the spot where the ascension (*miraj*) took place. Early Muslim accounts differ on the time and details of the miraculous journey.[10]

Two years later in 622, Muhammad was forced to flee to Medina (formerly Yathrib), about 250 miles north of Mecca. Muslims claim that his diplomatic skills were exhibited in initial peaceful coexistence with various Jewish tribes, Christians and pagan Arabs who lived in Medina. The famous *Constitution of Medina* (possibly referred to in surah 8:56) captures something of this serenity, though the prophet clearly has the upper hand. "Whenever you differ about a matter it must be referred to God and to Muhammad."[11]

According to Islamic tradition, the relative calm behind the *Constitution* gave way to increasing tensions, especially with the Jews who failed to accept Muhammad as the prophet.[12] The early attempt in Medina to harmonize Muslim rituals with Jewish tradition was abandoned, most notably in the facing of Mecca rather than Jerusalem for prayer. Muhammad's hope for unity with "People of the Book" became overshadowed by stronger warnings against Jews and Christians and claims that both groups had deliberately distorted their Scriptures.

For eight years the Prophet engaged in repeated military battles with his Meccan enemies. The early victory at the famous battle at Badr on March 15, 624, was used as proof that Allah gave His blessing to the strategy of *jihad*. Surah 3:123 states, "Allah had helped you at Badr, when ye were a contemptible little force; then fear Allah; thus May you show your gratitude." There is also a report that at Badr Muhammad threw stones at the enemy, which God used supernaturally to defeat them. A major setback at Uhud in 625 (the prophet was wounded) raised skepticism among some Muslims and the Jews of Medina, but there was no turning back for Muhammad.

His military focus has always been used against him by non-Muslim critics. Particular objection has been made to the death penalty he imposed on the Qurayzah, the last major Jewish clan left in Medina. He accused these Jews of complicity in the last Meccan attack on Medina in 626–627, known as the "War of the Trench." According to one account by Ibn Ishaq, the Prophet ordered the beheading of over 600 Jewish males. Surah 33:6 is said to refer to this episode. "And those of the People of the Book who aided them—Allah did take them down from their strongholds and cast terror into their hearts. (So that) some ye slew, and some ye made prisoners." The killing of the Jewish males and the subsequent enslavement of the Jewish women and children is often used as the centerpiece of claims that Muhammad was anti-Semitic.

An expedition against the Mustalik clan created a scandal in the Muslim community because of allegations of immorality against Aisha, one of Muhammad's wives. She had been accidentally left behind on the return trip to Medina. Rumors circulated about her and the lone Muslim soldier who brought her back to the camp. The stir in the Muslim community was quieted when Muhammad received a revelation exonerating Aisha. Surah 24:12 is said to address the gossip: "Why did not the believers—men and women—when you heard of the affair—put the best construction on it in their own minds and say, 'This (charge) is an obvious lie'?"[13]

## Wives of Muhammad

| Wife | Married |
| --- | --- |
| Khadijah bint Khuwaylid | 595–619 |
| Sawda bint Zam'a | 619–632 |
| Aisha bint Abi Bakr | 619–632 |
| Hafsa bint Umar | 624–632 |
| Zaynab bint Khuzayma | 625–627 |
| Hind bint Abi Umayya | 629–632 |
| Zaynab bint Jahsh | 627–632 |
| Juwayriya bint al-Harith | 628–632 |
| Ramlah bint Abi Sufyan | 628–632 |
| Rayhana bint Zayd | 629–631 |
| Safiyya bint Huyayy | 629–632 |
| Maymuna bint al-Harith | 630–632 |
| Maria al-Qibtiyya | 630–632 |

In 628, Muhammad led a group of his followers to Mecca and negotiated a treaty at al-Hudaybiyyah with his most powerful Meccan adversaries. At the same time, Muhammad also captured other regions of Arabia, including Khaybar, home to one of the Jewish tribes expelled earlier by Muhammad.[14] It is also claimed that the prophet wrote letters sometime in 628 or 629 demanding that the political leaders in Alexandria, Persia, Abyssinia and Byzantine convert to Islam. Muslims also believe that Muhammad carried on some correspondence with leaders in close proximity, including Mukawkis of Egypt.[15]

In 629, Muhammad made a pilgrimage to Mecca and reconciled with his own clan. In January of the next year he took control of Mecca and destroyed the idols in the Ka'ba. Muhammad was merciful in his triumph over his Meccan enemies.[16] In spite of his victory, Medina continued to be his home base. He led further military campaigns in northern Arabia.

By this time, according to traditional Muslim sources, Muhammad was widely recognized for his power, though some of his own followers tried to resist his plans for a raid to Tabuk (near Jordan's southern boundary).[17] According to traditional Muslim accounts, many tribes near Medina and in other parts of Arabia submitted to his leadership. Muslim sources also suggest that Muhammad's success was so great that the Byzantine emperor

Heraclius (who ruled AD 610–641) pondered surrender to Muhammad as long as the prophet advanced no further than northern Syria.[18]

Islamic tradition reports on a personal tragedy for the prophet Muhammad in 630. His only surviving son, Ibrahim, died in his second year. Muhammad was devastated. Tariq Ramadan has a very moving account:

> At the very time when the religion of the One was being established all over the Peninsula, with adversity constantly diminishing and the number of conversions continuing to grow, the Prophet saw his only son about to leave life and to leave him. He visited him every day and spent hours by his side. When the child eventually breathed his last, the Prophet took him in his arms and held him against his breast, tears streaming down his face, so deep was his sorrow.[19]

Muhammad returned to Mecca for a final pilgrimage in early 632. He was in poor health at the time and soon traveled back to Medina. He died, according to tradition, on June 8th of that year, in the

| Muhammad's Children | |
|---|---|
| Sons | Daughters |
| Qasim | Zainab |
| 'Abd-Allah | Ruqayyah |
| Ibrahim | Umm Kulthoom |
| | Fatimah Zahra |

embrace of Aisha. His burial place remains the second most important pilgrimage site in the Islamic world.

## Reza Aslan on Muhammad

Muhammad is the centerpiece of Reza Aslan's *No God but God*. Though he does not follow traditional Muslim views on every detail about Muhammad, Aslan paints an enormously positive picture of him. At the outset, Aslan quotes with approval the famous verdict of Ernest Renan that Muhammad lived "in the full view of history."[20] There is no duplication here of the skepticism employed on the historical Jesus in Aslan's *Zealot*. Aslan makes bold and confident assertions about Muhammad and basically adopts wholesale the main contours of the traditional Islamic view.

This is not to say that he accepts absolutely everything in traditional Islam about the prophet. For example, he denies that Muhammad's birth was in the year of the elephant. He also states that the miraculous reports about Muhammad's birth "are not intended to relate historical events" and that "the historicity of these topoi is irrelevant."[21] This, of course, parallels his treatment of the birth narratives and miraculous elements in the life of Jesus. Aslan also contends that Muhammad was not illiterate.

Apart from these items, Aslan adheres to orthodox Islamic views, and Muhammad comes across as a moral, political and social revolutionary of the highest caliber. Muhammad's message is one of "moral accountability and social egalitarianism." The prophet was "authoritative" and "trustworthy" and "he was able to establish a new kind of society, the likes of which had never before been seen in Arabia." More specifically, Aslan goes into detail to show that "perhaps nowhere was Muhammad's struggle for economic redistribution and social egalitarianism more evident than in the rights and privileges he bestowed upon the women in his community."[22]

Aslan articulates a supernatural grounding to Muhammad's prophetic call, one that began in 610 when "Muhammad had an encounter that would change the world." Aslan refers to Muhammad's revelations from the angel Gabriel as "indescribable supernatural experiences." He also regards Muhammad's creation of the Islamic ideal in Medina as so idyllic that it led Muslims to proclaim a new calendar based on the first year of the flight to the northern city, that is, AD 622.

Occasionally Aslan writes of Muhammad in far from academic tones. He quotes early Muslim reports about his "stately appearance" with his "wide black eyes" and "long thick hair." Later, Aslan draws this image of the prophet in his final days in Medina:

> But now, the sight of Muhammad standing at the entrance of the mosque, a smile wrinkling his bronzed face, dispels all those anxious rumors about his health. He looks lean, but surprisingly hearty for a man of his age. The long black hair he keeps twisted into plaits is thin and silver. His back bows a bit and his shoulders droop. But his face is as radiant as ever, and his eyes still smolder with the light of God.[23]

Given this sentimental physical portrait, it is no surprise that Aslan defends Muhammad at every turn in relation to the standard objections to Muhammad's greatness. He is the liberator of women. He is also the "perfect man" for political arbitrations, a leader who promoted forgiveness between enemies, and a prophet unjustly charged with sexual deviance, anti-Semitism and promoting violent jihad. As one would expect, Aslan glorifies Muhammad for being the recipient of the Qur'an. Aslan refers to the Qur'an as "Glorious" and claims that Muhammad recited its "entire text" during his prophetic career.

Aslan's high view of the Qur'an is in keeping with the traditional Muslim view that the sacred text is *the* great miracle of Muhammad's life. Some liberal Muslims downplay other miraculous elements in the prophet's earthly sojourn, even the famous Night Journey. While the Qur'an itself gives no clear testimony to nature miracles by Muhammad's hand, over time Islamic tradition became rife with supernatural tales.

Miracle stories abound in the sira and hadith material. The prophet was said to have split the moon in two to prove Islam. His chest was opened supernaturally by an angel, and his heart was washed. Like Jesus, Muhammad fed the multitudes. A wolf praised his ministry at one time, while trees moved to provide privacy for the prophet at another. Three thousand angels aided Muhammad in a crucial military battle.[24]

## Muslim Love for the Prophet

It is obvious from the aforementioned that the ideological worlds of Islam and that of Reza Aslan are dominated by a high view of Muhammad. This cannot be stressed enough, since criticism of Muhammad is tantamount to blasphemy, a sign of bad faith and virtually incomprehensible to most Muslims. While Muhammad is not to be worshiped, he is the object of tremendous praise from the earliest Muslim writers. Traditional Muslims often say or write "May peace be upon him" after mention of Muhammad.[25] One of the opening narratives in the first biography about Muhammad has this to say:

> The apostle of God grew up, God protecting him and keeping him from the vileness of heathenism because he wished to honor him with apostleship, until he grew up to be the finest of his people in manliness, the best in character, most noble in lineage, the best neighbor, the most kind, truthful, reliable, the furthest removed from filthiness and corrupt morals, through loftiness and mobility, somebody was known among his people as "the trustworthy" because of the good qualities which God had implanted in him.[26]

This lofty view of Muhammad dominates early Islam whether in the Muslim biographies, military histories, traditions about the prophet (hadith) or commentaries on the Qur'an. The adulation of the prophet among Muslims continues to the present day, as one would expect.

The Muslim writer Farida Khanam portrays him as meek, mild and full of love and compassion.

> His mission was to bring people abreast of the reality that all people—despite that they come from different countries and are seemingly different from one another in regards to their color, language, dress, and culture—are interconnected. Hence a proper relationship can only be established between all humans if they were to regard one another as sisters and brothers. Only then will proper feelings of love and respect prevail throughout the world.[27]

Safi-ur-Rahman al-Mubarakpuri, whose biography of Muhammad, *Ar-Raheeq Al-Makhtum (The Sealed Nectar),* won first prize in an international Muhammad biography competition held in Mecca in 1979, wrote, "the Prophet combined both perfection of creation and perfection of manners....The Prophet is the most just, the most decent, the most truthful at speech, and the honestest [*sic*] of all."[28]

Across the Muslim world poems are sung in praise of the prophet. Omid Safi quotes this poem in his *Memories of Muhammad*:

> O Muhammad
> Embodied Light
> My Beloved
> My Master
> You are:
> The image of the perfection of love
> The illumination of God's beauty[29]

Safi draws attention to Rumi's adulation of the prophet. Rumi (1207–1273) is the most famous mystical writer in Islam. After Rumi told the story of a napkin that the prophet used being supernaturally protected when it was tossed in the fire, Rumi wrote, "O heart who is fearful of the torment of hellfire, get acquainted with such a hand and such lips. If the prophet bestowed such honour upon an inanimate object, imagine what he would do to the soul of the lovers!"[30]

Safi also notes the Muslim tradition of offering daily blessings upon Muhammad. This latter practice is most famously associated with the *Dala'il al-Khayrat*, a work from Muhammad al-Jazuli (d. 1465), a Sufi master.[31] This extensive work provides long prayers of blessing for Muhammad for every day of the week.

Here is one of many prayers for Monday:

O Allah, bless our master Muhammad, and the family of our master Muhammad, his wives and offspring, and all the Prophets and Messengers, the angels, those who are near and all the righteous servants of Allah in quantity as great as all the rain of heaven since the time it was set up. Bless our master Muhammad in quantity as great as all the plants the earth has brought forth since the time it was spread out. Bless our master Muhammad in quantity as great as the stars in the sky, for You can count them, and bless our master Muhammad in quantity as great as the breaths breathed by souls since You created them. Bless our master Muhammad in quantity as great as what You have created and what You will create and what Your knowledge contains and the double of that.

There is a popular tradition among Muslims that Allah stated to the prophet: "Were it not for you, I would not have created the universe." While many Muslim scholars deny the validity of the hadith in question, it is argued that the sentiment of the verse is true.[32] Muslim love for the prophet involves obedience to his teachings and exacting duplication of his deeds. On the latter, the Islamic traditions (hadith) contain both Muhammad's sayings and actions, and these serve as a basis for the most mundane areas of life. For example, the prophet disapproved of biting one's nails. He taught that the right shoe is to be put on before the left. He advocated the use of a toothpick to clean teeth. While Islamic jurists had to figure out whether an action of the prophet makes something obligatory or just recommended, following the prophet's example is a major element in the Islamic ethic.[33]

## Non-Muslim Praise for the Prophet

While one step removed from Islamic orthodoxy, various modern writers have abandoned the nasty interpretation of the prophet that dominated Western reaction to Muhammad through the centuries.[34] Thus, Alphonse de LaMartaine in *A History of the Turks* (Paris, 1854) writes,

If greatness of purpose, smallness of means, and astonishing results are the three criteria of a human genius, who could dare compare any great man in history with Muhammad? The most famous men created arms, laws, and empires only. They founded, if anything at all, no more than material powers which often crumbled away before their eyes. This man moved not only armies, legislations, empires, peoples, dynasties, but millions of men in one-third of the then inhabited world; and more than that, he moved the altars, the gods, the religions, the ideas, the beliefs and the souls.[35]

Hans Küng, a Roman Catholic and one of the most famous theologians of modern times, first took up the question of Muhammad's status in his book *Christianity and the World Religions*. He presents seven parallels between Muhammad and the prophets of Israel, outlines the immense contribution of Muhammad and concludes by citing Vatican II. One of Council documents states that the Catholic Church "also looks upon the Muslims with great respect: They worship the one true God who has spoken to man."

Küng, who does not believe that Muhammad was sinless or that Islam is the one true religion, then offers this assessment: "In my opinion, that Church—and all the Christian Churches—must also 'look with great respect' upon the man whose name is omitted from the declaration out of embarrassment, although he alone led the Muslims to the worship of the one God, who spoke through him: Muhammad the Prophet."[36]

A high view of the prophet has also been advanced by William Montgomery Watt, Alfred Guillaume and Karen Armstrong, among others. Guillaume is of particular significance, given his scholarly work on Ibn Ishaq's *Sirat Rasul Allah*, the most famous Muslim biography of the prophet.[37] Watt is highly regarded for his two-volume biography of Muhammad.[38] Armstrong has gained acclaim among Muslims for her glowing portrait of the prophet.[39]

## You Must Know This Man

Of course, the praise of various non-Muslim writers for Muhammad never reaches the acclaim showered on him by Muslims themselves. One of the most famous modern encomiums to the prophet comes under the title "You Must Know This Man." It is offered in printed pamphlet form by the Islamic Circle of North America, and the text is quoted on many Muslim websites and even set to music on YouTube.[40] The following edited selection serves as a superb example of the idealization of Muhammad and the epistemic certainty surrounding his merits and those of Islam.

## You Must Know This Man

No matter what you are, and no matter what your religious and political beliefs, personal and social habits happen to be—YOU MUST STILL KNOW THIS MAN!

He was by far the most remarkable man that ever set foot on this earth. He preached a religion, founded a state, built a nation, laid down a moral code, initiated numberless social and political reforms, established a dynamic and powerful society to practice and represent his teachings, and completely revolutionized the worlds of human thought and action for all times to come.

HIS NAME IS MUHAMMAD, peace and blessings of Almighty God be upon him and he accomplished all these wonders in the unbelievably short span of twenty-three years.

Muhammad, peace and blessings of God Almighty be upon him was born in Arabia on the 20th of August, in the year 570 of the Christian era, and when he died after 63 years, the whole of the Arabian Peninsula had changed from paganism and idol-worship to the worship of One God; from tribal quarrels and wars to national solidarity and cohesion; from drunkenness and debauchery to sobriety and piety; from lawlessness and anarchy to disciplined living; from utter moral bankruptcy to the highest standards of moral excellence. Human history has never known such a complete transformation of a people or a place before or since!

Indeed no other human being ever accomplished so much, in such diverse fields of human thought and behavior, in so limited a space of time, as did Muhammad, peace and blessings of God Almighty be upon him. He was a religious teacher, a social reformer, a moral guide, a political thinker, a military genius, an administrative colossus, a faithful friend, a wonderful companion, a devoted husband, a loving father—all in one. No other man in history ever excelled or equaled him in any of these difficult departments of life.

Not only was he born in the fullest blaze of recorded history, but every detail of his private and public life, of his actions and utterances, has been accurately documented and faithfully preserved to our day. The authenticity of the information so preserved is vouched for not only by faithful followers but also by unbiased critics and open-minded scholars.

In a fast changing world, while other systems have undergone profound transformations, Islam alone has remained above all change and mutation and retained its original form for the past 1400 years. What is more, the positive changes that are taking place in the world of human thought and behavior, truly and consistently reflect the healthy influence of Islam in these areas. Further, it is not given to the best of thinkers to put their ideas completely into practice, and to see the seeds of their labors grow and bear fruit, in their own lifetime. Except of course, Muhammad, peace and blessings of God Almighty be upon him, who not only preached the most wonderful ideas but also successfully translated each one of them into practice in his own lifetime. At the time of his death his teachings were not mere precepts and ideas straining for fulfillment, but had become the very core of the life of tens of thousands of perfectly trained individuals, each one of whom was a marvelous personification of everything that Muhammad peace and blessings of God Almighty be upon him taught and stood for. At what other time or place and in relation to what other political, social, religious system, philosophy or ideology-did the world ever witness such a perfectly amazing phenomenon?

Indeed no other system or ideology secular or religious, social or political, ancient or modern—could ever claim the distinction of having been put into practice in its fullness and entirety EVEN ONCE in this world, either before or after the death of its founder. Except of course ISLAM, the ideology preached by Muhammad, peace and blessings of God Almighty be upon him which was established as a complete way of life by the teacher himself, before he departed from this world. History bears testimony to this fact and the greatest skeptics have no option but to concede this point.

Today after the lapse of some 1400 years the life and teachings of Prophet Muhammad, peace and blessings of God Almighty be upon him, have survived without the slightest loss, alteration or interpolation. Today they offer the same undying hope for treating mankind's many ills which they did when Prophet Muhammad, peace and blessings of God Almighty be upon him, was alive. This is our honest claim and this is the inescapable conclusion forced upon us by a critical and unbiased study of history.

## Summary

Three elements of this tribute are important for what follows in thinking about Muhammad. First, given the high regard for Muhammad, it is no wonder that critique of him creates such negativity among Muslims. The idealization of Muhammad creates a barrier to critique of the prophet. Second, this high regard is accompanied by an almost absolute dogmatic certainty in regards to the historicity of Muhammad and the supreme greatness of Islam. This again erects a roadblock to open investigation. Thirdly, and somewhat ironically, the high estimate of the prophet and the inner certainty of his greatness lead to invitations from Muslims to engage in serious investigation of the one Muslims call the final prophet of God. Omid Safi states,

> Whether some of us think of ourselves as Americans first or citizens of one shared planet first, it is simply part of being an educated citizen to have accurate knowledge about the faith of Islam. Muhammad stands at the center of this faith, and there is no way of being familiar with Islam without taking a long, hard, and close look at this figure.[41]

# Chapter 7

# How Reliable Is the Historical Record about Muhammad?

*Islamic Views Under Scrutiny*

Two large and controversial tasks face anyone who wants to adjudicate the merits of Aslan's vision of Muhammad, which amounts to the traditional Islamic perspective. First, it is necessary to assess the historical credibility of the orthodox Islamic view of Muhammad and the rise of Islam. Second, it is also crucial to probe whether the traditional Muslim portrait of the prophet has been skewed in order to hide unpleasant realities or avoid major indictments against the traditional view. These two tasks are complicated, of course, by the potential of violence or discrimination (even of the academic variety) towards anyone who dares question the prophet. Also, anyone with an open mind will acknowledge the inherent difficulties involved in sorting through the various academic ideologies, competing religious perspectives, and varied political and social narratives at play in interpreting a figure as colossal and controversial as Muhammad.

## The Qur'an and the Prophet

The casual reader of Reza Aslan's *No god but God* would probably think that the historical reliability of the traditional view of Muhammad is secure. Such is far from the case. Aslan admits that the Qur'an's direct material on the prophet is minimal, but he understates how seriously deficient the Muslim Scripture is in providing even indirect biographical information on Muhammad. The average person would expect that the Qur'an, as the sacred book, would be the greatest source for the prophet's life. This is particularly true if one accepts the traditional Muslim view

97

that the Qur'an was revealed directly to Muhammad and that the final rendition of the Qur'an dates to about AD 650.

Even a minimal acquaintance with the Qur'an shows clearly that it is not explicitly helpful on either the big picture or the details of Muhammad's life and mission. In all 114 chapters of the Qur'an, Muhammad is mentioned by name only four times. Here are the four passages:

1. "Muhammad is naught but a Messenger; Messengers have passed away before him. Why, if he should die or is slain, will you turn about on your heels? If any man should turn about on his heels, he will not harm God in any way; and God will recompense the thankful." 3:144

2. "Muhammad is not the father of any one of your men, but the Messenger of God, and the Seal of the Prophets; God has knowledge of everything." 33:40

3. "But those who believe and do righteous deeds and believe in what is sent down to Muhammad—and it is the truth from their Lord—He will acquit them of their evil deeds, and dispose their minds aright." 47:2

4. "Muhammad is the Messenger of God, and those who are with him are hard against the unbelievers, merciful one to another. Thou seest them bowing, prostrating, seeking bounty from God and good pleasure. Their mark is on their faces, the trace of prostration. That is their likeness in the Torah, and their likeness in the Gospel: as a seed that puts forth its shoot, and strengthens it, and it grows stout and rises straight upon its stalk, pleasing the sowers, that through them He may enrage the unbelievers. God has promised those of them who believe and do deeds of righteousness forgiveness and a mighty wage." 48:29

In spite of only four explicit uses of the name "Muhammad," Muslims use the Qur'an as a biographical source by assuming that Muhammad is the central figure of the Qur'an. Aslan clearly follows this agenda in his portrait of the prophet. Given this, Muslims posit that Muhammad is the major antagonist to his own tribe in Mecca (surah 9, for example) and the chief warner to the Jews and Christians of his day (see 2:119 and 5:54, for example). Muhammad is the warrior-leader in the battles alluded to in the sacred text, as at Badr (3:123). Without any mention of him by name, it is contended that Muhammad is a judge (4:65), that he is to be respected by his disciples (2:104; 4:46), and that Allah himself is a witness to his mission

(13:43; and 46:8). On the basis of the Qur'an, Muslims believe that both Moses (46:10) and Jesus (61:6) predicted the work of Muhammad. The latter text reads, "And when Jesus son of Mary said, 'Children of Israel, I am indeed the Messenger of God to you, confirming the Torah that is before me, and giving good tidings of a Messenger who shall come after me, whose name shall be Ahmad.' Then, when he brought them the clear signs, they said, 'This is a manifest sorcery.'"

Further, according to the traditional Islamic reading, the Qur'an teaches that Muhammad is the universal messenger from God (34:28) and the symbol of Allah's mercy to the world (9:61; 28:46–47; 76:24–26). The prophet is sincere (53:10–12), gentle (3:159), very concerned about his followers (9:128) and in deep distress for unbelievers (12:97; 25:30). It says he was a man of prayer (74:3) and had an "exalted standard of character" (68:4). Muhammad is told to adore Allah (96:19), remain faithful to the revealed message (46:9), follow Allah's duty for him (30:30) and work hard (66:9). According to surah 33, Muhammad's abrogation of traditional Arabic marriage norms is allowed by Allah. He can marry his cousins and any woman he wants "and any woman believer, if she give herself to the Prophet."

Surah 33 also illustrates some tension surrounding various social customs. Muhammad's followers are told to visit the prophet's home only when they have permission, to arrive right at mealtime (not before), leave quickly after the meal, and avoid "familiar talk" with the prophet. It is said "that is hurtful to the Prophet, and he is ashamed before you; but God is not ashamed before the truth" (33:53).

There is no explicit reason from within the Qur'an itself to claim that the various texts noted here are necessarily about Muhammad.[1] They may be about him, but the Qur'an itself does not say so. While this fact bothers neither Aslan nor most Muslims, the absence of incontrovertible material about major aspects of the prophet's life is very significant. Even if we accept that all of the Qur'an material quoted is about Muhammad, it is a rather minimal amount. This leaves us with the fact that we cannot turn to the Qur'an, the alleged holiest of books, for any clear detail on Muhammad's birth, his earliest years, his travels to Syria, his marriage to Khadijah, his first calling as a prophet, the nature of Meccan polytheism, his Night Journey to Jerusalem, the flight to Medina, his military battles with fellow Arabs, his killing of men from the Jewish Qurayzah, his conquest of Mecca, and his death. These are stunning silences in the sacred text.[2] This is noted by Michael Cook, the famous Princeton scholar: "To write the biography of the Prophet on the basis of the Koran alone is simply not an option."[3]

Muslims believe, of course, that this silence is more than compensated for by other Islamic sources. Most Muslims would argue that we have data in abundance about Muhammad in Islamic sira (biographies), maghazi (military history), hadith (traditions of the prophet), shariah (legal material) and tafsir (Muslim commentaries). For centuries data from these sources has been read back into the Qur'an, so that most Muslims would find it impossible and laughable to entertain any suggestion that the Qur'an is not clearly about Muhammad.

## Muhammad and Traditional Islamic Sources

Leaving aside the connection of the Qur'an with Muhammad, what is Aslan's view of the traditional sources for Muhammad? His portrait of the prophet is built largely on the sira material.[4] He is highly suspicious of the hadith and also contemptuous of the traditionalist figures behind Islamic shariah law. In spite of these reservations about the hadith and shariah law, he does not really face the enormous historical objections to the traditional Islamic narrative of Muhammad.

We noted the lack of detail in the Qur'an about Muhammad. Do the other traditional Islamic sources for Muhammad solve the historicity issue? Not at all. Consider the following facts about the sira, maghazi, hadith, shariah and tafsir material. All of these sources for the life of Muhammad date from long after his death. The earliest and most famous biography is the *Sirat Rasul Allah* of Ibn Ishaq. Muhammad b. Ishaq was born about 704, and he died in 767. While his biography dates from about 750, there is no copy from Ibn Ishaq directly. What we have is the version of Ibn Ishaq as given by his most famous disciple, Abd al-Malik b. Hisham, who died in about 830. If we place Ibn Hisham's rendition to about AD 800, this means that over a century and a half lies between Muhammad's death and the first extant biography.

Wim Raven concludes his even-tempered entry on the sira in the *Encyclopedia of Islam* (second edition) with these words:

> The *sīra* materials as a whole are so heterogeneous that a coherent image of the Prophet cannot be obtained from it. Can any of them be used at all for a historically reliable biography of Muḥammad, or for the historiography of early Islam? Several arguments plead against it: (1) Hardly any *sīra* text can be dated back to the first century of

Islam. (2) The various versions of a text often show discrepancies, both in chronology and in contents. (3) The later the sources are, the more they claim to know about the time of the Prophet. (4) Non-Islamic sources are often at variance with Islamic sources.[5]

Historical authenticity is no better with the maghazi material. The most famous account of the military battles connected to the prophet comes from Muhammad b. Umar al-Waqidi (747–822). His *al-Maghazi* dates from the same time period as Ibn Hisham; thus there is again a significant time between Muhammad's death and the military material about him.[6]

The situation is as bleak with the hadith records, the traditions about Muhammad. There are six standard hadith collections in Sunni Islam and two in Shia Islam. The most famous Sunni collection is the *al-Jāmi ʿ al-musnad al-ṣaḥīḥ al-mukhtaṣar* done by al-Bukhari (810–870). Known simply as the *al-sahih*, it dates from about 850, but there are no originals.[7] The hadith collection by Muslim b. al-Ḥajjāj (d. 875) is next to al-Bukhari in influence.

The tafsir material has a weak historical foundation, since it is totally dependent on the sira, maghazi and hadith literature.[8] The most well-known tafsir material comes from al-Tabari (d. 923) and dates from about AD 900. His material on the life of Muhammad is noted especially for his preoccupation with situating the prophet's life into the narratives and teachings in the Qur'an.[9] As with the sira, maghazi and hadith material, the late dating of al-Tabari must raise serious objections to any notion of historical certainty about the prophet. The same late-dating realities apply to Sunni and Shia legal traditions. They arise long after the prophet.

Muslims would argue, of course, that the late date of the material is no proof of inauthenticity. Islamic apologetic here involves two general points. First, it is contended that early Muslims cared deeply about remembering the prophet's deeds and teachings, and the biographical works, the military histories and the recording of traditions and the commentaries on the Qur'an are all proof of how much they cared. There is no need to distrust their memory. The trouble with such faith is that it overlooks the common realities of human forgetfulness and the ways in which people alter or even twist history to suit their own religious or other ideological agendas. Further, it is astounding that the earliest Muslims left no records of Muhammad.

Muslims, however, posit a second factor to buttress their belief in the historicity of the prophet. They contend that their scholars cared so much about accuracy that they developed a whole science related to studying the traditions (hadith) of the prophet to figure out which ones are authentic. This discipline of hadith analysis provides, according to traditional Islam, a secure epistemic foundation for the biographical and military histories of the prophet, the establishment of shariah law and the proper understanding of the Qur'an. The hadith material is only second to the Qur'an in terms of the grounding for authority in traditional Islam.

The actual realities about the hadith illustrate that things are far from adequate in terms of the historical memory of the earliest Muslim community. Al-Bukhari, the most trusted collector, is said to have sifted through 600,000 hadith, and yet his collection includes just over 7,000 as genuine. The amount of fraudulent or unsound material does not suggest great historical acumen among Islam's founding fathers.

As for the so-called genuine hadith, there are telling signs of shoddy record keeping. The entry on the hadith in *The Encyclopaedia of Islam* makes six telling points: (1) phrases from the Bible are put into the mouth of Muhammad, (2) towns yet to be conquered after Muhammad's death are included in narrative about the prophet, (3) later Muslim dynasties are mentioned as if existent during the prophet's life, (4) many miracles are recorded about the prophet even though never mentioned in the Qur'an, (5) elaborate details are given about the end of the world and (6) late legal rulings are written back into the prophet's life. Here is the balanced conclusion of the entry:

> While one does not feel justified in explaining away the whole body of Tradition on these lines, it is quite clear that much material coming from a later date has been attributed to the Prophet, and this makes it very difficult to find a satisfactory criterion by which one may recognize what is genuine.[10]

Unlike orthodox Muslims, Aslan dismisses the hadith material quite readily in his apologetic for Islam. In doing so, Aslan fails to realize the devastating implications of his rejection. The cost has been noted by Tom Holland in his bestseller *In the Shadow of the Sword*:

> Beginning in 1890 and continuing to the present day, a succession of scholars have delivered a series of body-blows to the credibility of the *hadiths* as a record of what Muhammad himself might truly have said. Even the greatest collectors, even al-Bukhari himself, had failed to spot the clues. Heroic though all their efforts at

panning for gold had undoubtedly been, yet their rigour had been largely in vain—for the ability to distinguish a fake will invariably require a certain measure of distance, both of sympathy and time. Modern scholars have been in a position to recognise, as al-Bukhari was not, how even the most seemingly authentic *hadiths* wear a glitter that is all too often that of fool's gold. Far from bearing witness to the opinions of Muhammad, they in truth bear the unmistakable stamp of controversies that were raging two whole centuries after the *hijra*. Over and again, the Prophet had been made to serve as the mouthpiece for a whole host of rival, and often directly antagonistic, traditions. Many of these, far from deriving from Muhammad, were not even Arab in origin, but originated instead in the laws, the customs, or the superstitions of infidel peoples. What the jurists of the early Caliphate had succeeded in pulling off, by means of "a fiction perhaps unequalled in the history of human thought," was the ultimate in lawyers' tricks: a quite breathtaking show of creativity and nerve. Stitching together a whole new legal framework for the infant empire, it had become the habit of these ingenious scholars to attribute their rulings, not to their own initiative or judgement, but rather to that ultimate in authorities: the Prophet.[11]

Muslim academics sometimes realize the wrench thrown into the traditional Islamic picture if the hadith are largely lost in the fog of ideology, empire building, legal machinations and careless memory. Fazlur Rahman, a famous Islamic scholar trained in Western scholarship, asked, "If all *Hadith* is given up, what remains but a yawning chasm of fourteen centuries between us and the Prophet?" He goes on:

And in the vacuity of this chasm not only must the Qur'an slip from our fingers under our subjective whims—for the only thing that anchors it is the Prophetic activity itself—but even the very existence and integrity of the Qur'an and, indeed, the existence of the Prophet himself become an unwarranted myth.[12]

## The Strange World of the Hadith

Traditional Islamic acceptance of the hadith (traditions) about Muhammad provides many Muslims with confidence about the historicity of the prophet. However, adopting the hadith as a reliable source comes at a great price in terms of moral and rational critique.

| Teaching | Hadith reference |
| --- | --- |
| Adam was 90 feet tall. | Al-Bukhari 4, #453 |
| Angels do not enter homes that have dogs. | Al-Bukhari 5, #338 |
| The evil eye is real. | Muslim 3, #5424–5427 |
| Gabriel has 600 wings. | Al-Bukhari 4, #455 |
| Women are a majority in hell. | Al-Bukhari 1, #28 |
| Jinn eat bones and dung. | Al-Bukhari 5, #200 |
| Satan eats food with his left hand. | Muslim 3, #5007, 8, 10 |
| Satan urinates in people's ears. | Al-Bukhari 2, #194 |
| Sex with female slaves is allowed. | Al-Bukhari 9, #506 |
| Wing of fly has healing in it. | Al-Bukhari 7, #673 |
| Women can be beaten for disobedience. | Al-Bukhari 7, #715 |

## Evidence from Non-Muslim Sources

The case for a reliable portrait of Muhammad diminishes in light of the study of non-Muslim sources at the time of the prophet. Simply put, there is hardly anything about Muhammad in any historical data from the 7th and 8th centuries AD. This is an astonishing vacuum given the spread of Islam after the death of Muhammad. The paucity here is described by Tom Holland in relation to evidence about the battle of Badr, said to have taken place in 624.

> Certainly, it can come as a jolt to discover that, with a single exception, we have no extant descriptions of the battle of Badr that date from before the ninth century ad. We do not even have Ibn Ishaq's original biography of Muhammad—only revisions and reworkings. As for the material on which Ibn Ishaq himself drew upon for his researches, it has long since vanished. Set against the triumphal hubbub raised by Arab historians in the ninth century, let alone the centuries that followed, the silence is deafening and perplexing.

The precise state of play bears spelling out. Over the course of almost two hundred years, the Arabs, a people never noted for their reticence, and whose motivation, we are told, had been an utterly consuming sense of religious certitude, had set themselves to conquering the world—and yet in all that time, they composed not a single record of their victories, not one, that has survived into the present day. How could this possibly have been so, when even on the most barbarous fringes of civilization, even in Britain, even in the north of England, books of history were being written during this same period, and copied, and lovingly tended? Why, when the savage Northumbrians were capable of preserving the writings of a scholar such as Bede, do we have no Muslim records from the age of Muhammad? Why not a single Arab account of his life, nor of his followers' conquests, nor of the progress of his religion, from the whole of the near two centuries that followed his death?[13]

The earliest non-Muslim material about Muhammad is provided in Robert Hoyland's work *Seeing Islam as Others Saw It*.[14] Hoyland collected references to Islam and Muhammad from the 7th and 8th centuries among Greek, Syrian, Coptic, Hebrew, Persian, and even Chinese sources.[15] On Muhammad, the material is sparse, though it seems clear that Muhammad is viewed as a historical person. Thomas the Presbyter writes of "a battle between the Romans and the Arabs of Muhammad" in the year 634. Muhammad is mentioned in early Christian sources as the leader of the sons of Ishmael. A Chronicler of Khuzistan does so in a document sometime after 650. John of Damascus, writing in the 730s, calls Muhammad a "false prophet" and references books from him, though John does not name any as the Qur'an. This non-Muslim material confirms some broad historical realities, like that Arabs took over Palestine and that Jews sometimes viewed them as protectors. In spite of these generalities, no biography of Muhammad can be constructed from Christian and Jewish sources after the death of the prophet. Aslan gives no serious attention to this enormous vacuum of history.

## The Patricia Crone Case

Aslan's defense of traditional Islam fails miserably in facing other historiographical issues. This can be shown in his discussion of Patricia Crone, one of the most erudite and famous scholars of Islam. Crone and Michael Cook gained notoriety in 1977 with the publication of their *Hagarism: The Making of the Islamic World*, a work that advanced a very skeptical attitude towards traditional Muslim views of the origin of Islam, the historicity of the prophet and the integrity of the Qur'an.[16] Both authors soon distanced themselves from various particulars in that early work, but Crone has continued to write critically of the standard Muslim paradigms related to early Islamic history.

How Reza Aslan deals with Crone's scholarship is very telling. First, one could never imagine from Aslan's discussion that Crone is one of the most distinguished historians of early Islam. This is true regardless of what anyone thinks about the particulars of her outlook on Muhammad, the Qur'an and the rise and spread of Islam.[17] Peter Brown, the great Princeton historian, recognized the stunning importance of Crone and Cook's work in a seminal analysis in *The New York Review of Books* in early 1979.[18]

Brown covers 11 different books (including several from Bernard Lewis, one of the most famous scholars of Islam) in his long essay but gives over 50 percent of space to Crone and Cook. He states that *Hagarism* is "a book to be taken seriously." He also adds that it is "of genuine historical importance" and an "enterprising and learned book." It is astounding that Aslan dismisses her so readily in a few lines.[19]

Second, Aslan engages in gross distortion of Crone's overall viewpoint. According to Aslan, Crone contends that

> everything we know about the pre-Islamic Ka'ba, indeed everything we know about the Prophet Muhammad and the rise of Islam in seventh century Arabia, is a complete fabrication created by Arab storytellers in the 8th and 9th centuries—a fiction containing not one kernel of sound historical evidence.[20]

This summary statement is outlandish, in relation not only to Crone's views in *Hagarism* but to her many writings and public talks since then. The skepticism in *Hagarism* is far more muted than Aslan's verdict implies. More important, Crone has never argued that Muhammad did not exist or that the traditional Muslim narrative of the rise of Islam is "a complete fabrication."[21]

Third, Aslan fails as well in his specific arguments against Crone's well-known doubts about the standard Muslim views of the Ka'ba and the issue of trade in Mecca. According to Crone, there is little historical proof that Mecca was a major trade route for Arabs in the 6th and 7th century, given its terrain and location. Aslan concedes her general point about geography but argues that Mecca became a center of trade because the Ka'ba was a central shrine for all Arabs.

Aslan argues that the leaders of Mecca "had developed an innovative religio-economic system that relied on control of the Ka'ba and its pilgrimage rites—rites in which nearly the whole of Arabia participated—to guarantee the economic, religious, and political supremacy of a single tribe, the Quraysh."[22] Aslan claims that the Abyssinians attacked Mecca in order to destroy the Ka'ba since it had created an economic rivalry to their pilgrimage site in Sana. Aslan provides no evidence for his assertions. The articles on Sana in the first and second editions of the authoritative *Encyclopaedia of Islam* give no support for Aslan's specific interpretation of the alleged Sana-Mecca rivalry.[23]

## Historical Puzzles

There are a whole number of historical puzzles related to early Islam that Aslan does not face. Given the prominence of Mecca in traditional Islamic sources, why is the city mentioned only once by name in the Qur'an, the earliest of Muslim sources? Why is there a lack of serious detail about Medina? Why do descriptions allegedly related to Mecca in the Qur'an not seem to match the topography or agriculture known about the city? What is to be done with evidence that the direction of prayer in the first mosques in Syria, Palestine and Iraq did not point to Mecca but to Petra in what is now southern Jordan?[24] Likewise, why are there hardly any references to Muhammad in non-Muslim sources throughout most of the 7th and 8th centuries? In his new book on the Islamic conquests Robert Hoyland writes, "we have no contemporary external sources to elucidate his life."[25]

There are further complications. As Holland notes, why is there no mention of Muhammad in the inscriptions, coins and documents from Muawiya, the first Umayyad caliph, who ruled from 661–680? It is astonishing that this famous Muslim ruler would seem to have no preoccupation with Islam's prophet. This certainly speaks to the case for being hesitant about the historical reliability of the traditional Islamic picture of Muhammad. The paucity of archeological data is seconded by Michael Bonner: After stating that "the earliest surviving fragments of sira and maghazi on papyrus do not bring us any earlier than the middle of the eighth century CE," he points out that "no inscriptions, coins, original documents, or archaeological findings provide direct corroboration for any of this information [in the sira and maghazi material], at least as it relates to the life and career of Muhammad in Arabia."[26] Crone and Martin Hinds add a similar verdict: "It is a striking fact that such documentary evidence as survives from the Sufyanid period (661–684) makes no mention of the messenger of God at all. The papyri do not refer to him."[27]

Hesitations about Muhammad and historicity also arise when one examines the ways in which traditional Islam owes much of its identity to the political, military, social and religious machinations of Abd al-Malik, whose caliphate lasted from 685 through 705. He is most famous for construction of the Dome of the Rock in Jerusalem and cementing of Umayyad rule in Arabia. Unlike Muawiya, Abd al-Malik gave clear indication of his linkage to Muhammad through inscriptions of the prophet's name on the Dome of the Rock. New coinage from his reign also make explicit Abd al-Malik's devotion to Islam. The issue of relevance here is why there is so little of Muhammad in earlier chapters of Islamic history, at least in inscriptions, coinage or extant documents.

The influence of Abd al-Malik on Islam is well known but has been interpreted in various ways. Fred Donner, a doyen of scholarship on Islam, argues that the Umayyad leader turned Islam away from its early ecumenical thrust.[28] Robert Spencer, a controversial critic of Islam, argues that Abd al-Malik may have "essentially" invented Islam or more likely "invested it with details about Muhammad and his teaching, to unify and strengthen his empire."[29] Spencer's case against the existence of Muhammad (or against the traditional narrative about Muhammad) will not likely convince moderate Muslims or even secular historians, but he and others give plenty of reason to doubt Renan's famous line that Muhammad was born in the full light of history.

## Summary

The absence of Muhammad in the Qur'an, the late-dating of other Islamic sources, the unreliability of the hadith traditions, and the silence about Muhammad in early non-Muslim history give every reason to be suspicious at the historical level of Reza Aslan's portrait of Muhammad and apologetic for Islam. He either ignores the issues, misrepresents the relevant scholarship or maligns scholars who oppose traditional Muslim views. The case for skepticism about the historical Muhammad does not demand denial of his existence, as Spencer notes, but it does warrant uncertainty about how much we can truly know about the details of Muhammad's life and mission. In this regard, the verdict of Jonathan A. C. Brown, a Western trained and believing Muslim scholar, is important: "As for the first crucial century of Islam, beyond its broad outlines, it lies out of historical sight."[30]

# Chapter 8

# Is Muhammad the Greatest Moral and Spiritual Model?

*Ethical Problems for Muslims*

What if readers want to bypass historiographical issues and assume that the traditional Muslim accounts of Muhammad in the sira, maghazi, hadith and tafsir are basically reliable? What would the impact be on the analysis of Reza Aslan's interpretation of the prophet and on the traditional Muslim view of Muhammad? Ironically, the bypass of the historicity question actually leads to more significant problems. If one takes all traditional sources for Muhammad at face value, huge burdens arise over major components in the prophet's life and teachings. Reza Aslan, like many Muslim apologists, either avoids these issues, breezes over them with a shallow apologetic or engages in misleading explanations.

Of course, the burden that Aslan and other Muslims face in defending Muhammad is nothing when contrasted to the threat of persecution or death that hangs over those who write about Muhammad in the wrong way or displease the wrong powers in the process. In our case, we wish to raise certain issues about Muhammad with Reza Aslan and ask him to come to Islam's defense and aid us in our mutual search for historical truth and spiritual and moral integrity. More important, given our skepticism about the historical reliability of the Qur'an, hadith, surah and maghazi, we do **not** know what Muhammad really said or did during his life. Our doubts also extend to the reliability of Islamic tradition beyond Muhammad's death.

Thus, we are asking questions of Aslan in relation to traditional Muslim views of the prophet. It is Islam itself that provides the standard biography of the prophet, and the questions to Aslan that follow arise from within that tradition. Ironically, we believe that Muslims worldwide would have enormous moral gains if they abandoned many of the traditions about the prophet. Regarding this, we suggest exploring the possibility that the real Muhammad of history is the early Meccan prophet who cared for the poor and was concerned about justice and absolute trust in God. Perhaps the Muhammad of later traditions was created by the leaders and scholars of 8th and 9th century Islam. Again, we have no way of knowing if our hypothesis is historically true, but we recommend it to the Muslim community as a solution to the problems here noted.

The items addressed in this chapter constitute the usual suspects when it comes to questions about Muhammad. At one level, Muslims apologists like Aslan must grow weary of the same topics being raised time and again about their prophet. From that angle, we certainly wish that the concerns of this chapter could be avoided or easily wiped away. If Muhammad is as great as Muslims believe, surely the famous objections to the prophet must arise out of serious historical error or some emotional and spiritual blindness. Is it not the fault of the critic of Islam for being closed to the beauty of the prophet? Is this chapter built simply on centuries of bigotry and misinformation? Or, does the image of traditional Islam leave much to be desired? This might explain why many ex-Muslims trace their apostasy to reading reports from the orthodox perspective on Muhammad.[1] We shall see.

In the following section, readers will note we use words like "alleged" or "seemed." This is to remind readers that we are addressing Muslim traditions and Muslim views. We are **not** saying that the traditions involved are true, accurate or historical. In our view, to quote the famous Islamic expression, only God knows.

## The Stepson's Wife

Critical assessments of the prophet Muhammad almost always mention the ethical issues raised by the prophet's supposed dealings with Zaynab, the former wife of Muhammad's stepson Zayd. Controversy has centered on the following narrative:

While the couple were married the prophet went to see Zayd at his home.

As Zayd was not home, the prophet was greeted by Zaynab who was not fully dressed.

She noticed that the prophet was attracted to her and mentioned this later to Zayd.

Zayd went to Muhammad and told him that he would divorce his wife so Muhammad could marry her.

Zayd and Zaynab divorced.

Muhammad was reluctant to pursue marriage to Zaynab after her divorce, but a divine revelation sanctioned the marriage to the prophet.

The prophet's taking of his adopted son's wife created controversy at the time and ever since.[2]

Before we assess Muslim apologetic on the matter, the documentation of primary source material is important. The famous Muslim historian al-Tabari gives two accounts. Here is the first:

The Messenger of God came to the house of Zayd b. Harithah. Perhaps the Messenger of God missed him at that moment, so as to ask, "Where is Zayd?" He came to his residence to look for him but did not find him. Zaynab bt. Jash, Zayd's wife, rose to meet him. Because she was dressed only in a shift, the Messenger of God turned away from her. She said: "He is not here, Messenger of God. Come in, you who are as dear to me as my father and mother!" The Messenger of God refused to enter. Zaynab had dressed in haste when she was told "the Messenger of God is at the door." She jumped up in haste and excited the admiration of the Messenger of God, so that he turned away murmuring something that could scarcely be understood. However, he did say overtly: "Glory be to God the Almighty! Glory be to God, who causes the hearts to turn!"

When Zayd came home, his wife told him that the Messenger of God had come to his house. Zayd said, "Why didn't you ask him to come in?" He replied, "I asked him, but he refused." "Did you hear him say anything?" he asked. She replied, "As he turned away, I heard him say: 'Glory be to God the Almighty! Glory be to God, who causes hearts to turn!'"

So Zayd left, and having come to the Messenger of God, he said: "Messenger of God, I have heard that you came to my house. Why didn't you go in, you who are as dear to me as my father and mother? Messenger of God, perhaps Zaynab has excited your admiration, and so I will separate myself from her." Zayd could find no possible way to [approach] her after that day. He would

111

come to the Messenger of God and tell him so, but the Messenger of God would say to him, "Keep your wife." Zayd separated from her and left her, and she became free.

In his second account, al-Tabari writes that Zayd told the prophet, "Perhaps [the problem is] that you like Zaynab? In that case, I shall divorce her." The Prophet said, "Keep your wife." After the couple divorced, al-Tabari claims that Muhammad was told by God to marry Zaynab. The account reads, "[One day], while talking to 'A'ishah, the Prophet fainted. On regaining consciousness he smiled and said 'Who will go to Zaynab to bring her the glad tidings that God from above gave her to me in marriage?'"

This narrative is said to provide the context for surah 33:36–38:

It is not for a believing man or a believing woman, when God and His messenger have decided a matter, to have the choice in their matter. Whoever disobeys God and His messenger has very clearly gone astray. (Remember) when you said to the one whom God had blessed, and whom you had blessed: "Keep your wife to yourself, and guard (yourself) against God," and you hid within yourself what God was going to reveal, and feared the people, when God had a better right that you feared Him. So when Zayd had gotten what he needed from her, We married her to you, so that there should not be any blame on the believers concerning the wives of their adopted sons, when they have gotten what they needed from them. The command of God was (to be) fulfilled. There is no blame on the prophet concerning what God has made obligatory for him.

Some of the famous Muslim commentaries on this issue add some important information. Al-Tabari states in his discussion of the Qur'anic passage the following: "When Zaid mentioned his intention to separate from Zainab to the prophet, the prophet told him, 'Retain thou thy wife' even though the prophet desired that they separate so that he could marry her." Another commentator contends that Allah sent a wind to lift the curtain to reveal Zaynab to Muhammad.

The Zaynab affair has led various critics to denounce Muhammad as evil.[3]

Without wanting to engage in rhetorical flourish, we would be interested to hear Reza Aslan's analysis. There is the historical question: Did the prophet marry his adopted son's wife? There are then larger moral questions: Does Aslan believe that it was morally right for the prophet to marry Zaynab? Did the prophet set a normative pattern for Muslims in his disruption of Zayd's marriage?[4] Is Aslan at all disturbed by the ways in which

Muhammad's self-interest seems to dovetail with what he claims is God's will in regard to Zaynab? The same occurs in the prophet's taking of more than four wives.[5]

## The Prophet and Slavery

It is a truism that slavery was condoned in the West for centuries. What is not as well known is that Islamic leaders fostered slavery in most Muslim empires and countries over the centuries as well. Madeline C. Zilfi notes, for example, "slavery was deeply rooted and ubiquitous in the vast, centuries-old Ottoman Empire. Although generally only the wealthier elements of society could afford to own slaves, slavery in numerous forms was practiced in every Ottoman province from the Balkans, Asia Minor, and the Caucasus to the Arabian Peninsula and North Africa."[6] Slavery was institutionalized in various African countries as Islam became dominant from the 7th century on.[7] Muslim conquerors enforced slavery in what is now Pakistan in the 8th century and a bit later in India, though Muslim control in India was muted early on by Hindu armies. The spread of Islam in southeast Asia in the 13th century led to the enslavement of non-Muslims almost immediately.[8]

It is tempting to avoid consideration of the dreadful reality of slavery in the history of humanity simply by noting that the practice, with rare exception, has been abolished throughout the world. Sadly, this tactic has to be avoided in our present context given that it appears that Muhammad himself owned slaves and sanctioned slavery. This is in keeping with the justification given to slavery in the pages of the Qur'an itself. Islamic legal schools built on the traditional legacy of the prophet and the Qur'an and gave approval to slavery. The spread of Islamic slavery is thus a tribute to its ideological foundation in the prophet's life, the pages of the Qur'an and shariah law.

But did the prophet really own slaves? Well, Islamic tradition is reasonably clear on the matter. Ibn Sa'd mentions that Muhammad had sexual relations with his Coptic slave Mariyah. It is said that she "was of white complexion, with curly hair and pretty."[9] Various hadith by Buhkari, the most famous of collectors, make pretty blunt reading on the prophet's advice on slaves:

Vol. 7-#137 Narrated Abu al-Khudri:

> We got female captives in the war booty and we used to do coitus interruptus with them. So we asked Allah's messenger about it and he said, "Do you really do that?" repeating the question thrice, "There is no soul that is destined to exist but will come into existence, till the Day of Resurrection."

A similar hadith adds more detail.

Vol. 5-#459 Narrated Ibn Muhairiz:

> I entered the mosque and saw Abu Khudri and sat beside him and asked him about coitus interruptus. Abu said, "We went out with Allah's messenger for the Ghazwa (attack upon) Banu Mustaliq and we received captives from among the Arab captives and we desired women and celibacy became hard on us and we loved to do coitus interruptus. So when we intended to do coitus interruptus we said "How can we do coitus interruptus without asking Allah's messenger while he is present among us?" We asked (him) about it and he said "It is better for you not to do so, for if any soul (till the Day of Resurrection) is predestined to exist, it will exist."

Other hadith mention that Aisha, one of the prophet's wives, had her own slave, and various Muslim leaders from the prophet's time had slaves as well, as the hadith document. Ali, the prophet's son-in-law, beat Aisha's slave in front of Muhammad, and the prophet did not object, at least according to the report. This makes a disturbing case since, according to Islamic tradition, Muhammad advised that slaves be treated well.

While it is true that the Qur'an moderates slavery and Islamic law places restrictions on abuses, it is singularly depressing that the prophet of Islam, the exemplar for morality, did not abolish the practice in its entirety, at least according to traditional Islam.[10] Rather, the evidence suggests that he owned slaves and gave his blessing to other Muslims who duplicated his practice. We would be interested in Aslan's view of slavery in relation to the prophet. We also have a question for Tariq Ramadan, the famous Oxford scholar and celebrated Muslim intellectual: In light of the traditional Islamic material about female slaves, do you stand by your view that Muhammad "expressed constant respect toward all women"?[11]

## Karen Armstrong on Muhammad

### Karen Armstrong vs. Robert Spencer

According to traditional Islamic sources, Muhammad owned slaves, allowed female slaves to be raped, sanctioned torture, allowed assassinations of his critics, ordered the beheadings of hundreds of Jewish men, ordered or took part in over twenty battles and did not critique his soldiers for killing an old woman by tying her between two camels and driving them off in opposite directions.

If the traditional view is right, who has a more accurate perspective of Muhammad: Karen Armstrong or Robert Spencer?

### Karen Armstrong on Muhammad

Muhammad is "one of the most remarkable human beings who ever lived...who pursued a daring, inspired policy of non-violence that was worthy of Gandhi" (11–12, 14).

(Preface to 2001 edition of *Muhammad: A Biography of the Prophet*)

### Robert Spencer on Muhammad

"Islamic apologists who quote instances of the Prophet of Islam being kind or gentle generally do not mention at all his exhortations to make war against unbelievers until they are converted or subjugated. They do not mention his raids, his battles, his joy at the assassinations of his enemies—assassinations he himself ordered."

(from *The Truth about Muhammad*)

If Karen Armstrong extended to Robert Spencer a modicum of the empathy she gives to Muhammad, world peace would ensue.

## The Case of the Young Bride

There is hardly a nastier accusation about Muhammad than the claim that he was a pedophile. This charge has circulated widely in recent years. Geert Wilders, the controversial Dutch politician, stated at a press conference in London on March 5, 2010, that Muhammad was a pedophile, along with being a mass murderer. Jerry Vines, a past president of the Southern Baptist convention, opined at their 2002 annual meeting, "Christianity was founded by the virgin-born Jesus Christ. Islam was founded by Mohammed, a demon-possessed pedophile who had twelve wives, and his last one was a nine-year-old girl." The same charge was featured in *Innocence of Muslims*, a trailer released in July 2012 by Nakoula Basseley Nakoula. Nakoula's 13-minute video resulted in demonstrations worldwide, with many arrests and over 50 deaths reported.

What is the explanation for this allegation against the prophet? It arises out of various Muslim reports concerning the prophet's marriage to Aisha when she was six or seven and subsequent consummation when she was nine. Here are some of the most important references:

> Khadija died three years before the Prophet departed to Medina. He stayed there for two years or so and then he married 'Aisha when she was a girl of six years of age, and he consumed that marriage when she was nine years old. (al-Bukhari 5, 58:236)

> Narrated 'Aisha: that the Prophet married her when she was six years old and he consummated his marriage when she was nine years old, and then she remained with him for nine years (i.e., till his death). (al-Bukhari 7, 62:64)

> 'A'isha (Allah be pleased with her) reported that Allah's Apostle (may peace be upon him) married her when she was seven years old, and he was taken to his house as a bride when she was nine, and her dolls were with her; and when he (the Holy Prophet) died she was 18 years old. (Muslim 8:3311)

> 'A'isha (Allah be pleased with her) reported that Allah's Apostle (may peace be upon him) married her when she was seven years old, and he was taken to his house as a bride when she was nine, and her dolls were with her; and when he (the Holy Prophet) died she was 18 years old. (Abu Dawud 2:2116)

> Narrated Aisha, Ummul Mu'minin: When we came to Medina, the women came to me when I was playing on the swing, and my hair was up to my ears. They brought me, prepared me, and decorated me. Then they brought me to the Apostle of Allah (peace be upon him) and he took up cohabitation with me, when I was nine. (Abu Dawud 41:4197)

> It was narrated from 'Aishah that the Messenger of Allah married her when she was six years old, and consummated the marriage with her when she was nine. (al Nasa'i 4:26:3257)

> Abd Allah b. Safwan together with another person came to Aishah and Aishah said (to the latter), "O so and so, have you heard what Hafsah has been saying?" He said, "Yes, o Mother of the Faithful." Abd Allah b. Safwan asked her, "What is that?" She replied, "There are nine

special features in me that have not been in any woman, except for what God bestowed on Maryam bt. Imran. By God, I do not say this to exalt myself over any of my companions." "What are these?" he asked. She replied, "The angel brought down my likeness; the Messenger of God married me when I was seven; my marriage was consummated when I was nine; he married me when I was a virgin, no other man having shared me with him; inspiration came to him when he and I were in a single blanket; I was one of the dearest people to him, a verse of the Qur'an was revealed concerning me when the community was almost destroyed; I saw Gabriel when none of his other wives saw him; and he was taken (that is, died) in his house when there was nobody with him but the angel and myself." (al-Tabari 7:6–7)

He married 'A'isha in Mecca when she was a child of seven and lived with her in Medina when she was nine or ten. She was the only virgin that he married. Her father, Abu Bakr, married her to him and the apostle gave her four hundred dirhams. (Ibn Ishaq, *The Life of Muhammad*, 792)

Readers unfamiliar with the sources might easily imagine that these quotations are from eccentric Muslim or anti-Muslim voices. One might wish for this to be the case, since it would aid in any Muslim-Christian dialogue. However, these are the most trusted Muslim historical sources used by traditional Muslims. Al-Bukhari and Muslim are the two most famous hadith collectors, as noted previously. Abu Dawud and Al Nasa'i are also prominent collectors of reliable hadith, at least according to traditional Sunni thinkers. It was noted earlier that al-Tabari is one of the most famous Muslim commentators.[12] Ibn Ishaq is the most influential biographer of the prophet.

The unanimity in the traditional Muslim sources has led the most famous non-Muslim biographers to assent to a young age for Aisha at the consummation of her marriage. W. Montgomery Watt, for example, states in one place, "the marriage was not consummated until some months after the *hidjra* (in Shawwāl 1 or 2/ April 623 or 624). 'Ā'isha went to live in an apartment in Muḥammad's house, later the mosque of Medina. She cannot have been more than ten years old at the time, and took her toys to her new home."[13]

Several caveats about Aisha's alleged early marriage to the prophet are in order. First, Shia Muslims do not hold Aisha in high regard, given her opposition to Ali's caliphate after the death of Muhammad. So, Shia Muslims distrust the hadith collectors noted previously. Second, various contemporary Sunni scholars seek to offset the traditional Sunni sources by arguing that

117

careful historical analysis shows that Aisha was in her mid-teens or later when her marriage was consummated. Reza Aslan asserts without evidence that it was simply a case of engagement.[14] Third, other Sunni Muslims contend that there is nothing immoral even if Aisha was only nine at the time, especially when one factors in the social context of the time. On this latter point, Robert Spencer notes, "the concept of pedophilia as a manifestation of deviant sexuality did not exist in the 7th century. In marrying Aisha, Muhammad was doing no more and no less than what was done by many men of his time, and no one thought twice about the matter until much later."[15]

Spencer goes on to argue that dismissal of the pedophilia charge still leaves the troubling reality that for Muslims Muhammad serves as the highest moral example for humanity. In Islamic history the prophet's alleged marriage to a very young Aisha set the stage for legal rulings that Muslim men can have young child brides. Spencer mentions that Ayatollah Khomeini married a ten-year-old girl and that Iran has set the legal age for girls at nine. *The Globe and Mail* (Toronto) reported on child brides in their 2009 series on women in Kandahar.[16] In 2008 *The New York Times* covered the courageous story of two child brides in Yemen who resisted their abusive husbands. The article notes that the fight against the marriage of young girls is difficult since "hard-line Islamic conservatives, whose influence has grown enormously in the past two decades, defend it, pointing to the Prophet Muhammad's marriage to a 9-year-old."[17] The child bride issue surfaced again in Yemen after a 2013 report on an eight-year-old Yemeni girl who died on her wedding night from internal bleeding caused by sex with her husband. We ask Aslan what he thinks of the many traditions supporting the view that Aisha was very young when the marriage was consummated. Does he accept the accounts as historical? If so, does he view the prophet as a great role model on this matter?

## Kinana's Misfortune

Any merit one gives to the U.S. attempts to liberate Iraq from the rule of Saddam Hussein must be offset by some rather huge negatives, not the least of which is the fact that some U.S. soldiers engaged in torture at Abu Ghraib. Further, the evidence is certainly strong that various U.S. leaders sanctioned torture in the interrogating of certain prisoners. Some critics have argued that U.S. involvement in torture played a significant part in pushing Muslims to support al-Qaeda and other militant groups.[18]

Critique of the United States on these matters is often countered by indictments about the use of torture among Muslim extremists. What is not often mentioned in the polemics about torture is that it seems to have been sanctioned by the prophet in the case of a Jewish leader named Kinana. He was connected to the Banu Nadir, one of the Jewish tribes in Medina. He had the misfortune to know where the treasure of his tribe was located. According to Ibn Ishaq's biography of the prophet, Kinana paid dearly for his reluctance to provide the whereabouts of the treasure. Here is the complete account from Ibn Ishaq:

> Kinana b. al-Rabi,' who had the custody of the treasure of B. al-Nadir, was brought to the apostle who asked him about it. He denied that he knew where it was. A Jew came to the apostle and said that he had seen Kinana going round a certain ruin every morning early. When the apostle said to Kinana, "Do you know that if we find you have it I shall kill you?" he said Yes. The apostle gave orders that the ruin was to be excavated and some of the treasure was found. When he asked him about the rest he refused to produce it, so the apostle gave orders to al-Zubayr b. al-'Awwam, "Torture him until you extract what he has," so he kindled a fire with flint and steel on his chest until he was nearly dead. Then the apostle delivered him to Muhammad b. Maslama and he struck off his head, in revenge for his brother Mahmud.

The torture of Kinana is also mentioned in al-Tabari's history. The relevant section reads,

> The Prophet gave orders concerning Kinanah to Zubayr, saying, "Torture him until you root out and extract what he has. So Zubayr kindled a fire on Kinanah's chest, twirling it with his firestick until Kinanah was near death. Then the Messenger gave him to Maslamah, who beheaded him."[19]

Does Aslan accept the authenticity of the reports from Ibn Ishaq, the most famous and influential biographer of the prophet, and from al-Tabari, the great historian of Islam?

## A Poet Dies

One of the most disturbing allegations against Muhammad is that he allowed and ordered the death of various critics. One of the most famous cases surrounds a poetess named Asma who mocked the men of her own tribe for not standing up to Muhammad. Ibn Ishaq narrates the rest of the story:

> When the apostle heard what she had said he said, "Who will rid me of Marwaan's daughter?" Umayr b. Adiy al-Khatmi who was with him heard him and that very night he went to her house and killed her. In the morning he came to the apostle and told him what he had done and he said, "You have helped God and His apostle, O 'Umayr!" When he asked if he would have to bear any evil consequences the apostle said, "Two goats won't butt their heads about her."

Again, does Aslan accept this report from the standard biography? Should Muslims be alarmed by this assassination? Sadly, these are not the only reports in the early Muslim community of killings that go well beyond standard military protocol. Al-Tabari reports a Muslim warrior who tied an old woman named Umm Qirfa to two camels and drove them in separate directions until she was torn in two.[20] There is no specific record of the prophet's reaction to her manner of death, but according to *Sahih Muslim*, one of the top hadith collections, the prophet had the old woman's daughter traded for some Muslim prisoners in Mecca.[21] The episode is used in an anti-Muslim comic book from Indonesia.[22]

We are not raising the issue of assassination to charge Muslims in general with moral approval of such deaths; nor are we drawing attention to them to prove anything about Islam per se. What is at issue for us is how Aslan specifically and other Muslims, particularly established leaders, interpret Muhammad in relation to these killings. Is Al-Tabari to be trusted or Ibn Ishaq or the hadith of al-Bukhari and Muslim in relation to such deaths? What do these reports suggest about the traditional Islamic portrait of Muhammad?

## Death for Apostasy

On June 23, 2014, a sigh of relief was heard around the world as news spread that Meriam Ibrahim, a Sudanese wife and mother, had her death penalty overturned. What was her crime? Sudanese courts had ruled that she was guilty of apostasy since she was born Muslim but had refused to give up her Christian faith. Her case received international attention. Amnesty International campaigned for her release, and U.S. Secretary of State John Kerry urged Sudan to release her. He urged Sudan to "repeal its laws that are inconsistent with its 2005 Interim Constitution, the Universal Declaration of Human Rights and the International Covenant on Civil and Political Rights. Such actions would help to demonstrate to the Sudanese people that their government intends to respect their fundamental freedoms and universal human rights."[23]

Sudan is not the only Islamic country to impose the death penalty on apostates. In 2006, Abdul Rahman of Afghanistan was charged with apostasy, and he escaped a death penalty only because of international pressure. Saudi Arabia law calls for the death penalty for apostasy. The most famous modern example of an imposition of the death penalty on an apostate involves Salman Rushdie. On February 14, 1989, Ayatollah Khomeini of Iran issued his infamous fatwa against the Indian born author for his book *The Satanic Verses*. The fatwa read,

> I am informing all brave Muslims of the world that the author of The Satanic Verses, a text written, edited and published against Islam, the Prophet of Islam, and the Qur'an, along with all the editors and publishers aware of its contents, are condemned to death. I call on all valiant Muslims wherever they may be in the world to kill them without delay, so that no one will dare insult the sacred beliefs of Muslims henceforth. And whoever is killed in this cause will be a martyr, Allah Willing.[24]

What is the background to contemporary cases of apostasy from Islam? As is reasonably well-known, the four schools of Sunni law advocate the death penalty for apostasy, though all schools provide an opportunity in most cases for the accused to repent. Frank Griffel notes,

> Concomitant with the establishment of the death penalty is the legal institution of the "invitation to repent" (istitāba). Every accused apostate is given the right to return to Islam. Only after this invitation is turned down for the third time may he or she be killed. The istitāba is a safeguard for an accused apostate, providing him or her with an opportunity to return to Islam, fully avert punishment, and recover all rights as a Muslim. This compulsory invitation insured that only those apostates who openly declared their breaking away from Islam and who maintained their rejection in the face of capital punishment would be punished.[25]

The Qur'an provides no earthly penalty for apostasy. In fact, Wael Hallaq shows that the Qur'an is very moderate on apostasy in contrast to later Islamic law. He suggests that the so-called wars of apostasy that took place after Muhammad's death set the stage for the harsh legal rulings to come. What makes discussion of the Qur'an and shariah somewhat complicated is some evidence in the hadith that Muhammad himself seems to have encouraged death for apostates. Hallaq writes this about the relevant hadith:

> On the authority of the Companion Ibn 'Abbās (d. 68/688), the Prophet is reported to have said, "He who changes his religion, kill him." Another ḥadīth from Ibn 'Abbās and the Prophet's wife 'Ā'isha states that the Prophet allowed the execution of anyone who abandoned Islam and dissented with the community. The Prophet is also reported to have given Mu'ādh b. Jabal the following order when he dispatched him to govern in the Yemen: "Any man who turns away from Islam, invite him [to return to it]; if he does not return, cut off his neck." The second half of the ḥadīth occurs also in a virtually identical formulation, but applies to women.[26]

The first reference Hallaq mentions is from al-Bukhari's collection of hadith (4, 52:260), so it is from the highest ranked source of the hadith. Another hadith from al-Bukhari mentions that the killing of a particular apostate (a Muslim who had returned to Judaism) resulted from the "judgment of Allah and His Apostle" (9, 84:58). Another hadith includes apostasy as grounds for capital punishment, along with illegal sexual intercourse and murder (9, 83:17). The same rule is noted in the hadith collection of Muslim, the second most influential collector (16:4152).

On this topic, Reza Aslan would applaud himself for his rejection of the hadith as a guide for modern Muslims. He would also join Hallaq in noting the Qur'an's moderation on the topic, a reality often mentioned on Muslim websites where one also finds frequent citation of the famous statement in surah 2:256: "There is no compulsion in religion."[27] In spite of this famous verse, the apparent record of Muhammad himself specifically and Islamic history here and there seems to include realities to the contrary. Is Aslan concerned about the traditional accounts of the prophet?

Related to this is the corresponding reality that the possibility of death in principle puts into immediate question the level of freedom any Muslim has in regard to religious belief. How can a person make a truly free choice with the sword of shariah law in the background? Those who value Article 18 of the Universal Declaration of Human Rights can only hope that all Muslims, traditional, moderate or otherwise, will work to abandon all Muslim laws or customs that demand or allow death for apostates from Islam. Further, the world will be a better place if all Muslim-majority countries and Islamic states allow for the same level of religious freedom for non-Muslims that Muslims have a right to expect in all the nations of the world.

## Four Schools of Sunni Law

| School | Founder | Muslim World Under School |
|---|---|---|
| Hanafi School | Imam Abu Hanifa (AD 699–767) from Iraq | 45% |
| Shafi'i | Imam al Shafi'i (AD 767–820) from Medina | 28% |
| Maliki | Imam Malik (c. AD 711–795) from Medina | 15% |
| Hanbali | Imam Ahmad bin Hanbal (AD 780–855) from Iraq | 2% |

## Summary

The gap between the high view of Muhammad in traditional Islam and the critical portrait of Muhammad outside of Islam is very significant. The divide is mainly a result of the issues noted in this chapter. How can Muhammad be the greatest light from God given the traditional Muslim teachings about Zaynab, slavery, Aisha, assassinations, torture and death for apostates? Many Muslims will not know details about these matters. For them and for those who are informed but remain deeply concerned we hope that Reza Aslan and other Muslims apologists will provide answers that go beyond simple Islamic retorts and probe these profound moral issues carefully.

# Chapter 9

# How Do Muslims View the Qur'an?

*Importance, Content and Origin of the Muslim Holy Scripture*

A slan's view of Jesus and the Qur'an is shaped by a traditional Islamic perspective, and his appreciation for the Qur'an runs deep throughout *No god but God*. Understanding the Qur'an, the Muslim holy book, is absolutely necessary in order to understand Islam and the views of Aslan or any other Muslim. Here we examine the traditional Muslim view of the Qur'an, its nature, origin and transmission.

## The Importance of the Qur'an

The standard Muslim view of the Qur'an has been captured eloquently by Hans Küng in his magisterial work *Islam: Past, Present & Future*. The famous Swiss scholar writes,

> The Qur'an is the center of Islam. For over 14 hundred years, Islam has time and again fundamentally changed its social order; one political ideology has given way to another and cultural systems have undergone epoch-making paradigm changes. What remained in all the changes of persons, structures, institutions and interpretations? The Qur'an is the origin, source and norm of all that is Islamic, all Islamic faith, action and life. It is given the highest, absolute, authority.[1]

Tariq Ramadan, a believing Muslim scholar, says this of the Qur'an:

> It is a reminder of the monotheistic messages of the past, the light of divine guidance for the future, and the miracle of the eternal and inevitable word conveyed to human beings at the heart of their history...By its highly evocative form and contents, as well as by its spiritual power, the Qur'an is Islam's miracle.[2]

The importance of the Qur'an in Islam can be perceived in the extensive rules about its handling and about belief in its contents and the dangers of skepticism towards the Qur'an. Consider these items from *Reliance of the Traveler,* a classic manual of Islamic law:

- The Qur'an can only be touched and recited in a state of ritual purity.
- The mouth has to be clean before reciting the Qur'an.
- Recitation is to be done while facing Mecca.
- Recitation is to be stopped if yawning.
- The Qur'an is not to be left open after putting it down.
- One should never enter a lavatory with a copy of the Qur'an.
- The Qur'an should be placed higher than all other books.
- One should not let a day pass without looking at its pages.

The manual states that belief in the Qur'an is part of necessary "sacred knowledge" and that denial of any verse of the Qur'an is proof of apostasy.[3] The high status of the Qur'an is also shown by its unique presence in Islamic art and architecture. Images of the prophet Muhammad are often forbidden, but passages of the Qur'an are displayed in mosques and other buildings.[4] As is well known, the Qur'an's importance is illustrated through elaborate calligraphy (as on the cover of tombs in Iran or on a medicinal cup in 17th century India, for example).[5] Further, the enormous emphasis on the recitation and memorization of the Qur'an speaks to the supreme significance of the Qur'an.[6]

## The Qur'an on Itself[7]

- The Qur'an often calls itself "the Book" (*al-kitab* in Arabic).
- The term al-Qur'an (which means "the Recitation") occurs 70 times.
- It is the "blessed" book (38:29).
- It is "the wise book" (10:1, 31:2).
- It is a "glorious" book (50:1).
- The Qur'an is "sent down" or "brought down" from heaven (56:80).
- The Qur'an is "an Arabic" book (43:2–4).
- If the Qur'an had been sent down on a mountain the mountain would have humbled and split apart (59:21).

## Basics about the Qur'an

There are some commonly known facts about the Qur'an. The Qur'an is about the size of the New Testament. A typical English translation can run close to 600 pages, as is the case with Yusaf Ali's famous rendition. The Qur'an is composed of 114 surahs (chapters). The standard Arabic translation has 6,236 verses and 77,807 words.[8] After the famous but short first chapter (called the Fatiha, which is used in the five daily prayers), the remaining surahs are arranged, with a few exceptions, in order of length, from the longest to the shortest. As an example of the range of verses, surah 2 has 286 verses, surah 47 has 38 verses, and surah 90 has 20, while both surahs 108 and 110 have only three.

---

## The Fatiha (Surah 1 of the Qur'an)

**1** In the Name of God, the Merciful, the Compassionate.
**2** Praise (be) to God, Lord of the worlds, **3** the Merciful, the
Compassionate, **4** Master of the Day of Judgment. **5** You we
serve and You we seek for help. **6** Guide us to the straight path:
**7** the path of those whom You have blessed, not (the path) of
those on whom (Your) anger falls, nor of those who go astray.

This opening of the Qur'an is a prayer that is recited 17 times every
day as part of the five daily prayers.

Sunni Muslims end the Fatiha by saying amin (amen).

This surah is often called the quintessence of the Qur'an.

The first sentence of the prayer, "In the Name of God, the Merciful,
the Compassionate," is known as the bismillah (or basmala) and is
found at the start of every surah except the ninth. The bismillah is
also given in surah 27:30.

In the standard Cairo edition of the Qur'an the bismillah is not
counted as a verse except in this first surah.

Muslim tradition usually places the Fatiha as an early revelation to
Muhammad.

This is the most famous surah of the Qur'an.

The Fatiha is used in healing rituals, as an invocation against evil
spirits, as a prayer at circumcisions and burials or as part of various
covenants, including marriage.

The Fatiha is often said as a means to gain courage for battle.

Some Muslims believe this is the oldest surah.[9]

Most Muslim scholars believe that the contents of the Qur'an are in
reverse order in terms of when they were revealed by God. Thus, surahs
that come just after the Fatiha (surah 1) are actually from a later time
period in the life of the prophet. Or, to put it another way, surah 114, the
last in terms of page count, was given to Muhammad many years before
surah 2. A traditional Muslim would argue that if one wants to read the
Qur'an in chronological order then one should start at the back of the
text.[10] Most Western scholars of Islam share this traditional Islamic perspective about the chronological order, though many remain skeptical

about whether or not the contents of the Qur'an are necessarily related to Muhammad.

The titles of the various chapters are often based on some word, idea, person or event that appears in the chapter, though the titles do not necessarily suggest the main theme of the chapter, if there is one. Very few surahs have just one theme or topic, though surahs 12 (on Joseph) and 71 (on Noah) are major exceptions. The numbering of verses in the Qur'an varies in different Arabic texts. The two dominant versions are the Cairo edition of 1924 and one done earlier by Gustav Flügel in 1834. The main difference between the two versions has to do with whether the *bismillah* ("In the Name of God, the Merciful, the Compassionate") is counted as a verse.

---

## Miracle Proofs for the Qur'an

Many Muslims believe that the Qur'an is inspired by God because of its miraculous elements. There are said to be scientific, prophetic, medical, historical and mathematic miracles in the Muslim Scripture, in addition to the fact that the Qur'an is a literary miracle. One Muslim website lists 113 scientific miracles of the Qur'an, including its description of radar technology, quasars, black holes, radio receivers, the ozone layer, the moon's orbit and so on. It is argued that the number 19 is used in the Qur'an in ways that offer mathematical proof of divine authorship. As well, surah 18:65 has the Arabic letters DNA in the text. This is particularly significant since 1865 is the year that the science of genetics began, at least according to the website. One of the most popular books defending the scientific integrity of the Qur'an was published by Maurice Bucaille (1920–1998) in the 1970s under the title *The Bible, the Qur'an and Science*.[11]

---

## Ten Major Themes of the Qur'an

Many first-time readers of the Qur'an find it confusing. It is not an orderly text, as most Muslims will acknowledge. It is not a narrative document, by and large, though there are narrative sections. It is by no means systematic. The chapters are not arranged by content, as noted earlier. It is not necessarily being impious to say that the Qur'an is a very disjointed work. Further, there are numerous difficult terms and textual puzzles that have never been solved. Of the latter, the most famous conundrum is the fact that 29 surahs have a letter or letters just after the *bismillah* that make no obvious sense. For example, surah 11 has "Alif Lam Ra" at the beginning while surah 32 starts with "Alif Lam Mim." The guesswork from commentators on these mysterious letters is wide-ranging.[12]

In addition, the fact that there are such diverse and opposing evaluations of the Qur'an would make anyone conclude that it must be a very difficult book to understand. The gap, for example, between Reza Aslan and Robert Spencer on the beauty, integrity and value of the Qur'an is so wide that it is easy to imagine that they are writing about different books.

In spite of the real problems of wildly differing interpretations and lack of order, the basic message or messages of the Qur'an can be grasped. This is due to three factors. First, in spite of its length there are not that many major subjects in the whole document. Second, the basic themes are repeated over and over again, and the message gets through in spite of a disorderly text. Finally, the Qur'an is not written in an esoteric style; nor is it full of philosophical abstraction. It is also not a scientific treatise, a technical manual or a dense legal document (in spite of the prominence of law in Islamic orthodoxy), and it does not dwell on arcane, unusual topics.

1.  The Qur'an is about God or Allah, the common Arabic word for God. The Qur'an is absolutely dominated by references to Allah. The word "Allah" appears over 2,500 times. Anyone who says that the Qur'an is mainly about something else has never read the Qur'an. It is a book saturated with references to God.

---

## Basics about Allah

1. He is the Creator.

"He is God, the Creator, the Maker, the Shaper. To Him belong the Names Most Beautiful. All that is in the heavens and the earth magnifies Him; He is the All-mighty, the All-wise" (59:24).

2. Allah is Eternal.

"God, the Everlasting Refuge" (112: 2).

---

3. Allah is the Guardian.

"Lord of the East and the West—(there is) no god but Him, so take Him as a guardian" (73:9).

4. Allah is Holy.

"All that is in the heavens and the earth magnifies God, the King, the All-holy, the All-mighty, the All-wise" (73:9).

5. Allah is All-Knowing.

"God knows the Unseen in the heavens and the earth; He knows the thoughts within the breasts." An earlier surah also reads, "He knows all that goes into the earth, and all that comes out thereof; all that comes down from the sky and all that ascends thereto" (35:38).

6. Allah alone is God. He has no partners.

"He is God; there is no god but He. He is the King, the All-holy, the All-peaceable, the All-faithful, the All-preserver, the All-mighty, the All-compeller, the All-sublime. Glory be to God, above that they associate!" (59:23).

7. Allah is Merciful.

"He is the most merciful of the merciful!" (12:64).

8. God is the Revealer.

"And some there are of the People of the Book who believe in God, and what has been sent down unto you, and what has been sent down unto them, men humble to God, not selling the signs of God for a small price…" (3:199).

9. Allah is the Sustainer.

"Surely your Lord is God, who created the heavens and the earth in six days—then sat Himself upon the Throne, covering the day with the night it pursues urgently—and the sun, and the moon, and the stars subservient, by His command. Verily, His are the creation and the command. Blessed be God, the Lord of all Being!" (7:54).

10. Allah is the Judge.

"Judgment (belongs) only to God. He recounts the truth, and He is the best of judges" (6:57).

2.  The Qur'an is about a new prophet or new prophets who are chosen by Allah in the time of the Qur'an to continue the same prophetic message as given earlier to Jews and Christians. Of course, all Muslims and most scholars believe that the recipient of the Qur'an is Muhammad, the "seal" of the prophets. We already noted how he is read into countless verses, even though he is only mentioned by name four times.

3.  The Qur'an is preoccupied with itself. The Qur'an says of itself that it is clear, understandable, written in pure Arabic and free from error and that it contains the universal message, one that will guide its hearers into eternal salvation.

4.  The Qur'an is a repository of material from, or at least related to, the Bible. It gives enormous attention to various Old and New Testament figures, narratives from the Old Testament and teachings from Jewish and Christian Scriptures. Of biblical figures, Moses gets the most mention, with more than five hundred verses or almost 10 percent of the Qur'anic text dealing with him. The Qur'an also gives significant attention to Noah, Abraham, Joshua, David, Mary and others.

5.  As presented in detail in two other chapters, the Qur'an views Jesus as a central prophet in Allah's revelation to humanity. While he is not viewed as the Son of God or part of a Trinity, he is highly regarded, a worker of miracles, born of the Virgin Mary and a sign from God.

6.  The Qur'an describes the characteristics, attitudes and actions of Allah's true believers. This is in keeping with the common assertion that Islam is a religion about the right path much more than it is a religion about right ideas. Even though Islam is a religion of law, the Qur'an is focused more on the larger spiritual and moral principles behind the law. Shariah law, in all of its enormous detail, builds on the more minimal doctrinal and moral framework of the Qur'an. As a case in point, the Qur'an affirms the famous five pillars of Sunni Islam: *shahada*: "I testify that there is no god but God and I testify that Muhammad is the messenger of God,"[13] *salat* (prayer), *zakat* (tithing), fasting (sawm) during Ramadan and the *hajj* (pilgrimage to Mecca), but one has to look in the shariah for details of the relevant rituals.[14] The same is true of the ten Ancillaries in Twelver Shia Islam.[15]

# Bible Names in the Qur'an

| Name in the Bible | Name in the Qur'an |
| --- | --- |
| Aaron | *Hārūn* |
| Abraham | *Ibrāhīm* |
| Adam | *Ādam* |
| Christians | *Naṣārā* |
| David | *Dāwūd* |
| Elijah | *Ilyās* |
| Elisha | *Alyasa or al-Yasa* |
| Enoch | *Idrīs* |
| Ezra | *Uzayr* |
| Gabriel | *Jibrīl* |
| Goliath | *Jālūt* |
| Isaac | *Is'ḥāq* |
| Ishmael | *Ismā'īl* |
| Israel | *Is'ḥāq* |
| Jacob | *Ya'qūb* |
| Jesus | *'Īsā* |
| Job | *Ayyūb* |
| John the Baptist | *Yaḥyā* |
| Jonah | *Yūnus* |
| Joseph | *Yūsuf* |
| Lot | *Lūṭ* |
| Mary | *Maryam* |
| Messiah | *al-Masīḥ* |
| Michael | *Mīkāl* |
| Moses | *Mūsā* |
| Noah | *Nūḥ* |
| Pharaoh | *Fir'awn* |
| Satan/Devil | *Iblīs* |
| Saul | *Ṭālūt* |
| Sheba | *Sabā'* |
| Solomon | *Sulaymān* |
| Zachariah | *Zakariyyā* |

## The Qur'an on the Believer

- Worships Allah alone
- A person of prayer and contemplation
- Faithful, humble, forgiving
- Protects other Muslims
- Charitable
- Does not gamble
- Does not drink alcohol
- Does not engage in usury
- Muslim male has no more than four wives
- Practices modesty
- Fasts
- Avoids excess in religion
- Believes in the equality of all humans

7. The Qur'an also gives major attention to unbelievers who stand against Allah's divine revelations and will. The whole human setting of the Qur'an involves the storm created by the prophetic call to decision and the subsequent division between belief and unbelief. Those who reject Allah's message are deaf, blind and full of disease. They are arrogant and foolish, hate the truth and live in delusion, and their prayers are in vain. The unbeliever is a liar, a coward, vain and a deceiver. Muslims should avoid unbelievers, given their perversity.

8. The Qur'an gives enormous weight to life after death, and heaven is one of the related themes. Though Muslim scholars debate to what extent certain verses about heaven are to be taken literally, the overall message is clear. Heaven is pictured like a garden paradise, with mansions, fountains, food and drink and sexual pleasure, where believers are full of happiness, peace and joy in the presence of God.

## Virgins or Grapes?

The usual translations of the Qur'an suggest that the heavenly reward for Muslim males will include access to a number of virgins. One passage reads, "And theirs shall be the dark-eyed houris, chaste as hidden pearls: a guerdon for their deeds...We created the houris and made them virgins, loving companions for those on the right hand."

Considerable attention has been given in recent years to the controversial claims of Christoph Luxenberg, the pseudonymous author of *The Syro-Aramaic Reading of the Qur'an*. He has argued that the passages that speak about virgins in paradise are actually based on Syriac wording that is really a reference to raisins or grapes. The Qur'an, according to Luxenberg, is talking about heavenly rewards of food and drink, not sexual rewards.

Heaven is for both males and females. This needs some mention given media focus on Islamic teaching about the alleged 72 virgins who await Muslim martyrs (presumably male). While the specific hadith behind this particular number of virgins is questioned by some scholars, in general both the Qur'an and hadith are clear on the substantial sexual rewards that await martyrs and non-martyrs.[16]

## The Qur'an on Paradise

4:57　　　But those who believe and do righteous deeds—We shall cause them to enter Gardens through which rivers flow, there to remain forever. There they will have pure spouses, and We shall cause them to enter sheltering shade.

10:9　　　Surely those who believe and do righteous deeds—their Lord guides them for their belief. Beneath them rivers flow in Gardens of Bliss.

18:31　　　Those—for them (there are) Gardens of Eden through which rivers flow. There they will be adorned with bracelets of gold, and they will wear green clothes of silk and brocade, reclining there on couches. Excellent is the reward, and good the resting place!

43:68–70　My servants! (There is) no fear on you today, nor will you sorrow **69**—those (of you) who believed in Our signs and submitted. **70** Enter the Garden, you and your wives, you will be made happy!

44:51–55　Surely the ones who guard (themselves) are in a secure place, **52** in (the midst of) gardens and springs, **53** wearing clothes of silk and brocade, facing each other. **54** So (it is), and We shall marry them to (maidens) with dark, wide eyes. **55** There they will call for every (kind of) fruit, secure.

52:19–20,　**19** 'Eat and drink with satisfaction, (in return) for what you have done.' **20** (There they will be) reclining on couches lined up, and We shall marry them to (maidens) with dark, wide eyes.

56:35–40　Surely We produced them specially, **36** and made them virgins, **37** amorous, (all) of the same age, **38** for the companions on the right. **39** A host from the ones of old, **40** and a host from the later (generations).

78:31–36　Surely for the ones who guard (themselves) (there is) a (place of) safety: **32** orchards and grapes, **33** and full-breasted (maidens), (all) of the same age, **34** and a cup full (of wine) **35**—in which they will not hear any frivolous talk, nor any lying **36**—a payment from your Lord, a gift, a reckoning!

9. The Qur'an also gives much space to hell and the wrath of Allah. The unbelievers will taste the boiling fluids of hell, with their faces covered in flame. They will wear garments of fire, will live in eternal regret at the folly of their rebellion against Allah and will beg for destruction. The Day of Judgment is an absolute certainty, according to the Qur'an, though the righteous have no reason for fear of hell. Justice will be done, and human deeds will be weighed in the balance, when the Last Trumpet sounds. While clear on the reality of heaven, hell and the last judgment, the Qur'an is not specific on a timetable or even the major events related to the end of time. This detail comes later in the hadith and in commentaries.

---

## The Qur'an on Hell

2:81    Yes indeed! Whoever commits evil and is encompassed by his sin—those are the companions of the Fire. There they will remain.

7:179    Certainly We have created for Gehenna many of the jinn and humans: they have hearts, but they do not understand with them; they have eyes, but they do not see with them; they have ears, but they do not hear with them. Those (people) are like cattle—No! They are (even) farther astray! Those—they are the oblivious.

11:106    As for those who are miserable, (they will be) in the Fire, where (there will be) a moaning and panting for them.

20:74    Surely the one who comes to his Lord as a sinner, surely for him (there is) Gehenna, where he will neither die nor live.

21:98–100 Surely you, and what you were serving instead of God, are coals for Gehenna—you will go down to it.' If these had been gods, they would not have gone down to it, but everyone (of them) will remain in it. In it (there is) a moaning for them, and in it they do not hear (anything else).

25:11–12 No! They have called the Hour a lie—and We have prepared a blazing (Fire) for whoever calls the Hour a lie. When it sees them from a place far off, they will hear its raging and moaning.

---

| 38:55–58 | (All) this! But surely for the insolent transgressors (there is) indeed an evil (place of) return: Gehenna, (where) they will burn—it is an evil bed! (All) this! So make them taste it—boiling (water) and rotten (food), and other (torments) of (this) kind in pairs. |
| 40:49–50 | Those who are in the Fire will say to the keepers of Gehenna, 'Call on your Lord to lighten for us one day of the punishment!' They will say, 'Did your messengers not bring you the clear signs?' They will say, 'Yes indeed!' They will say, 'Then call!' But the call of the disbelievers only goes astray. |
| 73:12–13 | Surely We have chains and a Furnace, and food that chokes, and a painful punishment, |
| 104:4–9 | By no means! Indeed He will be tossed into al-Ḥuṭama. And what will make you know what al-Ḥuṭama is? The Fire of God ignited, which rises up to the hearts. Surely it (will be) closed over them in extended columns (of flame). |

10. As an aspect of the Qur'an's teaching about unbelief and wrath, significant attention is given to the failures of Jews and Christians to accept the message of Muhammad and the Qur'an. There is, of course, much debate about the way in which the Islamic sacred text relates historically to specific pagan, Christian and Jewish groups and traditions. Regardless, the Jewish and Christian presence in the Qur'an is impossible to miss.

## The Words Christian/Christians in Qur'an

| 2:62 | Surely those who believe, and those who are Jews, and the Christians, and the Sabians—whoever believes in God and the Last Day, and does righteousness—they have their reward with their Lord. (There will be) no fear on them, nor will they sorrow. |
| 2:111 | They say, 'No one will enter the Garden unless they are Jews or Christians.' That is their wishful thinking. Say: 'Bring your proof, if you are truthful.' |

| | |
|---|---|
| 2:113 | The Jews say, 'The Christians have no ground to stand on'; and the Christians say, 'The Jews have no ground to stand on,' though they (both) recite the Book. In this way those who have no knowledge say something similar to their saying. God will judge between them on the Day of Resurrection concerning their differences. |
| 2:120 | Neither the Jews nor the Christians will ever be pleased with you until you follow their creed. Say: 'Surely the guidance of God—it is the (true) guidance.' If indeed you follow their (vain) desires, after the knowledge which has come to you, you will have no ally and no helper against God. |
| 2:135 | They say, 'Be Jews or Christians, (and then) you will be (rightly) guided.' Say: 'No! The creed of Abraham the Ḥanīf. He was not one of the idolaters.' |
| 2:140 | Or do you say, "Abraham, and Ishmael, and Isaac, and Jacob, and the tribes were Jews or Christians"? |
| 3:67 | Abraham was not a Jew, nor a Christian, but he was a Ḥanīf, a Muslim. |
| 5:14 | And with those who say, 'Surely we are Christians,' We took a covenant, but they have forgotten part of what they were reminded of. So We stirred up enmity and hatred among them, until the Day of Resurrection, and (then) God will inform them about what they have done. |
| 5:18 | The Jews and the Christians say, 'We are the sons of God, and His beloved.' Say: 'Then why does He punish you for your sins? No! You are human beings, (part) of what He created. He forgives whomever He pleases and He punishes whomever He pleases. To God (belongs) the kingdom of the heavens and the earth, and whatever is between them. To Him is the (final) destination.' |
| 5:51 | You who believe! Do not take the Jews and the Christians as allies. They are allies of each other. Whoever of you takes them as allies is already one of them. Surely God does not guide the people who are evildoers. |
| 5:69 | Surely those who believe, and those who are Jews, and the Sabians, and the Christians—whoever believes in GOD and the Last Day, and does righteousness—(there will be) no fear on them, nor will they sorrow. |

| 5:82 | Certainly you will find that the most violent of people in enmity to the believers are the Jews and the idolaters. Certainly you will find that the closest of them in affection to the believers are those who say, 'We are Christians.' That is because (there are) priests and monks among them, and because they are not arrogant. 83 When they hear what has been sent down to the messenger, you see their eyes overflowing with tears because of what they recognize of the truth. |
|---|---|
| 9:30 | The Jews say, 'Ezra is the son of God,' and the Christians say, 'The Messiah is the son of God.' That is their saying with their mouths. They imitate the saying of those who disbelieved before (them). (May) God fight them. How are they (so) deluded? 31 They have taken their teachers and their monks as Lords instead of God, and (also) the Messiah, son of Mary, when they were only commanded to serve one God. (There is) no god but Him. Glory to Him above what they associate! |
| 22:17 | Surely those who believe, and those who are Jews, and the Sabians, and the Christians, and the Magians, and the idolaters– surely God will distinguish between them on the Day of Resurrection. Surely God is a witness over everything. |

## Traditional Islam on the Origin and Transmission of the Qur'an

The traditional Muslim understanding of the origin of the Qur'an is at once both simple and complex. On the one hand, Islamic orthodoxy stipulates that the Qur'an is totally from Allah. He is the sole author. The Qur'an is utterly unique as the perfect, absolute Word of God. There is no mixture of human authorship in the text. Orthodox Muslims believe that the Christian and Jewish Scriptures have been corrupted, whereas the Qur'an is pure and unadulterated. It is a perfect divine revelation sent down from heaven to Muhammad. Whether one believes this perspective or not, the basic Muslim view is easy to understand at first glance.

Complexities arose, however, once Muslim scholars started thinking more deeply about the origins of the sacred Word. For example, is the Qur'an created or eternal? Is the Qur'an part of a larger divine corpus in a heavenly realm? Is the inspiration process of the Qur'an similar to divine inspiration to earlier prophets like Moses, for example?[17] Was the Qur'an revealed all at once or over time? When did Muhammad first receive revelation?

---

## Early Muslim Leaders (623-683)

- Muhammad (623–632).
- First Caliph: Abu Bakr (632–634), father-in-law of prophet.
- Second Caliph: Umar I (634–644).
- Third Caliph: Uthman ibn Affan (644–656), Muhammad's son-in-law and a member of the Umayyad tribe. Uthman was murdered by an Islamic mob.
- Fourth Caliph and first Shi'a Imam: Ali Ben Abu Talib (656–661), Muhammad's son-in-law. Ali was resented by Umayyads and was killed in 661.
- al-Hasan (661–669), second Imam, grandson of prophet and older brother of Husayn.
- Muawiyah I ibn Abu Sufyan (661–680), first leader of Umayyad dynasty.
- al-Husayn (669–680), third Imam and grandson of Muhammad; Husayn was killed at Karbala.
- Yazid I ibn Muawiyah (680–683), second Umayyad caliph.

---

Getting into the details of the traditional Muslim debates on these matters is not important for our purposes. It is sufficient to note that orthodox Muslims hold the following views:

- The Qur'an is eternal and not created. By this Muslims mean that the current Qur'an as a written Arabic text did not ultimately originate in a moment of time, whether in the mind of Muhammad or in written form through scribes.

- The Qur'an is part of a larger heavenly corpus whose contents are known only to Allah.

- The Qur'anic revelation to Muhammad is somewhat similar in process to the revelations given to other prophets like Moses or Jesus.

- The Qur'an, though eternal, was revealed over time to the prophet Muhammad.

- The first revelation (usually said to be surah 96) was given in AD 610 and the final revelation came to the prophet a short while before his death in June of AD 632.[18]

What do traditional Muslims believe about the development of the written text of the Qur'an? While the debates on this are legion and involve complex issues, the orthodox Sunni perspective is again quite clear in its basic answer. There are seven stages in the emergence of the written Qur'an.

Stage One: Gabriel revealed the Qur'an to Muhammad and checked the revelations every year from 610 to 631 and twice in the last year of the prophet's life.[19]

Stage Two: Muhammad recited revelations first to his wife and then to other followers (including later wives, especially Aisha) until his death. The earliest Muslims memorized the recitations of the prophet.

Stage Three: After Muhammad's death Abu Bakr (first Islamic caliph, 632–34) ordered Zayd bin Thabit to make a complete written collection of the revelations. Zayd collected the texts within two years of the prophet's death.

Stage Four: Abu Bakr's collection was given to Umar I (second caliph, 634–44) and then this collection was given to Umar's daughter Hafsa (one of Muhammad's widows).

Stage Six: Uthman (third caliph, 644–56) ordered Zayd to compare various collections and make the final version of the Qur'an.

Stage Seven: Uthman sent his codex to Mecca, Bazra, Kufa and Damascus. Uthman then ordered Muslim leaders to destroy other versions of the Qur'an. The Kufan leader Abdallah bin Masud (d. circa 653) refused. His codex was said to have differences with the Uthmanic one.

Abdallah's version was suppressed to some degree by al-Hajjaj bin Yusuf (d. AD 714), a governor in Iraq, but Masud's reading was not completely crushed until the tenth century, when Ibn Mujahid (859–936) had one of his opponents flogged for following the alternative Masud rendition. Thereafter, the text from Uthman reigned supreme.[20]

Traditional Sunni Muslims believe that the version of the Qur'an done by Uthman was basically copied perfectly from his day to the present so that contemporary Muslims are reading the same Arabic text as the first Muslims, apart from the reality that the earliest texts have no vowels.[21] The Egyptian government noted that there were some variations in the Arabic Qur'ans being used in schools in Egypt at the end of the 19th century and the beginning of the 20th. This led to the publication of what is viewed as the standard edition of the Qur'an in Cairo in 1924. It is said to be based on a recitation/reading of the Qur'an from a scholar named Hafs bin Sulayman (d. AD 796) who was dependent on a scholar named Asim bin Abi l-Najud Bahdala (d. 744–745).[22]

Regardless of acceptance, the Qur'an is one of the most influential books in the history of humanity.[23] Along with the vast majority of Muslims, Reza Aslan believes that the Qur'an is one of the greatest gifts of God to humanity. While he is not orthodox in all respects, Aslan accepts the Qur'an as a divine revelation to Muhammad. He retains a high view of the textual integrity of the Islamic Scripture and basically accepts the teachings of the Qur'an at face value, though he resists conservative Islamic interpretation on various matters. Given the influence of the Qur'an, both within and outside the Muslim world, it is a text to be investigated. To this we turn in the next chapter.

# Chapter 10

# Is the Qur'an
# God's Infallible Word?

*The Qur'an's Textual, Historical and Moral Reliability*

## Qur'an under Critique

In the world of religion there is hardly a higher claim of epistemic certainty than what most Muslims make for their holy book. It is, according to traditional Islam, an infallible book, uncreated, delivered by an angel to the final prophet Muhammad. He, as the perfect model for humanity, lived the ideals of the Qur'an, and his example and teachings are given there and in sacred tradition (hadith). The Qur'an, according to traditional Islam, was copied carefully by early Muslims, and the original version has been preserved ever since. Muslims also claim that Jews and Christians corrupted their Scriptures but Muslims have never altered their sacred text.[1]

## Textual Transmission

What should be made of the basic claim that the Qur'an has been transmitted without change since the original revelations to Muhammad were provided in their final, complete form by Uthman?

Though traditional Muslims are very confident and dogmatic on this high view of the Qur'an, the case for it is very weak.[2]

The following points represent the heart of a more skeptical view.

1. There is no confirmed extant manuscript (i.e., original) of any of the revelations given to Muhammad, dating to his lifetime or the first decades after his death. This is noted in Etan Kohlberg and Mohammad Ali Amir-Moezzi's introduction to their *Revelation and Falsification*: "There is no autograph of Muhammad or his

145

scribes."[3] Frederik Leehmuis notes, "until the present day, no pre-'Uthmānic codices of the Qur'ān have been discovered and definitively identified."[4]

2. Likewise, there are no original copies of the alleged Uthmanic rendition and no consensus on the dating of the early extant codices. Of course, many Western scholars have accepted the basic idea of an Uthmanic text without acceptance of its divine origin or transmission and without dogmatism about the details of how it links with Muhammad.

3. The earliest fragments of the Qur'an are probably from the late 600s or early 700s, but the limited study of them has not settled anything about the dating and textual reliability of the original Qur'an other than to increase skepticism about the traditional Muslim view.

4. The earliest Muslim reports about the transmission of the Qur'an are not as dogmatic as later Muslim orthodoxy. Keith Small, one of the leading scholars of textual criticism of the Qur'an, states, "the early view of the Qur'an from hadith and in tafsir and available literature shows that the Qur'an was viewed as incomplete, with textual problems, and a more flexible attitude toward its degree of fixity. It was in later centuries that the attitude hardened and that the equation was made that Uthman's text=Muhammad's text, together with the justifications needed to support this equation."[5]

5. Dogmatism about the Uthmanic text holds only for the Sunni Muslim majority. Various Shia Muslim leaders believed that changes were made in the original Qur'an in order to lessen the influence of Ali, the son-in-law of the prophet.

6. In general, all scholars, Muslim and otherwise, agree that there are variants in the Qur'an. Those who inclined to a greater skepticism about the rise of such variants believe, with Fred Donner, that "we cannot conceptualize the Qur'an as a text that crystallized into a single, immutable codified form at an early date (e. g. within one generation of Muhammad)."[6]

7. As noted in the last chapter, the increasing stress on a uniform text of the Qur'an led to the destruction and suppression of alternate versions of the Qur'an. Keith Small puts it this way: "the primary task in Qur'anic textual criticism, as practiced historically in Islam has been instead to justify one form of the text against many others. And the efforts to establish and justify one text from among a group of collections of material, both oral and written, has resulted in the irreparable loss of the earliest authoritative forms of the text."[7]

For the most part, skepticism among Western scholars ranges from general acceptance of a basic Uthmanic Qur'an (Motzki)[8] without claiming infallibility for the text or its transmission, to the view that the Qur'an is largely a product of the late 7th century and had little to do with Uthman, to a perspective that it is the creation of a non-Muslim milieu well into the 8th century. This latter view, most famously argued by John Wansbrough, has become impossible to maintain in light of the discovery of early Qur'an manuscripts.[9]

All in all, given the seven points listed, Western critics contend that there is no strong historical justification for the traditional Islamic view. Given the absence of an original Qur'an, the variations in early Qur'an manuscripts, suppression of alternate versions, enormous difficulties created by recitation of the Qur'an and convoluted textual history that led to the current Cairo edition, the burden is on traditional Muslims to prove their view.[10] Of course, some Muslim scholars attempt to disprove the typical Western critiques and argue for the traditional Islamic perspective, but they are facing an immense uphill battle.[11]

## The Satanic Verses

In spite of scholarly consensus that the text of the current Qur'an cannot be traced back to Uthman, Western scholars recognize that the text of the Qur'an has been quite stable since the beginning of the 8th century AD and that variants have not been that significant. There are exceptions. One of the most notable involves the so-called episode of the "satanic verses." According to early Muslim reports, Satan fooled Muhammad into thinking that true followers of Allah could worship three Arab deities (mentioned in surah 53:19–20), and this sanction was at one time in the Qur'an. As soon as Gabriel told Muhammad of the deception by Satan (or, in another version, as soon as he realized his error), the offending teaching was removed from the Qur'an. It is from this incident that Salman Rushdie titled his controversial novel.

The satanic verses episode is mentioned in almost every commentary on the Qur'an in the first two centuries of Islam. It is also mentioned in the sira and maghazi material from the same time period. Here is the wording from Ibn Ishaq, the most famous biographer, on the angelic correction:

Then Gabriel came to the apostle and said, "What have you done, Muhammad? You have read to these people something I did not bring you from Allah and you have said what He did not say to you." The apostle was bitterly grieved and was greatly in fear of God. So Allah sent down (a revelation), for He was merciful to him, comforting him and making light of the affair and telling him that every prophet and apostle before him desired as he desired and wanted what he wanted and Satan interjected something into his desires as he had on his tongue. So Allah annulled what Satan had suggested and Allah established His verses, i.e. you are just like the prophets and apostle.[12]

The satanic verses incident was accepted as historical by various classical Muslim writers, including al-Tabari (d. 923) and al-Wawardi (d. 1058). There were also strong objections to the reliability of the story in the classical period, notably from al-Yahsubi (d. 1149) and Imad al-Din b. Kathir (d. 1373). Shia scholars have rejected the incident, believing, alongside various Sunni authors, that the incident threatens the doctrine of *isma*, that God will protect prophets from sin and error. Contemporary Muslim scholars deny the incident or that it was ever in the Qur'an, while many Western scholars accept that the Qur'an originally recorded the story.[13]

## Very Human and Fallible Sources: Four Examples

Beyond issues of textual integrity, the Qur'an must be called into question on grounds that various teachings or verses actually come from non-Qur'anic sources and not from direct eternal inspiration. The shaping of the Qur'an here is probably oral, as Muhammad and the earliest Muslim community heard stories from Christians and Jews in 7th century Arabia.[14]

### Sleepers in the Cave

One of the constant critiques of the Qur'an involves the fact that its contents are often baffling, strange, unclear, and lacking in inner logic. This can be illustrated from four narratives, three from surah 18 and one from surah 27. The first involves a narrative about young men in a cave. The text from surah 18 reads,

9 Or did you think that the companions of the cave and al-Raqīm were an amazing thing among Our signs? 10 (Remember) when the young men took refuge in the cave, and said, "Our Lord, grant us mercy from Yourself, and furnish the right (course) for us in our situation." 11 So We sealed up their ears in the cave for a number of

years, 12 and then We raised them up (again), so that We might know which of the two factions would better count (the length of) time (they had) remained (there).

13 We shall recount to you their story in truth: Surely they were young men who believed in their Lord, and We increased them in guidance. 14 We strengthened their hearts, when they stood up and said, "Our Lord is the Lord of the heavens and the earth. We do not call on any god other than Him. Certainly we would then have spoken an outrageous thing. 15 These people of ours have taken gods other than Him. If only they would bring some clear authority concerning them! Who is more evil than the one who forges a lie against GOD? 16 When you have withdrawn from them and what they serve instead of GOD, take refuge in the cave. Your Lord will display some of His mercy to you, and will furnish some relief for you in your situation."

17 And you (would) see the sun when it rose, inclining from their cave toward the right, and when it set, passing them by on the left, while they were in the open part of it. That was one of the signs of GOD. Whoever GOD guides is the (rightly) guided one, and whoever He leads astray—you will not find for him an ally guiding (him). 18 And you (would) think them awake, even though they were asleep, and We were turning them (now) to the right and (now) to the left, while their dog (lay) stretched out (with) its front paws at the door (of the cave). If you (had) observed them, you would indeed have turned away from them in flight, and indeed been filled (with) dread because of them.

19 So We raised them up (again) that they might ask questions among themselves. A speaker among them said, "How long have you remained (here)?" Some said, "We have (only) remained (here) a day, or part of a day." Others said, "Your Lord knows how long you have remained (here). So send one of you with this paper (money) of yours to the city, and let him see which (part) of it (has the) purest food, and let him bring you a supply of it. But let him be astute, and let no one realize (who) you (are). 20 Surely they—if they become aware of you—they will stone you, or make you return to their creed, and then you will never prosper." 21 So We caused (the people of the city) to stumble upon them, in order that they might know that the promise of GOD is true, and that the Hour—(there is) no doubt about it.

When they argued among themselves about their situation, they said, "Build over them a building. Their Lord knows about them." Those who prevailed over their situation said, "We shall indeed take (to building) a place of worship over them."

22 Some say, "(There were) three, the fourth of them was their dog." But others say, "(There were) five, the sixth of them was their dog"—guessing about what is unknown. Still others say, "(There

149

were) seven, the eighth of them was their dog." Say: "My Lord knows about their number. No one knows (about) them except a few." So do not dispute about them, except (on) an obvious point, and do not ask for a pronouncement about them from any of them. 23 And do not say of anything, "Surely I am going to do that tomorrow," 24 except (with the proviso): "If GOD pleases." And remember your Lord, when you forget, and say, "It may be that my Lord will guide me to something nearer the right (way) than this."

25 They remained in their cave for three hundred years and (some) add nine (more). 26 Say: "GOD knows about how long they remained (there). To Him (belongs) the unseen of the heavens and the earth. How well He sees and hears! They have no ally other than Him, and He does not associate anyone in His judgment."

Apart from the obvious infelicities of style, one can ask whether Aslan believes this account in the Qur'an to be historical. Do Muslims, including Aslan, realize that this sleeper story circulated among Syriac Christians long before it was adapted for use in the Qur'an? Are these sleepers Muslims? The implications of the Qur'an's borrowing here are very significant proof of the human origins of the Muslim sacred text.

## Moses and the Green Man

The second story from surah 18 involves a report about Moses and a young man that the Qur'an identifies as al-Khadr or al-Khidr (often referred to as the green man in Muslim exegesis), who go on a trip. Here is the passage from the Qur'an:

(Remember) when Moses said to his young man, "I shall not give up until I reach the junction of the two seas, or (else) I shall go on for a long time." 61 When they reached the junction of them, they forgot their fish, (for) it had taken its way into the sea, swimming off. 62 So when they had passed beyond (that place), he said to his young man, "Bring us our morning meal. We have indeed become weary from this journey of ours." 63 He said, "Did you see when we took refuge at the rock? Surely I forgot the fish—none other than Satan made me forget to remember it—and it took its way into the sea—an amazing thing!" 64 He said, "That is what we were seeking!" So they returned, retracing their footsteps. 65 And they found a servant, one of Our servants to whom We had given mercy from Us, and whom We had taught knowledge from Us. 66 Moses said to him, "Shall I follow you on (the condition) that you teach me some of what you have been taught (of) right (knowledge)?" 67 He said, "Surely you will not be able (to have) patience with me. 68 How could you have patience for what you cannot encompass in (your) awareness of it?" 69 He said, "You will find me, if GOD pleases, patient, and I shall not disobey you in any command." 70 He said, "If you follow (me), do not ask me about anything, until I mention it to you."

71 So they both set out (and continued on) until, when they sailed in the ship, he made a hole in it. He said, "Have you made a hole in it in order to drown its passengers? You have indeed done a dreadful thing!" 72 He said, "Did I not say, "Surely you will not be able (to have) patience with me?"" 73 He said, "Do not take me to task for what I forgot, and do not burden me (with) hardship in my affair." 74 So they both set out (and continued on) until, when they met a young boy, he killed him. He said, "Have you killed an innocent person, other than (in retaliation) for a person? Certainly you have done a terrible thing!" 75 He said, "Did I not say to you, "Surely you will not be able (to have) patience with me?"" 76 He said, "If I ask you about anything after this, do not keep me as a companion. You have had enough excuses from me." 77 So they both set out (and continued on) until, when they came to the people of a town, they asked its people for food, but they refused to offer them hospitality. They both found in it a wall on the verge of collapse, and he set it up. He said, "If you had wished, you could indeed have taken a reward for that." 78 He said, "This is the parting between me and you. (Now) I shall inform you about the interpretation of what you were not able (to have) patience with. 79 As for the ship, it belonged to poor people working on the sea, and I wanted to damage it, (because) behind them (there) was a king seizing every ship by force. 80 As for the young boy, his parents were believers, and we feared that he would burden them both (with) insolent transgression and disbelief. 81 We wanted their Lord to give to them both in exchange (one) better than him in purity, and closer (to them) in affection. 82 As for the wall, it belonged to two orphan boys in the city, and underneath it was a treasure belonging to them both, (for) their father had been a righteous man. Your Lord wanted them both to reach their maturity, and bring forth their treasure as a mercy from your Lord. I did not do it on my (own) command. That is the interpretation (of) what you were not able (to have) patience with."

There is no basis for this story in the biblical material on Moses. If it should be taken as historical, then its criminality is evident with the one act of murder. It reads like folklore and is at best a garbled legend of unknown origin. The varied and contradictory explanations among Muslim scholars for all aspects of the Moses/al-Khidr narrative are abundant proof why some sections of the Qur'an have a very questionable origin.[15]

## Alexander the Great in the Qur'an

After the story of Moses and the young man, surah 18 continues with a famous narrative of a figure named Dhu-l-Qarnayn, usually understood in Muslim exegesis to be Alexander the Great. Here is the text from Qur'an 18:83–102:

83 They ask you about Dhk-l-Qarnayn. Say: I shall recite to you a remembrance of him. 84 Surely We established him on the earth and gave him a way of access to everything. 85 He followed (one such) way of access 86 until, when he reached the setting of the sun, he found it setting in a muddy spring, and he found next to it a people. We said, "Dhū-l-Qarnayn! Either punish (them) or do them (some) good." 87 He said, "As for the one who does evil, we shall punish him. Then he will be returned to his Lord, and He will punish him (with) a terrible punishment. 88 But as for the one who believes, and does righteousness, for him (there is) the good payment, and we shall speak to him something easy from our command." 89 Then he followed (another) way of access 90 until, when he reached the rising (place) of the sun, he found it rising on a people for whom We had not provided any shelter from it. 91 So (it was), but We had already encompassed what his situation was in (our) awareness. 92 Then he followed (another) way of access 93 until, when he arrived (at the place) between the two barriers, he found on this side of them a people hardly able to understand (his) speech. 94 They said, "Dhū-l-Qarnayn! Surely Yajūj and Majūj are fomenting corruption on the earth. Shall we pay tribute to you on (the condition) that you construct a barrier between us and them?" 95 He said, "What my Lord has established me with is better. Help me with a force, (and) I shall construct a rampart between you and them. 96 Bring me blocks of iron!"—Until, when he had made level (the gap) between the two cliffs, he said, "Blow!"—Until, when he had made it a fire, he said, "Bring me (blocks of brass)! I will pour molten brass over it. " 97 So they were not able to surmount it, nor were they able (to make) a hole in it. 98 He said, "This is a mercy from my Lord. But when the promise of my Lord comes, He will shatter it. The promise of my Lord is true." 99 We shall leave some of them on that Day crashing into each other, and there will be a blast on the trumpet, and We shall gather them all together. 100 We shall present Gehennaon that Day to the disbelievers, 101 whose eyes were covered from My remembrance and (who) were not capable (of) hearing. 102 Do those who disbelieve think that they can take My servants as allies instead of Me? Surely We have prepared Gehenna as a reception for the disbelievers.

Three things are important to note. First, as with the story of the men in the cave and the travels of Moses and al-Khidr, the narrative about Dhu-l-Qarnayn is confusing and the wording very unclear. Is this really the infallible Word of God? Second, the text also forces questions about historicity. Did Alexander the Great go to "the rising place of the sun"? Did he construct a barrier to resist Yajuj and Majuj (possibly Muslim terms for Gog and Magog)? Third, is this report about Dhu-l-Qarnayn in the Qur'an basically an adaptation from a Syriac legend about Alexander the Great that was in circulation about the time of Muhammad?

In 1889, E. A. Wallis Budge drew attention to what is now called "the Alexander Legend," a Syriac text about Alexander the Great that was distinct from the famous Alexander Romance. In 1890, the great German scholar Theodor Noldeke argued in a brief discussion that the Alexander legend was the source for surah 18's narrative about Dhu-l-Qarnayn. This has now been documented conclusively by Kevin Van Bladel in a magisterial analysis.[16] Van Bladel shows that the Qur'an's five-part narration about Alexander parallels the structure in the Syriac legend. While the Syriac legend is longer and the Qur'an has a different eschatological framework, the similarity in word usage and the duplication in order is striking. One can see the resemblances simply by reading Budge's translation and surah 18 for themselves. Van Bladel writes, "Many of the correspondences between the Syriac and the Arabic stories are so obvious that they do not need special attention. Simply relating both stories together establishes their extraordinary similarity." He also states,

> the correspondences shown earlier are still so exact that it is obvious in comparison that the two texts are at least connected very closely. They relate the same story in precisely the same order of events using many of the same particular details. Every part of the Qur'anic passage has its counterpart in the Syriac, except that in the Qur'an the story is told through the first-person account of God.[17]

Van Bladel dates the Alexander legend between AD 628 and AD 630 and presents a clear argument why it is the source for the Qur'an and not the reverse. He also shows why the legend was significant for the Muslim community of the 7th century, though it cannot be known exactly when the Alexander legend material made it into the Qur'an. What Van Bladel's research shows beyond doubt is that surah 18:83–102 is not a direct revelation from Allah unless one imagines that Allah enjoys following and adapting Syriac Christian legends for Muhammad and his followers.

## Solomon and the Queen of Sheba

The Qur'anic account of Solomon and the queen of Sheba duplicates the al-Khidr narrative in lack of clarity (just like the stories of the sleepers in the cave and Alexander the Great). Further, the narrative is the Qur'an is probably an adaptation from a prior source. Here is the account from surah 27:15–44:

> 15 Certainly We gave David and Solomon knowledge, and they said, "Praise (be) to GOD, who has favored us over many of His believing servants!" 16 Solomon inherited (it) from David, and said, "People! We have been taught the speech of birds, and we have been given (some) of everything. Surely this—it indeed is clear favor." 17 Gathered before Solomon were his forces—jinn, and men, and birds—and they were arranged (in rows) 18—until, when they came upon the Wādi of the Ants, an ant said, "Ants! Enter your dwellings, or Solomon and his forces will crush you without realizing (it)." 19 But he smiled, laughing at its words, and said, "My Lord, (so) dispose me that I may be thankful for your blessing with which You have blessed me and my parents, and that I may do righteousness (that) pleases You, and cause me to enter, by Your mercy, among your righteous servants."
>
> 20 He reviewed the birds, and said, "Why do I not see the hud-hud? Or is it one of the absent? 21 I shall indeed punish it severely, or slaughter it, or it will bring me a clear authority." 22 But it did not stay (away) for long, and said, "I have encompassed what you have not encompassed, and I have brought you reliable news from (the people of) Sheba. 23 Surely I found a woman ruling over them, and she has been given (some) of everything, and she has a great throne. 24 I found her and her people prostrating themselves before the sun instead of GOD. Satan has made their deeds appear enticing to them, and he has kept them from the way, and they are not (rightly) guided. 25 (He did this) so that they would not prostrate themselves before GOD, who brings forth what is hidden in the heavens and the earth. He knows what you hide and what you speak aloud. 26 GOD—(there is) no god but Him, Lord of the great throne." 27 He said, "We shall see whether you have spoken the truth or are one of the liars. 28 Go with this letter of mine, and cast it (down) to them. Then turn away from them and see what they return."
>
> 29 She said, "Assembly! Surely an honorable letter has been cast (down) to me. 30 Surely it is from Solomon, and surely it (reads): "In the Name of GOD, the Merciful, the Compassionate. 31 Do not

exalt yourselves over me, but come to me in surrender. " 32 She said, "Assembly! Make a pronouncement to me about my affair. I do not decide any affair until you bear me witness." 33 They said, "We are full of strength and full of harsh violence, but the affair (belongs) to you. See what you will command." 34 She said, "Surely kings, when they enter a town, corrupt it, and make the upper class of its people the lowest, and that is what they will do. 35 Surely I am going to send a gift to them, and see what the envoys bring back."

36 When he came to Solomon, he said, "Would you increase me with wealth, when what GOD has given me is better than what He has given you? No! (It is) you (who) gloat over your own gift. 37 Return to them! We shall indeed come upon them with forces which they have no power to face, and we shall indeed expel them from there in humiliation, and they will be disgraced." 38 He said, "Assembly! Which of you will bring me her throne before they come to me in surrender?" 39 A crafty one of the jinn said, "I shall bring it to you before you (can) rise from your place. Surely I have strength for it (and am) trustworthy." 40 One who had knowledge of the Book said, "I will bring it to you in the wink of an eye." So when he saw it set before him, he said, "This is from the favor of my Lord to test me (to see) whether I am thankful or ungrateful. Whoever is thankful is thankful only for his own good, and whoever is ungrateful—surely my Lord is wealthy, generous." 41 He said, "Disguise her throne for her. We shall see whether she is (rightly) guided or is one of those who are not (rightly) guided." 42 So when she came, it was said, "Is your throne like this?" She said, "It seems like it." "And we had been given the knowledge before her, and were in surrender, 43 but what she served, instead of GOD, kept her back. Surely she was from a disbelieving people." 44 It was said to her, "Enter the palace." When she saw it, she thought it was a pool (of water), and she uncovered her legs. He said, "Surely it is a polished palace of crystal." She said, "My Lord, surely I have done myself evil. I surrender with Solomon to GOD, Lord of the worlds."

While most readers will see readily that the narrative of the Qur'an is confusing and strange, it is the historical questions that are most important. Does Reza Aslan believe that Solomon understood the speech of birds? Can ants talk? Did a hoopoe bird bring Solomon news about the queen of Sheba? Did Solomon really send a letter to her that read "In the Name of God, the Merciful, the Compassionate"? Did Solomon trick her and lead her to Islam?

In addition to the intrinsic difficulties in the Qur'an story, doubt is also warranted by the fact that the Solomon/Sheba material is probably borrowed from a Jewish work known as the *Targum Sheni to the Book of Esther*, at least if one accepts an early date for the Targum, as advanced by Bernard Grossfeld in his recent *Critical Edition*. Regardless of dating, in the Qur'anic account we certainly hear echoes of some of the Jewish legends that grew up around Solomon. These legends include his mastery over demons and evil spirits (jinn), as we find in the apocryphal work the *Testament of Solomon*, which began to circulate sometime in the late first century AD.[18]

## Other Borrowings

In addition, various teachings about Jesus in the Qur'an are actually borrowed from extra-biblical sources. This will be examined in detail in the next chapter. There are other examples of the Qur'an's dependence on other sources. For example, consider the famous statement in surah 5:32: "whoever kills a person...(it is) as if he had killed all the people. And whoever gives (a person) life, (it is) as if he had given all the people life." This is remarkably similar to a saying in the Jewish Mishnah that predates the Qur'an by several centuries: "Whoever saves a single life, the Torah considers it as is if that person had saved an entire world. But whoever destroys a single life, the Torah considers it is as if that person had destroyed an entire world."[19] Likewise, the report in surah 21:68 about God saving Abraham from death by his enemies after he destroyed the idols is not found in Genesis but is available in later Jewish tradition.[20] In the Qur'anic account of Abraham's sacrifice of his son, the son (unnamed in the Qur'an) knows of the intended death and encourages his father. This has no parallel in the Genesis material but is part of the rabbinical tradition prior to the time of Muhammad.[21]

It must be constantly remembered that the objections raised here concerning the Qur'an's borrowing of material from prior sources arises only because of the traditional Muslim claim that the Qur'an is an eternal book dictated from the angel to the prophet. If the Qur'an is an eternal book from God, why does the text show the Qur'an's reliance on earthly, human sources? The fact that the Qur'an borrows Jewish and Christian material serves as powerful evidence that it is a human product and not an eternal Scripture given straight from heaven.

Our objections would not apply to a moderate Muslim view that claims that Muhammad or someone else is the inspired human author of the Qur'an, who quoted and used material from his day. This moderate perspective would parallel the way that biblical authors use other sources.

## More Troubles in the Qur'an

Beyond the issues of textual transmission, the Satanic Verses, and dependence on other sources, there are several further troubling elements in the Qur'an that are inconsistent with its alleged divine origin. Three items deserve attention for the remainder of this chapter.

### Jews as Apes and Pigs

In relation to questionable morality, the Qur'an contains startling passages that imply that Allah has occasionally turned Jews into apes and pigs. Surah 5:60 says to the People of the Book, "Shall I inform you of (something) worse than that? Retribution with GOD! Whomever GOD has cursed, and whomever He is angry with—some of whom He made apes, and pigs."[22] The same nasty judgment is mentioned in surah 2:65 and 7:163–167.[23] The surah 7 passage is about Jewish disobedience in relation to the Sabbath. While some Muslim commentators treat the passages as metaphorical, the idea of God turning Jews into apes and pigs has been part of anti-Jewish rhetoric in both Sunni and Shia circles. In January of 2013 Mohammed Morsi, former president of Egypt, created controversy over his alleged reference to Jews as "descendants of apes and pigs."[24] As another example, the Al-Azhar Sheik Muhammad Sayyid Tantawi used this language of Jews in a sermon in April 2002. Muslim tradition claims that the prophet Muhammad called Jewish tribal members "brothers of monkeys" just before he had the Jews put to death.[25]

### Confusions, Disorder and Contradictions

Given the incredible claims made by Muslims about the Qur'an, the uninformed reader would have every right to imagine that the Muslim sacred text is without peer in terms of clarity and order. Surely God would communicate in straightforward and illuminating fashion, especially since the topics are of temporal and eternal importance.[26] There are, of course, crystal clear teachings and beautiful passages in the Qur'an. However, sadly, the dominant impression a first reader has is that the text is often jumbled, unclear, disorderly, and contradictory.

Theodor Noldeke, a famous early scholar, has this balanced assessment: "On the whole, while many parts of the Qur'an undoubtedly have considerable rhetorical power, even over an unbelieving reader, the book, aesthetically considered, is by no means a first-rate performance."[27] This has been the verdict of other readers of the Qur'an. For example, Edward Gibbon said that the Qur'an is an "endless incoherent rhapsody of fable and precept." Thomas Carlyle opined that it was "as toilsome reading as I ever undertook; a wearisome, confused jumble, crude, incondite."[28]

Traditional Muslims explain negative verdicts about the Qur'an as a result of spiritual blindness. The same line of argument is given in the Qur'an itself. Regardless of this ad hominem answer, the evidence for Qur'anic obscurity and contradictions are in the text itself where words are unknown, verses are expressly unclear, discrepancies exist and passages are strung together with no apparent order. For example, no one knows what Alif, Lam and Mim stand for at the start of many surahs.[29] Likewise, the middle phrase in surah 2:29 is very confusing: "It is He who created for you all that is in the earth, then He lifted Himself to heaven and levelled them seven heavens; and He has knowledge of everything." For problems and contradictions in the Qur'an, we can note a false teaching, that Jews taught that "Ezra is the Son of God" (9:30) or that Mary is the sister of Aaron (19:27–28) or that there are seven earths (65:2) or whether Noah's son drowned (11:42–43).[30]

The next two chapters will examine the ways in which the Jesus of the Qur'an stands in contradiction to the Jesus presented in New Testament material. That discrepancy is a subset of a larger problem with the Qur'an itself in that the Muslim text shows little respect or regard for the Jewish and Christian Scriptures. While the Qur'an sometimes agrees with biblical data, all too often its specific teachings and overall spirit are contradictory to what is presented in the Old and New Testament.[31] Narratives in the Qur'an often depart from the strata of the biblical world. Teachings about Adam, Noah, Moses and Abraham do not match Old Testament material. Even more important, the grace motif in the New Testament is largely absent from the Qur'an.

While Muslims explain these contradictions as proof that Jews and Christians corrupted their Scriptures, it is obvious that the writers behind the Qur'an did not know biblical material very well. As we will see in the next chapter, this comes out with absolute clarity in the fact that the Qur'an has a truncated and distorted treatment of Jesus.

The Muslim argument that the Qur'an trumps the Old and New Testaments amounts to a case of special pleading. The Qur'an is given priority because of Islamic dogmatism about its inerrancy and the alleged corruption of Jewish and Christian Scripture. We have already seen how strong the case is for the textual stability of the New Testament. The same applies to the Old Testament text.

## Summary

The evidence in this chapter shows that the Qur'an is of human origin, borrows material from earlier sources and contains insurmountable moral problems and clear errors. Beyond this, common sense demands that texts of the Jewish Scripture and texts of Christian Scripture be granted epistemic preference over the Qur'an when it comes to persons, events and teachings from Old and New Testament times. Why would anyone give preference to an Arabic text five centuries removed from the time of Jesus or Paul, not to mention the many more centuries that the Qur'an is removed from King David, Moses, Abraham, and Noah?

Chapter 11

# Does the Qur'an Get Jesus Right?

*The Birth and Childhood of Jesus in the Qur'an and Islamic Tradition*

It will come as a surprise to many to learn that Jesus is referenced several times in the Qur'an and in later Islamic tradition. All of these references are positive and respectful. Muhammad (c. 570—c. 632) clearly admired Jesus, but he had a lot of problems with Christians and simply did not agree with the way Christians told the story of Jesus and understood his teachings.

According to Muslim tradition, Muhammad was familiar with Christianity, particularly in its Syrian form. He conversed with his wife's cousin, who was a Christian, and was aware of Jewish beliefs and criticisms of Christianity. He accepted Jewish monotheism but resented Jewish criticism of Jesus. He admired Jesus and accepted much of his teaching, but he rejected the idea that Jesus was divine. In 610, at the age of 40, Muhammad began his mission—to convert his polytheistic Arab people, chastise Jews and correct Christians.[1] The Qur'an echoes Muhammad, and in its 114 surahs (or chapters) we have the earliest Muslim teachings about Jesus.

## Jesus in the Qur'an[2]

Jesus, called *'Īsā* in the Qur'an,[3] is often referred to as the "son of Mary" (see Mark 6:3: "Is not this the carpenter, the son of Mary...?"), sometimes with the full title "Christ Jesus, the son of Mary" (surah 3:45).[4] The Qur'an states that Jesus was strengthened with the Holy Spirit (surah 2:87, 253) and that he received revelation from Allah (the Arabic term for God).[5] We are told that Jesus is "held in honor in this world and in the hereafter" and is "of those nearest to Allah" (surah 3:45). He is also of the company

161

"of the righteous" (surah 3:46). All in all, these are very positive statements. But before we explore further what the Qur'an says about Jesus, let's back up a bit and trace what in effect is Muhammad's understanding of the origins of Mary and her famous son.

The story begins in surah 3, a section of the Qur'an devoted to the family of Imran, from whom Mary the mother of Jesus descended.[6] What we find in this surah are echoes of the infancy account of Luke, as well as some second- and third-century legends about the birth of Mary. In the Qur'an, the story begins with the prayer of a woman of the family of Imran:[7] "My Lord! Surely I vow to you what is in my womb, to be devoted (to your service). Accept therefore from me, surely you are the Hearing, the Knowing" (surah 3:35). Her petition granted, the woman gives birth to a girl, whom she names Mary (surah 3:36) and then gives to an old man named Zachariah, who will look after the child in the temple (surah 3:37). Zachariah then prays to Allah for offspring (surah 3:38). As he prays in the temple angels call out to him, proclaiming "the good news of (the birth) of Yahya," or John, who is described as "honorable and chaste and a prophet" (surah 3:39). Zachariah wonders how this can be, since he is old and his wife is barren (surah 3:40). Allah promises the man a sign: he will not be able to speak for three days except by making signs (surah 3:41). More will be said about this part of the story shortly.

Several elements of the infancy story in the Gospel of Luke are echoed in the Qur'an's account. However, the account begins with allusions to the story of the miraculous birth of Mary, a story that is not found in the New Testament Gospels but is found in one form or another in a late second-century work variously called in its surviving oldest copies *The Birth of Mary* and *the Revelation of James*, parts of which appear in a much later work (fifth century?) called *Arabic Gospel of the Infancy*.[8] This legendary account circulated under a variety of titles. Most today call it *Protevangelium of James*, or "First Gospel of James," meaning the Gospel story that preceded the well-known Gospel narratives found in Matthew, Mark, Luke and John. *Protevangelium of James* not only defends the virginal conception and birth of Jesus but also advances the idea of Mary's perpetual virginity.[9]

According to *Protevangelium of James*, the elderly and righteous but childless couple Joachim and Anna pray for a child. Wandering into the wilderness to meditate and pray, Joachim recalls the aged patriarch Abraham, how near the end of his life God gave him Isaac. While Anna looks heavenward and laments, an angel appears to her and says, "Anna, Anna, the Lord has heard your prayer. You will conceive a child and give birth." Anna replies that she will offer her child—boy or girl—to God, to minister to him his or her entire life. In time Anna conceives and gives birth to a baby girl, whom she names Mary. When Mary reaches the age of three years Anna and Joachim take her to the temple in fulfillment of their vow. Mary then grows up in the temple and at the age of twelve is betrothed to the elderly Joseph, a widower and father of children. Joseph takes Mary to his home but has no sexual relations with her. In time Mary becomes acquainted with her relative Elizabeth and her husband, Zachariah. Here the account in *Protevangelium of James* begins to overlap with Luke's infancy narrative (Luke 1–2).[10]

There is little doubt that the legendary traditions of *Protevangelium of James*, along with other related traditions, became part of the pool of material with which Muhammad and some of his followers were familiar.[11] These traditions, which were made up of material from the New Testament Gospels—especially Luke's story of the infancy—and much later apocryphal writings, circulated in the Middle East for centuries and were very popular. In this blend of early and late versions of the infancy a few things became mixed up (such as having Mary given to Zachariah rather than to Joseph; cf. surah 3:37). Even so, the parallels are pretty close.

Of course, no serious historian accepts as factual the legendary additions found in *Protevangelium of James*, *Arabic Gospel of the Infancy* or *Infancy Gospel of Thomas*. Under what circumstances Mary was born is simply not known. If the genealogy found in Luke 3:23–38 is Mary's rather than Joseph's (as it is in Matt 1:1–16), then we may know the name of her father, but that is uncertain, and in any event it is not Joachim.

In the Qur'an there are also obvious parallels with Luke's infancy narrative. To return to where we left off previously, the Qur'an mentions the elderly Zachariah, who is apparently a priest, for he serves in the temple (surah 3:37–38). Angels assure him that he will have a son, a prophet named John (surah 3:39), even though his wife is elderly and barren (surah 3:40). The sign that this will be fulfilled will be Zachariah's inability to speak, making it necessary for him to communicate using signs (surah 3:41).

What we find in the Qur'an is a version of the story of the aged priest Zachariah (or Zechariah) and his wife, Elizabeth (Luke 1:8–23). While serving in the temple an angel appears to Zachariah and assures him that Elizabeth will give birth to a son and they will name him John. Zachariah finds this news hard to believe, given his and his wife's old age. The angel rebukes Zachariah for his lack of faith, telling him that he will be unable to speak until the child is born. When the priest comes out of the temple, he cannot speak but has to communicate by making signs. When his son finally arrives, Zachariah is able to speak, declaring that the boy's name is John (Luke 1:63).

The Qur'an has more to say about the birth and ministry of Jesus. Echoing the angelic annunciation found in Luke 1:26–38, the Qur'an tells us,

> "O Mary! Allah gives you good news with a word from him: His name will be Messiah Jesus, son of Mary…He shall speak to the people when in the cradle and when of old age…" And she said, "My Lord, when shall there be a son (born) to me, since man has not touched me?" He said, "Even so, Allah creates what he pleases…" (surah 3:45–47; cf. 19:20–22; 21:91)

In this convoluted passage we hear unmistakable allusions to Luke's account. These include allusions to the angel Gabriel's announcement to Mary ("Hail, O favored one"), to the effect that she will conceive and give birth to a son, whose name will be Jesus (Luke 1:28, 31), to Mary's puzzlement because she is a virgin (1:34) and to the angel's explanation (1:35). Of course, the version in the Qur'an says nothing about Jesus being recognized as the "Son of the Most High" and "Son of God," as in the angel's announcement in Luke 1:32 and 1:35, for Muhammad rejected the divinity of Jesus and the doctrine of the Trinity (see surah 4:171: "Say not 'Trinity'!"; cf. 5:17, 72, 75, 116; 9:30–31; 19:19, 88, 91–92).[12] Nevertheless, Muhammad appears to have accepted most of the Christian tradition regarding the annunciation, the immaculate conception, the virgin birth and presentation of the youthful Jesus in the temple.[13]

The Qur'an's comment that Jesus "shall speak to the people when in the cradle" (surah 3:46) is odd. It probably alludes to the apocryphal story in the already mentioned *Arabic Gospel of the Infancy*. In this very late work the infant Jesus quite literally speaks from the cradle.[14] The *Arabic Gospel of the Infancy* has drawn from the Gospel of Luke and some later apocryphal traditions. The idea that as a child Jesus was a prodigy may owe its inspiration to the much older story of the 12-year old Jesus, who discusses theology with the religious leaders in the temple precincts (Luke 2:46–52). This theme is elaborated in later apocryphal sources, where we hear stories of Jesus who as a young child astounds the teachers of Israel. One of the better known examples is *Infancy Gospel of Thomas*, where we are told that Jesus stupefies one Zacchaeus, a schoolteacher, with his great knowledge (*Infan. Thom.* 6–8). Humiliated, Zacchaeus confesses that he has been bested by a child and says to Joseph, "What kind of great thing he could be—whether a divine being or an angel—I do not know even what to say" (*Infan. Thom.* 7:4).[15] We suspect that traditions such as what we find in *Arabic Gospel of the Infancy* and *Infancy Gospel of Thomas* lie behind surah 3:46.

The passage in the Qur'an goes on to say that "Allah will teach him the Book and Wisdom, the Law and the Gospel" (surah 3:48). These items probably refer to the Jewish and Christian Scriptures. Of course, the "Gospel" (Arabic: *injeel*), which is derived from the older Greek word *euangelion*, could refer to the message that Jesus was to proclaim throughout his ministry and not necessarily to the New Testament Gospels themselves, though sometimes this word does.[16] Because Jesus has been well instructed, he is in a position to act as Allah's messenger and teach the people of Israel.

The next verse in the Qur'an is quite revealing. Allah will appoint Jesus to serve as "a messenger to the children of Israel." Jesus is to say to the Jewish people,

> I have come to you, with a sign from your Lord, in that I make for you out of clay, as it were, the figure of a bird, and breathe into it, and it becomes a bird by Allah's leave: And I heal those born blind and the lepers, and I quicken the dead, by Allah's leave; and I declare to you what you eat and what you store in your houses. Surely therein is a sign for you if you did believe. (Surah 3:49; cf. 5:110)

The story of making a bird out of clay and then breathing life into it is drawn from another story recounted in the *Infancy Gospel of Thomas*:

> When this child Jesus was five years old, he was playing by the ford of a stream; and he gathered the flowing waters into pools and made them instantly pure. These things he ordered simply by speaking the word. He then made some soft mud and fashioned twelve sparrows from it. It was the Sabbath when he did this. There were also a number of other children playing with him. When a certain Jew saw what Jesus was doing while playing on the Sabbath, he left right away and reported to his father, Joseph, "Look, your child is at the stream and he has taken mud and formed twelve sparrows. He has profaned the Sabbath!" When Joseph came to the place and looked, he cried out

to him, "Why are you doing what is forbidden on the Sabbath?" But Jesus clapped his hands and cried to the sparrows, "Be gone!" And the sparrows took flight and went off, chirping. When the Jews saw this they were amazed; and they went away and reported to their leaders what they had seen Jesus do. (*Infan. Thom.* 2:1–5)[17]

---

## Was Jesus a Muslim?

Muslims claim that Jesus was a Muslim. Besides it being implicitly anachronistic (after all, as most people know, Islam did not arise until some 600 years after the time of Jesus—so in what sense could Jesus have been a Muslim?), there are several factors that call such a claim into question. Let's review some of them.

1. First, Jesus' attitude toward women is out of step with Islamic teaching. Jesus allowed women to touch him. One immediately thinks of the woman suffering from an ongoing hemorrhage who touched Jesus. Jesus did not rebuke her but assured her that she was healed, telling her, "Daughter, your faith has made you well; go in peace, and be healed of your disease" (Mark 5:25–34, NASB). On another occasion Jesus spent time with a woman alone, instructing her (John 4:7–29). Jesus, in fact, allowed women to sit at his feet and hear his teaching (Luke 10:39). Perhaps the most inspiring example of all was the woman who anointed Jesus' head. "She has done a beautiful thing to me," Jesus said in response (Mark 14:3–9, NIV). It is not easy to see how examples like these fit Islam's rules about relations between men and women.

2. Second, Jesus' use of alcohol does not conform to later Islamic teaching and practice. Jesus frequently associated with sinners and outcasts (e.g., Mark 2:15–17). Because Jesus was willing to drink wine with these people and with others, his critics vilified him, describing him as "a glutton and a drunkard, a friend of tax collectors and 'sinners'"! (Matt 11:19, NIV = Luke 7:34). On one occasion Jesus turned water into wine (John 2:1–11), and, of course, when he ate the last meal with his disciples, he drank wine (Mark 14:23–25). Jesus' behavior was hardly that of a devout Muslim.

3. Third, Jesus opposed legalism. He taught righteousness but not endless rules. He sometimes ate with unwashed hands (Mark 7:1–13). Many other examples could be cited. How does this behavior conform with Islamic teaching? It does not.

4. Fourth, Jesus' teaching regarding prayer was simple. He taught his disciples the famous Lord's Prayer: "Our Father which art in heaven, Hallowed be thy name. Thy kingdom come" (Matt 6:9–13, KJV = Luke 11:2–4). His follower the apostle Paul tells Christians to pray "with thanksgiving" and to "let your requests be made known to God" (Phil 4:6, NASB). In contrast to this simplicity, Muslims are required to follow hundreds of detailed rules about prayer.

5. Finally, Jesus allowed his followers to worship him. On this, see the account of Jesus walking on water in Matthew 14:22–33. It says of his disciples, "Then those in the boat worshiped him, saying, 'Truly you are the Son of God'" (NIV).

No, Jesus was not a Muslim; neither were his followers.

Jesus giving life to birds made of mud (or clay) is but one of several extraordinary (and utterly unhistorical) miracles the child Jesus performs in *Infancy Gospel of Thomas* and in other related writings. It is on this very story that Qur'an surah 3:49 is based. In *Infancy Gospel of Thomas* Jesus makes birds from mud; in the Qur'an he makes a bird from dust. In *Thomas* Jesus claps his hands and the mud bird becomes a living, flying bird; in the Qur'an Jesus breathes into the form of the bird made from dust (cf. Gen 2:7) and it becomes a bird. This story appears in the so-called *Arabic Infancy Gospel*, which originated in the fifth or sixth century and which made use of *Protevangelium of James* and *Infancy Gospel of Thomas* (see *Arab. Infan.* 46 for the story of the clay birds).[18] It is probable that Muhammad was familiar with some of the infancy stories and perhaps had himself heard a version of *Arabic Infancy Gospel*. It is not necessary to think that Muhammad was familiar with the teaching of Basilides or some other Gnostic.

According to the Qur'an, Jesus further claimed, "I heal those born blind and the lepers, and I quicken the dead." We again have a tradition that ultimately derives from the Gospel of Luke, for the Qur'an's words constitute an unmistakable allusion to Jesus' reply to John the Baptist: "Go and tell John what you have seen and heard: the *blind* receive their sight, the lame walk, *lepers* are cleansed, and the deaf hear, the *dead* are raised up, the poor have good news preached to them" (Luke 7:22, emphasis added; cf. Matt 11:5). We have emphasized the three elements found in the

Qur'an (viz. blind, lepers, dead) that have been drawn from Luke 7. One will note that these three elements appear *in the same order* as in the Gospel of Luke. We should add that this does not mean that Muhammad or any of his followers actually possessed direct knowledge of the Gospel of Luke or any of the other New Testament writings. It is only to say that Qur'an surah 3:49 contains an echo of tradition that may be traced back to the first century New Testament Gospels of Luke and Matthew.

---

## ✸ Muslim Writers Who Pass on Sayings Attributed to Jesus

- Abdallah ibn Omar al-Baidawi (d. c. 1286)
- 'Abd al-Jabbar (d. 1025)
- Abu Hamid al-Ghazzali (d. 1111)
- al-Abi (d. 1030)
- Ibn 'Asakir (d. 1175)
- Ibn Hanbal (d. 855)

---

One of the boldest claims in the Qur'an concerning Jesus is what appears to be a denial of his death on a Roman cross. The strange statement appears in surah 4, a section of the Qur'an that is concerned with laws and teaching relating to women. This passage will be discussed in the following chapter, but before we do, it will be helpful to back up and acquire a better sense of the context in which this passage is located. The context directly relates to what the Qur'an says about the birth of Jesus.

Our passage appears in a section that expresses criticism of unbelievers, especially Jews. We find references to Moses, Mount Sinai, the covenant, the Sabbath and a number of laws or allusions to laws (see surah 4:153–55). The Jews stand condemned, the Qur'an says, "for their having uttered against Mary a grievous insult" (surah 4:156). Although the insult is not spelled out, it is probably the claim found in rabbinic literature, especially in the tractate known as the *Toledot Yeshu* (lit. "Generations of Jesus"), to the effect that Mary conceived Jesus through adultery.[19] For example, in the Talmud (where some of this material appears) we find,

"She [Mary] who was the descendant of princes and governors played the harlot with carpenters [Joseph]" (*b. Sanh.* 106a).

The slander that Mary was an adulteress is what lies behind the habit of referring to Jesus as "Jesus ben Pantera" (as in the story of the man named Jacob who offered to heal someone "in the name of Jesus ben Pantera").[20] The sobriquet "ben Pantera" means "son of the panther." The Latin word for "panther" is *panthera*, which happened to be a popular name with Roman soldiers. We do not know the origin of the slur. It may have begun with Celsus, who authored an anti-Christian tract called *True Doctrine* (c. 170). Speaking of Mary, he says, "when she was pregnant she was turned out of doors by the carpenter to whom she had been betrothed, as having been guilty of adultery, and she bore a child to a certain soldier named Panthera" (according to Origen, *Against Celsus* 1.32).[21] Celsus goes on to claim that Jesus learned magic in Egypt (probably an idea based on the holy family's sojourn in Egypt; cf. Matt 2:13–15) and "on account of those powers gave himself the title of God" (according to Origen, *Against Celsus* 1.38).

But did the slander of Jesus' illegitimate birth originate with the pagan Celsus in the late second century? The charge of black magic appears in the first-century New Testament Gospels (see Mark 3:22), a century or more before the time Celsus wrote.[22] The charge of illegitimacy might also reach back to the first century. In fact, we may have hints of it in the Gospel of John (c. 90). In a very polemical context, Jesus' critics ask him, "Where is your Father?" (John 8:19). The question is ambiguous, in part playing off of the idea of Jesus' heavenly origin and his claim that in fact God is his Father (John 5:18; 8:54). But the question may also hint at the uncertainty of Jesus' birth (despite what his disciples had earlier stated in John 1:45: "We have found him of whom Moses in the law and also the prophets wrote, Jesus of Nazareth, the son of Joseph"). Perhaps the assertion "we do not know where he comes from" (John 9:29) hints at the same question (later, in v. 34, the religious teachers insult the man healed by Jesus by asserting that he had been "born in utter sin").[23]

Doubts about the legitimacy of Jesus' conception and birth seem to lie behind yet another assertion offered by his critics: "We were not born of fornication" (John 8:41).[24] In my view, the statement is elliptical, in that lying behind it is an unstated but understood contrast. If we fully write out the insinuation, his critics were saying, "We were not born of fornication [but you were]."[25] Even the reference to Jesus as "the son of Mary" (Mark 6:3) may have been based on the uncertainty of Jesus' paternity. In the second-century apocryphal work the *Acts of Pilate*, the implied logic of the ellipsis we just considered is stated rather matter-of-factly. Jesus' critics say to him, "You were born of fornication" (*Acts of Pilate* 2:3).

Although we cannot be sure of the origin of the allegation that Jesus was conceived out of wedlock, there is little question that by the time of the second century, perhaps earlier, slanders against Mary and Jesus could be heard in both Jewish and pagan circles. Whatever its origin, the "ben Pantera" sobriquet suggested that Jesus was the illegitimate son of a Roman soldier with whom Mary had had a dalliance (or by whom she had been raped). What makes the sobriquet so delightful from a rabbinic perspective is that the Latin *panthera* may well have been understood as a wordplay on the Greek *parthenos*, "virgin." That is, Jesus was the son of the virgin Mary all right—but not in the way you think! Muhammad found this slander highly offensive (and no doubt Christians did too) and spoke against it in surah 4:156.[26] We think the Qur'an's reference to the Jewish insult to Mary sets up the criticism that follows in 4.157–58, which will be considered in the next chapter.

## Summary

The Qur'an's traditions about Mary and the birth and childhood of Jesus are based on limited acquaintance with the infancy narratives of the New Testament's Gospel of Luke (relating both to John the Baptist and to Jesus) and the fanciful infancy narratives found in the second-century apocryphal works *Protevangelium of James* and *Infancy Gospel of Thomas*. No properly trained historian views the latter two works as offering us factual history. It is unfortunate that Muhammad made use of their traditions. The best explanation for this lies in what was said previously. Muhammad drew upon a pool of tradition that was made up of stories of Jesus as well as the Jewish and Christian biblical materials.[27] The evidence suggests that Muhammad did not know the difference between the early canonical writings and the later apocryphal materials. He made use of whatever traditions served his purposes.

In the next chapter we will review what the Qur'an says about the death of Jesus. We will again inquire into Muhammad's sources and evaluate their usefulness for historical research.

# Chapter 12

# Does the Qur'an Get the Death of Jesus Right?

*The Death of Jesus in the Qur'an and Islamic Tradition*

P erhaps the most controversial element in the Qur'an, as it relates to Jesus, is the apparent denial of Jesus' death. For Christians the death of Jesus on a Roman cross is not only a given, it is of vital theological importance. All four Gospels narrate the crucifixion, death and burial of Jesus. Paul presupposes the crucifixion and death of Jesus throughout his letters. The author of the book of Hebrews develops a major part of his theology—that Jesus became the sacrifice that never needs to be repeated—in his writing. Could all of these writers be wrong? Could the disciples and family of Jesus have misunderstood what really happened to Jesus? Could the Christian Church have been so grossly wrong for more than half a millennium? Could Muhammad be right, even though he lived more than 500 years after the fact? To these questions we now turn.

## The Death of Jesus in the Qur'an

In Qur'an surah 4:156, Muhammad complains of the Jewish insult to Mary (and Jesus) to the effect that she had committed adultery. In the next two verses (surah 4:157–58) Muhammad rails against the Jews for boasting that they put to death Jesus. Again Muhammad was probably reacting to rabbinic tradition that claims that very thing. In the Talmud we read,

> On the eve of Passover they hanged Jesus the Nazarene. And a herald went out, in front of him, for 40 days saying: "He is going to be stoned, because he practiced sorcery and enticed and led Israel astray. Anyone who knows anything in his favor, let him come and plead in his behalf." But, not having found anything in his favor, they hanged him on the eve of Passover. (b. Sanh. 43a)

By "hanging" one should understand crucifixion, in which one was hanged on a cross until dead. The threat of being stoned reflects the Old Testament law that prescribed such punishment for idolaters and practitioners of black magic, even if they offered signs and miracles that seemingly supported their claims (see Deut 13). This is what Jesus is accused of here: "he practiced magic and led Israel astray."[1]

Muhammad was apparently familiar with these Jewish polemics. In a passage that parallels and expands on 3.49, the giving of life to the clay bird and the healing of the blind, the lepers and the dead are linked to the charge of practicing magic. Allah assures Jesus, "I restrained the children of Israel from (doing violence to) you when you showed them the clear signs, and the unbelievers among them said, 'This is nothing but magic'" (surah 5:110; cf. 61:6: "This is sorcery!"). As we have seen, the charge of magic originated in the time of Jesus, as reported in all three of the Synoptic Gospels (Matt 12:24; Mark 3:22; Luke 11:15), and were echoed in second-century pagan writers like Celsus.

We now come to a very difficult passage. In surah 4:155–58 the Qur'an says,

> Allah set a seal upon them (the Jews) owing to their unbelief, so they shall not believe except a few...for they say: "Surely we have killed the Messiah, Jesus son of Mary, the apostle of Allah." Nay, they did not kill him, nor did they crucify him, but it was made to appear so to them. Those who argued this matter are uncertain; they have no knowledge about it except by speculation. In certainty they did not kill him, for Allah took him up to himself.

Although it is debated, the vast majority of Muslim laity and clerics understand this passage as saying that Jesus did not in fact die on the cross.[2] The Qur'an explicitly and emphatically states that contrary to what the Jews claim, "they did not kill him, nor did they crucify him."[3] The difficulty is in understanding what is meant by the words "a likeness made to appear to them" (Arabic: *walākin shubbiha lahum*).[4] These words seem to mean that it only appeared to the Jews that Jesus had been crucified. But in what sense did Jesus only *appear* to have been crucified?

The answer to this question may lie in the obscure comment about the uncertainty, lack of knowledge and speculation on the part of those who "argued this matter." These two elements—the appearance of the crucifixion, when in fact Jesus was not crucified, and the subsequent futile debate over what really happened—are clarified by the second-century debate instigated by one Basilides, a Gnostic heretic, who suggested that it was not Jesus who was crucified but Simon of Cyrene, the man who assisted Jesus with the cross (Mark 15:21). This strange hypothesis is sharply criticized by the influential Church Father Irenaeus (c. AD 180), who describes the view of Basilides as follows:

> He (Jesus) appeared, then, on earth as a man, to the nations of these powers, and worked miracles. Therefore he did not himself suffer death, but Simon, a certain man of Cyrene, being compelled, bore the cross in his stead; so that this latter being transfigured by him, that he might be thought to be Jesus, was crucified, through ignorance and error, while Jesus himself received the form of Simon, and, standing by, laughed at them. For since he was an incorporeal power…he ascended to him who sent him. (*Against Heresies* 1.24.4)

Irenaeus' description of what Basilides taught coheres with the Qur'an's claims: It really wasn't Jesus who was crucified; it only seemed to be. Jesus (or an angel) transformed the hapless Simon to look like Jesus, while Jesus was transformed to look like Simon. Rather than dying on the cross, as everybody thought, Jesus was taken up to God (which likely reflects the ascension; cf. Luke 24:50–53; Acts 1:9–12). It is this debate between Basilides and docetic Gnostics on the one hand and Irenaeus and the proto-orthodox Christians on the other that the Qur'an's references to uncertainty and speculation should be understood to be about. Although Gnosticism as a serious threat had receded by the time of Muhammad (seventh century), some of its distinctive ideas lingered, especially in the East.

It is important to emphasize that the Qur'an is not asserting *Docetism* (i.e., that Jesus only *seemed* to be physical), which was the perspective that Basilides and other Gnostics were attempting to defend. Muhammad never doubted the reality of Jesus' physical humanity, his mortality or even his vulnerability.

Whereas Basilides suggested that the man who was crucified was Simon of Cyrene, Islamic tradition came to believe that it was Judas Iscariot. Writing c. AD 995, 'Abd al-Jabbar (d. 1025), chief judge of Rayy (today's Teheran), claimed that through angelic intervention the "shape of Jesus was put upon Judas who had pointed him out, and they crucified him instead, supposing that he was Jesus. After three hours God took Jesus to himself and raised him up to heaven."[5] There is, however, absolutely no evidence before the time of Muhammad for the idea that Judas was crucified in the place of Jesus. Some Muslims think there is.

Muslims sometimes appeal to a work called the *Gospel of Barnabas* for proof that Jesus really was not crucified, as the Qur'an seems to say. As we just noted in 'Abd al-Jabbar, so also in the *Gospel of Barnabas* it is the betrayer Judas Iscariot who is crucified (*Gos. Barn.* 220). As in the Qur'an's account, so in the *Gospel of Barnabas*, Jesus is taken up into heaven. But what of the discovery of the empty tomb, reported in all four of the Christian Gospels? According to *Gospel of Barnabas,* some of Jesus' less enlightened, less spiritual disciples came by night and stole the body of Judas, thinking it was the body of Jesus. For this reason there arose the belief that Jesus had been crucified, buried and resurrected. Muslims especially like the *Gospel of Barnabas* because in it Jesus teaches that the chosen line descends through Ishmael, not Isaac (*Gos. Barn.* 43), he denies that he is the Son of God (*Gos. Barn.* 53) and he prophesies the coming of Muhammad (implicitly in *Gos. Barn.* 43; explicitly in *Gos. Barn.* 97, 163; cf. Qur'an surah 61:6, where Jesus shares the "good news of an apostle who will come after me, his name being Ahmad"[6]).

What should we think of this *Gospel of Barnabas*? Is it a credible source? Does it overturn the witnesses of the four New Testament Gospels? Historians don't think so. The *Gospel of Barnabas* is a medieval forgery, though it may contain a few fragments of an earlier work. In places it shows contact with Tatian's harmony of the four New Testament Gospels known as the *Diatessaron* (c. 170).[7]

Scholars readily recognize the lateness of the *Gospel of Barnabas* and its unreliability because of its many historical errors and anachronisms. Because this apocryphal Gospel dates to the 13th or 14th century, it can hardly rival the testimony of the four first-century New Testament Gospels. Historians always prefer older sources, sources that originate close to the time that they narrate. Historians know that the closer in time a source is to the events that source describes, the more likely its reliability.

The errors in the *Gospel of Barnabas* are numerous and for the most part quite obvious. Among these errors and anachronisms is the statement that Jesus was born during the administration of Pontius Pilate, governor of Judea and Samaria (AD 25–36). Not so; Jesus was born around 4 or 5 BC, shortly before the death of Herod the Great. The author of the *Gospel of Barnabas* describes Jesus as crossing the Sea of Galilee and landing *at*

*Nazareth* (*Gos. Barn.* 20–21)! The author evidently does not know that Nazareth is several miles inland. The author thinks wine was stored in wooden casks (*Gos. Barn.* 152). This is medieval practice, not ancient practice. In antiquity wine was stored in skins and ceramic jars called amphorae.

There's more. The author of the *Gospel of Barnabas* apparently does not know that "Christ" (from Greek, meaning "anointed") and "Messiah" (from Hebrew, also meaning "anointed") are the same word. We observe this when the *Gospel of Barnabas* refers to Jesus as "Jesus Christ" and then has him state that he is not the Messiah (*Gos. Barn.* 42). The author appears to be oblivious to the contradiction. There are further indications of lateness. Old Testament quotations and allusions in the *Gospel of Barnabas* reflect the Latin Vulgate, which was the Christian Bible of medieval Europe. There are even words and turns-of-phrase in the *Gospel of Barnabas* that have been drawn from Dante (1265–1321), the author of the *Inferno*. Throughout, the *Gospel of Barnabas* presupposes the feudalism and lifestyle of medieval Europe. In short, the *Gospel of Barnabas* utterly lacks verisimilitude. It does not reflect life in first-century Jewish Palestine. For this reason historians do not regard it as a helpful source in the study of Jesus.

If the *Gospel of Barnabas* provides no historical confirmation for the claim that Jesus really did not die on the cross, then on what basis did Muhammad deny that Jesus died on the cross? All early sources—with no exception—claim that Jesus died on the cross. All four New Testament Gospels say he did. The apostle Paul, who wrote his letters to various Christian churches and leaders from the late 40s to the early 60s, frequently makes reference to the crucifixion or cross of Jesus. Other New Testament writings allude to it.[8] It will be helpful to elaborate on two important lines of evidence: one from the Gospel of John and the other from Paul's letters.

As just mentioned, all four Gospels describe the crucifixion of Jesus. The Qur'an suggests, probably following the novel suggestion by the second-century heretic Basilides, that it was not Jesus who was crucified but someone who looked like him. We must ask, how realistic is this idea? After all, according to the Gospel of John, Mary the mother of Jesus was at the foot of the cross (John 19:25, "standing by the cross of Jesus were his mother, and his mother's sister...and Mary Mag'dalene"). What the fourth evangelist then narrates is quite important for our discussion:

> When Jesus saw his mother, and the disciple whom he loved stand-
> ing near, he said to his mother, "Woman, behold, your son!" Then
> he said to the disciple, "Behold, your mother!" And from that hour
> the disciple took her to his own home. (John 19:26–27)

Jesus has told his mother that she should now regard his disciple as her son, and he has told his disciple that he should regard Mary as his mother. After that, the disciple "took her to his own home." If the Qur'an's version of events is correct, then it was Simon of Cyrene (or Judas Iscariot, if we follow the apocryphal *Gospel of Barnabas*!) who spoke to Mary. Can we really believe that Mary had no idea that the man speaking to her from the cross was not her son? The whole idea is fantastic.

In Paul we have early and very important evidence that relates to the question of Jesus' death. Ten times Paul mentions the cross, that is, the cross on which Jesus suffered death by crucifixion. In poetic praise Paul says Jesus "humbled himself and became obedient unto death, even death on a cross" (Phil 2:8). Ten times Paul uses the verb crucify/crucified. Almost every occurrence is to the crucifixion of Jesus: "We preach Christ crucified" (1 Cor 1:23); "Jesus Christ and him crucified" (1 Cor 2:2); "he was crucified in weakness" (2 Cor 13:4). Dozens of times Paul speaks of the death of Jesus: "who was put to death for our trespasses" (Rom 4:25); "Christ died for the ungodly" (Rom 5:6); "the death of his Son" (Rom 5:10); "the death he died he died to sin" (Rom 6:10). Paul also repeats the words Jesus spoke during his final meal with his disciples (1 Cor 11:23–25).

In reminding the Christians of Corinth of the importance of the resurrection, Paul rehearses the tradition that he had "received," namely, "that Christ died for our sins in accordance with the scriptures, that he was buried, that he was raised on the third day in accordance with the scriptures" (1 Cor 15:3–4). This pre-Pauline tradition is very ancient, dating to the first year of the Christian movement.[9] Paul recounts the resurrection appearances to Cephas (Peter), the twelve, "more than five hundred brethren at one time" (most of whom were still living at the time of writing 1 Corinthians), James, "all the apostles," and finally Paul himself (vv. 5–8). Paul's preaching of the resurrection of Jesus, a proclamation that lies at the very heart of the Christian message, clearly presupposes the death of Jesus on a Roman cross. It is inconceivable that Paul and the original followers of Jesus were mistaken on this point.

There is little doubt that the writers of the New Testament and all of the leaders of the early Church either directly witnessed the death of Jesus or knew those who had witnessed the death of Jesus. There was never any doubt of it. Is there early evidence outside the early Christian community?

## Early Non-Christian References to the Death of Jesus

There are several important references to the death of Jesus in non-Christian sources. The most important witness is the Jewish historian Josephus, who survived the Jewish rebellion against Rome (AD 66–73) and went on to write several important works. He mentions the crucifixion of Jesus under the Roman governor Pilate. Writing in the early 90s AD, the Jewish historian and apologist explains to his readers who the Christians were, why they were called "Christians" and what happened to their founder:

> At this time there appeared Jesus, a wise man, *if indeed one ought to call him a man.* For he was a doer of amazing deeds, a teacher of persons who receive truth with pleasure. He won over many Jews and many of the Greeks. *He was the Messiah.* And when Pilate condemned him to the cross, the leading men among us having accused him, those who loved him from the first did not cease to do so. *For he appeared to them the third day alive again, the divine prophets having spoken these things and a myriad of other marvels concerning him.* And to the present the tribe of Christians, named after this person, has not disappeared. (*Ant.* 18.63–64)

This paragraph is known as the Testimonium Flavianum (i.e., "the Flavius [Josephus] testimony"). The words placed in italics are widely regarded as later Christian interpolations, to bring the testimony of Josephus into closer alignment with Christian beliefs about Jesus. Most scholars today accept the rest of the paragraph as genuine.[10] Note that Josephus says, "Pilate condemned him [Jesus] to the cross." An early form of the passage, minus some of the Christian additions, was known to Arab writers in the medieval period. In Agapius, *Kitab al-Unwan* (*Book of the Title*), we read very similarly, "Pilate condemned him to be crucified and to die."[11]

## Josephus on Jesus and James

He (Ananus) convened the council of judges and brought before it the brother of Jesus—the one called "Christ"—whose name was James, and certain others. Accusing them of transgressing the law he delivered them up for stoning. But those of the city considered the most fair-minded and strict concerning the laws were offended at this and sent to the king secretly urging him to order Ananus to take such actions no longer. (*Ant.* 20.200–201)

The reference to "Jesus—the one called 'Christ'" argues for the authenticity of the earlier mention of Jesus in *Antiquities* 20.

Another early and important witness to the death of Jesus is found in the letter of the Syriac-speaking Mara bar Serapion. He writes to his son sometime after the year AD 73, after his city has been conquered by the Romans and he himself has been taken prisoner. He tries to console his son with the thought that conquerors who act unjustly will in the end pay the price. In this context he refers to Jesus as the Jews' "wise king":

What else can we say, when the wise are forcibly dragged off by tyrants, their wisdom is captured by insults, and their minds are oppressed and without defense? For what advantage did the Athenians gain by the murder of Socrates, the recompense of which they received in famine and pestilence? Or the people of Samos by the burning of Pythagoras, because in one hour their country was entirely covered in sand? Or the Jews by the death of their wise king, because from that same time their kingdom was taken away? God justly avenged these three wise men: the Athenians died of hunger; the Samians were overwhelmed by the sea; the Jews, ruined and driven from their land, live in complete dispersion. But Socrates did not die for good; he lived on in the teaching of Plato. Pythagoras did not die for good; he lived on in the statue of Hera. Nor did the wise king die for good; he lived on in the teaching which he had given.[12]

Comparing Jesus to Socrates and Pythagoras is quite remarkable (and implicitly comparing himself to these men and to Jesus is rather immodest on the part of Mara bar Serapion, it might be added). But for the point at hand, what is important is bar Serapion's knowledge that the death of Jesus was in some way the responsibility of the Jewish leadership and for that "their kingdom was taken away," by which he means the Roman victory over the Jewish rebels and the destruction of the city of Jerusalem.

Early second-century Roman historian and anti-Semite Cornelius Tacitus (c. AD 56–118) speaks of Jesus' death in the context of his explanation of the hated emperor Nero and the widespread suspicion that he was the cause of the fire that destroyed almost half of the city of Rome. In *Annals* 15.44 (written c. AD 110) Tacitus says,

> Therefore, to squelch the rumor [that the burning of Rome had taken place by order], Nero supplied [as culprits] and punished in the most extraordinary fashion those hated for their vice, whom the crowd called "Christians." Christus, the author of their name, had suffered the death penalty during the reign of Tiberius, by sentence of the procurator Pontius Pilate. The pernicious superstition was checked for a time, only to break out once more, not merely in Judea, the origin of the evil, but in the capital itself, where all things horrible and shameful collect and are practiced.

The hostility toward Christians in general and the failure to mention the resurrection of Jesus are strong arguments for the authenticity of the passage, as well as for its independence. Arguments that Christian editors tampered with the passage have not been persuasive.[13] Tacitus does not specifically mention crucifixion, but he does state that Jesus "suffered the death penalty," under the author of Pilate the governor of Judea, during the rule of emperor Tiberius.

Trypho the Jew (early second century AD) expresses admiration for Jesus—for his miracles and his teaching—but he is reluctant to accept him as Israel's Messiah because of his shameful death on the cross: "Prove to us whether he must be crucified and die so disgracefully and dishonorably by the death cursed in the Law. For we cannot bring ourselves even to think of this" (Justin Martyr, *Dialogue with Trypho* 90).[14] Had Jesus not been crucified, Justin Martyr (c. AD 100–165) would have had a much easier time trying to persuade Trypho. But Jesus had in fact suffered crucifixion, so it was necessary for Justin to find an explanation in the Jewish Scriptures that would satisfy the skeptic Trypho.

Writing late in the second century, Lucian of Samosata (c. 115–200) mocks Christians in his tract on the charlatan Peregrinus, who, to gain the emperor's attention, set himself on fire. Lucian tells us that for a time

Peregrinus associated with Christians. In reference to Jesus, the Christians' "first lawgiver," he says,

> Furthermore, their first lawgiver persuaded them that they are all brothers of one another after they have transgressed once for all by denying the Greek gods and by worshipping that crucified sophist himself and living according to his laws. Therefore they despise all things equally and regard them common, without certain evidence accepting such things. (Lucian, *Peregrinus* §13; cf. §11).

There is no doubt in the mind of this unfriendly critic that the "sophist" Jesus was crucified.[15]

Celsus, author of *True Doctrine* (*c.* AD 170), saw in the crucifixion of Jesus evidence that he was neither divine nor anyone special (Origen, *Against Celsus* 2.34–39; 39: "[Jesus] underwent these punishments and sufferings").[16] Writing in the third century, Porphyry, biographer of the philosopher Plotinus and acquainted with Origen, wrote *Against the Christians*, a highly polemical work. Among other things, Porphyry wonders why after his crucifixion and supposed resurrection Jesus did not "appear to Pilate, who had punished him saying he had done nothing worthy of execution" (*Apocriticus* 2.14–15).[17] Porphyry's rejection of the resurrection presupposes the reality of the crucifixion. There is no doubt in the minds of Celsus and Porphyry that Jesus died on a Roman cross and for that reason cannot be what Christians claim him to be.

Every ancient source that has anything to say on the matter explicitly states or assumes the death of Jesus of Nazareth by crucifixion, on the orders of the Roman governor Pontius Pilate, just outside the walls of Jerusalem. There are simply no sources[18] that deny the crucifixion and death of Jesus. Virtually all historians today—apart from some Muslim historians—agree that Jesus died on a Roman cross. Even Muslim author Reza Aslan believes that Jesus died on the cross.[19]

## Summary

The Qur'an's claim that Jesus was not crucified but that it only appeared so flies in the face of all historical evidence, from the very beginning of the Christian movement and on into the first three centuries of the new era. Every single source that has anything relevant to say about the matter refers to Jesus' death on the cross or at least presupposes it. The only exception is the odd notion put forth in the second century by Basilides, more than one hundred years after the beginning of the Christian Church and some sixty to seventy years after the New Testament Gospels were written. Historians past and present wisely choose to follow the preponderance of the evidence. It is regrettable that Muhammad was misled by Basilides and those who passed on his bizarre assertion. No doubt the founder of Islam thought he was defending the honor of Jesus against yet another Jewish criticism, but in this case he was wildly off the mark.[20]

In this chapter and in the previous chapter we have considered what is said about Jesus primarily in the Qur'an. In the chapter that follows we shall consider that is said about Jesus in early Islamic writers.

# Chapter 13

# Does Islamic Tradition
# Get Jesus Right?

T he Qur'an's Jesus tradition sometimes exhibits a form of Ascetism that
is reminiscent of Encratism, which referred to various groups who advocated strict "self-control" (the meaning of the Greek word *egkrateia*). This
movement arose in Syria in the second century and became very influential
in the Middle East. Encratites, as adherents were called, tended to be ascetic
in the extreme, which meant they ate simple food, were usually vegetarians,
avoided wine, dressed simply, avoided the comforts of life, refrained from
marriage and sex, and were critical of the wealthy.

The historical Jesus, who is described in the New Testament's four
Gospels—all of which were written in the first century, a few decades after
Jesus lived—was not ascetic. But those sectarian Christians who advocated the
ascetic lifestyle began in the second century and later to write new accounts
that depicted Jesus as an advocate of asceticism. This was a common feature
in late, apocryphal works, not the older works that were written in the first century when Jesus' original followers and family members were still living.

In this chapter, we explore the implications of the appearance of traditions in which Jesus is portrayed as an ascetic, if not a full-fledged Encratite,
in early Islamic tradition that often complement and sometimes extend tendencies found in the Qur'an itself. To these traditions we now turn.

## Jesus in Early Islamic Tradition

Outside the Qur'an but still in the Islamic tradition we find a number of stories and sayings attributed to Jesus. One of the stories in Islamic tradition

gives clear expression to the Encratite tendencies just described. Muslim writer Ibn 'Asakir (d. 1175) tells us,

> Jesus son of Mary used to eat barley, walk on foot and did not ride donkeys. He did not live in a house, nor did he use lamps for light. He neither dressed in cotton, nor touched women, nor used perfume. He never mixed his drink with anything, nor cooled it. He never greased or washed his hair or his beard. He never had anything between his skin and the ground, except his garment. He had no concern for lunch or dinner, and coveted nothing of the desires of this world. He used to consort with the weak, the chronically sick and the poor. Whenever food was offered him, he would place it on the ground, and he never ate meat. Of food, he ate little, saying: "This is too much for one who has to die and answer for his deeds."[1]

The Jesus of this imaginative description is thoroughly ascetic. He eats simple food (barley, not meat) and not much of it. He avoids women. His grooming is simple. He makes no use of perfume or oil for his hair. He lives outdoors, and he has no bed but sleeps on the ground. Jesus always walks and never rides an animal. He consorts with the poor and sick, not the wealthy and powerful.

Some of this description ultimately derives from the New Testament Gospels. In these first-century sources, Jesus is said to eat and drink with sinners (Matt 9:10; Luke 15:1–2). He often heals the sick (Matt 4:24; 8:16). He urges the wealthy to give to the poor. Jesus is remembered to have said, "Foxes have holes, and birds of the air have nests; but the Son of man has nowhere to lay his head" (Matt 8:20 = Luke 9:58).

But there are details about Jesus' life and habits that do not square with the Islamic description. Although Jesus was not married, women were in his company and were allowed to learn from him (e.g., Luke 10:38–42). Jesus permitted a woman to wash his feet with her tears and them apply perfume to his feet (Luke 7:36–50). He allowed another woman to anoint his head with oil (Mark 14:3–9). He helped a Gentile woman who petitioned him (Mark 7:24–30). He did not rebuke the woman who touched him, although she was afflicted with a condition that rendered her impure (Mark 5:24–34). Jesus associated with outcasts, to be sure, but he was hardly ascetic in food and drink. Indeed, his dining with such people led some critics to say of him, "Behold, a glutton and a drunkard, a friend of tax collectors and sinners!" (Matt 11:19 = Luke 7:34; cf. Luke 15:1–2: "This man receives sinners and eats with them"). When the wine ran out at a wedding feast, Jesus accommodated the crowd by turning one hundred gallons of water into high quality wine (John 2:1–11).

Our earliest sources (i.e., the New Testament writings), which actually overlap with the lives of those who personally knew Jesus, do agree with some of the claims we find in the Islamic description of Jesus. But many other descriptions of Jesus in Islamic tradition are not based on early, authentic materials. Indeed, the Islamic description of Jesus owes as much to imagination as it does to early, reliable sources. As already mentioned, the tendency to exaggerate the ascetic side of Jesus' life probably reflects the Encratism of second- and third-century Syria, which left traces in the Middle East on into the time of Muhammad. We see this tendency in other sayings about Jesus that we find in early Islamic sources.

Encratism's negative view of women and wine is heard in a saying preserved by Ibn Hanbal (d. 855), in which Jesus is supposed to have said, "The greatest sin is love of the world. Women are the ropes of Satan. Wine is the key to every evil."[2] Jesus said nothing of the sort, but we probably do hear echoes of warnings found in the New Testament and in later Church Fathers. The statement that the "greatest sin is love of the world" likely reflects the command of the Christian leader in Ephesus, who exhorted Christians, "Do not love the world" (1 John 2:15). It may also reflect the idea that "love of money is the root of all evils" (1 Tim 6:10; cf. Heb 13:5). These concerns are expressed by later Christian writers (e.g., Polycarp, *Philippians* 9:2, "they did not love the present world"; 11:2, "who does not avoid love of money will be polluted by idolatry"). But nowhere does Jesus describe women as "the ropes of Satan."[3] The historical Jesus was very accepting of women and included them among his disciples. And although Jewish and Christian Scriptures warn against drunkenness (e.g., Isa 5:11; 28:7; Hab 2:5; Prov 20:1; Eph 5:18), nowhere is wine itself described as "the key to every evil."[4] There is nothing from early, credible sources to suggest that Jesus regarded wine as something to be avoided.[5]

Ibn Hanbal provides another saying in which Jesus is supposed to have said, "Place your treasures in heaven, for the heart of man is where his treasure is."[6] This saying is an adaptation and abridgement of Matthew 6:19–21, where in the Sermon on the Mount Jesus exhorts his disciples, "Do not lay up for yourselves treasures on earth, where moth and rust consume and where thieves break in and steal, but lay up for yourselves treasures in heaven, where neither moth nor rust consumes and where thieves do not break in and steal. For where your treasure is, there will your heart be also."

The two elements of the abridged version show up in writings that were probably read by ascetics and Gnostics in Egypt and elsewhere in the Middle East. The exhortation to "lay up treasures in heaven" is echoed in a work called the *Teaching of Silvanus*, a second-century ascetic work possibly written by a monk.[7] The last part of Jesus' saying is found in the much talked about *Gospel of Mary*, a second-century Gnostic work.[8] The Islamic form of the saying, where the two elements appear together, is consistent with this pattern.

The vegetarian perspective of asceticism, if not Encratism, is seen in this story and saying preserved by al-Abi (d. 1030): "Jesus passed by a man eating meat. He said: 'Flesh eating flesh, what a despicable thing!'"[9] Radical vegetarianism is attested in the *Gospel of Thomas*, a work that originated in second-century Syria, as we see in several sayings—all attributed to Jesus. These include the comments "wretched is the body that depends on a body" (*Gos. Thom.* §87) and "woe to the soul that depends on flesh" (*Gos. Thom.* §112). Living in Syria shortly before the *Gospel of Thomas* was written, Justin Martyr's student Tatian, who was labelled the "father of the Encratites" (Eusebius, *Hist. eccl.* 4.29.1–2), was remembered to have taught that it was necessary to abstain from meat (Irenaeus, *Adv. Haer.* 1.28.1; Jerome, *Adv. Jovinianum* 1.3) and from wine (Jerome, *Comm. Amos* 2:12).

'Abd al-Jabbar (d. 1025) preserves a tradition in which Jesus is called on to act as an arbitrator in a dispute between brothers: "A person said to him: 'Master, my brother (wants) to share (with me) my father's blessing.' (Jesus) said to him: 'Who placed me over you (to determine your) share?'"[10] The story and saying are drawn from the Gospel of Luke: "One of the multitude said to him, 'Teacher, bid my brother divide the inheritance with me.' But he said to him, 'Man, who made me a judge or divider over you?'" (Luke 12:13–14). A slightly different form of the saying appears in the second-century Syrian *Gospel of Thomas* (saying §72). We may also have an allusion to Luke 12:13–14 in the Babylonian recension of the Talmud (*b. Shabbat* 116b).[11]

'Abd al-Jabbar provides us with another early Islamic tradition, in which the purpose of Jesus' ministry is explained:

The Messiah came to revive the Law and to put it into practice, and said: "I have come to act according to the Law and the orders of the Prophets before me. I have not come to abolish but to complete. It is easier in God's eyes for heaven to fall upon the earth than to abolish anything from the Law of Moses. So if any person sets aside anything of this, that person will be called small in the kingdom of heaven."[12]

We again have a paraphrase of a passage from the Sermon on the Mount. It is where Jesus declares his purpose with respect to the Law and the Prophets: He has come to fulfill them, not abolish them (Matt 5:17–19). The Islamic paraphrase offers a close approximation. Part of the saying (Matt 5:18 = Luke 16:17) is echoed in the *Gospel of Thomas*: "This heaven will pass away, and the one above it will pass away" (*Gos. Thom.* §11). In keeping with its ascetic orientation, the point of the saying in the *Gospel of Thomas* is not the eternal validity of Jesus' teaching but the transitory nature of the present world. Jesus' teaching is echoed in the Talmud: "The (Christian) philosopher said to them (Rabban Gamaliel and two others), 'Look at the end of the Gospel, where it is written, "I have not come to abolish the Law of Moses, nor to add to the Law of Moses"'" (b. *Shabbat* 116b, according to the Oxford Codex, which reads "Gospel" instead of "book").

Abu Hamid al-Ghazzali (d. 1111) tells us that Jesus said, "Whoever knows and does and teaches will be called great in the kingdom of heaven."[13] The saying here takes us back to Matthew 5:19, where Jesus says, "he who does them and teaches them shall be called great in the kingdom of heaven." The only difference in the Islamic version of Jesus' saying is the appearance the verb "know." This may again reflect Syrian tradition, in which emphasis is placed on knowing or possessing esoteric knowledge. We see this in the oft referenced *Gospel of Thomas*. Here are two examples: "Whoever *knows* himself will find (the kingdom). And when you *know* yourselves, you will understand" (*Gos. Thom.* §3, according to P. Oxy. 654, with emphasis added); and "*Know* what is before your face, and what is hidden will be disclosed to you" (*Gos. Thom.* §5, according to P.Oxy. 654, emphasis added).[14]

Abu Hamid al-Ghazzali provides another saying, in which Jesus is supposed to have said,

> Evil scholars are like a rock that has fallen at the mouth of a brook; it does not drink the water, nor does it let the water flow to the plants. And evil scholars are like the drainpipe of a latrine that is plastered outside but filthy inside; or like graves that are decorated outside but contain dead people's bones inside.[15]

The three similes (rock, drainpipe and graves) are proverbial. The first one, which compares evil scholars to a rock that blocks the flow of water but does not drink, is similar to Jesus' complaint that the scribes and Pharisees shut people out of the kingdom and do not enter it themselves (Matt 23:13) and his warning that the Jewish legal authorities take away the key of knowledge but do not themselves enter (Luke 11:52). The latter form of the saying appears in the *Gospel of Thomas*.[16] The second simile in the Islamic saying, which speaks of the drainpipe that is plastered outside but filthy inside, is reminiscent of Jesus' saying about the cup that has been cleaned on the outside but not inside (Matt 23:25–26 = Luke 11:39–40). The third simile, which speaks of decorated graves that contain bones of the dead, clearly echoes Jesus' saying about whitewashed tombs, "which outwardly appear beautiful, but within they are full of dead men's bones" (Matt 23:27 = Luke 11:44).

We may review very briefly a few more sayings Abu Hamid al-Ghazzali attributes to Jesus:

> "Blessed is he who relinquishes present desire for an absent promise which he has not yet seen."
> "The love of this world and of the life to come cannot co-exist in the believer's heart, any more than water and fire can co-exist in the same vessel."
> "He who seeks the world is like a man who drinks sea-water: The more he drinks, the more thirsty he becomes, until at last it kills him."[17]

The first two sayings echo the teaching of Jesus and some of the New Testament writers. All three sayings are consistent with ascetic perspectives. The first saying about relinquishing present desire for a not-yet-fulfilled promise reminds us of the assurance Jesus gave his disciples, after Peter had exclaimed that they had given up everything to follow Jesus (Matt 19:27; Mark 10:28; Luke 18:28): "Truly, I say to you, there is no one who has left house or brothers or sisters or mother or father or children or lands, for my sake and for the gospel, who will not receive a hundredfold now in this time, houses and brothers and sisters and mothers and children and lands, with persecutions, and in the age to come eternal life" (Mark 10:29–30; cf. Matt 19:28–29; Luke 18:29–30). Reference to the "promise which he has not seen" recalls Paul's words that believers "walk by faith, not by sight" (2 Cor 5:7) and the definition of faith in the book of Hebrews: "faith is the assurance of things hoped for, the conviction of things not seen" (Heb 11:1).

The second saying about the impossibility of water and fire co-existing recalls Jesus' teaching that one cannot serve God and mammon (wealth): "No one can serve two masters; for either he will hate the one and love the other, or he will be devoted to the one and despise the other. You cannot serve God and mammon" (Matt 6:24 = Luke 16:13).

The third saying about the impossibility of having one's thirst quenched by sea water may well reflect what Jesus said to the woman at the well of Jacob: "Every one who drinks of this water will thirst again, but whoever drinks of the water that I shall give him will never thirst; the water that I shall give him will become in him a spring of water welling up to eternal life" (John 4:13–14). The water of Jesus quenches thirst forever, but ordinary water cannot. Abu Hamid al-Ghazzali's form of the saying plays on the two types of water: fresh water that quenches thirst and salt water that does not.

The last example that we consider in this survey is found inscribed on a mosque in India. The inscription reads, "Jesus said: 'The world is a bridge. Pass over it, but do not build your dwelling there.'"[18] A similar saying is found in al-Baidawi's thirteenth-century commentary on the Qur'an. It reads, "Jesus said, 'Be in the midst, but walk on one side.'"[19] These sayings are probably related in a general sense to *Gos. Thom.* §42: "Jesus says, 'Become passersby.'" It is unclear if this saying is based on anything that Jesus actually said.[20] One thinks of an exhortation offered by Philo (c. 20 BC—AD 50), the Jewish scholar who lived in Alexandria, Egypt: "Let us then, without any delay, attempt to proceed by the royal road, since we think fit to pass by all earthly things" (*Unchangeable* 159; cf. *Migration* 146). Although not a form of the saying, an early rabbinic proverb seems to give expression to the same basic idea: "Rabbi Jacob [c. AD 200] said: 'The world is like an antechamber before the world to come. Prepare yourself in the antechamber so that you may enter into the banqueting hall'" (m. *'Abot* 4.16).[21]

## Jesus in Muslim Eschatology

There is no total unanimity among Muslims about the details of the Last Days. There are, of course, divisions between Sunni and Shia Muslims about eschatology, particularly in relation to the view of the hidden imam in Shi'ite Islam. Among most Muslims there is belief that a false Messiah or Antichrist will appear from the east. Muslims refer to him as the Dajjal. Sunni Muslims usually believe that a messianic figure known as the Mahdi will arise on earth to transform the world. He will be from the family of Muhammad and will lead Muslim warriors carrying black flags. The Mahdi will defeat the Antichrist, Israel will be conquered and all Jews and Christians will realize that Islam is the true religion. Many Muslims believe that Jesus will return to assist the Mahdi. Before the final judgment, Allah will defeat evil forces from Gog and Magog.

For further study see David Cook, *Contemporary Muslim Apocalyptic Literature* (Syracuse: Syracuse University Press, 2005) and Jean-Pierre Filiu, *Apocalypse in Islam* (Los Angeles: University of California, 2011).

There are many other sayings in Islamic tradition that are attributed to Jesus. Many of them are reminiscent of sayings found in the New Testament Gospels. But what we often see are new traditions or alterations in the older traditions that reflect new ideas that emerged in the second century and later, often in Syria or elsewhere in the Middle East. It is interesting to observe how often distinctive sayings in the Qur'an or in other Islamic traditions correspond to the newer material that began to circulate in Syria, the likely place of origin of the *Gospel of Thomas*, and points further east.[22] The ascetic teachings attributed to Jesus also reflect the asceticism and Encratism that took hold in second-century Syria and became so popular.[23]

## Summary

Virtually everything about Jesus in the Qur'an and other early Islamic sources that does not itself derive from the New Testament Gospels themselves has no claim to great antiquity or authenticity. Again and again we hear vague echoes of things Jesus said or did according to the New Testament Gospels. Other times we hear echoes of things Jesus said or did according to late, dubious traditions, often found in Middle Eastern settings, such as Syria. These late, dubious traditions are sometimes Christian, Gnostic, Jewish or even pagan. They may have originated in order to have Jesus say something that endorses someone's preferred view, or they may be due to simple confusion and misidentification of a source.

The extreme asceticism in the distinctive Jesus traditions in the Qur'an and Islamic traditions outside the Qur'an, some of which likely originated in Encratite circles, provides another clue that these traditions are late and secondary. We have seen many of these tendencies in stories and sayings attributed to Jesus in Islamic tradition outside the Qur'an, but these tendencies can be seen in the Qur'an itself. These tendencies, which do not square with the older sources, suggest that the Islamic traditions about Jesus do not reach back to the time and place of Jesus of Nazareth and his Galilean disciples.

Not everything said about Jesus in the Qur'an and Islamic tradition is inaccurate or false, nor is everything about Jesus in the Talmud and other Rabbinic sources inaccurate or false, but much of it is. The real problem is that these traditions are not *historical* traditions as such. Rather, they reflect opinions, polemic, legends, rumors and popular beliefs held by Jews, Christians, pagans or Muhammad himself and some of his first followers. The Jesus of the Qur'an reflects the time of Muhammad, not the time of Jesus. Keith Small remarks,

> The Jesus speaking in the Qur'an uses words and thoughts that could only have arisen in a milieu that is post-Nicea and post-Chalcedon, relying on information from apocryphal sources in oral circulation, rather than being a revelation giving the words of someone speaking from the first-century.[24]

The evidence fully supports his assessment.

Sometimes what is said in reference to Jesus may not have been about Jesus originally; it may have been about someone else. The Qur'an and the Talmud are not sources of history, and they contain virtually nothing that historians today would regard as true biography. To supplement, or even correct, the New Testament Gospels, which were written in the first century, a few decades after the death and resurrection of Jesus, with the distinctive traditions found in the Qur'an is hardly sound historical procedure. Historians prefer sources that originated close to the persons and events narrated.

We should agree with historians that the New Testament Gospels should be preferred over the much later Qur'an and even later Islamic traditions. But that does not mean our work is finished. Historians will also give a hard look at an ancient source, even if it was composed within a generation or so of the events it describes. After all, an ancient source is not necessarily a reliable source. As we have seen in chapter 1, critical examination of the New Testament Gospels shows them to be reliable sources. They contain the kind of reliable data that historians need in order to write history, in order to describe the life and teaching of Jesus.

# Chapter 14

# Does Islam Liberate Women?

*Veils, Wife Beating and Other Contested Issues*

Reza Aslan's passion in defending Islam comes through on many topics, particularly on the treatment of women. As with many Muslim apologists, Aslan believes that women gain true freedom in Islam, that the Prophet liberated females, that there is essential equality between males and females and that non-Muslims have basically misunderstood the whole topic. Of course, everyone knows that this standard Islamic perspective is met by the polar opposite in anti-Muslim polemics. In that world, women are in bondage in Islam, the Prophet was abusive to women and the Qur'an contains very offensive material about women. Many non-Muslims believe that Islamic law views women as second-class citizens and that women are subject to abuse in most Muslim countries of the world. The difference in perspectives is so extreme that one wonders if the same subject is being debated.

## The Greatest for Women

In *No god but God*, Aslan paints an incredibly positive view of the first Muslim community in Medina. According to him, Muhammad created a "new and radically innovative" tribe[1] once he left Mecca and had the opportunity to construct what Allah wanted for humanity. "By enacting a series of radical religious, social, and economic reforms, he was able to establish a new kind of society, the likes of which had never before been seen in Arabia."[2] For Aslan, Medina's greatness can be measured best in relation to females. "Perhaps nowhere was Muhammad's struggle for economic redistribution and social egalitarianism more evident than in the rights and privileges he bestowed upon the women in his community."[3]

In Medina, as in the Qur'an (4:1 and 7:189), men and women are equal but have separate roles. Women, Muhammad instructed, could inherit property, keep their dowries and divorce their husbands. The Qur'an set boundaries on polygamy and has monogamy as the ideal. Muhammad was tough on Muslim males in Medina who opposed his empowerment of women.[4] For Aslan, "Islam is above all the egalitarian religion."[5]

Aslan's glowing portrait of the Islamic ideal lived out in Medina fits with the high view offered by other Muslim leaders. Here are, for example, ten points made by Hammudah Abdalati and Jamal A. Badawi, two respected Muslim authorities.

- Islam stopped the practice of female infanticide in the Arab world.
- Women are allowed to receive education just like men.
- Women are to be given freedom of expression.
- Marriage and family life are very sacred.
- Motherhood is given incredible honor in Islam.
- Husbands are to love their wives and treat them kindly.
- Husbands are to make sure their wives are satisfied sexually.
- The separation of females in worship is done for reasons of purity.
- Divorce is to be allowed only when absolutely necessary.
- Women receive a just inheritance in Islamic family law.

In one of Badawi's essays on the status of women, he quotes surah 4:1 from the Qur'an: "O mankind! reverence your Guardian-Lord, who created you from a single person, created, of like nature, His mate, and from them twain scattered (like seeds) countless men and women."

Of this passage, Badawi writes, "In the midst of the darkness that engulfed the world, the divine revelation echoed in the wide desert of Arabia with a fresh, noble, and universal message to humanity." He then cites an unnamed scholar on the same text: "It is believed that there is no text, old or new, that deals with the humanity of the woman from all aspects with such amazing brevity, eloquence, depth, and originality as this divine decree."[6]

Aslan and these other scholars properly note some egalitarian elements in the Qur'an. One of the most famous passages reads, "For Muslim men and women—for believing men and women, for devout men and women, for true men and women, for men and women who are patient and constant, for men and women who humble themselves, for men and women who give in Charity, for men and women who fast (and deny themselves), for men and women who guard their chastity, and for men and women who engage much in God's praise—for them has God prepared forgiveness and great reward" (33:35). The Qur'an also describes husbands and wives as friends (4:36), and says that there is to be "tranquility, love and mercy" between them (30:21). In heaven, there will be delight, love, and joy between spouses (36:55–57, 55:51-53). If divorce occurs in this life, women are to be treated with grace (2:237) and justice (2:231 and 65:2). There should be arbitration in conflict (4:35).

## Major Concerns about Islam and Women

Aslan realizes that stereotypes abound about Islam and the treatment of women. He works hard to allay fears that women have anything to fear in relation to Muhammad in particular and Islam in general. We already dealt with Aslan's weak defense of the prophet's marriage to Aisha when she was very young. Beyond this specific, Aslan attempts to dismiss popular attacks on the prophet's alleged licentiousness with minimal discussion. His argument that Muhammad's marriages were political, not sexual, unions is only partly true. If they were not sexual, why does Aslan bother to state that Muhammad was "a man with a robust and healthy libido"?[7]

In general, Aslan is content to assert how egalitarian the prophet was in his teachings and practice, though he is short on details about actual life for Muslim women in Medina. He spends most of his time on three larger issues: (1) the veil, (2) hadith and legal traditions on women and (3) a controversial passage in the Qur'an about wife beating.

### The Veil

Aslan is clearly opposed to what he calls the stereotypical use of the veil to show that women in Islam are oppressed.[8] His points are the following:

- Veiling and seclusion was borrowed from Iranian and Syrian upper classes.

- Veiling applied only to Muhammad's wives in the early years. They were the only ones who "observed hijab" during the prophet's lifetime.

- The Qur'an instructs all Muslim females to "draw their clothes around them a little to be recognized as believers" (surah 33:59) and "guard their private parts" and "drape a cover over their breasts." (24:31–32).

- After referencing Leila Ahmed, the famous Muslim feminist, Aslan states that "nowhere in the whole of the Quran is the term hijab applied to any woman other than the wives of Muhammad."

- The custom of Muslim females wearing a veil most likely started "long after the prophet's death."

- The veil is not necessarily a symbol of female empowerment or oppression. Wearing a veil should be a matter of individual choice for any Muslim woman.[9]

These simple statements and Aslan's brief and dogmatic analysis belie the enormous controversy and complexities involved in thinking about the veil. Aslan's discussion is somewhat misleading because his terminology shifts between popular meanings of veiling and technical points about various Arabic terms in the Qur'an. For example, you would never know from his analysis that the term "hijab" is **never** used in the Qur'an about clothing in regard to women, whether Muhammad's wives or otherwise.[10] Further, on the broader historical timeline, there is really little data to settle when veiling became customary for Muslim females. Of course, traditional Muslim exegetes are dogmatic on the matter since, unlike Aslan, they trust the hadith and shariah law. The various schools of law each teach that their particular rules on clothing go right back to Muhammad and the earliest Muslim community in Medina.[11]

Aslan is quite eloquent on Western stereotypes about the veil. Further, and more important, he is balanced in his realization that (a) Muslim women are sometimes abused in Islamic societies, (b) the meaning of the veil has to be decided individually and contextually, and (c) Islamic women should be free to decide on whether or not to wear the veil. Of course, his assertions and our appreciation and agreement of his perspective on veiling do not settle the matters easily. Rahela Nayebzadah states in her brilliant analysis,

No other item of clothing compares to the veil. The veil is always being defined, and each definition involves some level of distortion. The veil cannot escape egregious interpretations or dichotomous relationships: it is an area of interest for both the West and the East, the Muslim and the non-Muslim, the veiled and the unveiled.[12]

---

## Use of Veil in Qur'an

"Between both (groups) of them (there is) a partition." (7:46)

"When you recite the Qur'an, We place between you and those who do not believe in the Hereafter an obscuring veil." (17:45)

"And remember in the Book Mary: When she withdrew from her family to an eastern place, and took a veil apart from them..." (19:17)

"When you ask them for anything, ask them from behind a veil. That is purer for your hearts and their hearts." (33:53)

"When the standing horses were presented before him in the evening, he said, 'Surely I have loved the love of good (things) more than the remembrance of my Lord, until the sun has (now) been hidden by the veil.'" (38:32)

"They say, 'Our hearts are covered from what you call us to, and (there is) a heaviness in our ears, and between us and you (there is) a veil.'" (41:5)

"It is not (fitting) for any human being that God should speak to him, except (by) inspiration, or from behind a veil..." (42:51)

"By no means! Surely on that Day they will indeed be veiled from their Lord." (83:15)

---

## Misogynist Traditions

Aslan believes that the early egalitarianism in Medina was slowly wiped away by the dominant chauvinist tendencies in Arabia and the Middle East. Muslim males avoided the ideals of the Qur'an and used their power to fabricate false traditions about the prophet's teachings, make laws that restricted the rights of women and engage in misogynist exegesis of the sacred text. Here Aslan shows his basic contempt for three huge sources of authority in orthodox Islam: the hadith, shariah and tafsir (commentaries on the Qur'an).

We noted in an earlier chapter that the hadith are traditions supposedly from and about the prophet Muhammad. For Aslan they are largely unsound reports since they were "muddled and totally unregulated, making their authentication almost impossible."[13] While dismissing the hadith comes at the expense of sacrificing much that makes up the framework and detail of the prophet's biography, Aslan's removal of the hadith as authoritative gives him grounds to set aside its misogynist elements, especially those related to the prophet. Aslan adopts the same approach to shariah laws that restrict the rights of women.

Aslan is correct that the hadith and legal verdicts are often misogynist. If one takes some of the hadith or shariah statements at face value, then (1) the prophet taught that there are more women in hell than men, (2) the prophet believed brief contractual marriages are sometimes right, given the sexual needs of males, (3) the prophet asserted that women are mentally inferior to men, (4) the prophet believed that the prayer of a man is invalid if a donkey, dog or woman walks in front of him while praying, (5) the prophet believed that the testimony of women is worth only half that of males, (6) the prophet granted more power to husbands in divorce proceedings, (7) the prophet gave greater inheritance rights to males than females and (8) the prophet taught that it was proper for a husband to beat his wife in certain circumstances.

## An Infamous and Controversial Verse

This last point about the hadith on wife-beating always leads to debate about one of the most contested verses in the Qur'an, surah 4:34. Aslan discusses this passage immediately after bemoaning the dominance of male exegetes. He writes,

The fact is that for fourteen centuries, the science of Quranic commentary has been the exclusive domain of Muslim men. And because each one of these exegetes inevitably brings to the Quran his own ideology and his own preconceived notions, it should not be surprising to learn that certain verses have most often been read in their most misogynist interpretation.[14]

Aslan then provides two stunningly different translations of 4:34. The first is from Ahmed Ali and the second is from Majid Fakhry. Aslan provides Arabic transliteration in parenthesis. (Emphasis in bold added.)

"Men are the **support** of women [*qawwamuna 'ala an-nisa*] as God gives some more means than others, and because they spend of their wealth (to provide for them)....As for women you feel are averse, talk to them suasively; then leave them alone in bed (without molesting them) and **go to bed** with them (when they are willing)."

"Men are in **charge** of women, because Allah has made some of them excel the others, and because they spend some of their wealth.... And for those [women] that you fear might rebel, admonish them and abandon them in their beds and **beat** them [*adribuhunna*]."

Aslan makes his verdict on the two renditions:

Because of the variability of the Arabic language, both of these translations are grammatically, syntactically and definitionally correct. The phrase *qawwamuna 'ala an-nisa* can be understood as "watch over," "protect," "support," "attend to," "look after" or "be in charge of" women. The final word in the verse, *adribuhunna*, which Fakhry has rendered as "beat them," can equally mean "turn away from them," "go along with them" and, remarkably, even "have consensual intercourse with them."

Aslan concludes, "If religion is indeed interpretation, then which meaning one chooses to accept and follow depends on what one is trying to extract from the text." The choice is either one of "empowering women" or looking to the Qur'an "to justify violence against women."[15]

Is the proper translation of the Qur'an so easily settled? Are both translations correct on 4:34? While translation does involve choice, things are not quite as simple as Aslan suggests, and he fails to disclose some important issues. First, neither version of the Qur'an he chooses to use have been given stellar reviews in scholarship.[16] Second, he neglects to inform his readership that the most distinguished translations of the Qur'an follow Fakhry. Here are six major translators on 4:34.

> "As for those from whom ye fear rebellion, admonish them and banish them to beds apart, and scourge them." (Pickthall)

> "As to those women on whose part ye fear disloyalty and ill-conduct, admonish them (first), (Next), refuse to share their beds, (And last) beat them (lightly)." (Yusuf Ali)

> "and (as to) those on whose part you fear desertion, admonish them, and leave them alone in the sleeping-places and beat them." (Shakir)

> "(As for) those women whom you fear may be rebellious: admonish them, avoid them in bed, and (finally) strike them." (Arthur Droge)

> "If you fear high-handedness from your wives, remind them [of the teachings of God], then ignore them when you go to bed, then hit them." (Abdel Haleem)

> "And those you fear may be rebellious admonish; banish them to their couches, and beat them." (Arberry)

Arberry's translation may be the most significant since his translation is often regarded as the best by Western scholars.[17]

While Aslan may dismiss all of these translators as either traditional Muslims or chauvinists, such an ad hominem approach would only cheapen his already strained apologetic about the passage. Sooner or later one has to move back to the foundational grammar, syntax and definition of words under debate. On this, Ahmed Ali's translation of the Arabic term as "go to bed with them" represents a very strained reading, one far removed from the usual meaning of the Arabic term.[18]

Aslan's apologetic here and Ali's translation of 4:34 shows how hard it is for moderate Muslims to simply go against the plain teaching of the Qur'an. It is far easier for them to adopt minority, strained, truncated or even tortuous explanations of the Qur'an than to openly question the sacred text. On the issue of minority translations, Aslan might have been better off to quote the wording of Laleh Bakhtiar, the first woman to translate the Qur'an.[19] She offers a less startling rendering than Ahmed Ali but still avoids the use of "strike" or "hit" or "beat" or any synonym. Her translation reads, "But those whose resistance you fear, then admonish them and abandon them in their sleeping place then go away from them."[20]

Whether Ali or Bakhtiar, however, troublesome issues remain for Aslan's apologetic on 4:34. David Cook, a scholar of Islam at Rice University, states,

> creative re-interpretations of this verse, coupled with other attempts by feminists to get around the plain meaning of the text, tell us much about the defensive attitude towards the verses and are more about the translators themselves and their difficult relationship with the text than they are about the meaning of the Qur'an.[21]

He notes that some translators, including Ahmed Ali, cite the hadith, which states, "Do not beat God's handmaidens."[22] Cook writes,

> It is of course arbitrary and intellectually dishonest for Ahmed Ali, who just finished telling us in his Qur'anic translation that the verb *daraba* does not mean 'to beat' but 'to go to bed with' to then inform us that this new and unusual interpretation is *proved* by a tradition that uses the verb *daraba* to indicate the prohibition of beating.[23]

In relation to surah 4:34, Ayesha S. Chaudhry's new book *Domestic Violence and the Islamic Tradition* is important in terms of dealing with dissonance with objectionable material in the Qur'an. She recounts, as a Canadian Muslim academic, her journey to face her own difficulties with the text of surah 4:34.[24] The passage disturbed her first in middle school and then through her university studies. She asks of the Qur'an, "Why are men allowed to hit their wives at all, however lightly? Why is violence ever the correct answer to marital dispute? And why had God interrupted human history to divinely sanction the right of husbands to hit their wives?"[25]

Chaudhry went on in her doctoral work to examine pre-colonial Islamic thinkers on the interpretation of 4:34. She was astonished to discover that "not a single pre-colonial Islamic jurist or exegete interpreted Q. 4:34 in a way that forbids husbands from hitting their wives."[26] Her dismay was balanced by the discovery that post-colonial Muslim scholars have questioned the traditionalist narrative. Chaudhry stresses the value of the Muslim's "performative relationship" with both the Qur'an and the varied Muslim communities who respond to the text in different and complex ways.

Chaudhry wants to avoid a PR image "of a presentable and palatable Islam" where uncomfortable issues are avoided. While she shares Aslan's postmodern hermeneutic, her treatment of 4:34 does not duplicate his rather facile handling.[27] Also, unlike him, she faces clearly difficult reports about

Muhammad's alleged approval of wife beating. Chaudhry's difficulties come at the level of whether her sophisticated "performative relationship" with the Qur'an comes at too great a price in terms of its subjectivity. While she is properly concerned about "text fundamentalism," an overemphasis on community hearing can lead to text obliteration.[28]

---

## The Issue of Female Circumcision

In recent years, the world community has been alarmed by the practice of female circumcision, which is also known as Female Genital Mutilation (FGM).[29] This ritual is done in approximately 30 countries worldwide but not always for reasons related to Islam. It involves different procedures depending on how much removal takes place. The World Health Organization issued a statement against female circumcision in 1997 and another in 2008.[30]

No one seems to trace the practice to the Qur'an, but some Muslims defend it on the basis of several hadith. The Shafi school of law mandates it for both males and females, while the other Sunni schools obligate it for males but allow it for females.[31] Bohra Muslims (a branch of Shia Islam) practice it in some parts of India and Pakistan. Those Muslims who advocate female circumcision claim that the practice has some benefits: (a) protects girls from sexual temptation, (b) increases the wife's sexual satisfaction during intercourse and (c) surrounds girls in love during the ceremony itself. Voices against the practice are growing stronger in the worldwide Muslim community, with some websites presenting graphic pictures of the rituals to raise awareness.[32]

---

## Troublesome Issues in the Qur'an

At the outset of this chapter, we quoted Aslan's high estimate of the Qur'an on women and highlighted some very positive statements from the Qur'an itself. Aslan and most Muslims are reluctant to admit that the Qur'an contains very troubling passages in regard to the status and treatment of women. Aslan admits that the Qur'an "was deeply affected by the cultural norms of society in which it was revealed"[33] but says nothing directly against any specific Qur'anic material. Aslan obviously admires Muslim female scholars who argue that the Qur'an and its "message of revolution-ary social egalitarianism—must be separated from the cultural prejudices of seventh century Arabia."[34] This, however, does not change some problem-atic teachings that come in the Qur'an itself.

Such realities are covered in Ruth Roded's masterful survey "Women and the Qur'ān."[35] She writes that "symbolically, the concept of woman in the Qur'an is undoubtedly that of a being who is considered to be weak, flawed or passive." Menstruation is viewed disparagingly (see surah 2:222). Women, Roded claims, are viewed in a "subaltern" manner (surah 4:2–3, 75, 98, 127). The rights of women are sometimes lower than men (surah 2:228), and a woman's testimony is not equal to a man's (surah 2:282). She draws attention to the famous and controversial passage in the Qur'an that a Muslim man "may conclude an agreement with a virtuous woman for sexual relations in return for a fee and this is not considered illicit" (surah 4:24). This is the classic verse used to support temporary marriages in Shia Islam.[36] While Roded celebrates various high points in the Qur'an on women, includ-ing property rights, and documents the feminist turn in scholarship on the Qur'an as Aslan does, she contends that "the overall image of women in the Qur'an is ambivalent."

## Women in Modern Islam

As complex as the debate is over the ideals of Islamic orthodoxy, it is obviously much more difficult to write with accuracy about the actual realities of life for Muslim women in a global setting. Given the global Muslim population, the diversity of Muslim states, the power of feminism, the power of traditionalist perspectives, the astonishing debates over the veil and the use of gender as a way to critique Islam, the only thing that is certain is that no one picture can capture what it is like to be a Muslim woman in our day.

Here are some varied snapshots:

Samira Ahmed covers opposing views of the veil among Muslim women globally in the BBC documentary *Islam Unveiled*. She reports, for example, on college students in the United Kingdom who find freedom in veiling, while interviews with an Iranian couple see them choosing to let their nine-year-old go unveiled.

Phyllis Chesler states that honor killings were on the rise in the period between 1989 and 2009. The vast majority of those killed worldwide are Muslim females. There are about five thousand honor killings every year.[37]

Jennifer Zobair, a Muslim American novelist, argues,

> It's time for the media to ask more of itself when portraying Muslim American women. Relentlessly trafficking in stereotypes hurts Muslim women in obvious ways. But it hurts non-Muslims as well. When you hide an entire group of women behind lazy, monolithic and often inaccurate clichés, you impede the understanding and respect that come when people from different backgrounds get to know one another. You discount that we have something to learn from each other. You preclude the possibility of affection. In effect, you keep us from being friends, and that is a loss for all of us.[38]

The Muslim women who make up the Women's Islamic Initiative in Spirituality and Equality (WISE), founded in 2006, contend that "the Muslim woman is worthy of respect and dignity, that as a legal individual, spiritual being, social person, responsible agent, free citizen and servant of God, she holds fundamentally equal rights to exercise her abilities and talents in all areas of human activity."[39]

The 2013 Gender Gap Index shows that most of the lowest ranking nations in the listing of 136 are Muslim majority countries.[40]

Only two females make the list of the top 50 most influential Muslims in the 2013–2014 listing of *The Muslim 500*.[41] They are Her Holiness Sheikha Moza of Qatar and Her Majesty Queen Rania of Jordan.

Mona Eltahawy, an Egyptian-American journalist, wrote the April 23, 2012, cover story for *Foreign Policy* magazine, "Why Do They Hate Us?" with the subtitle "The real war on women is in the Middle East." Her piece created controversy in part because of provocative images of women.

Fareena Alam, born in London and of Bangladeshi heritage, started the website "Islam—The Modern Religion" at age 18. She believes that "Islam's attitude toward woman is a dream come true for anyone who is interested in equal rights and feminism." She has gone on to become a major public figure in Islamic discourse.

Karamah (which means "dignity" in Arabic) was founded in 1993 by Dr. Azizah al-Hibri, a law professor and Islamic scholar at the University of Richmond, in order to establish freedom for Muslim women all over the globe.[42]

204

Farah El-Sharif, a graduate of Georgetown, writes of the liberation she experienced as a Muslim woman during her first *hajj* (pilgrimage to Mecca). She asked her mother to hold her hands as she closed her eyes and walked towards the Ka'ba.

"When Mama said 'We're here, open your eyes,' my lips mumbled a little prayer and my eyes sprung open. It was as if my entire life was leading up to that moment. I felt like I had known this place since birth; like it had been waiting for me, perhaps because I turned my face to it five times, every day. As if pulled by a magnetic field, I began to float in circles around it and praised my Creator and Sustainer for inviting me here. My heart fluttered, and I felt wiped clean with the wings of angels. I had never felt such joy in my life! I prayed for the eternal joy of this *ummah*, my extended Muslim family."[43]

On November 16, 1999, the Taliban held a public execution of a woman named Zarmeena at the Ghazi sports stadium. She had been convicted of killing her abusive husband while he slept.

Irshad Manji (b. 1968) is a public Muslim intellectual who is pro-lesbian, pro-democratic, pro-Palestinian and pro-Israeli. *The New York Times* called her "Osama bin Laden's worst nightmare." She is director of the Moral Courage Project at New York University and the creator of the PBC documentary *Faith without Fear*. Author of *The Trouble with Islam Today* and *Allah, Liberty and Love*, Manji is the executive producer of Moral Courage TV.[44]

## Summary

These various profiles duplicate the ambivalent realities about women in the life of Muhammad, the Qur'an, shariah law, and Islamic tradition. In general, Islam remains a contested place about and for women. Thankfully, Muslim women are gaining a stronger voice to assert their own identity and framework in some parts of the contemporary Islamic world, but there is a long way to go, a journey complicated by some sad realities in Muslim history, in the Qur'an and even in the traditional Islamic understanding of the prophet Muhammad.

# Chapter 15

# Is Islam a Religion of Peace?

*Jihad, Crusades, Colonialism and the Rise of Terrorism*

September 11, 2001, has forever altered the significance of the word "jihad" to the modern world. While many Muslims assert that the word simply means spiritual struggle, other Muslims use the term in the sense of just war, and still others take "jihad" to mean everything implied in the world of terrorism.

In February 1998, three and a half years before September 11, Osama bin Laden made his own views clear. Along with other extremists from Egypt, Pakistan, and Bangladesh, he issued a fatwa or ruling that called on Muslims "to kill the Americans and their allies—civilian and military." He said that this is "an individual duty for every Muslim who can do it in any country in which it is possible to do it."[1]

The events of 9/11 brought to the fore longstanding debates about jihad, the Crusades, colonialism and the Israel-Palestinian conflict, all of which serve as fodder in the perennial question, Is Islam a religion of peace? The answer to this broad and controversial query depends in part on responses on other questions: What is the teaching of the Qur'an on jihad? How does Muhammad's life and teaching impact understanding of jihad? Is it true that Islam spread by the sword after Muhammad's death? What does shariah law mandate on jihad?

## Aslan's Perspective under Scrutiny

Reza Aslan devotes a whole chapter of *No god but God* to jihad. His overall position can be captured in 15 key points, ones that would be held by most mainstream Muslims in the West and the rest of the world.

1. The perception of Islam as "a warrior religion" is a "deep-rooted stereotype" that "has its origins in the papal propaganda of the Crusades when Muslims were depicted as the soldiers of the antichrist in blasphemous occupation of the Holy Lands (and, far more importantly, of the silk route to China)" (80).

2. "European colonialists systematically plundered the natural resources of the Middle East and North Africa" and "inadvertently" created "a rabid political and religious backlash" that produced "Islamic fundamentalism." This resulted in "the image of the dreaded Muslim warrior" (80).

3. "Today, the traditional image of the Muslim horde has been more or less replaced by a new image: the Islamic terrorist, strapped with explosives, ready to be martyred for God, eager to take as many innocent people as possible with him" (80).

4. "What has not changed, however, is the notion that Islam is a religion whose adherents have been embroiled in a perpetual state of holy war, or *jihad*, from the time of Mohammed to this very day" (80).

5. The doctrine of jihad "was not fully developed as an ideological expression until long after Muhammad's death, when Muslim conquerors began absorbing the cultures and practices of the Near East." The Muslim armies "simply joined in the existing fracas." Every religion of the time was "a religion of the sword" (80–81).

6. The Muslim conquerors did not force conversion upon the conquered peoples (81).

7. "Holy war" was not a term used by Muslim conquerors, and it is in no way a proper definition of the word *jihad* (82).

8. Jihad means "a struggle" "striving" "a great effort" (82).

9. Early Muslim understanding of jihad amounted to "a primitive just war theory" (82) but one way ahead of its time in terms of forbidding killing of non-combatants (85).

10. The true understanding of jihad involves an "outright prohibition of all but strictly defensive wars." See surah 2:190 and 22:39 (85).

11. The negative verses in the Qur'an about attacking others (9:5, for example) were "directed specifically at the Quraysh," the tribe in Mecca that opposed Muhammad (86).

12. The division of the world into the "house of Islam" and the "house of war" is a creation of later Muslim legal scholars who were influenced by the Crusades (86).

13. The just war theories of the Qur'an and the prophet were recaptured by Ibn Taymiyya (1263–1328), who resisted the classical Islamic war theories that allowed non-Muslims who did not convert to Islam to be put to death. Ibn Taymiyya's moderate views influenced Sayyid Ahmed Khan (1817–1898), Chiragh Ali (1844–1895) and Mahmud Shaltut (1897–1963) (86–87).

14. The "colonial experience" in the Middle East in the nineteenth century "gave birth to a new kind of Islamic radicalism." The ensuing Jihadist movements (like that of Osama bin Laden) were shaped in the late twentieth century by figures like the Ayatollah Khomeini and Abdullah Yusuf Azzam (1941–1989) (87).

15. Radical jihadism is "roundly condemned by the vast majority of the world's Muslims" (88).

It is obvious from Aslan's chapter and from this 15-point summary that the last thing Aslan wants to do is link "true" Islam and especially the prophet Muhammad with the dark images associated with the popular understanding of jihad. Proper assessment of Aslan and his mainstream Islamic understanding involves study in six major areas: the teaching and actions of Muhammad, the place of jihad in the Qur'an, the nature of the early Muslim conquests, the development of a doctrine of jihad in Islamic law, the nature of the Crusades and the influence of colonialism in the rise of radical Islam.

## Muhammad and Jihad

Keeping in mind our position that we cannot know with any certainty historical details of Muhammad, we will explore the relationship of jihad and the traditional Islamic understanding of Muhammad's life as a warrior. Reza Aslan works hard to offer a soft version of the prophet in battle. He makes light of the caravan raids that Muhammad led, arguing that they cannot be "considered stealing" even though the raid involved carrying off "whatever they could get their hands on before being discovered."[2] As well, Aslan fails to note the utter significance of these raids as offensive in nature since they involved a military targeting of the Meccan caravans. Al-Waqidi lists seven raids in the first 18 months after the prophet arrives in Medina.[3] Aslan's claim that Muhammad only engaged in the first battle of Badr (624) when attacked rings hollow in light of the fact that Badr's direct cause was the Muslim raid on a large Meccan caravan.[4] Aslan also minimizes the nasty side of that war.[5]

In contrast, Aslan paints a grisly picture of Muslim losses at the battle of Uhud in 625, including the image of a woman named Hind who, in revenge, eats the liver of one of her Muslim enemies. Whether on the caravan raids or major battles, Aslan offers no questioning of Muhammad's motives or actions, no matter the nature of the aggression or the body count. While Aslan is right to note that Muhammad could be magnanimous in victory, as at Badr in 624 and Mecca in 630, the prophet could also be incredibly brutal and unforgiving, at least in the detail of traditional Islam.

This dark side of the traditional Muhammad can be illustrated in many episodes in his life after the exodus to Medina. Three incidents will suffice. First, Muhammad showed no qualms in having hundreds of Jewish men from the tribe of Qurayza beheaded at the infamous Battle of the Trench in 627. While Aslan notes the alleged treachery of this remaining Jewish tribe in Medina, there is something disheartening about Aslan's failure to lament the lack of any grace or pity on the part of Muhammad.[6]

The second incident happened in AD 628 when a Muslim group captured some men who had stolen from the prophet. The hadith on the matter states that the prophet ordered their hands and feet cut off and that "their eyes were branded with heated pieces of iron."[7] Other hadith on the same event report that their limbs were not cauterized and they were left to die. A third event shows that Muhammad's actions were not always defensive in nature. He sent Khalid ibn Walid and other Muslim warriors to attack a Christian prince named Ukaydir in an area known as Duma. There Ukaydir was captured and his brother killed, and the prince was forced to pay tribute to Muhammad.[8]

It is imperative to consider the overarching reality about the traditional Muslim reports. Regardless of the details on this or that raid or battle, once the prophet got power after his exile to Medina the choice was simple: either submit to him or face slavery, subjection or death. This is expressed clearly even by Watt, a very sympathetic biographer. He notes that by 630 "non-Muslim tribes were given the choice between accepting Islam and paying annual tribute. In either case they became members of the Islamic security system. If they refused that, they were killed or enslaved."[9] On balance, it should be obvious that the image of Islam as a warrior religion owes much to the actions of Muhammad as portrayed in Islamic orthodoxy.[10]

This tragic aspect to Muhammad's later prophetic life has been captured in the concerns of Marshall G. S. Hodgson, one of the magisterial historians of Islam.

> It is not just a Christian squeamishness, I think, that points to Muhammad's military measures as a central problem in his prophethood. Every virtue carries with it its own characteristic defects, every perception of truth is accompanied by its own temptations to falsehood. In any tradition, greatness is in part to be measured by success in overcoming the peculiar failings which necessarily accompany the peculiar excellences of the tradition. Christianity has its own pitfalls. A peculiar test of Islam lies in how Muslims can meet the question of war.... Muhammad's prophethood, in fulfilling the monotheistic tendency toward a total religious community, at the same time left his community confronted with that temptation to a spirit of exclusivity that went with any vision of a total community and that received appropriate expression in warfare. The resulting problems came to form a persistent theme of Muslim history.[11]

Here it is altogether significant that Hans Küng shares Hodgson's measured critique of Muhammad on the matter of violence. In his tour de force on Islam, Küng defends the prophet from simplistic allegations about abuse of power but goes on to write,

> Perhaps Muslims would have done better to say more unequivocally that even the Prophet was not a morally perfect man; that possibly he submitted too much to the unwritten laws of old Arab society; that he broke treaties both with the Jews and Meccans simply out of suspicion; that at least in two cases he failed to observe recognized rules of war (for example attacking at a holy time and felling palms) and that he did not shrink from political murder (of Jews), thus causing widespread fear.[12]

Aslan and all Muslims would do well to listen to the wisdom from Hodgson and Küng about Muhammad. As hard as it is, Muslims today could also learn from Muhammad's wife Aisha, who may have had the courage to recognize weaknesses in his actions.[13]

## Jihad and the Qur'an

Aslan's discussion of jihad in relation to the Qur'an is somewhat muddled. This is not surprising since, as Ella Landau-Tasseron notes, "there is no one coherent doctrine of warfare in the Qur'an."[14] Aslan is correct in noting the root meaning of "jihad" as "struggle, striving, great effort." As well, there are some verses in the Qur'an that support his contention that jihad should be understood as a "primitive just war theory."[15] Like many Muslims, Aslan makes too much of the distinction between the "greater jihad" (struggling to obey God) and the "lesser jihad" (which can include military effort). Aslan downplays the extent of the emphasis on the "lesser jihad" throughout Islamic history. On this issue, David Cook makes some cogent observations: "The spiritual, internal jihad is the derivative form, and not the contrary. This is clear from the absence of any mention of the 'greater jihad' in the earliest hadith books.... Nor does the 'greater jihad' find any mention in the later literature on jihad, except occasionally in the most perfunctory form."[16]

Aslan's treatment of jihad is off in other ways. He states, for example, that "war, according to the Quran, is either just or unjust; it is never 'holy.'" While his point is technically correct, Aslan fails to explain why so many experts on jihad have no problem in linking the military understanding of jihad with the words "holy war."[17] He also does not appreciate the fact that the Qur'an justifies the basic idea of holy war without using the term itself. If holy war is the common way of referencing a war that is sanctioned and sometimes even ordered by God, much of the Qur'anic material fits the use of holy war. On this, it is significant that the term "holy war" is used in the very first article of the famous Constitution of Medina.[18]

In spite of the importance and complexity of the topic, Aslan offers a very truncated analysis of jihad and warfare in the Qur'an. His apologetical bias comes out in his simplistic reading of the famous "sword verses" of the Qur'an. The most famous is surah 9:5: "Then, when the sacred months have passed, kill the idolaters wherever you find them, and seize them, and besiege them, and sit (in wait) for them at every place of ambush. If they turn (in repentance), and observe the prayer and give the alms, let them go their way. Surely God is forgiving, compassionate."[19] Aslan also cites the first part of surah 9:29, "Fight those who do not believe in God or the Last Day" and surah 9:73, "carry the struggle to the hypocrites who deny the faith." Aslan writes that "it must be understood that these verses were directed specifically at the Quraysh and their clandestine partisans."[20] Several replies are in order. First, it would be nice for Aslan to show some sympathy for whoever was the target of such sword verses, the Quraysh or whoever. Second, Aslan ignores that the traditional Muslim history of Muhammad claims that the prophet adopted the jihad of the sword verses to those who were not Quraysh. Third, the sword verses were adopted as a key element in traditional Islamic understanding of war.[21]

Aslan argues that these sword verses have been grossly misinterpreted by extremists.[22] This view lies behind the popular sentiment that the militants have hijacked Islam, as President George W. Bush stated just after 9/11.[23] Thankfully, as Aslan points out, the vast majority of Muslims agree with Bush on this point and have contempt for the Islamic terrorist agenda.

As one might expect, Aslan places great emphasis on the "peace" passages of the Qur'an. These verses, of course, must not be ignored, minimized or dismissed, as is the case among some extreme critics of Islam. However, the error in that direction should not be matched by Aslan's failure the other way. The famous and wonderful words of surah 2:256 ("Let there be no compulsion in religion") and of surah 5:32 ("whoever kills a person, except (in retaliation) for another, or (for) fomenting corruption on the earth, (it is) as if he had killed all the people. And whoever gives (a person) life, (it is) as if he had given all the people life") cannot work like a magic wand to erase the reality of the many brutal verses in the Islamic sacred text.[24] This is especially true given the influence of the Qur'anic material immediately following Muhammad's death, not to mention the ways in which Muslim law came to emphasize the sword verses.

## Early Muslim Conquests

Three claims in *No god but God* are of immediate relevance in examining martial developments in the Muslim community after the demise of Muhammad. (1) Aslan states that the "the most important innovation" in jihad teaching involved the "outright prohibition of all but strictly defensive wars."[25] (2) In relation to the expansion of Islam, he argues that "the Muslim conquerors did not force conversion upon the conquered peoples; indeed, they did not even encourage it." (3) After the prophet's death Muslims built their understanding of war in part from the religious ideologies of the Persian and Byzantine empires and their various land grabs. In those days, Aslan states, "*every* religion was a religion of the sword."[26]

These points seem designed to dull any real or deep concern about the early Muslim conquests. In response, things are not as cozy as Aslan suggests. First, the conquests immediately after Muhammad's death were anything but defensive. These are known as the *ridda wars* and took place from 632–634. During this time Muslim soldiers subdued all of Arabia under the banner of Islam.[27] Second, after the subjection of all of Arabia to Muslim rule, the Islamic armies swept across the Middle East, through North Africa, into Spain, into southern Europe, and conquered territory as far east as modern-day Pakistan. Large areas of the Byzantine Empire came under Islamic control, and the Sasanian Empire was basically crushed. While most Jews, Christians and Zoroastrians were allowed to practice their religion, they became subject to the laws of *dhimmitude*. While dhimmi status is not slavery, it was certainly, with rare exception, second-class citizenry.[28]

Aslan emphasizes that Muslim soldiers did not force conversion by the sword as they swept out of Arabia. As Patricia Crone has noted, this fact is well known by almost all scholars, but it is overplayed by both Muslim apologists like Aslan and other scholars who should know better. Crone has a blistering attack on Fred Donner's equivocations on the early Muslim conquests in his new book *Among the Believers*.

Crone writes,

> The claim that the "violent conquest" model should be discarded is ultra-revisionist: It goes against the testimony of *both* contemporary sources (as Donner acknowledges) *and* the later tradition, about which he himself has written a well-known book. Now he speaks of the "conquerors" and "conquered" people in quotation marks. But at the same time he still grants that there were campaigns and battles; he even gives us a summary based on his 1981 book, *The Early Islamic Conquests*. He also admits that there was some pillaging and taking of captives, though (once more going against the contemporary sources) he does his best to belittle both activities. But if you occupy a country by means of battles, in what sense have you *not* engaged in "violent conquest"? The expression is surely a tautology. What Donner turns out to mean is simply the well-known fact that the Muslims did not engage in systematic destruction of towns, churches, and other religious buildings, and that they were not out to impose their religion by force. The "violent conquest" model is wrong, he tells us, because it is predicated on the mistaken notion that the "conquerors" (his quotation marks) came with the intention of imposing a new religion by force on local populations. How seriously is one

meant to take this? No scholar believes that the Muslim conquerors were out to impose their religion by force; even going back a century or more I cannot think of any who has espoused this view.[29]

While it is comforting to know that Jews, Christians and Zoroastrians were not converted at the point of a sword,[30] Aslan should not make too much of that, given the coercive and often brutal nature of the conquests, as Crone argues. It is also telling that Aslan shows absolutely no angst over the fact that polytheists and pagans were often told to convert or be killed. This grim reality gets one parenthetical sentence in his treatment of jihad.[31]

It is also significant to note that Aslan cannot seem to make up his own mind about Islam as a warrior religion. On one page of *No god but God* he calls the charge a stereotype, while on the very next page he admits it is a "religion of the sword."[32] On this, one can easily imagine that many of the victims of various Muslim conquests would have used exactly that description of Islam as they experienced the terrors, muted or otherwise, connected with military invasion.[33]

## Jihad and Islamic Law

As with his discussion of jihad in the Qur'an, Aslan offers a jumbled treatment of jihad in Islamic law. He regards classical jihad theory in Islamic law as distinct from the "just war theories of the Qur'an and the prophet." Aslan argues, as noted previously, that classical shariah law "allowed non-Muslims who did not convert to Islam to be put to death." Aslan is trying to make too fine a point. First, the inconsistent teaching of the Qur'an on jihad means that the Islamic Scripture hardly works as a stellar example of a just-war document. Second, and more important, the Muhammad of the *sira* and *maghazi* literature offers no real clarity, given the contradictory data about him in relation to just-war practice. Third, classical Islamic jurists who wrote on jihad often have elements of a "just war" perspective in their rulings and guidelines.[34] This was accented just after 9/11 when the Islamic Research Council at Al-Azhar in Cairo declared,

> Islam provides clear rules and ethical norms that forbid the killing of noncombatants, as well as women, children, and the elderly, and also forbids the pursuit of the enemy in defeat, the execution of those who surrender, the infliction of harm on prisoners of war, and the destruction of property that is not being used in the hostilities.[35]

215

The same outlook was adopted in September 2014 when major Sunni scholars wrote "An Open Letter to Al-Baghdadi" (the leader of the Islamic State) and offered a just-war critique of the actions of the terrorist group. "Jihad in Islam is defensive war. It is not permissible without the right cause, the right purpose and without the right rules of conduct."[36] One could only wish that the Islamic terrorists would follow the Al-Azhar perspective and the views defended in the open letter to the head of the Islamic State.

---

## Canadian Council of Imams Statement on ISIS

"We categorically condemn the actions of this group and its monstrous crimes against humanity, absolutely and without equivocation. ISIS has manifested some of the worst and barbaric human behaviour by mercilessly and brutally killing innocent people, looting, robbing, kidnapping and enslaving hundreds of Muslim and non-Muslim women and children and committing all kinds of atrocities against religious minorities. We call upon all Canadian Muslims to denounce this deliberate perversion of the Muslim faith and to dissociate themselves totally from such a despicable ideology and dangerous people who intentionally use the name of Islam in their ongoing campaign of distortion and destruction."

Quotation from http://www.canadiancouncilofimams.com

---

## Jihad and the Crusades

Like many Muslims, Aslan distorts the nature of the infamous Christian Crusades of the Middle Ages and makes some serious historical errors. First, the view that Islam is a warrior religion started long before the Crusades, so Aslan is wrong to assert that the papal propaganda of the Crusades provides the roots of the stereotype.[37] Second, the division of the world by Islamic jurists into *dar al-Islam* and *dar al-Harb* occurred two or three centuries before Pope Urban II started the First Crusade in 1095. Scholars of jihad trace the division back to the eighth century AD.[38]

Third, on a more technical point, Aslan has misinterpreted the major Islamic figure Ibn Taymiyya (1263–1328) as an influence on later moderate Muslims.[39] Contrary to Aslan, this medieval Muslim thinker was no moderate. Rather, he had a significant impact on the founder of the Wahhabi movement in Saudi Arabia[40] and later radical Islamists like Hasan al-Banna (1906–1949), Sayyid Qutb (1906–1966) and Mawlana Mawdudi (1903–1979).[41]

Fourth, major scholars of the Crusades would not support Aslan's innuendo that the Christian soldiers were after "the silk route to China." Thomas Madden writes, "I know of no other instance in human history in which so many soldiers marched thousands of miles from their home and endured numerous hardships deep in enemy territory for no good strategic or economic reasons. Their reasons had much more to do with the next world than with this one."[42] There is no mention at all of the "silk route" in *God's War*, Christopher Tyerman's massive and authoritative work on the Crusades.[43]

Regardless of this detail, in the large scheme of things Aslan is following standard Muslim and anti-Western apologetic about the Crusades.[44] While nothing can excuse the brutality of the Crusades, particularly in the capture of Jerusalem (1099) and the sack of Constantinople (1204), the Christian Crusades were essentially a religious and military response to the Islamic crusades of the preceding centuries and the Muslim takeover of lands once held by Christian powers.

All in all, no amount of vilification of the Western crusaders can erase the fact that Muhammad engaged in his own conquests, as did the Muslim armies after him, at least if Islamic tradition is accepted at face value. Jihad as military conquest is part of Muslim history from Muhammad to the present. Muslim military campaigns continued after the initial Islamic conquests in the seventh century. Whether under Muhammad bin Qasim at Debal in India (711), Saladin at the Battle of Hittin (1187), Timur at the sacking of Delhi (1398) or Mehmed II at the fall of Constantinople (1453), Muslim armies readily matched Christian Crusaders in brutality. One eyewitness at Constantinople wrote,

> Nothing will ever equal the horror of this harrowing and terrible spectacle. People frightened by the shouting ran out of their houses and were cut down by the sword before they knew what was happening. And some were massacred in their houses where they tried to hide, and some in churches where they sought refuge. The enraged Turkish soldiers...gave no quarter. When they had massacred and there was no longer any resistance, they were intent on pillage and roamed through the town stealing, disrobing, pillaging, killing, raping, taking captive men, women, children, old men, young men, monks, priests, people of all sorts and conditions.[45]

As with the military leaders in the Christian Crusades, Muslim leaders framed their battles in religious discourse. Saladin is the most famous Muslim warrior through the time of the Crusades. In 1181, he claimed that he would keep on fighting "until the word of God is supreme and the Abbasid caliphate has wiped the world clean, turning the churches into mosques." Later, he told of plans to cross the sea to the islands of the Crusaders "to pursue them until there remains no one on the face of the earth who does not acknowledge Allah."[46] Current radical Muslim groups claim to be standing in the tradition of the prophet and warriors like Saladin.[47]

## Colonialism and the Rise of Militant Islam

Parallel to the use of the Crusades for polemical purposes, Aslan and other Muslims often use the foil of colonialism in writing about militant Islam and terrorism. Once again, nothing here is meant to excuse all the evils connected with colonialism. Some of Aslan's depictions on the matter make very depressing reading, most notably his searing indictment of British colonialism in India and Egypt. Further, Islamic complaints about American imperialism are sometimes on target, though often overdone and one-sided.

What Aslan specifically and Muslims generally need to resist is the urge to draw only one causal line—a colonial one—from Islam at the start of modernity to the rise of jihadism or from the realities of British, French, German, American or Dutch imperialism to the emergence of figures like Ayatollah Khomeini and Osama bin Laden. The causal factors and the connections are there but need to be expressed with care and balance.[48] Otherwise, it is too often the case that insufficient attention is paid to other factors, especially internal ones, in the rise of Islamic militancy and terrorism. One thinks immediately of various elements in the traditional Islamic view of Muhammad, the dark currents of Muslim history and the use of the sword verses of the Qur'an.

## A Self-Critical Stance

The enormous failures in the West must not keep Muslims from self-critical awareness about horrendous aspects of various Islamic societies and movements in the past and around the globe today. In terms of near history, the connections between Nazi leaders, including Hitler, and various Islamic figures, especially Amin al-Husaini (one-time Grand Mufti of Jerusalem), are enormously troubling.[49] Al-Husaini managed to exploit British, German and French colonialists in his long hatred of the Jews. Tragically, there is growth of radical anti-Semitism in contemporary Turkish circles, even among the educated and political elite, where Hitler is celebrated.[50] Of course, adherents of every religion or ideology need to be self-critical and aware of how corruption permeates all political, secular and religious enterprises. On this score, Robert Fisk, though not without fault, is helpful for his multi-faceted and searing indictment of all sides in the Middle East tragedy of the last century and more.[51]

Is Reza Aslan self-critical about his analysis of Islam? The record is divided. On the one hand, he realizes the enormous costs paid in liberty and life in various historical and modern corruptions of the higher Islam he defends. Thus, he is properly critical of many aspects of traditionalist Islam. As well, he has warned about the persecution of Christians in the Middle East.[52] These gains are offset, however, by his inability to critique the standard Muslim view of Muhammad, the Qur'an and jihad. This leaves Aslan blind on many topics, as we have shown.

---

### Aslan on Iran

In *No god but God* Aslan makes an offhand comment about modern Iran that is stunning. After noting "the corruption and ineptitude" of Iranian authorities and uncertainty about "whether the Iranian experiment will ultimately prove successful" Aslan writes, "However, not since the Prophet Muhammad attempted to build a new kind of society in Medina has a more significant experiment in nation building been attempted."[53]

---

Sadly, events since *No god but God* was revised and published in 2011 have done little to justify his optimism about Iran or the new Islamic reformation that he claimed has already started. Nevertheless, those like him and Mustafa Akyol, author of *Islam without Extremes*, who argue for liberty on the basis of Islam should be celebrated on that fundamental matter, as much as one disagrees with them on other issues.[54]

The theme of Islamic self-criticism has been accented by Kanan Makiya, author of the famous works *Republic of Fear* (on Saddam's Iraq) and *Cruelty and Silence.*[55] He wrote in London's *Observer* just after 9/11 that Muslims will pray a price if they continue to wallow in the sense of one's own victimhood to the point of losing the essentially universal idea of human dignity and worth that is the only true measure of civility. Arabs and Muslims need today to face up to the fact that their resentment of America has long since become unmoored from any rational underpinnings it might once have had; like the anti-Semitism of the interwar years, it is today steeped in deeply embedded conspiratorial patterns of thought rooted in profound ignorance of how a society and a polity like the United States, much less Israel, functions. After reference to the greater jihad (the spiritual fight to be faithful to God) he mentions "the terrorists and suicide bombers and all those who applaud or find excuses for them" and states "to exorcise what they have done in our name is the civilizational challenge of the twenty-first century for every Arab and Muslim in the world today."[56]

The issue of jihad and its relation to Islamic identity has emerged again as a global issue in 2014 with the kidnapping of girls from a school in Nigeria by Boko Haram and the emergence of the Islamic State with its beheadings of journalists, calls for sexual jihad, killings of non-combatants and rape of enslaved captives.[57] In the frenzied reactions to this new round of terrorism, debates return to the questions that arose after 9/11: What is jihad?[58] Is Muhammad a prophet of peace? Is Islam a religion of peace?

Obvious truths are missed whenever issues are controversial, and such is the case in the debate over the proper analysis of Islam. In spite of that, we have no hesitation in answering the three questions. Based on our study, we believe that the truth is obvious except to those blinded by ignorance, political correctness (even and sometimes especially among scholars) or zeal for Islam.

What is jihad? According to traditional Islamic sources, it is the term for both inner spiritual struggle and external battle against the enemies of Islam. The latter includes warfare. This answer, based on the Qur'an, sira, maghazi material, hadith and shariah law, opposes those who argue that jihad is only inner struggle. Scholars who say the latter are allowing political correctness to blind them to the obvious.

Is Muhammad a prophet of peace? If we accept the Qur'an and other traditional Islamic sources (sira, hadith, maghazi and tafsir material) at face value, any argument that Muhammad is a prophet of peace or that he could be a peacemaker at times must include penetrating recognition that he conquered enemies as a warrior, engaged in killings, fostered slavery, ordered torture and approved of assassinations. In other words, contrary to Karen Armstrong, the traditional Muhammad is no Gandhi.

Is Islam a religion of peace? Thankfully, it has been at various times in various countries and is today in various settings a religion of peace. However, sadly, both in the past and today, it is sometimes not a religion of peace but one of conflict, war and terror. Those who say Islam is a religion of peace without qualification are missing the obvious elements against peace in the Qur'an, the traditional view of the prophet, Islamic history and shariah law.

## Which Path to Follow?

| Allow, Encourage or Permit? | Liberal/ Moderate Islam | Al-Qaeda/ Islamic State | Traditional Muhammad of Qur'an, Sira, Maghazi, Hadith and shariah law* | Jesus of New Testament |
|---|---|---|---|---|
| Female Genital Circumcision | No | Yes | Yes | No |
| Stoning for Adultery | No | Yes | Yes | No |
| Hands Cut Off for Stealing | No | Yes | Yes | No |
| Raping Slaves | No | Yes | Yes | No |
| Beheadings | No | Yes | Yes | No |
| Wife Beatings | No | Yes | Yes | No |
| Torture | No | Yes | Yes | No |
| Death of Apostates | No | Yes | Yes | No |

*As noted in earlier chapters, there is divided evidence on some issues in the list. For example, the Qur'an does not command death to apostates. Likewise, not all schools of Islamic law mandate female circumcision and the evidence for female circumcision is weak in the hadith literature, though not totally absent. Even with these nuances, however, the traditional sources create very troubling realities for moderate Muslims. How their vision of Islam is to be reconciled with the traditional Muhammad is their most significant intellectual and moral challenge.

Our answers to these three questions suggest very stark and unsettling aspects to Islam. This cannot be denied. The same applies to Christian faith if one has in mind some of the military passages in the Old Testament and aspects of Christian history after Constantine wedded Christian faith to state power.

Does this mean that Islam and Christianity are on equal footing? In many respects, yes, given their bloody histories. However, they are not on equal ground if one studies the traditional life of Muhammad and the Jesus pictured in the New Testament. Jesus commanded love for enemies, did not engage in war, had no army, did not sanction torture, did not own slaves and ordered no assassinations. Unfortunately, the traditional Muhammad of Medina did not follow the path of Jesus. In light of this, we suggest that that the gospel of Jesus is a better alternative than Islam, and to this we offer some conclusions in our final chapter.

# Chapter 16

---

# Easter Truths, Muslim Realities and Common Hope

## *Missing Jesus*

M issing the truth about Jesus of Nazareth is a tragedy. For the vast majority of Muslims this involves denial of the deity of Christ, his death on the cross and his resurrection. While Reza Aslan recognizes that Jesus died on the cross, he misinterprets the nature and meaning of Calvary because of his implausible zealot thesis. Most Muslims miss Easter truths because they deny Calvary, whereas Aslan misses Easter because of his skepticism about miracles in the New Testament.[1] In either case, missing Jesus is the saddest reality to note about Islam.

This verdict depends, of course, on seeing the implications of the argument of our book.

We believe that the evidence presented in our chapters clearly shows five basic truths:

The New Testament is the most important and trustworthy source about Jesus of Nazareth.

Reza Aslan is a very unreliable guide on Jesus (and Islam).

The Qur'an and Islamic tradition are untrustworthy guides on Jesus.

The traditional Muslim view of Muhammad is not supported historically.

The traditional Muslim view of Muhammad has serious moral problems.

If accepted, these fundamental points lead obviously to an epistemic crisis for Muslims, regardless of whether or not Islam is a religion of peace. Even if all Muslims were pacifist and jihad was never about war or terror, many of Islam's essential teachings are not true. The falsity of Islam overall does not mean that the Qur'an is totally wrong or that the traditional Muhammad of Islamic faith is without any merit. Nevertheless, if Muslims care about Jesus as a prophet from Allah, they must turn to the New Testament as the true source for the deeds and teaching of Jesus.

So, as the introduction noted, we extend to our Muslim readers and every non-Christian an invitation to consider the gospel of Jesus Christ as presented in the New Testament as the highest gift God has ever given to humanity. As we said in the introduction, we are not claiming that Christianity has no problems.[2] We struggle, for example, with issues like pain and evil, tough passages in Jewish and Christian Scriptures, and the mysteries of the Trinity. In the end, however, we believe that the beauty and truth of Jesus as Savior and Lord outweigh doubt and difficulties in the Christian story.[3]

Do we expect Reza Aslan and other Muslims to become followers of the Jesus of the New Testament? Well, we hope so. However, even with all that is meant by the miraculous realities of the first Easter, we are realistic about how hard conversion would be for Muslims. Most Muslims are simply unable to hear of any critique of Muhammad or the Qur'an. As well, it is humanly impossible for the majority of Muslims to even contemplate the worship of Jesus, especially given the anti-Trinitarian overtones in the Qur'an.[4] We also recognize that conversion to Jesus means family and social breakup and in some Muslim countries death for apostasy.

Why then persist in evangelism about the gospel? With other Christians, we do so because we believe this is the command of Jesus. We respect the Muslim's right to evangelism (dawah) and sharing what he or she believes to be true. Reciprocally, we hope Muslims will understand our desire to share what we believe is true, especially regarding the positive news of the gospel.[5]

For Muslims, embracing the gospel will mean a deeper understanding of God the Father's grace, the filling of the Holy Spirit, assurance of salvation, liberation from the demands of Islamic law, and a new life rooted in a grasp of the truths of the death and resurrection of Jesus.[6] In this regard, we believe that the argument of our book places Muslims in the same situation that the apostle Paul faced when he was on the road to Damascus. In his case we find a radical monotheist faced with the evidence that Jesus is the risen Savior, Son of God and Lord. As the New Testament reports, Paul turned to Jesus and claimed that it was more than worth the cost he paid.

## Aslan on Miracles and Easter

Reza Aslan is confused on both the issue of miracles and Easter. First, he cannot seem to make up his mind on the reality of the super-natural. In *Zealot* his Enlightenment rationalism is on full display, as he regularly dismisses miracle claims about Jesus by simple dictate.[7] In *No god but God*, however, he implicitly accepts the Qur'an as the "miracle" text given to Muhammad and writes constantly of the Qur'an as a "revealed" text.[8] So, God can speak a miracle text through Muhammad but cannot do a miraculous deed through Jesus?

Second, Aslan allows his Enlightenment skepticism to unduly shape his attitude toward historical analysis of miracle claims. Aslan wants to drive a wedge between history and faith. Thus, after conceding that belief in the resurrection of Jesus was part of the earliest Christian testimony, Aslan writes, "the fact remains that the resurrection is not a historical event. It may have had historical ripples, but the event itself falls outside the scope of history and into the realm of faith."[9] Later, he claims that belief in Jesus rising from the dead "is, in the end, purely a matter of faith."[10]

There is no need for Aslan to follow Lessing and Hume in advancing such a gap between history and faith. Serious historians and philosophers remain convinced that Hume's argument against miracles was confusing and logically flawed.[11] Further, historians and philosophers continue to study the resurrection of Jesus as a historical possibility. Antony Flew, the famous atheist philosopher turned deist, thought the evidence for the resurrection of Jesus was very impressive.[12]

While Aslan is ultimately doubtful of the resurrection of Jesus, he does not dismiss the claim as readily as most Muslims. He writes,

> But these first followers of Jesus were not being asked to reject matters of faith based on events that took place centuries, if not millennia, before. They were being asked to deny something they themselves personally, directly encountered. The disciples were themselves fugitives in Jerusalem,

complicit in the sedition that led to Jesus's crucifixion. They were repeatedly arrested and abused for their preaching; more than once their leaders had been brought before the Sanhedrin to answer charges of blasphemy. They were beaten, whipped, stoned, and crucified, yet they would not cease proclaiming the risen Jesus. And it worked! Perhaps the most obvious reason not to dismiss the disciples' resurrection experiences out of hand is that, among all the other failed messiahs who came before and after him, Jesus alone is still called messiah. It was precisely the fervor with which the followers of Jesus believed in his resurrection that transformed this tiny Jewish sect into the largest religion in the world.[13]

At times Aslan's discussion of the resurrection of Jesus is so positive that he sounds like he could be convinced to return to Christian faith.

## Signs of Hope, Paths to Peace

As Christians, our belief in the power of the Easter message provides us some hope in facing Muslim-Christian-Jewish tensions, in spite of the failure of the Arab Spring, the rise of the Islamic State, dreadful military campaigns in Iraq and Syria, terrorist acts in other countries of the world, ongoing hatreds in Israel-Palestinian dynamics,[14] rising tensions in Pakistan and Afghanistan and the blunders of Western powers in the mix of all these tragic realities.[15]

We suggest the following to all parties interested in peaceful resolutions between Muslims and Christians. In spite of all the darkness in radical Islam, the reality of moderate Islam must not be minimized. According to Gallup surveys, more than 90 percent of Muslims worldwide reject radical Islam. In this regard, the 2007 Common Word project initiated by major leaders of Islam is a sign for hope, given its clarion call to pursue peace between Christians and Muslims. The open letter from the Common Word states, "So let our differences not cause hatred and strife between us. Let us vie with each other only in righteousness and good works. Let us respect each other, be fair, just and kind to another and live in sincere peace, harmony and mutual goodwill."[16]

From another angle, it is not hard to find Muslim thinkers who defend a tolerant, open Islam. For example, Khaled Abou El Fadl's *The Great Theft* is a powerful argument against Islamic terrorism and radicalism.[17] Haroon

Sidiqqi, one of the major Muslim leaders in Canada, presents a great version of moderate Islam in his book *Being Muslim*.[18] A major statement from The Canadian Council of Imams offers a peaceful interpretation of Islam.[19] H. R. H. Prince Ghazi bin Muhammad's *Love in the Holy Quran* illustrates clearly that Islam can have a gentle touch.[20] The same is true for the works of Seyyed Hossein Nasr, the great Shia writer and professor at Georgetown.[21] Futher, the global work of Prince Karim Aga Khan IV and his Aga Khan Foundation must be noted as a great example of pluralistic vision for Islam and the world.[22] As much as we have been critical of Islam in this book, nothing is meant to downplay the depth and extent of passion among Muslims for global peace. As well, nothing is meant to minimize great elements in the life of Muhammad, profound passages in the Qur'an or the deep moral integrity of Muslims all over the world.

Conversely, the depth of Christian longing for peace, even among conservative Christians, must be noted. Evangelical Christian leaders (including Lynn Green, Cathy Nobles and Matthew Hand) organized a Reconciliation Walk from 1996 through 1999 to trace the route of the Crusaders and apologize to local Jews, Muslims and Orthodox Christians for the atrocities of the Crusades nine centuries earlier.[23] Rick Love, an American, shared Jesus among Indonesian Muslims for eight years and then worked with the Frontiers mission organization (with its motto "With love and respect, inviting all Muslim peoples to follow Jesus") from 1992 through 2007. After study and work in the Reconciliation program at Yale, he now leads Peace Catalyst International and serves as associate director of the World Evangelical Peace and Reconciliation Initiative.[24] He was also behind the Grace and Truth Affirmation (2009), signed by 50 evangelicals, that offers a very balanced framework. While the signatories could not resolve issues of just war, there was unity on this conclusion: "The commission to 'make disciples of all nations' has not been rescinded. Neither have the commands to demonstrate sacrificial love and to work toward peace. There is no separate gospel for wartime and peacetime."[25]

The same peaceful evangelical stance can be found in the work of Joseph Cumming, pastor of the International Church at Yale and international director of Doulos ministries (Mauritania) and former director of the Reconciliation Program at Yale University's Center for Faith and Culture.[26] Cumming urged Yale University Press not to publish the controversial cartoons of the prophet

Muhammad in their book on the subject. Carl Medearis is another evangelical leader working for peaceful relations with Muslims. Medearis has lived in the Middle East and works on dialogue with all Muslims, including radicals.[27]

It should also help in Muslim-Christian conversation to realize that even strong Christian critics of Islam argue for human rights for Muslims. One thinks here, for example, of Norman Geisler, Christine Schirrmacher, Dudley Woodberry and Lamin Sanneh.[28] Sanneh, an ex-Muslim Yale professor and Roman Catholic, is a critic of Islam but combines that with deep respect for many aspects of his previous religion.[29] Jay Smith, the famous debater of Muslims in Hyde Park (London), and Robert Spencer, the founder of Jihad Watch, are two other examples of note. Even with their strong critiques of Islam, they argue for fundamental liberties for Muslims in spite of verbal and physical threat from various elements in the Islamic world.[30]

Given these signals of hope among Muslims and Christians, given that almost all Muslims, Jews and Christians long for peace, there is no need to overplay whatever "clash of civilizations" truly exists or to demonize everyone who has strong opinions on the Muslim-Christian-Jewish divide. Too much energy is wasted on name-calling (Islamophobic/Islamophile) or categorically questioning the motives of those who have strong opinions about radical Islam, conservative Christianity, the existence of Israel and so on.[31]

Thankfully, even in the stories of Christian crusades and Muslim jihads, there are bright moments. In 1219, during the Fifth Crusade, St. Francis (d. 1221) braved enemy lines to talk peace with the Egyptian sultan. Francis may have been naïve and overly optimistic, but one likes to think he was heading in the right direction.[32] Muslims and Christians today should emulate the willingness of Francis and his Muslim interlocutor to pursue peace. This does not mean avoiding tough realities about Muslim-Christian differences and the dark state of the world but in light of them to work as hard at peace as others do for war and hate.[33]

# Appendix 1

# Reza Aslan's *Zealot*: Wrong at Many Points

There are many curious statements in Reza Aslan's *Zealot: The Life and Times of Jesus of Nazareth*, as well as a number of errors of fact. Often, the problem is one of nuance, in which the reader is left with the impression that what Aslan says represents a widely held opinion among scholars. Frequently, what is said may well be held by some scholars, but there are many others who hold to a different view. In what follows, we review some of what we regard as the most important examples.

In his introduction, Aslan states that Jesus "was a man of profound contradictions" (xxiv), but the evidence he cites for this claim (e.g., in one place Jesus commands his disciples to preach only to Israel and in another he commands them to preach to the Gentiles as well) shows that Aslan has little understanding of the way the Jesus tradition has been edited and compiled in the Gospels. At an early stage in his ministry, Jesus commanded his disciples to preach only to Israel. Later in his ministry, probably in anticipation of the great missionary commission, Jesus commanded his disciples to proclaim the good news of the kingdom of God to the Gentiles. The evangelist Matthew assembles the related missionary teaching in one discourse (Matt 10).

Aslan's discussion of the genre of the Gospels (xxvi–xxvii), their dates of composition and their relationship to eyewitness testimony does not reflect mainstream views. He shows little awareness of the best and most recent scholarship.[1] When he does engage proper works he tends to choose the eccentric and extreme options.

The description of the sacrificial system in the precincts of the Jerusalem temple (4–6) in Aslan's book is quite imaginative, even fanciful, and in places potentially insulting. His description of the "stink of carnage" that "clings to the skin, the hair" and an "insufferable stench of slaughter" (5–6) is illustrative of a remarkable license.

Aslan claims there was no synagogue in Nazareth (25, 35), notwithstanding the fact that the first-century Gospels say there was (Matt 13:53–58 = Mark 6:1–6 = Luke 4:16–30). How does Aslan know there was no synagogue? One pre-AD 70 synagogue after another has been unearthed in archaeological excavations in recent years. When E. P. Sanders published in 1993 *The Historical Figure of Jesus*, he spoke of three pre-AD 70 synagogues that have been found.[2] Twenty years later we now speak of ten, with two additional candidates in the wings.[3] The problem with excavating Nazareth, of course, is that it is a living city. It's not easy to dig beneath homes, businesses and streets. This is why there has been relatively little excavation in Nazareth, which in turn explains why the first-century synagogue has not yet been uncovered (though someday it might be). In any case, several pre-AD 70 synagogues have in fact been found in Galilee, Gaulanitis and Judea. There is no reason to think that there would not have been a synagogue in Nazareth.

Further, Aslan gratuitously asserts that in Nazareth in the time of Jesus "there was little for a woodworker to do" (34). Where does he get that idea? Aslan goes on to inform his readers that as a woodworker, "Jesus would have belonged to the lowest class of peasants in first-century Palestine, just above the indigent, the beggar, and the slave" (34). How does Aslan know this? Later we are told "Nazareth was just a day's walk from…Sepphoris" (38). Actually, it is about a two-hour walk, 45 minutes if one jogs. Aslan speaks of the zealots of Sepphoris. This is highly doubtful. In the time of Jesus, the city, still very Jewish and Torah-observant (as archaeology shows), was accepting of Roman rule.

Demonstrating an argument from omission, Aslan finds the story of Jesus' rebuff at Nazareth suspect (Luke 4:16–30) because "there is no cliff to be pushed off in Nazareth, just a gently sloping hillside" (94–95). Yes, now. But what was the topography 2,000 years ago? Today's "gently sloping hillside" could easily have been a steep drop in the time of Jesus.

Similarly, Aslan's talk of the change in Galilee that took place during the brief interval between Jesus' visit to John the Baptist in Judea and his return home is simply mind-boggling. In this interval, Aslan tells us, the Galilee that Jesus had known—one of "family farms and open fields, of blooming orchards and vast meadows bursting with wildflowers"—had been transformed into something that was "urbanized, Hellenized, iniquitous, and stratified between those who had and those who had not" (93). This is imagination run amok.

Aslan tells us that Capernaum, the small town where Jesus established his headquarters, "stretched along a wide expanse of the seacoast, allowing the cool salt air to nurture all manner of plants and trees" (95). In reading such a misinformed statement, one wonders if anyone proofread Aslan's manuscript. A blunder of this nature is disgraceful and it reflects poorly on the publisher. Aslan is referring, of course, to the body of water popularly known as the Sea of Galilee. It is a fresh-water lake. (Kinneret Lake was its proper name.) There was no cool *salt* air that nurtured anything. In fact, for most of the year the air isn't cool. At 630 feet below sea level, the Sea Galilee is a warm place. Informed readers may be forgiven for suspecting that Aslan has never visited the land where the principal figure of his book once taught and ministered.

Regarding Q, the non-Markan source utilized by the evangelists Matthew and Luke, Aslan makes an odd comment. "The Q material," Aslan writes, "makes no mention of anything that happened before Jesus's baptism by John the Baptist" (29). This is a strange thing to say. Gospel scholars view Q as containing a large portion of Jesus' (and John's) teaching. Why should we expect Q to contain earlier, pre-ministry stories and sayings? One wonders if Aslan actually knows what Q is. The reason there was a Q at all is because John and Jesus were public figures with disciples. These disciples memorized and passed on their masters' teaching, which in time was committed to writing and was eventually taken up in the Gospels of Matthew and Luke. These disciples did not follow John and Jesus when they were children or teenagers, so of course Q preserves nothing earlier than the beginning of their respective adult ministries.

Moreover, Aslan's skepticism with regard to the census, Joseph's journey to Bethlehem and Joseph's belonging to the family of David (29–31) is unnuanced and shows little acquaintance with the best of scholarship relating to the infancy narratives. Aslan does not engage Raymond Brown's learned and detailed *The Birth of the Messiah*.[4]

Aslan tells us that the prophet Jesus ben Ananias, who began preaching in AD 62 or 63, proclaimed "the imminent return of the messiah" (53). This man did no such thing. Josephus, our only source for the activities of this Jesus ben

Ananias (*Jewish Wars* 6.300–309), says the prophet proclaimed the doom of Jerusalem and temple. Ben Ananias said nothing of a return of the Messiah.

Aslan says the "Greek translations of the New Testament" are his. This statement implies an ability to read Greek, but the presence of elementary mistakes leave us wondering. For example, he tells his readers that the Greek word for Jesus' "ambassadors" is *apostolou* (98). That's the genitive singular form ("of an apostle"), which doesn't fit the context. Aslan should have written the plural nominative form *apostoloi* ("apostles"). Some of his translation choices also raise doubts about his competence.

Aslan asserts "all of Jesus's miracle stories were embellished with the passage of time and convoluted with Christological significance" (104). Most scholars would require such a statement to be qualified; others would view it as flat out wrong.

Aslan is correct to say that Jesus was widely viewed as a miracle worker and exorcist, but his assertion that "Jesus was just one of an untold number of diviners and dream interpreters, magicians and medicine men who wandered Judea and Galilee" (105) is confusing and misleading. The confusion is compounded when Aslan later asserts "no doubt Jesus uses a magician's techniques—incantations, rehearsed formulae, spitting, repeated supplications—in some of his miracles" (109). On the contrary, there is plenty of doubt. In two miracles—both healings of a blind person—Jesus touches the eyes of the sufferer with spittle. However, we never hear of incantations, formulae, repeated supplications. It is gratuitous to assert, as Aslan does, that Jesus' utterance in Aramaic, "be opened," was "chanted" (109). In short, Jesus was very different from the professional healers and exorcists. He did not rely on talismans, charms and incantations supposedly handed down from Solomon. He touched or simply spoke the word, and the sufferer was healed. This is a big part of the reason people exclaimed when Jesus performed a work of power: "We never saw anything like this!" (Mark 2:12). If Jesus was no different from "an untold number" of magicians and medicine men, why would people say this?

When Jesus told the man whom he had healed of leprosy to go show himself to the village priest, as the Law of Moses commands in cases of remission (Mark 1:40–45; see Lev 14:2–20), Aslan tells us that "Jesus is joking. His command to the leper is a jest" (112). The suggestion is as ludicrous as it is gratuitous. Aslan's explanation shows that he does not understand the cultural and scriptural background to this story.

Because Jesus' teaching that one should turn the other cheek (Matt 5:39 = Luke 6:29), love one's enemies (Matt 5:44 = Luke 6:27, 35) and pray for those who persecute (Matt 5:44 = Luke 6:28) conflicts with his thesis of Jesus as a zealot, Aslan declares this "picture of Jesus" is "a complete fabrication" (120). We have again nothing more than special pleading. Jesus' teaching conflicts with Aslan's thesis because Aslan's thesis is off target.

The assertion "there is no reason to consider Jesus' conception of his neighbors and enemies to have been any more or less expansive than that of any other Jew of his time" (122) is another completely gratuitous claim. The parable of the Good Samaritan (Luke 10:30–37) suggests that Jesus' conception of his neighbors and enemies was indeed quite different from that of most of his contemporaries.

Aslan's discussion of the trial of Jesus (146–59) is problematic throughout. The trial before Pilate is "pure fantasy," we are told (156). Well, not so pure, it seems. Aslan will later admit to the story containing a "kernel of truth" (158). The Mishnah, a compilation of Jewish interpretations of the Law of Moses, published in the early third century AD, is cited by Aslan as proof that what the New Testament Gospels say about the trial of Jesus is inaccurate. Why a third century AD source, written from an idealized, ahistorical perspective, should trump four first-century sources is not explained.

In keeping with his view that they contain no eyewitness material and really aren't historical works, Aslan assigns remarkably late dates to the New Testament Gospels. He tells his readers that Matthew and Luke were composed "between 90 and 100" AD. Very few scholars date these Gospels that late. Aslan tells us that John was composed "between 100 and 120" AD (190) and that the book of Acts was composed about 40 years after the death of Paul, which would give it a date of about 105 AD (184). These late dates do not represent the mainstream of scholarship. Aslan's reasoning is circular: Because the Gospels are late, they are unhistorical; because they are unhistorical, they should be given late dates. And, of course, because they are late and unhistorical, they contain no eyewitness testimony.

More examples could be cited, but we think these are sufficient. *Zealot: The Life and Times of Jesus of Nazareth* makes for entertaining reading, but the book is rife with errors and dubious choices among the scholarly options. Aslan writes as one who is acquainted with the discipline, but not as one who possesses mastery of the material.[5] His intellectual stature is diminished by his failure to respond to many devastating critiques of *Zealot* (see, most notably, the reviews by Robert Gundry, Allan Nadler, Richard Horsley, John Dickson, Larry Behrebdt, Bart Ehrman, Simon Joseph and Anthony Le Donne) and by his breathless advancing of various inane views, including the one-liner that "all interpretations are valid."

It was announced in late 2013 that Lionsgate plans to turn Reza Aslan's *Zealot* into a movie. David Heyman, famous for his work on the Harry Potter films, is slated as a producer, along with Jeffrey Clifford. It is depressing that Aslan's shoddy book on Jesus might make it to the big screen. More important, there is something deeply unethical in any movie that turns Jesus into a Marxist, zealous revolutionary or Christian jihadist. Is there not enough pushing of violence in our world already? Adding Jesus to that mix made and makes Aslan's book a dishonest and immoral enterprise. Hollywood should not join him.

# Appendix 2

# Was Jesus Married to Mary Magdalene?

Since Muslims have adopted various dubious theories about Jesus, some attention should be given to recent false theories about a so-called lost Gospel. Simcha Jacobovici, producer and host of the Canadian television program *The Naked Archaeologist*, has published another book in which he attempts to undermine the Christian faith. In *The Lost Gospel: Decoding the Sacred Text that Reveals Jesus' Marriage to Mary Magdalene* (HarperCollins, 2014), co-authored with Barrie Wilson, Jacobovici claims to have found and deciphered an ancient text that reveals the truth about Jesus' marital status and relationship to Mary of Magdala.

This newest theory is no more persuasive than his previous ones. Indeed, its misrepresentation of evidence is much more outlandish than usual. No doubt some readers will recall that in 2007 Jacobovici and James Cameron, producer of the movies *Robocop* and *Titanic*, claimed that a tomb south of Jerusalem, in Talpiot, contained the remains of Jesus of Nazareth and Mary Magdalene. Because the DNA samples recovered from their respective burial receptacles (aka bone boxes or ossuaries) indicated that "Jesus" and "Mary" were not blood relatives, Jacobovici concluded that they must have been married.

Immediately archaeologists and historians cried foul, noting that the evidence had been mishandled and some of the authorities that had been interviewed for the documentary had been either misquoted or quoted out of context. Two or three of those interviewed complained of being pressured and harangued. In 2008, a conference was convened in Jerusalem to review the Talpiot evidence. Virtually every scholar present (some 48 out of 50), including Jews and

Christians, historians, archaeologists and biblical scholars, concluded that the Talpiot tomb had nothing to do with Jesus and his family. Unfazed by this almost unanimous conclusion, Jacobovici claimed in the media that he had been "vindicated." Nothing could have been further from the truth.

To compound the silliness, a few years later Jacobovici claimed that he had found a second tomb at Talpiot, about 50 meters from the first tomb, that he believes is a Christian tomb. The appearance of a Christian tomb in the vicinity of the first tomb confirms, Jacobovici thinks, the claim that Jesus was indeed buried in the first tomb. And why does Jacobovici think the second tomb is also a Christian tomb? Because inscribed words and a picture seem to celebrate the resurrection of Jesus. But wait a minute: If the first tomb proves that Jesus was not resurrected but remained in his tomb (enabling the intrepid Jacobovici to recover DNA samples), how do we then explain a nearby tomb celebrating a resurrection that did not take place? Jacobovici doesn't seem to be aware of the breakdown in logic. In any event, it really doesn't matter, for no properly trained archaeologist believes any of it. Serious, sensible scholars in the fields of archaeology and biblical scholarship have ignored Jacobovici's claims.

But Jacobovici doesn't give up easily. He is confident that he has found an old manuscript that confirms his earlier claims. And once again the evidence has been mishandled and egregiously misinterpreted. The old text Jacobovici is talking about in his latest book is actually quite well known. It's a fictional account of Joseph, son of Jacob the patriarch, and his romance and eventual marriage to Asenath, the daughter of an Egyptian priest. The book of Genesis tells us that Joseph married the daughter of the priest of On (Genesis 41:45, 50; 46:20), which embarrassed later conservative Jews. How could Joseph marry a pagan, the daughter of a pagan priest, no less? Good question. Indeed, it is an awkward question that needs to be answered. So somebody wrote *The History of Joseph and Aseneth*, which, among other things, is careful to show that Asenath (also spelled Aseneth) repents of her idolatry and becomes a devout Jewish convert. Then she and Joseph prevent an assassination of Pharaoh, get married and live happily ever after. Jacobovici will have us believe *The History of Joseph and Aseneth* is not really a story about Joseph and Aseneth but an allegory about Jesus and Mary Magdalene in which "Joseph" refers to Jesus and "Aseneth" refers to Mary. No scholar agrees with this.

The long-lost manuscript that Jacobovici is talking about is a sixth-century Syriac translation of the original Greek *The History of Joseph and Aseneth*, a work composed in either the first century BC or the first century AD.[1] The work was never "lost," and it is not a "Gospel," as Jacobovici claims. His assertions could not be more misleading. Neither is the writing an allegory, hinting at and alluding to the story of Jesus and Mary.

*The History of Joseph and Aseneth* is a well-known piece of fiction, which appeared in an English translation and introduction some thirty years ago in a popular and widely read two-volume collection of extra-biblical writings known as the Old Testament Pseudepigrapha.[2] Jacobovici's claim that this is a "lost work" that contains stunning new information, even confirmation of the utterly unsubstantiated hypothesis that Jesus and Mary were married and had children, is blatantly false. Scholars know this; unfortunately many in the reading public do not know this and so will be confused or misled.

What is also unfortunate is that these misrepresentations of evidence discredit the legitimate work that properly trained historians and archaeologists do. We worry that the general public no longer will be able to distinguish reports of genuine and truly significant finds from the exaggerated and false claims made by the hacks and self-promoters like Jacobovici. As a case in point, the synagogue of first-century Magdala, home of Mary of Magdala (i.e., Mary Magdalene), has been uncovered in the last few years. This is truly a significant find. Ongoing work will likely shed further light on what surely was an important village in the public preaching and travels of Jesus. It may also shed light on Mary herself, one of the women privileged to have been numbered among the original followers of Jesus. But will a jaundiced public be receptive to the reports about Magdala that are beginning to be published? Or will the public turn a deaf ear, suspecting (wrongly but understandably) that the discoveries at Magdala are yet more examples of the kind of nonsense that have been advanced in recent years?

We can only hope that the public will be both patient and discerning, knowing that there is real scholarship and honest archaeology, which usually is not sensational or attention-grabbing. In contrast to the charlatans who seek the spotlight, real scholars work more slowly, more carefully, discussing their work with colleagues and eventually publishing after their work has been properly vetted and criticized.

The Jesus and Mary romance theme likely will not disappear any time soon. The profit potential, as demonstrated by Dan Brown's all-time bestselling *DaVinci Code,* is simply too great for the charlatans to abandon. Let us hope that scholars will be willing to be diverted from time to time from their serious work, to correct the false claims and exaggerations of the profiteers and hacks.

# Appendix 3

# Modern Studies on the Qur'an

| Date | Studies |
|------|---------|
| 1534 | Latin translation of Qur'an by Robert of Ketton |
| 1547 | Italian translation by Andrea Arrivabene |
| 1647 | French translation by André du Ryer |
| 1649 | English translation published by Alexander Ross |
| 1658 | Dutch translation by Jan Glazemaker |
| 1698 | Latin translation of Qur'an by Fr. Ludovico Marracci (1612–1700) |
| 1716 | Russian translation by Petr Vasilyevic Pos(t)nikov |
| 1734 | G. Sale, *The Koran, Commonly called The Alcoran of Mohammed* |
| 1806 | Ross version of Qur'an published in USA |
| 1834 | Gustav Flugel edition of Qur'an |
| 1835 | Abraham Geiger writes on Jewish influence on Qur'an |
| 1843 | Gustav Weil (1808–1889), *Mohammed, der Prophet* |
| 1860 | Th. Nöldeke, *Geschichte des Qorāns* |
| 1851 | Aloys Sprenger, *The Life of Mohammad* |
| 1878 | William Muir, *The Life of Mahomet* (1–2 vols. 1858, 3–4 vols. 1861) |
| 1889–1890 | Ignaz Goldziher (Muslim Studies) 1909 Second edition of Nöldeke (with material from F. Schwally) |
| 1918 | Tor Andrae (1885–1947), life of Muhammad |
| 1924 July 10 | Publication of standard Egyptian edition |
| 1930 | Muhammad Marmaduke Pickthall translation |
| 1933 August | Bergstrasser dies hiking |

| | |
|---|---|
| 1933 | Otto Pretzel continues Bergstrasser's work in Munich |
| 1933 | C. C. Torrey, *The Jewish Foundation of Islam* |
| 1934 | Yusaf Ali translation |
| 1936 | Faruq edition of the Cairo Qur'an |
| 1937 | Arthur Jeffery, *Materials for the History of the Text of the Qur'an* |
| 1937–1939 | Translation by Richard Bell (1876–1952) |
| 1938 | Third edition of Nöldeke (with material from Schwally, Bergstrasser and Pretzl) |
| 1938 | Jeffery, *The Foreign Vocabulary of the Qur'an* |
| 1941 October 28 | Pretzel dies in plane crash |
| 1944 | British air force bombs Bavarian Academy of Science |
| 1950 | Joseph Schacht, *Origins of Muslim Jurisprudence* |
| 1955 | Alfred Guillaume translation of Ibn Ishaq |
| 1955 | A. J. Arberry translation |
| 1956 | N. J. Dawood translation |
| 1959 | Jeffery dies on August 2 |
| 1972 | Discovery of Qur'an manuscripts in Sana, Yemen |
| 1974 | Gunter Luling, *Über den Ur-Qur'an* |
| 1977 | John Wansbrough, *Quranic Studies* |
| 1977 | Patricia Crone and Michael Cook, *Hagarism: The Making of the Islamic World* |
| 1977 | John Burton, *The Collection of the Qur'an* |
| 1983 | *Mu'jam al-qira'at al-qur'aniyya* reference work on variants in Qur'an |
| 1987 | Crone, *Meccan Trade and the Rise of Islam* |
| c. 1990 | Spitaler tells Angelika Neuwirth that Qur'an archive not destroyed in 1944 |
| 1992 | Yehuda Nevo dies |
| 1996 | G.-R. Puin, "Observations on Early Qur'an Manuscripts in San 'a,'" in *The Qur'an as Text*, ed. S. Wild (Leiden: Brill, 1996), 107–11 |
| 1999 | "What is the Koran?" *Atlantic Monthly* (Toby Lester) |
| 1999 | G. R. Hawting, *The Idea of Idolatry and the Emergence of Islam* |
| 2000 | Christoph Luxenberg, *Die syro-aramäische Lesart des Koran* |

| | |
|---|---|
| 2001 | Andrew Rippin, *The Qur'an and Its Interpretative Tradition* |
| 2003 | Death of Spitaler |
| 2003 | Yehuda Nevo and Judieth Koren (ed.), *Crossroads to Islam* |
| 2004 | Gunter Luling, *A Challenge to Islam for Reformation* |
| 2005 | Gerd Puin, *Die Dunklen Anfange* |
| 2006–2011 | *Encyclopedia of the Qur'an* (ed. Jane McAuliffe) |
| 2007 | Corpus Coranicum (Angelika Neuwirth, Free University of Berlin) |
| 2007 | Luxenberg, *The Syro-Aramaic Reading of the Koran* (English translation of 2000 work) |
| 2008 | Andrew Higgins, "The Lost Archive," *Wall Street Journal* (January 12) |
| 2009 | G.-R. Puin, *The Hidden Origins of Islam* |
| 2011 | Keith Small, *Textual Criticism and Qur'an Manuscripts* |
| 2012 | International Qur'anic Studies Association (IQSA) founded |
| 2013 | A.J. Droge annotated translation |
| 2013 | Francois Deroche, *Qur'ans of the Umayyads* |
| 2015 | Seyyed Hossein Nasr, Caner K. Dagli, Maria Massi Dakake, Joseph E.B. Lumbard (eds.) *The Study Quran* |

# Appendix 4

---

# New Testament Background and the Growth of Christianity

| | |
|---|---|
| 587 B.C. | The capture of Jerusalem, the destruction of the temple, and the deportation of many Jews to Babylonia. Isaiah 55–66 were written in the aftermath of these events, perhaps as late as 530 BC. One century later, Ezra was a principal figure in the return of some Jews to Jerusalem. |
| 333–32 B.C. | Alexander the Great sweeps through Israel, conquers the Middle East. |
| 324 B.C. | The death of Aristotle, tutor of Alexander. |
| 323 B.C. | The death of Alexander. |
| 270 B.C. | The death of Epicurus (founder of Epicureanism). |
| c. 265 B.C. | The death of Zeno (founder of Cynicism). |
| c. 250 B.C. | The beginning of the work of translation leading to the Septuagint (LXX). |
| c. 180 B.C. | Sirach (or Ecclesiasticus) was written in Hebrew, translated into Greek approximately 50 years later. |
| 167 B.C. | Desecration of the temple by the Seleucid ruler, Antiochus IV "Epiphanes" (i.e. "[Divine] Manifestation"), who ruled 175–164 B.C. Daniel was written shortly thereafter. Material in 1 Enoch began to be compiled; Wisdom of Solomon was perhaps written in the following century. |
| 164 B.C. | Judas Maccabeus (the "hammer") defeats General Lysias; Antiochus IV dies; Judas rules Judea, begins to enlarge borders, Israel as nation is re-established; Hasmonean dynasty is founded; brothers Jonathan and Simon succeed Judas. |
| 160 B.C. | The death of Judas; succeeded by Jonathan. |

| | |
|---|---|
| 142 B.C. | The death of Jonathan; succeeded by Simon. |
| 134 B.C. | The death of Simon; succeeded by John Hyrcanus I. |
| 104 B.C. | The death of John Hyrcanus I (son of Simon); succeeded by Aristobulus I. |
| 103 B.C. | The death of Aristobulus I (son of John Hyrcanus I); succeeded by Alexander Janneus. |
| 76 B.C. | The death of Alexander Janneus (son of John Hyrcanus I). |
| 67 B.C. | The death of Alexandra (wife of Alexander Janneus). |
| 67–63 B.C. | Aristobulus II rules briefly amidst dissension; people appeal to Rome. |
| 63 B.C. | Pompey enters Jerusalem, thus beginning the era of Roman dominance. *Psalms of Solomon* were composed not long after this event. Hyrcanus II (son of Alexander Janneus) is made High Priest. |
| 48 B.C. | Julius Caesar gains mastery over Roman Empire. |
| 44 B.C. | Julius Caesar is assassinated; Mark Antony and young Octavian (grandnephew of Caesar) avenge Caesar's murder and establish Second Triumvirate. |
| 40 B.C. | Roman senate, at prompting of Mark Antony, declares Herod (son of Antipater II) "King of the Jews"; Parthians support Antigonus (son of Aristobulus II). |
| 37 B.C. | Herod defeats Antigonus, last of the Hasmonean rulers, and becomes king of Israel in fact; marries Mariamne (granddaughter of Hyrcanus II); during his reign he rebuilds Jerusalem and the Temple; founds several cities and fortresses; and marries and divorces or murders ten wives. |
| 31 B.C. | Octavian defeats Mark Antony and Cleopatra at Actium; becomes Roman emperor; forgives Herod for siding with Mark Antony; confirms Herod's kingship. |
| 28 B.C. | Octavian assumes the name Augustus. |
| 6 or 5 B.C. | The birth of Jesus. |
| 4 B.C. | The death of Herod the Great. |
| 6 | Archelaus (son of Herod the Great) is deposed. |
| 6–15 | Annas (or Ananus) is appointed high priest. |
| 14 | The death of Augustus; succeeded by stepson Tiberius. |

| | |
|---|---|
| 18 | Joseph bar Caiaphas (son-in-law of Annas) is appointed high priest. |
| 30 or 33 | Jesus is crucified. |
| 34 | The death of Herod Philip (son of Herod the Great). |
| 36 or 37 | Pontius Pilate and Joseph bar Caiaphas are removed from office. |
| 37 | The death of Tiberius; succeeded by Gaius Caligula; the birth of Josephus. |
| 39 | Caligula banishes Herod Antipas (son of Herod the Great) to Gaul. |
| 41 | The death of Caligula; succeeded by Claudius. |
| 44 | The death of (Herod) Agrippa I (son of Aristobulus and Bernice, grandson of Herod the Great), after brief rule over Israel (41–44); cf. Acts 12:1–23. |
| c. 50 | The death of Philo of Alexandria. |
| 51–52 | Tenure of the Roman governor Gallio in Corinth. |
| 52–60 | Tenure of the Roman governor Felix in Caesarea. |
| c. 53 | Paul writes letter to the churches of Galatia. |
| 54 | The death of Claudius; succeeded by Nero. |
| c. 55–56 | Paul writes several letters to the church at Corinth. |
| c. 57 | Paul writes letter to the church at Rome. |
| 60–62 | Tenure of the Roman governor Festus in Caesarea. |
| 62 | Ananus (son of Annas) becomes high priest, without Roman approval convenes Jewish council and puts to death James the brother of Jesus; Albinus removes Ananus from office. |
| 62–64 | Tenure of the Roman governor Albinus in Caesarea. |
| 64–66 | Tenure of the Roman governor Gessius Florus in Caesarea. |
| 64 | Fire destroys half of Rome. |
| 65 | The deaths of Seneca, Peter, and (perhaps) Paul. |
| 66 | The Jewish revolt begins; Roman governor Florus is (perhaps) murdered. |
| 68 | The death of Nero; succeeded by Galba. |
| 68–69 | Brief reigns of Galba, Otho and Vitellius. |
| 69 | General Vespasian, commander of the Roman forces against the Jews, is proclaimed emperor. |
| c. 69 | The Gospel of Mark is published. |

| | |
|---|---|
| 70 | Jerusalem is captured by Titus (son of Vespasian); temple is badly damaged by fire; it is later demolished. |
| 71 | Vespasian and Titus hold great triumph in Rome, celebrating victory over Israel. |
| 73 | General Silva captures Masada. |
| c. 78 | Josephus publishes *The Jewish War*. |
| 79 | The death of Vespasian; succeeded by Titus. |
| 79 | Eruption of Mount Vesuvius; Pompeii and Herculanean are buried. |
| 81 | The death of Titus; succeeded by Domitian (brother of Titus). |
| c. 85 | Revision of twelfth benediction; Christians are excluded from synagogues. |
| c. 93 | The death of Agrippa II (son of Agrippa I), after ruling portions of Israel beginning in 49 (cf. Acts 25:13–26:32); Bernice was his sister. |
| 96 | The death of Domitian; succeeded by Nerva. |
| 98 | The death of Nerva; succeeded by Trajan; death of Josephus (?). |
| c. 112 | The death of Ignatius. |
| 115 | Jewish revolt in North Africa. |
| 117 | Revolt put down; the death of Trajan, succeeded by Hadrian. |
| c. 120 | Tacitus publishes *The Annals*. |
| 132–135 | The great Jewish revolt led by Simon ben Kosiba, dubbed "bar Kokhba." |
| c. 135 | The death of Papias, author of *Expositions of the Sayings of the Lord*. |
| 138 | The death of Hadrian; succeeded by Antoninus Pius. |
| c. 159 | The death of Marcion, whose "canon" excluded the Jewish parts of the New Testament. |
| c. 165 | The death of Justin Martyr, author of *1 Apology*. |
| c. 170 | The death of the gnostic Valentinus; early recognition of the New Testament canon, as reflected in the Muratorian fragment. |
| c. 172 | Tatian, in eastern Syria, publishes the *Diatessaron*, a harmony of the four Gospels (Matthew, Mark, Luke and John). |

| | |
|---|---|
| c. 178 | Celsus publishes *True Doctrine,* in which he criticizes Christianity and mocks the Gospels. |
| c. 180 | Publication of *Against All Heresies* by Irenaeus of Lyons, in which the fourfold canon of the Gospels (Matthew, Mark, Luke and John) was vigorously defended. |
| c. 180 | The publication, in eastern Syria, of an early edition of the *Gospel of Thomas.* |
| c. 185 | Birth of Origen of Alexandria. |
| c. 200 | The final editing and publication of the Mishnah. |
| 217 | The publication of *The Life of Apollonius of Tyana*, by Philostratus. |
| c. 248 | Origen publishes *Against Celsus.* |
| c. 253 | The death of Origen, editor of the *Hexapla* and numerous commentaries. |
| 313 | Edict of Milan, whereby Christianity and all religions are legalized in the Roman Empire. |
| 325 | The Council of Nicea, formulating Christian "orthodoxy." |
| 337 | The death of Constantine, first Christian emperor. |
| 339 | The death of Eusebius, author of *Ecclesiastical History.* |
| c. 360 | The production of the Coptic gnostic library found at Nag Hammadi. |
| 373 | The death of Athanasius, whose festal letter of 367 marks an important moment in the acceptance of the canon of the New Testament. |
| 381 | First Council of Constantinople, convened to unite eastern Church. |
| 420 | The death of Jerome, principal editor and translator of the Latin translation of the Bible, later called the Vulgate. |
| 430 | The death of Augustin(e), author of *City of God.* |
| 431 | Council of Ephesus, convened to deal with Nestorianism. |
| c. 450 | Compilation and publication of the Palestinian version of the Talmud. |
| 451 | The Council of Chalcedon, convened to clarify aspects of Christology and the trinity. |
| c. 550 | Compilation and publication of the Babylonian version of the Talmud. |
| 553 | Second Council of Constantinople. |

# Timeline of Islam

| | |
|---|---|
| 525 | Ethiopian Christians wipe out Arab Jews of Himyar |
| 527 | Justinian becomes Byzantine emperor (r. 527–565) |
| 530 | Beginning of rule of Sassanid Persian emperor Khusro I (r. 530–579) |
| 537 | Dedication of the church of Hagia Sophia in Constantinople |
| 540 | Khusro I takes Antioch, beginning of war between Persia and Byzantium |
| 554 | Byzantine conquest of southern Spain |
| 565 | End of Justinian's rule |
| c. 570 | Birth of Muhammad |
| 582 | Maurice (r. 582–602) becomes Byzantine emperor |
| 591 | Khusro II (r. 591–628) becomes emperor of Persia |
| 602 | Persian/Byzantine warfare (602–629) |
| 610 | Heraclius becomes Byzantine emperor (r. 610–641) |
| 610 | Muhammad's first vision |
| 613 | Persians conquer Antioch |
| 614 | Persians conquer Jerusalem |
| 619 | Persians conquer Alexandria |
| 622 | Muhammad's flight to Medina |
| 622 | Beginning of the Muslim Era (16 July) |
| 629 | Muslims take Mecca |
| 630 | Heraclius returns relics of the Cross to Jerusalem |
| 632 | Death of Muhammad |
| 632 | Abū Bakr becomes caliph or successor to Muhammad |
| 634 | Death of Abū Bakr, the first caliph or successor to Muhammad |
| 636 | Battle of Yarmuk (Muslim control over Syria) |
| 638 | Battle of al-Qadisyya and capture of Jerusalem |

| | |
|---|---|
| 640 | Conquest of Egypt |
| 641 | Capture of Caesarea |
| 642 | Battle of Nihawand (Arabs vs. Persian army) |
| 644 | Death of Umar I (r. 634–644), second caliph |
| 646 | Muslims retake Alexandria |
| 649 | Raid on Cyprus |
| 650–653 | Truce between Byzantines and Arabs |
| 654 | Battle of the Masts (Byzantine loss to Arab sailors) |
| 656 | Death of Uthman (r. 644–656), third caliph |
| 656 | Battle of the Camel (Aisha vs. Ali) |
| 657 | Battle of Siffin (Ali vs. Muawiya) |
| 661 | Assassination of Ali, the fourth caliph from Muhammad and first Shi'a imam |
| 661 | Muawiya I bin Abi Sufyan (r. 661–680), first leader of Umayyad dynasty which ruled from Damascus |
| 668 | Constantine IV begins Byzantine rule (r. 668–685) |
| 668–670 | Attacks on Constantinople |
| 669 | Death of al-Hasan (r. 661–669), second Shi'a imam |
| 680 | Battle of Karbala and murder of Husayn, son of Ali and grandson of the Prophet |
| 680 | Yazid I (r. 680–683), second Umayyad caliph, begins rule |
| 683–692 | Second Civil war |
| 683 | Muawiya II (third Umayyad caliph) |
| 684 | Marwan I (fourth caliph) |
| 685 | Abd al-Malik (r. 685–705), fifth Umayyad caliph and major leader in Islam |
| 69 | Construction of the Dome of the Rock in Jerusalem |
| 691 | Dome of the Rock completed |
| 695 | First Muslim coins are minted |
| 698 | Muslims take Carthage |
| 710 | Arab expansion into Sind |
| 711 | Tareq ibn Zaid invades Spain |
| 715 | Great Mosque of Damascus is completed |
| 717–718 | Muslims are defeated at Constantinople |
| 720 | Muslim attack on Sicily fails |
| 724 | Hisham begins rule as caliph (r. 724–743) |
| 728 | Death of Hasan al-Basri |

| | |
|---|---|
| 732 | Muslims defeated at Battle of Tours (Charles Martel) |
| 750 | Rise of the Abbasid Dynasty (r. 750–1258), based in Baghdad |
| 755 | Rise of independent Umayyad Dynasty in Spain |
| 762 | Baghdad is made Abbasid capital |
| 765 | Split among Shi'ite Muslims over new leader |
| 767 | Death of Ibn Ishaq (b. circa 704) |
| 767 | Death of Abu Hanifa (leading jurist for Indian and Middle East Muslims) |
| 786 | Harun al-Rashid (r. 786–809), Abbasid caliph, begins rule |
| 795 | Death of Malik b. Anas (law maker), author of *Muwatta* |
| 800 | Charlemagne crowned "emperor of the Romans" by Pope Leo III |
| 809 | Fall of Sardinia |
| 818 | Fall of Majorca |
| 820 | Death of al-Safi (law maker) |
| 824 | Fall of Crete |
| 831 | Fall of Palermo |
| 835 | Fall of Malta |
| 850 | Death of al-Bukhari, specialist on Islamic *hadith* |
| 851 | Martyrdom of Christians at Cordova by Muslims |
| 855 | Death of Ahmad ibn Hanbal (b. 780) |
| 870 | Possible Greek translation of the Qur'an by Nicetas Byzantius |
| 871 | Fall of Syracuse |
| 884 | First reported translation of the Qur'an in Alwar (Sindh, formerly India but now part of Pakistan) |
| 902 | Fall of Taormina |
| 923 | Death of al-Tabiri, Muslim historian |
| 940 | Twelfth Shi'a Imam becomes the "hidden imam" |
| 950 | Death of Al-Farabi, the Muslim Aristotle |
| 972 | Founding of Al-Azhar university in Cairo |
| 1017 | Mahmud of Ghazni (d. 1030) plunders north India |
| 1037 | Death of Ibn Sina (aka Avicenna), a great Islamic philosopher |
| 1037 | Ghazni sacked by Tughril |
| 1040 | Seljuk Turks defeat Ghaznavids at Battle of Dandanaqan |
| 1058 | Birth of al-Ghazali in Tus |
| 1064 | Alp Arslan succeeds Kutalmish as Seljuk leader |

| | |
|---|---|
| 1071 | Seljuk Turks defeat Byzantine army at Battle of Manzikert |
| 1072 | Alp Arslan assassinated |
| 1085 | Fall of Toledo |
| 1092 | Nizam al-Mulk murdered by Assassins (October 14) |
| 1094 | El Cid conquers Valencia |
| 1095 | Start of First Crusade by Pope Urban II |
| 1098 | Fall of Antioch to Crusaders (June 3) |
| 1099 | Crusaders capture Jerusalem (July 15) |
| 1111 | Death of al-Ghazali, author of *The Revival of the Religious Sciences* |
| 1118 | Hugh of Payns created Templars |
| 1128 | *In Praise of the New Chivalry*, Bernard |
| 1137 | Birth of Saladin |
| 1144 | Zengi captures Edessa |
| 1145 | Eugenius III launches Second Crusade with *Quantum Praedecessores* |
| 1146 | Bernard of Clairvaux promotes Crusade |
| 1147 | Birth of Ibn Qudamah, prominent Hanbal jurist |
| 1154 | Nur ad-Din captures Damascus |
| 1163 | Saladin sent to Egypt by Nur ad-Din |
| 1175 | Saladin captures areas of Syria |
| 1185 | Saladin makes treaty with Byzantine |
| 1187 | Saladin won Battle of Hattin (July 4) and captured Jerusalem (Oct. 2) |
| 1191 | Battle of Arsuf (Richard vs. Saladin) Third Crusade |
| 1192 | Treaty of Ramla between Richard and Saladin |
| 1193 | Death of Saladin |
| 1196 | Muslim victory at Battle of Alarcos |
| 1198 | Fourth Crusade called by Innocent III |
| 1202 | Zara sacked by Crusaders |
| 1204 | Western Crusaders sack Constantinople |
| 1208 | Albigensian Crusade called by Innocent III |
| 1212 | Battle of Las Navas de Tolosa |
| 1215 | Fifth Crusade called in Ad liberandam during Fourth Lateran Council |
| 1219 | St. Francis meets with al-Kamil during Crusade |
| 1221 | Crusaders surrender in Nile Delta |

| 1229 | Frederick II captures Jerusalem (Sixth Crusade) February |
|------|---------|
| 1236 | Muslim rule lost in Cordoba |
| 1248 | King Louis IX departed for East during Seventh Crusade |
| 1258 | Mongols sack Baghdad |
| 1273 | Death of Rumi (b. 1207) |
| 1291 | Fall of Acre |
| 1295 | Mongol dynasty converts to Islam |
| 1300 | Rise of Ottoman Empire |
| 1307 | Templars suppressed by King Philip IV |
| 1315 | Death of Raymond Lull, Christian missionary to Muslims |
| 1328 | Death of Ibn Taymiyya, leading Hanbali jurist |
| 1356 | Alexandria sacked by Peter I of Cyprus |
| 1389 | Ottomans defeat Serbs at Battle of Kosovo |
| 1426 | Cyprus under Egyptian control |
| 1453 | Ottomans capture Constantinople and rename it Istanbul |
| 1478 | Start of Spanish Inquisition |
| 1492 | Fall of Granada and end of Muslim rule in Spain |
| 1517 | Salim I (Ottoman) conquers Egypt |
| 1520 | Rise of Suleiman the Magnificent, the Ottoman emperor |
| 1526 | Muslim armies under Babur enter India |
| 1530s | Ahmad Gran gains temporary control of large parts of Ethiopia |
| 1563 | Akbar gains power in India |
| 1566 | Death of Suleiman |
| 1570 | Battle of Lepanto |
| 1683 | Ottoman forces defeated at Battle of Vienna |
| 1744 | Pact between Muhammad bin Saud and Muhammad ibn Abd al-Wahhab |
| 1774 | Treaty of Kuchuk Kainardji (Ottoman and Russia) |
| 1791 | Peace reached between Ottomans and Habsburgs |
| 1792 | Death of Muhammad bin 'Abd al-Wahhab (b. 1703) |
| 1796 | Treaty of Tripoli |
| 1798 | Napoleon in Egypt |
| 1803 | Louisiana Purchase |
| 1803 | Wahhabi movement gains control in Saudi Arabia |
| 1806 | End of Holy Roman Empire (Francis II abdicates imperial throne) |

| 1815 | Napoleon defeated at Waterloo |
| 1818 | Muhammad Ali defeats Saudi forces |
| 1830 | France occupies Algeria |
| 1831 | Sayyid Ahmad Shahid killed by Sikhs |
| 1854–1856 | Crimean War |
| 1857 | Indian Mutiny |
| 1881 | British take control of Egypt |
| 1893 | Alexander Russell Webb at World's Parliament of Religions |
| 1897 | Jamal ad-Din al-Afghani dies (March 9) |
| 1897 | First Zionist Congress in Basle (Aug. 29–31) |
| 1902 | Qasim Amin pioneers feminism in Egypt |
| 1902 | Start of third Saudi dynasty |
| 1910 | Oil prospects in Persia |
| 1914 | Start of World War I (Aug. 4) |
| 1914 | Ottoman Empire declares war against Allies (Nov. 11) |
| 1915 | British and French forces defeated at Gallipoli (April) |
| 1915 | Beginning of Armenian genocide |
| 1916 | Arab revolt led by Sharif Hussein against Ottoman rule |
| 1916 | Sykes-Picot agreement between Britain and France |
| 1917 | Balfour Declaration (November) |
| 1920 | San Remo conference |
| 1920 | Lebanon separated from Syria by French |
| 1920 | Arab revolts in Jerusalem (April) |
| 1920 | Formation of the Haganah (Jewish underground militia) |
| 1923 | Turkey becomes republic under Mustafa Kemal Atatürk |
| 1925 | Abdul Aziz ibn Saud captures Mecca from Sharif Hussein |
| 1928 | Muslim Brotherhood founded by Hassan al-Banna (b. 1906) |
| 1929 | Jews killed by Arabs at Hebron (August) |
| 1931 | Formation of the Irgun |
| 1932 | Political independence in Iraq |
| 1936 | Arab revolt in Palestine led by Haj Amin Al-Husseini |
| 1936 | Peel Commission on Palestine mandate (report: 1937) |
| 1939 | Start of World War II (Sept. 3) |
| 1941 | Mohammad Reza Pahlavi becomes Shah of Iran |
| 1946 | Syria gains independence from France |
| 1946 | Irgun bombing of King David Hotel (July 22) |
| 1947 | Creation of Pakistan |

| | |
|---|---|
| 1948 | Jewish attack on Deir Yassan (April 9) |
| 1948 | Founding of the State of Israel (May 14) |
| 1949 | Hassan al-Banna assassinated (Feb. 12) |
| 1952 | Nasser leads coup in Egypt |
| 1953 | CIA aids coup against Iranian leader Mohammad Mosaddeq |
| 1954 | Algerian war of independence begins |
| 1955 | Sudan gains independence from British-French rule |
| 1956 | Suez Canal crisis |
| 1962 | Algeria gains independence |
| 1964 | Formation of the Palestinian Liberation Organization |
| 1965 | Assassination of Malcolm X in New York City |
| 1966 | Sayyid Qutb executed in Egypt (Aug. 29) |
| 1967 | Six-Day War between Israel and Egypt (June 5–10) |
| 1969 | Qaddafi stages coup in Libya |
| 1970 | Death of Egypt president Nasser (Sept. 28) |
| 1972 | "Black September" attack on Israeli Olympic athletes (Sept. 5) |
| 1973 | October War between Israel and Arabs |
| 1974 | Peace treaty between Jordan and Israel |
| 1975 | Start of civil war in Lebanon |
| 1977 | Anwar Sadat makes historic peace trip to Jerusalem (Nov. 19) |
| 1978 | Saddam Hussein controls Baath party in Iraq |
| 1979 | Islamic revolution in Iran under Khomeini (February) |
| 1979 | USSR invades Afghanistan |
| 1979 | Iranian hostage crisis (Nov. 4) |
| 1979 | Seizure of Mecca's Grand Mosque by Juhayman al-Otaybi (Nov. 20) |
| 1980 | Iran-Iraq War (Sept. 22, 1980–Aug. 20, 1988) |
| 1981 | Release of U.S. hostages in Iran (Jan. 20) |
| 1981 | Israel destroys nuclear reactor in Iraq (June 7) |
| 1981 | Assassination of Anwar Sadat (October 6) |
| 1981 | Universal Islamic Declaration of Human Rights |
| 1982 | Syrian army massacres Muslim Brothers in Hama (February) |
| 1982 | Execution (April 15) of Muhammad 'Abd al-Salam Faraj, author of *Jihad: The Neglected Duty* |
| 1982 | Israeli invasion of Lebanon (June 6) |
| 1982 | Massacre at Sabra and Shatila camps in Beirut (Sept. 16–19) |
| 1983 | Attack on U.S. and French soldiers in Beirut (Oct. 23) |

| 1985 | Muḥammad Maḥmūd Ṭāhā executed on January 18 in Sudan for apostasy |
|------|------|
| 1985 | Palestinian terrorists hijack *Achille Lauro* (Oct. 7) |
| 1986 | Killing of Ismail and Lois al-Faruqi (May 27, 1986) |
| 1987 | Meena Keshwar Kamal assassinated (Feb. 4) |
| 1987 | Intifada begins in Palestine |
| 1988 | Pan Am flight 103 blown up over Lockerbie, Scotland |
| 1989 | Muḥammad al-Ghazali writes book against Wahhabi version of Islam |
| 1989 | Iranian *fatwa* against Salman Rushdie for *The Satanic Verses* |
| 1989 | Abdullah Azzam assassinated in Peshawar (Nov. 24) |
| 1991 | Gulf War to liberate Kuwait |
| 1991 | Military conflicts begin in former Yugoslavia |
| 1992 | Siege of Sarajevo begins (April 1992–Feb. 1996) |
| 1992 | Farag Foda (aka Faraj Fawda) executed by jihadists (June 8) in Cairo |
| 1993 | Bombing of the World Trade Center (Feb. 26) |
| 1993 | Oslo Accords (Washington signing Sept. 13) |
| 1994 | Jordan recognizes State of Israel |
| 1995 | Killing of more than 8,000 Muslims in Srebrenica (July) |
| 1995 | Nasr Abu Zaid leaves Egypt on July 23 and settles in Netherlands |
| 1995 | Assassination of Yitzhak Rabin (Nov. 4) |
| 1996 | Osama bin Laden announces Jihad against the U.S. |
| 1996 | Taliban take control of Kabul |
| 1996 | Mullah Omar, Taliban leader, meets Osama bin Laden |
| 1997 | Collapse of Albania |
| 1998 | World Islamic Front issues Declaration against the U.S. (Feb. 23) |
| 1998 | U.S. embassies in Kenya and Tanzania bombed (Aug. 7) |
| 1999 | War in Kosovo |
| 1999 | Second Chechen War and insurgency (1999–2009) |
| 2000 | Vatican issues Lenten apology |
| 2000 | Breakdown of President Clinton's Israel-Palestine peace talks |
| 2000 | USS *Cole* attacked in Yemen (Oct. 12) |
| 2001 | September 11 terrorist attack on America |
| 2001 | Defeat of Taliban in Afghanistan |

| | |
|---|---|
| 2002 | Daniel Pearl murdered in Pakistan (Feb. 1) |
| 2002 | Muslim girls burn to death in school in Mecca (March) |
| 2002 | Heightened suicide bombings in Israel |
| 2002 | Israel government approves security wall |
| 2002 | Terrorist bombing in Bali kills 202 (Oct. 12) |
| 2002 | Moscow theater hostage crisis (Oct. 23–26) |
| 2003 | U.S. attacks Iraq (March 19) |
| 2004 | Crisis in Darfur escalates |
| 2004 | Madrid train bombings (March 11) |
| 2004 | Film *Submission* (Ayaan Hirsi Ali and Theo van Gogh) shown on Dutch TV |
| 2004 | 385 die in Beslan school hostage crisis (Sept. 1-3) |
| 2004 | Killing of Dutch filmmaker Theo van Gogh (Nov. 2) |
| 2004 | Death of Arafat (Nov. 11) |
| 2005 | Mahmoud Abbas elected Palestinian leader |
| 2005 | Rafik Hariri killed in Beirut (Feb. 14) |
| 2005 | Amina Wadud leads mixed gender worship in Manhattan (March 18) |
| 2005 | London bombings (July 7) |
| 2005 | Israeli forces leave Gaza and West Bank (August) |
| 2005 | Ontario government in Canada says no to shariah law |
| 2005 | Danish cartoon controversy erupts (September–December) |
| 2006 | Hamas defeats Fatah in general election (January) |
| 2006 | Arrest of suspected terrorists in Toronto (June 3) |
| 2006 | Killing of Abu Musab al-Zarqawi (June 8) |
| 2006 | Israeli-Lebanese war (July 12–Aug 14) |
| 2006 | Pope Benedict XVI controversy (September) |
| 2006 | "An Open Letter to the Pope" (Oct. 13) |
| 2007 | Fighting between Hamas and Fatah in Gaza |
| 2007 | A Common Word October 13 (Muslim leaders appeal to Christians) |
| 2008 | Nov. 26–29 Shooting and bomb attacks in Mumbai |
| 2008 | Gaza under Israeli attack (Dec. 27–Jan. 19, 2009) |
| 2009 | President Obama Speech in Cairo (June 4) |
| 2009 | Major Nidal Hasan kills 13 at Fort Hood base (November 5) |
| 2010 | Negotiations on Israel-Palestinian conflict |
| 2010 | Pastor Terry Jones announces plan to burn Qur'an (July 12) |

| | |
|---|---|
| 2010 | Controversy over mosque proposal at Ground Zero |
| 2010 | Mohamed Bouazizi sets himself on fire in Tunisia (Dec. 17) |
| 2011 | Florida pastor Terry Jones burns Qur'an (March 21) |
| 2011 | Killing of Osama bin Laden (May 2) |
| 2011 | Bombings in Mumbai (July 13) |
| 2011 | Anders Breivik kills 77 in Norway attacks (July 22) |
| 2011 | Revolutions in Tunisia, Egypt, Libya, Yemen, Syria, and Bahrain |
| 2012 | Mohammed Shafia, wife and son found guilty in honor killings (Jan. 28) |
| 2012 | Innocence of Muslims uploaded to YouTube (July) |
| 2012 | U.S. Ambassador Christopher Stevens killed in Benghazi (Sept. 12) |
| 2012 | Controversy over British historian Tom Holland's work on Islam |
| 2013 | British soldier Lee Rigby killed on London street (May 22) |
| 2013 | Boston Marathon bombings (April 15) |
| 2013 | Egyptian military overthrows Mohamed Morsi (July 3) |
| 2014 | Myanmar Buddhists attack Muslims (January) |
| 2014 | Al-Qaeda separates from Islamic State (Feb. 3) |
| 2014 | Christian militias seek revenge on Muslims in Central African Republic |
| 2014 | Boko Haram kidnap 276 girls (April 14) |
| 2014 | Kidnapping of three Jewish teenagers (June 12) and Gaza-Israeli war |
| 2014 | Malaysia's top court bans non-Muslims from using word Allah |
| 2014 | Islamic State announces Abu Bakr al-Baghdadi as Caliph (June 29) |
| 2014 | Sheikh Moktar Ali Zubeyr (al-Shabab) killed in air strike (Sept. 1) |
| 2014 | Beheading of James Foley (Aug 19), Steven Sotloff (Sept. 2) and Alan Henning (c. Oct. 3) |
| 2014 | Ayman al-Zawahri announces new Al-Qaeda affiliate in India (Sept. 3) |
| 2014 | Coalition airstrikes begin against Islamic State (Sept. 23) |
| 2014 | Open Letter to Al-Baghdadi (Sept. 24) |

| | |
|---|---|
| 2014 | Malala Yousafzai announced as 2014 Nobel Peace Prize winner |
| 2014 | Killing of Canadian soldier near Montreal (Oct. 20) and death of another soldier in attack on Parliament Building in Ottawa (Oct. 22) |
| 2014 | Ahmadiyya Muslim Youth Association in Canada launches Stop the CrISIS campaign |
| 2014 | Beheading of Peter Kassig by Islamic State (November) |
| 2014 | Hostage crisis in Sydney (Dec. 15) |
| 2014 | Taliban attack on Army Public School in Peshawar (Dec. 16) |
| 2015 | 12 killed in attack on Charlie Hebdo (Jan. 7) |
| 2015 | Graeme Wood article "What ISIS Really Wants" in *The Atlantic* (online in February) |
| 2015 | 21 Coptic Christians beheaded in Libya |
| 2015 | Controversy over wearing of niqab in Canada |
| 2015 | Shooting at Bardo Museum in Tunis (March 18) |
| 2015 | Mosque bombings in Yemen (March 20) |
| 2015 | Saudi Arabia leads coalition against Houthi rebels (late March) |
| 2015 | Al-Shabab militants kill nearly 150 in Kenyan college attack |
| 2015 | Two gunmen killed at Muhammad Art Exhibit & Contest in Texas (May 3) |

# Appendix 6

# The Islamic State and *The Atlantic*

In February 2015, *The Atlantic* released Graeme Wood's article "What ISIS Really Wants" online. The 10,000 word piece (the cover for the March print version) created instant and enormous controversy, with thousands of comments online, huge media reaction (including CNN) and a war among academics over the proper interpretation of the article's most explosive claims. Most scholars have recognized the significant contribution of Wood on the history, beliefs (particularly eschatology) and practices of the Islamic State (aka ISIS, ISIL, Daesh). The disagreement and vitriol focuses largely on the following statements from Wood and Princeton scholar Bernard Haykel that seem to validate the Islamic State:

> The reality is that the Islamic State is Islamic. *Very* Islamic. Yes, it has attracted psychopaths and adventure seekers, drawn largely from the disaffected populations of the Middle East and Europe. But the religion preached by its most ardent followers derives from coherent and even learned interpretations of Islam.

> …Muslims who call the Islamic State un-Islamic are typically, as the Princeton scholar Bernard Haykel, the leading expert on the group's theology, told me, "embarrassed and politically correct, with a cotton-candy view of their own religion" that neglects "what their religion has historically and legally required." Many denials of the Islamic State's religious nature, he said, are rooted in an "interfaith-Christian-nonsense tradition."

> [Haykel] regards the claim that the Islamic State has distorted the texts of Islam as preposterous, sustainable only through willful ignorance. "People want to absolve Islam," he said. "It's this 'Islam is a religion of peace' mantra. As if there is such a thing as 'Islam'! It's what Muslims do, and how they interpret their texts." Those texts are

shared by all Sunni Muslims, not just the Islamic State. "And these guys have just as much legitimacy as anyone else."

In Haykel's estimation, the fighters of the Islamic State are authentic throwbacks to early Islam and are faithfully reproducing its norms of war....Leaders of the Islamic State have taken emulation of Muhammad as strict duty, and have revived traditions that have been dormant for hundreds of years. "What's striking about them is not just the literalism, but also the seriousness with which they read these texts," Haykel said. "There is an assiduous, obsessive seriousness that Muslims don't normally have."

Both Wood and the Princeton professor have argued that they have been read in a naïve manner and that their comments have been taken out of context.[1] Both have received great praise and severe critique. On the latter, one writer railed against the "cotton-candy professor" and the "juvenile journalist."

Beyond the rhetoric, the battle over the article illustrates one of the chief points made in this book. Our globe in general, the West more specifically, and, most significantly, the Muslim world faces an epistemic crisis over what constitutes authentic Islam. While *The Atlantic* piece has led to more debate, nasty and otherwise, about the essence of Islam, the extreme statements do provide a context for noting four different interpretations of Islam and the Islamic State. They range from the most positive towards the Islamic State to the most negative.

1.  The Islamic State represents what Islam is like when it is based on the model of the prophet Muhammad, the teachings of the Qur'an, and the teachings of shariah law. All other forms of Islam are false. This is the view of the Islamic State itself.[2]

2.  The Islamic State is a modern perversion of Islam, a distortion largely caused by the political and social vortex in Iraq and Syria post 9/11 and the American-led assault against Saddam Hussein. The theology and practice of the Islamic State is often contrary to the established traditions in Muhammad's day, especially in regards to the wanton violence of ISIS. Islam as given by the prophet Muhammad and in the Qur'an and in shariah law is a religion of peace.

    This is the view of both traditional Sunni and Shia Muslims. It is also a popular view among many academics, Muslim and otherwise, who study Islam.[3] Scholars who study Islam generally adopt a pluralist vision and argue that Islam, like all religions, is malleable and not static. Many non-Muslims (scholars or otherwise) would second, to varying degrees, the traditional Muslim critique of American imperialism.[4] As well, the point about Islam as a religion of peace has been advanced by both President George W. Bush and President Obama, though mainly for political purposes.[5]

3. The Islamic State distorts early Islam and the teachings and example of the prophet and the Qur'an in key ways. Thus, the Islamic State must not be identified with Islam per se. As well, failures in Western responses to the Middle East have, in fact, contributed to the rise of ISIS.[6] However, some of the most disturbing views and practices of ISIS find ready parallels and justification in the traditional interpretation of Muhammad, the Qur'an, and shariah law. Given this, early Islam was not and is not a completely viable ethical or intellectual path. While the Islamic State must be distinguished from Islam per se, Islam is in many ways not a religion of peace.[7] This is the view adopted by many critics of Islam. Bill Maher, for example, argued that Islam is too much like ISIS. Maher was in turn attacked for his views by Reza Aslan, among others.[8]

4. The Islamic State is faithful to and identical with the original Islam of the seventh and eight centuries and as such is proof that Islam is not a religion of peace and is essentially evil. The Islamic State is adequate illustration that the West has to be at war, ideologically and otherwise, with Islam. This is the perspective of some conservative critics of Islam.[9]

On the preceding, thankfully only ISIS members celebrate their version of Islam. While the differences between perspectives 3 and 4 are worth noting, the major ideological gap in interpreting Islam lies between those who basically celebrate Islam as a great path (#1 and #2) and those who do not (#3 and #4). While it is virtually impossible to imagine ISIS joining a campaign for peace, one can hope that a more moderate Islam will take deeper root throughout the Muslim world.[10]

In the end, the Islamic State provides part of the evidence for our earlier argument that Islam can be a religion of war. However, it must not be forgotten that it also can be a religion of peace. This balanced assessment is faithful to the overall realities of history, and adopting this approach, one taken by the great scholar Bernard Lewis, saves us from needless binary options.[11]

On the bottom line, the question whether the Islamic State is Islamic is a lot like the question whether Islam is a religion of peace. Both questions are usually approached from pre-set ideological positions with little interest in nuance. What is most important in debates about the Islamic State and Islam is to move as soon as possible beyond the false dichotomies and careless generalities that plague the discussion in order to face every major negative reality in ISIS, in Islam and in every religion and ideology that impedes genuine human peace and goodwill.[12]

# Appendix 7

# The Infamous
# Fox News Interview

A s Reza Aslan knows, the sales of *Zealot* and the current plans for a movie owe a lot to the 2013 Fox News interview with him that went viral. Despite weaknesses in Lauren Green's probing, many mainline media writers went overboard against her and should have paid attention to serious issues and falsehoods in Aslan's rejoinders to her, in addition to his frequent mentions of his PhD.

We note four matters:

1. How does Aslan reconcile his status as "a prominent Muslim thinker" with his claims that "Jesus was most definitely crucified" (something almost all Muslims deny) and that *Zealot* "overturns pretty much everything that Islam" thinks about Jesus? Why does Aslan remain a Muslim if he believes Islam does not even get Jesus right?

2. Does Aslan really think his book is not an attack on Christianity when he tries to destroy the integrity of Paul, denies the accuracy of many Gospel accounts of Jesus, dismisses the historicity of the miracles of Jesus, negates the divinity of Jesus and denies the resurrection of Jesus? If this does not amount to an attack on Christianity, we wonder what does.

3. In spite of his repeated claims in the interview to "two decades" of research, Aslan cites only three articles on Jesus from the ten years before *Zealot* was published. While Aslan has every right to do a book about Jesus (and Green never disputed that right), his swagger about his scholarship is not matched by reality.

Given his paucity of research and his outdated, careless scholarship, now documented in many reviews and in our book, it is clear that Lauren Green was basically on to something in her skepticism about Aslan's credentials.

4. Does Aslan stand by his claim in the interview that in his endnotes he cites "every scholar" who disagrees with him and "every scholar" who agrees? Was Aslan having a Brian Williams' moment? There are no references in *Zealot* to Wolfhart Pannenberg, Helmut Koester, Stephen Davis, Dale Allison, Michael Licona, Richard Bauckham, Birger Gerhardsson, Gary Habermas, John Kloppenborg, Ben Meyer, Graham Stanton, William Lane Craig, Bart Ehrman, Ben Witherington, Larry Hurtado, Paul Meier, Mark Goodacre, Gerald O'Collins, Joel Marcus, Darrell Bock, Steve Mason, Simon Joseph, David F. Watson, Chris Keith, Craig Keener, Gregory Boyd, Dale Martin or Paula Fredriksen, all scholars of the historical Jesus who are well-known and highly regarded.

# Resources

## Books on Jesus, the Bible and Christian Faith

Richard Bauckham, *Jesus and the Eyewitnesses: The Gospels as Eyewitness Testimony* (Grand Rapids: Eerdmans, 2006).

Richard Bauckham, *Jesus: A Very Short Introduction* (Oxford: Oxford University Press, 2011).

Darrell L. Bock, *Jesus according to Scripture: Restoring the Portrait from the Gospels* (Grand Rapids: Baker Academic, 2002).

F. F. Bruce, *The New Testament Documents: Are They Reliable?* (reprinted 6th ed., 1981, with foreword by N. T. Wright, Downers Grove: InterVarsity Press, 2003).

Paul R. Eddy and Gregory A. Boyd, *The Jesus Legend: A Case for the Historical Reliability of the Synoptic Jesus Tradition* (Grand Rapids: Baker Academic, 2007).

Craig A. Evans, *Fabricating Jesus: How Modern Scholars Distort the Gospels* (Downers Grove: InterVarsity Press, 2006).

Craig A. Evans and N. T. Wright, *Jesus, the Final Days* (London: SPCK, 2008; Louisville: Westminster John Knox Press, 2009).

Gordon D. Fee and Douglas Stuart, *How to Read the Bible Book by Book: A Guided Tour* (Grand Rapids: Zondervan, 2002).

Craig S. Keener, *Miracles: The Credibility of the New Testament Accounts* (2 vols., Grand Rapids: Baker Academic, 2011).

J. Ed Komoszewski, M. James Sawyer, and Daniel B. Wallace, *Reinventing Jesus* (Grand Rapids: Kregel, 2006).

Michael R. Licona, *The Resurrection of Jesus: A New Historiographical Approach* (Downers Grove: InterVarsity Press, 2010).

## Websites on Jesus, the Bible and Christian Faith

www.bible.org

www.bibleplaces.com

www.christianthinkers.com

www.dannyzacharias.net

http://embracethetruth.org

www.ntgateway.com

www.reasonablefaith.org

www.rzim.org

## Books on Islam

David Cook, *Understanding Jihad* (Berkeley: University of California Press, 2005).

Daveed Gartenstein-Ross, *Bin Laden's Legacy* (Hoboken: John Wiley & Sons, 2011).

Bruce Hoffman, *Inside Terrorism* (rev. ed., New York: Columbia University Press, 2006).

Tom Holland, *In the Shadow of the Sword* (London: Little, Brown, 2012).

Robert Hoyland, *In God's Path* (New York: Oxford, 2014).

Hans Küng, *Islam* (London: Oneworld, 2007).

Nabeel Qureshi, *Seeking Allah, Finding Jesus* (Grand Rapids: Zondervan, 2014).

Andrew Rippin, *Muslims* (London: Routledge, 2000).

Robert Spencer, *Did Muhammad Exist?* (Wilmington: ISI Books, 2012).

James White, *What Every Christian Should Know about the Qur'an* (Bloomington: Bethany, 2013).

Lawrence Wright, *The Looming Tower* (New York: Knopf, 2006).

## Websites on Islam

Answering Islam: www.answering-islam.org

Answering Muslims (David Wood): www.answeringmuslims.com

Carl Ernst: http://www.unc.edu/~cernst/index.html

Foundation for Defense of Democracies: http://defenddemocracy.org

Islam and Islamic Studies Resources (Alan Godlas): http://islam.uga.edu

Jihad Watch (Robert Spencer): www.jihadwatch.org

Jihadology (Aaron Zelin): http://jihadology.net

Thomas Joscelyn: www.longwarjournal.org/

Martin Kramer: www.martinkramer.org

Qur'an and Injil (Gordon Nickel): www.quranandinjil.org

Daniel Pipes: www.danielpipes.org

# Endnotes

## Chapter 1–Are the New Testament Gospels Reliable?

[1] For a recent and widely respected study of the New Testament Gospels as biographies, see R. A. Burridge, *What Are the Gospels? A Comparison with Graeco-Roman Biography* (2nd ed., Grand Rapids: Eerdmans, 2004).

[2] The traditional Muslim view is that the Qur'an was finally gathered by about 650 during the caliphate of Uthman. This is very debatable, as we will show in chapter 10. Also, see the forthcoming work of Gordon Nickel, a Canadian scholar of Islam, called *Gentle Answer,* which builds on his website www.quranandinjil.org.

[3] See K. Small, *Textual Criticism and Qur'ān Manuscripts* (Lanham and New York: Rowman & Littlefield, 2011), 165–66.

[4] The reason Jesus was born in the "before Christ" era is due to a mistake in the calendar, which was rectified later. Rather than change the dates in the present, which would have been very impractical, the dates of the past were pushed back. Thus, the birth of Jesus went from AD 1 to 5 BC (or 2 BC). For scholarly discussion of the date of the birth of Jesus see H. W. Hoehner, *Chronological Aspects of the Life of Christ* (Grand Rapids: Zondervan, 1977), 11–27. Hoehner opts for either December 5 BC or January 4 BC. Two of the reasons there is uncertainty surrounding these dates are that the Gospels themselves do not provide many dates, and Josephus, the first-century Jewish historian and apologist, sometimes provides faulty chronological data.

[5] If Jesus was born in 2 BC, then when his ministry began in AD 28 he would have been almost exactly 30 years old. For discussion of the date when the ministry of Jesus began see Hoehner, *Chronological Aspects,* 29–44. Hoehner opts for early AD 29. He also opts for AD 33 as the date

of Jesus' death. This is a date that many scholars accept. If AD 33 is the date of Jesus' death, then his ministry would have lasted about four years.

[6] For a learned study of memory in antiquity and how it is quite likely that many early Christian teachers had memorized the whole of Jesus' teaching and regularly repeated it to those they taught, see B. Gerhardsson, *Memory and Manuscript: Oral Tradition and Written Transmission in Rabbinic Judaism and Early Christianity* (Lund: Gleerup, 1961; repr. Grand Rapids: Eerdmans, 1998).

[7] We also refer to the hypothetical source known as Q. It is made up mostly of sayings material and is found in Matthew and Luke, who made use of it to supplement the Gospel of Mark. Some of this Q material also overlaps with Mark.

[8] Papias (c. AD 60–130) was bishop of Hierapolis, Asia Minor, and author of *An Explanation of the Sayings of the Lord.* English translations of the surviving fragments of his work can be found in J. B. Lightfoot, J. R. Harmer, and M. W. Holmes, *The Apostolic Fathers* (rev. ed., Grand Rapids: Baker, 1989), 307–29.

[9] The early Church believed, and many modern scholars agree, that Luke wrote both the Gospel of Luke and the book of Acts. In the later work, the author sometimes uses the first person plural ("we"). On these occasions it would seem that Luke himself is traveling with Paul and his companions.

[10] For further study on this important subject see J. D. G. Dunn, "Jesus Tradition in Paul," in B. D. Chilton and C. A. Evans (eds.), *Studying the Historical Jesus: Evaluations of the State of Current Research* (Leiden: Brill, 1994), 155–78; D. B. Capes, "Paul, Jesus Tradition in," in *Encyclopedia of the Historical Jesus*, ed. C. A. Evans (New York and London: Routledge, 2008), 446–50. Dunn argues persuasively that Paul's allusions to the teaching of Jesus would have brought into the minds of his readers the full teaching.

[11] The more obvious examples include James 1:5, 17 (Matt 7:7, 11); James 1:6 (Matt 21:21); James 1:22–23 (Matt 7:21, 24–27); James 4:12 (Matt 7:1); James 5:12 (Matt 5:34–37). Although some scholars assign a late date to the letter of James, we think its contents argue for an early date, in the late 40s or early 50s.

[12] Ironically, the earliest biography of the life of Muhammad (Ibn Ishaq's *Sirat Rasul Allah*) was composed about 145 years after his death.

[13] This point is acknowledged in Tarif al-Khalidi, *The Muslim Jesus: Sayings and Stories in Islamic Literature* (Cambridge: Harvard University Press, 2001). Khalidi argues that the images of Jesus expressed in the Qur'an and early Islamic literature were shaped according to the needs and imagination of diverse authorities and groups of Muslims. In an interview, Khalidi insightfully and succinctly remarks, "The Jesus of the Qur'ān is essentially a theological argument and not a narrative." See S. Tamari, "The Fifth Gospel: Tarif Khalidi on Jesus in the 'Muslim Gospel,'" *Jerusalem Quarterly* 15 (2002): 38–41, with quotation from 39; J. Sabih, "The *'Īsā* Narrative in the Qur'an: The Making of a Prophet," in T. L. Thompson and T. S. Verenna (eds.), *'Is This Not the Carpenter?' The Question of the Historicity of the Figure of Jesus* (Copenhagen International Seminar; Sheffield: Equinox Publishing, 2012), 216–32. Sabih rightly notes that the materials in the Qur'an are not narratives but proclamations, as though Allah is himself speaking (see esp. 218). No historical portrait of Jesus can be extracted from the Qur'an.

[14] Nowhere in *Zealot: The Life and Times of Jesus of Nazareth* (New York: Random House, 2013) does Reza Aslan call upon the Qur'an or other Islamic traditions, such as those reviewed in our book, to learn more about who Jesus was and what he taught. This is one reason why some of the criticism of Aslan's book in the popular media was so off target. Aslan's book does not represent a Qur'anic or Muslim perspective. In his portrait of Jesus, Aslan wisely relies on the Christian Gospels, not much later Islamic sources.

[15] Aslan, *Zealot*, xxvi. Aslan tells us "the only writings about Jesus that existed in 70 C.E. were the letters of Paul," 214. Really? Many scholars believe Mark circulated before 70.

[16] Some of the many problems with Aslan's *Zealot* are discussed in one of the appendices.

[17] J. D. G. Dunn, *Jesus Remembered* (Grand Rapids: Eerdmans, 2003).

[18] S. Byrskog, *Story as History—History as Story* (Tübingen: Mohr Siebeck, 2000), and "The transmission of the Jesus tradition: old and new insights," *Early Christianity* 1 (2010): 441–68. Standing in the scholarly tradition of Birger Gerhardsson, Byrskog rightly underscores the importance of the role of memory in the ancient world, especially among the Jewish teachers. On this point see Byrskog's recent study "From memory to memoirs. Tracing the background of a literary genre,"

in Magnus Zetterholm and Samuel Byrskog (eds.), *The Making of Christianity: Conflicts, Contacts, and Constructions. Essays in Honor of Bengt Holmberg* (Winona Lake: Eisenbrauns, 2012), 1–21.

[19] For recent studies see R. J. Bauckham, *Jesus and the Eyewitnesses: The Gospels as Eyewitness Testimony* (Grand Rapids: Eerdmans, 2006); R. J. Bauckham, "The Gospel of Mark: Origins and Eyewitnesses," in M. F. Bird and J. Maston (eds.), *Earliest Christian History: History, Literature, and Theology. Essays from the Tyndale Fellowship in Honor of Martin Hengel* (Tübingen: Mohr Siebeck, 2012), 145–69.

[20] Bauckham, *Jesus and the Eyewitnesses*, 12–38, carefully reviews what the early second-century Church Father Papias had to say about the "living voice" that was still available well past the middle of the first century. For a helpful study that shows that a number of eyewitness were still living when the Gospels were composed, see R. K. McIver, *Memory, Jesus, and the Synoptic Gospels* (Atlanta: Society of Biblical Literature, 2011).

[21] The historian seeks verisimilitude, not necessarily exactitude. On this important point see L. Gottschalk, America's doyen of history in the previous century, "The Historian and the Historical Document," in L. Gottschalk, C. Kluckhohn, and R. Angell, *The Use of Personal Documents in History, Anthropology, and Sociology* (New York: Social Science Research Council, 1945), 35.

[22] Archaeologists and historians ask if there is a correlation between text and *realia*. If there is, then we may speak of verisimilitude. The point has been well stated by R. S. Hendel, "Giants at Jericho," *Biblical Archaeology Review* 35, no. 2 (2009): 20, 66: "Biblical archeology...involves the rigorous correlation of textual data from the Bible and material evidence from archaeology." It is to this principle that A. N. Sherwin-White alludes when he says, "The basic reason for this confidence is, if put summarily, the existence of external confirmations." See Sherwin-White, *Roman Society and Roman Law in the New Testament: The Sarum Lectures 1960–61* (Oxford: Oxford University Press, 1963), 186–87. The historical and geographical verisimilitude of the New Testament Gospels was long ago noted by Henry Thayer in his 1895 Society of Biblical Literature presidential address. See J. H. Thayer, "The Historical Element in the New Testament," *Journal of Biblical Literature* 14 (1895), 1–18, esp. 15.

[23] We bring Acts into the discussion at this point because it, like the four Gospels, describes persons and events in first-century Jewish Palestine.

[24] J. H. Charlesworth (ed.), *Jesus and Archaeology* (Grand Rapids: Eerdmans, 2006).

## Chapter 2–Are the Manuscripts of the New Testament Gospels Reliable?

[1] The 1516 edition was entitled *Novum Instrumentum omne* ("all the New Teaching"). The remainder of the editions, beginning with the 1519 edition, were given the more familiar title *Novum Testamentum omne* ("all the New Testament"). Only one of Erasmus's manuscripts contained the Book of Revelation, and even it was missing the last six verses of the last chapter, which made it necessary for Erasmus to back-translate the Latin into the Greek. To call it a "critical edition" by today's standards is to be very generous. The 1516 edition was rife with errors. It was not the first printed edition, it should be pointed out. The first printed edition of the Greek New Testament, the *Complutensian Polyglot*, appeared in 1514.

[2] The most important of these witnesses are customarily listed in the front of modern editions of the Greek New Testament. The most commonly used texts are B. Aland, K. Aland, J. Karavidopoulos, C. M. Martini, and B. M. Metzger (eds.), *The Greek New Testament* (4th ed., Stuttgart: Deutsche Bibelgesellschaft and United Bible Societies, 1993); B. Aland, K. Aland, J. Karavidopoulos, C. M. Martini, and B. M. Metzger (eds.), *Novum Testamentum Graece* (28th ed., Stuttgart: Deutsche Bibelgesellschaft, 2012); and M. W. Holmes (ed.), *The Greek New Testament SBL Ed.* (Atlanta: Scholars Press, 2010). The latter takes an approach somewhat different from the first two.

[3] Respected textual critic Larry Hurtado speaks of a stable New Testament text. See L. Hurtado, "What Do the Earliest Christian Manuscripts Tell Us about Their Readers?" in *The World of Jesus and the Early Church: Identity and Interpretation in the Early Communities of Faith*, ed. C. A. Evans (Peabody: Hendrickson Publishers, 2011), 179–92, esp. 189–90. See also Stanley E. Porter, *How We Got the New Testament: Text, Transmission, Translation* (Grand Rapids: Baker Academic, 2013), 24. For an estimation that today's Greek New Testament is 98 percent or 99 percent in agreement with the original text, see Daniel B. Wallace, "The Majority Text and the Original Text: Are They Identical?" *Bibliotheca Sacra* 148 (1991): 158–66. Well known and widely respected New Testament textual critic Bruce Metzger estimates that of the approximate

20,000 lines of text only 40 are truly in doubt, not one of which involves a major Christian teaching.

[4] K. E. Small, *Textual Criticism and Qur'ān Manuscripts* (Lanham: Lexington Books, 2011), 3 (emphasis added).

[5] K. E. Small, *Holy Books Have a History: Textual Histories of the New Testament and the Qur'an* (Monument: Snowfall Press, 2009), vii–viii.

[6] E. A. Rezvan, "The Qur'ān and Its World: VI. Emergence of the Canon: The Struggle for Uniformity," *Manuscripta Orientalia* 4 (1998): 13–54, quotation from 23.

[7] This textual fiction is maintained in M. Abul-Fadl, *Introducing Islam From Within* (Leicester: Islamic Foundation, 1991), 92. Small, *Holy Books*, 26, finds this failure to acknowledge reality puzzling in light of the fact that "early and medieval Islamic scholarship openly acknowledges textual variants for the Qur'an that are intentional."

[8] For examples of Islamic efforts to impede textual study of the Qur'an see Small, *Holy Books*, 69–71; *Textual Criticism and Qur'ān Manuscripts*, 165–66.

[9] Small, *Textual Criticism and Qur'ān Manuscripts*, 11. See also Small, *Holy Books*, 61–62. Small notes that only *one* written form of the consonantal Qur'anic text has been preserved well.

[10] In the Qur'an and Islamic tradition one will encounter the word *taḥrīf*, which basically means "textual corruption." It reflects the belief that the Bible has been changed (see, e.g., surah 2:75–76; 4:46; 5:13, 41), the expression means either changing the meaning or changing the reading of the text. To speak this way of the Bible, especially the New Testament, in view of the textual realities of the Qur'an is remarkably unfair and naïve. The textual realities of the Qur'an suggest that *taḥrīf* is a far bigger problem for the Qur'an than it is for the New Testament.

[11] Small, *Textual Criticism and Qur'ān Manuscripts*, 179, 180. Small, *Holy Books*, 16, remarks, "once you start looking for firm answers to questions about the history of the text of the Qur'ān on a level that has been done with the New Testament, one finds almost a black hole."

[12] Small, *Textual Criticism and Qur'ān Manuscripts*, 179. See also F. M. Donner, "The Qur'ān in Recent Scholarship: Challenges and Desiderata," in G. Reynolds (ed.), *The Qur'ān in its Historical Context* (London: Routledge, 2008), 29–50, quotation from 31.

[13] See M. I. Finley, *Ancient History: Evidence and Models* (New York: Penguin Books, 1985), 8–9.

[14] Besides Arrian's *Anabasis of Alexander*, we have Diodorus' *Historical Library*, Book 17 (first century BC), Quintus Curtius Rufus' *History of Alexander the Great* (mid-first century AD), Plutarch's *Life of Alexander* (early 2nd century AD), Justin's *Epitome*, Books 11–12 (c. AD 200) and a few others still later. For critical assessment of these sources see A. Zambrini, "The Historians of Alexander the Great," in J. Marincola (ed.), *A Companion to Greek and Roman Historiography* (2 vols., Oxford: Blackwell, 2007–8) 1:210–20.

[15] For example see J. R. Hale, *Lords of the Sea: The Epic Story of the Athenian Navy and the Birth of Democracy* (New York: Viking, 2009). It is hard to imagine how Hale, a former student of historian Donald Kagan and now Director of Liberal Studies at the University of Louisville, could have written his brilliant history of the Athenian Navy (c. 480–330 BC) had he viewed the histories of Herodotus, Thucydides and Xenophon—not to mention their surviving manuscripts—with the degree of skepticism that some biblical scholars think is warranted with respect to writings from late antiquity.

For another recent example see R. M. Errington, *A History of the Hellenistic World 323–30 BC* (Oxford: Blackwell, 2008). For discussion of ancient sources see 6–8. Errington's history of Greece presupposes the general reliability of the sources. Errington is Emeritus Professor of Ancient History at the University of Marburg, Germany.

The same observation applies to the critically acclaimed works of D. Kagan, *The Peloponnesian War* (New York: Viking, 2003) and *Thucydides: The Reinvention of History* (New York: Penguin Books, 2009). Kagan is Sterling Professor of Classics and History at Yale University. One should also be reminded of the comments in A. N. Sherwin-White, *Roman Society and Roman Law in the New Testament: The Sarum Lectures 1960–61* (Oxford: Oxford University Press, 1963; repr. Grand Rapids: Baker, 1978, 1992), 186–93.

[16] On the importance of Paul's acquaintance with Peter see J. D. G. Dunn, "Jesus Tradition in Paul," in B. D. Chilton and C. A. Evans (eds.), *Studying the Historical Jesus: Evaluations of the State of Current Research* (Leiden: Brill, 1994), 155–78, especially 157; "The Relationship between Paul and Jerusalem according to Galatians 1 and

2," *New Testament Studies* 28 (1982): 461–78, especially 463–66; and "Once More—Gal 1.18: *historesai Kephan* in Reply to Otfried Hofius," *Zeitschrift für die Neutestamentliche Wissenschaft* 76 (1985): 138–39. Dunn understands Paul's *historesai Kephan* as "to get information from Cephas." It is from *historia* ("inquiry") that we get our word "history."

[17] For further comparisons of the textual histories of the New Testament and the Qur'an, see K. E. Small, "Textual Variants in the New Testament and Qur'ānic Manuscript Traditions," in K. H. Ohlig and M. Gross (eds.), *Schlaglichter: Die beiden ersten islamischen Jahrhunderte* (Berlin: Hans Schiler, 2008), 572–93.

## Chapter 3–How Did Jesus Understand Himself and His Mission?

[1] See H. Lenowitz, *The Jewish Messiahs: From Galilee to Crown Heights* (Oxford: Oxford University Press, 1998), 20: "These figures may call themselves messiahs, though generally they prefer to have others call them that."

[2] For a concise statement see L. W. Hurtado, "Monotheism," in J. J. Collins and D. C. Harlow (eds.), *The Eerdmans Dictionary of Early Judaism* (Grand Rapids: Eerdmans, 2010), 961–64. For more detail see L. W. Hurtado, *Lord Jesus Christ: Devotion to Jesus in Earliest Christianity* (Grand Rapids: Eerdmans, 2003), 29–53.

[3] The word *henotheism* is Greek (from *hen*, meaning "one," and *theos*, meaning "God") and implies loyalty to *one* God, not necessarily the belief that there is *only* one God. The word *monotheism* is Greek (from *mono*, meaning "only" or "alone," and *theos*). The word *polytheism* is also Greek (from *poly*, meaning "many"). On Israel's historic struggle to embrace monotheism see M. S. Smith, *The Early History of God: Yahweh and Other Deities in Ancient Israel* (San Francisco: Harper & Row, 1990).

[4] In this respect, it is very important to properly understand the phrase "worship of angels" (Greek: *threskeia ton aggelon*), in Colossians 2:18. Paul is not saying that the persons he is criticizing worshipped angels (where the genitive *ton aggelon* is understood grammatically as objective), but rather that these persons, having entered heaven (as they supposed), worship God, as the angels do (where the genitive *ton aggelon* is understood as subjective).

[5] C. A. Evans, "Messianic Hopes and Messianic Figures in Late Antiquity," *Journal for Greco-Roman Christianity and Judaism* 3 (2006): 9–40.

[6] Translation based on M. O. Wise, M. G. Abegg Jr., and E. M. Cook, *The Dead Sea Scrolls: A New Translation* (San Francisco: HarperCollins, 1996), 269–70.

[7] Translation based on Wise, Abegg Jr., and Cook, *The Dead Sea Scrolls*, 421. There is missing text in the Hebrew.

[8] For a survey of messianic texts found at Qumran see M. G. Abegg Jr., and C. A. Evans, "Messianic Passages in the Dead Sea Scrolls," in J. H. Charlesworth, H. Lichtenberger, and G. S. Oegema (eds.), *Qumran-Messianism: Studies on the Messianic Expectations in the Dead Sea Scrolls* (Tübingen: Mohr Siebeck, 1998), 191–203. See also J. J. Collins, *The Scepter and the Star: The Messiahs of the Dead Sea Scrolls and Other Ancient Literature* (New York: Doubleday, 1995).

[9] For further discussion of Jewish messianic expectations see J. Neusner et al. (eds.), *Judaisms and Their Messiahs at the Turn of the Christian Era* (Cambridge: Cambridge University Press, 1987); J. H. Charlesworth (ed.), *The Messiah: Developments in Earliest Judaism and Christianity* (Minneapolis: Fortress, 1992); G. S. Oegema, *The Anointed and His People: Messianic Expectations from the Maccabees to Bar Kochba* (Sheffield: Sheffield Academic Press, 1998); J. J. Collins and A. Yarbro Collins, *King and Messiah as Son of God: Divine, Human, and Angelic Messianic Figures* (Grand Rapids: Eerdmans, 2009).

[10] For concise and persuasive arguments that Jesus' self-reference "the son of man" alludes to Daniel 7 see C. F. D. Moule, "Neglected Features in the Problem of the 'Son of Man,'" in J. Gnilka (ed.), *Neues Testament und Kirche: Für Rudolf Schnackenburg* (Freiburg: Herder, 1974), 413–28, and *The Origin of Christology* (Cambridge and New York: Cambridge University Press, 1977), 11–22.

[11] See R. J. Bauckham, *Jesus and the Eyewitnesses: The Gospels as Eyewitness Testimony* (Grand Rapids: Eerdmans, 2006), 358–471.

[12] For critical study of the angelic "I have come" statements see S. J. Gathercole, *The Pre-existent Son: Recovering the Christologies of Matthew, Mark, and Luke* (Grand Rapids: Eerdmans, 2006), 113–47. Most of our examples have come from Gathercole's excellent study.

[13] For assessment of Jesus' "I have come" sayings see Gathercole, *The Pre-existent Son*, 148–76.

[14] For scholarly discussion of the parable of the vineyard see K. R. Snodgrass, *Stories with Intent: A Comprehensive Guide to the Parables of Jesus* (Grand Rapids: Eerdmans, 2007), 276–99.

[15] D. C. Allison Jr., *Constructing Jesus: Memory, Imagination, and History* (Grand Rapids: Baker Academic, 2010), 304. See Allison's critical survey of Synoptic materials, 227–32. Allison remarks that all of the contributors to these materials "are united in one particular: when they look into the future, they see Jesus, and indeed Jesus front and center," 231.

[16] D. B. Capes, *Old Testament Yahweh Texts in Paul's Christology* (Tübingen: Mohr Siebeck, 1992). See also L. J. Kreitzer, *Jesus and God in Paul's Eschatology* (Sheffield: JSOT Press, 1987).

## Chapter 4–Did James and Paul Preach a Different Gospel?

[1] This is seen in places in the book of Acts (e.g., chaps. 11 and 15) and especially in Paul's letter to the Galatian churches.

[2] This position sometimes suggests that the exalted view of Jesus as God's Son was largely a Pauline doctrine, not the doctrine of the original apostles. In the preceding chapter, we concluded that Paul's high Christology in fact reflects the high Christology of Jesus himself, as found in the earliest Gospel traditions.

[3] Reza Aslan, *Zealot: The Life and Times of Jesus of Nazareth* (New York: Random House, 2013), 190. Elsewhere Aslan makes similar extreme claims.

[4] See the arguments in the commentaries by W. F. Brosend II, *James and Jude* (New York: Cambridge University Press, 2004), 5; P. H. Davids, *The Epistle of James: A Commentary on the Greek Text* (Grand Rapids: Eerdmans, 1982), 2–22; L. T. Johnson, *The Letter of James* (Garden City: Doubleday, 1995), 92–106; and S. McKnight, *The Letter of James* (Grand Rapids: Eerdmans, 2011), 13–38.

[5] Jesus' statement "You…must be perfect, as your heavenly Father is perfect" (Matt 5:48), is analogous to the logic expressed in the Holiness Code: "And the LORD said to Moses, 'Say to all the congregation of the people of Israel, You shall be holy; for I the LORD your God am holy'" (Lev 19:1–2). It is in this context that the command to love one's neighbor as oneself appears (i.e., 19:18).

[6] On Leviticus 19:18 and the "royal law," see McKnight, *The Letter of James*, 206–7; W. Popkes, *Der Brief des Jakobus* (Leipzig: Evangelische Verlagsanstalt, 2001), 171–75.

[7] R. J. Bauckham, "For What Offence was James Put to Death?" in B. D. Chilton and C. A. Evans (eds.), *James the Just and Christian Origins* (Leiden: Brill, 1999), 199–232, especially 207.

[8] As Luther states in his preface to the New Testament, 1522; cf. M. Luther, *Luther's Works*, 55 vols., ed. H. C. Oswald et al. (Saint Louis: Concordia Publishing House, 1955–), 35:362.

[9] The text is known as 4QMMT (*Miqsat Ma'aseh ha-Torah* = "Some of the Works of the Law").

[10] Translation based on M. O. Wise, M. G. Abegg Jr., and E. M. Cook, *The Dead Sea Scrolls: A New Translation* (San Francisco: HarperCollins, 1996), 364.

[11] See C. A. Evans, "Israel according to the Book of Hebrews and the General Epistles," in D. L. Bock and M. Glaser (eds.), *The People, the Land and the Future of Israel: A Biblical Theology of Israel and the Jewish People* (Grand Rapids: Kregel Academic, 2014), 133–46, 331–32 (footnotes), especially 139.

# Chapter 5–Was Jesus a Zealot?

[1] The work originally appeared anonymously and in German under the title *Von dem Zwecke Jesu und seiner Jünger: Noch ein Fragment des Wolfenbüttelschen Ungenannten*, ed. G. E. Lessing (Braunschweig: [n.p.], 1778). Even the publisher did not identify himself. Lessing published this volume (or fragment) and six previous ones. English versions are *Fragments from Reimarus consisting of Brief Critical Remarks on the Object of Jesus and His Disciples*, ed. C. Voysey (London: Williams and Norgate, 1879), *Reimarus: Fragments*, ed. C. H. Talbert (Philadelphia: Fortress, 1970 and London: SCM Press, 1971) and *The Goal of Jesus and his Disciples*, ed. G. W. Buchanan (Leiden: Brill, 1970). *Von dem Zwecke Jesu und seiner Jünger* was part of a larger (at that time), unpublished manuscript entitled *Apologie oder Schutzschrift für die vernünftigen Verehre Gottes*, which today in its entirety is available, ed. G. Alexander (Frankfurt: Joachim Jungius-Gesellschaft, 1972).

[2] R. Eisler, *The Messiah Jesus and John the Baptist*, trans. A. H. Krappe (London: Methuen; New York: Dial, 1931). The original work appeared in German in two volumes, in 1929 and 1930. The works of Josephus are extant in Greek. However, portions also survive in Hebrew (aka the Josippon), and Old Slavonic or Old Russian. The latter contains passages not found in the Greek.

[3] S. G. F. Brandon, *The Fall of Jerusalem and the Christian Church: A Study of the Effects of the Jewish Overthrow of A.D. 70 on Christianity*

(London: SPCK, 1951; 2nd ed., 1957); *Jesus and the Zealots: A Study of the Political Factor in Primitive Christianity* (New York: Scribner's Sons, 1967); *The Trial of Jesus of Nazareth* (New York: Stein and Day, 1968). In all of these books Brandon discusses Eisler's views, especially in *The Fall of Jerusalem*, 115–22.

[4] M. Hengel, *War Jesus Revolutionär?* (Stuttgart: Calwer, 1970). For an English translation see M. Hengel, *Was Jesus a Revolutionist?* (Philadelphia: Fortress, 1971). For a more nuanced and balanced view of the context in which Jesus' style of leadership should be viewed see M. Hengel, *The Charismatic Leader and His Followers* (Edinburgh: T & T Clark, 1981; repr., with new preface, 1996). For expert analysis of Jewish zealotry in the approximate time of Jesus see M. Hengel, *The Zealots: Investigations into the Jewish Freedom Movement in the Period from Herod I until 70 A.D.* (Edinburgh: T & T Clark, 1989).

[5] E. P. Sanders, *Jesus and Judaism* (London: SCM Press, 1985), 68, 367n53.

[6] As does Richard Horsley in a number of publications. See R. A. Horsley, *Jesus and the Spiral of Violence: Popular Jewish Resistance in Roman Palestine* (San Francisco: Harper & Row, 1987).

[7] R. Aslan, *Zealot: The Life and Times of Jesus of Nazareth* (New York: Random House, 2013).

[8] Aslan, *Zealot*, 73–79, quotation from 75.

[9] The action of these teachers in the temple precincts is compared to the action that Jesus a generation later will take in those same precincts in B. D. Chilton, *Pure Kingdom: Jesus' Vision of God* (Grand Rapids: Eerdmans, 1996), 118–23. The actions of the teachers and Jesus are comparable in a general sense in that they were public protests, but the action of Jesus was not destructive.

[10] Aslan, *Zealot*, 73–79.

[11] Aslan, *Zealot*, 79. In referring to "the Zealot Party" (where capitalized letters are used), I wonder if Aslan has been taken in by Josephus, who wants his Roman readers to think of militant Jews, called zealots, as a fourth political party, rather than what they really were: zealous Jews strongly committed to Israel's religious faith and heritage.

[12] Aslan, *Zealot*, 79.

[13] Aslan, *Zealot*, 78–79.

[14] This is one of the reasons scholars never followed S. F. G. Brandon when he first proposed the thesis of a militant, zealot Jesus and why scholars are not now following Reza Aslan's updated version of this faulty thesis.

## Chapter 6–How Do Muslims View Muhammad?

[1] The year of the elephant refers to an attack on Mecca by Abraha, a Christian ruler from Yemen. Scholars dispute that this took place in 570 and put the attack much earlier. Surah 105 is said to refer to the attack. See discussion in Buhl and Welch, "Muhammad," in *Encyclopaedia of Islam* (2nd ed., Brill Online Books and Journals).

[2] Ibn Ishaq, *The Life of Muhammad*, trans. Alfred Guillaume (New York: Oxford University Press, 1970), 69.

[3] See A. J. Droge, *The Qur'an: A New Annotated Translation* (Sheffield: Equinox, 2013, 438.

[4] Ibn Ishaq, *The Life of Muhammad*, 81.

[5] W. M. Watt, "Khadīdja," in *Encyclopaedia of Islam* (2nd ed., Brill Online Books and Journals).

[6] Sebastian Günther notes that "ummi" and its plural forms "suggest a spectrum of ideas, which includes (a), someone belonging to a people (umma)—the Arabs—who were a nation without a scripture as yet; (b), someone without a scripture and thus not reading it; and (c), someone not reading a scripture and, therefore, not being taught or educated [by something or somebody]." See "Ummī," in *Encyclopaedia of the Qur'ān* (online).

[7] See Buhl and Welch, "Muhammad," *Encyclopaedia of Islam* (2nd ed., Brill Online Books and Journals). These two scholars suggest that the story might have "some historical kernel" behind it.

[8] See Jacqueline Chabbi, "jinn," in *Encyclopaedia of the Qur'ān* (Brill Online Books and Journals). Iblis (the Qur'anic term for Satan) is identified as a jinn in surah 18:50.

[9] For study of the early Western attacks on Muhammad see Norman Daniel's magnificently detailed study *Islam and the West: The Making of an Image* (Oxford: Oneworld Publications, 1993). This is the revised edition of his original 1960 publication, which received rave notice. See, for example, H. A. R. Gibb, "The Arabic Sources for the Life of Saladin," *Speculum* 37, no. 2 (April 1962): 269–270, Nabia Abbott in *Journal of Near Eastern Studies* 21, no. 2 (April 1962): 155–156 and James Kritzeck in *The Catholic Historical Review* 47, no. 1 (April 1961),

51–53. Reviews of the 1993 version continue the praise. See, for example, Feroz Ahmad in *International Journal of Middle East Studies* 26, no. 3 (August 1994), 510–511. There are some scholars who believe that Daniel was too harsh on critics of the prophet and not sufficiently alarmed by real weaknesses in Muhammad.

[10] On the Night Journey see Christine J. Gruber, "al-Burāq," in *Encyclopaedia of Islam* (3rd ed., online) and Michael Sells, "Ascension," in *Encyclopaedia of the Qur'ān* (Brill Online Books and Journals). Sells notes that the grounding for the journey in the text of the Qur'an is "tenuous."

[11] Michael Lecker's translation has a slight variation: "Whatever you differ about should be brought before God and Muḥammad." See Lecker, "Constitution of Medina," in *Encyclopaedia of Islam* (3rd ed., Brill Online Books and Journals).

[12] For analysis of the *Constitution* see Awad Halabi, "Constitution of Medina," in *The Oxford Encyclopedia of the Islamic World* (online). Michael Lecker calls the Constitution "the most significant document surviving from the time of the Prophet Muhammad." See Lecker, "Constitution of Medina," *Encyclopaedia of Islam* (3rd ed., Brill Online Books and Journals) and also note Lecker, *The Constitution of Medina* (Princeton: Princeton University Press, 2004).

[13] The incident is known as the affair of the necklace because Aisha remained behind to search for a lost necklace. For details see Denise A. Spellberg, "ʿĀʾisha bint Abī Bakr," in *Encyclopaedia of the Qur'ān* (Brill Online Books and Journals). Generally, Sunni Muslims hold Aisha in high regard, whereas Shia Muslims are more critical since Aisha resisted the political leadership of Ali (son-in-law of the prophet). For a sympathetic account of the necklace affair see Martin Lings, *Muhammad* (Rochester: Inner Traditions, 1983), 240–246.

[14] On Khaybar see Tariq Ramadan, *In the Footsteps of the Prophet: Lessons from the Life of Muhammad* (Oxford: Oxford University Press, 2007), 162–163, and Shari Lowin, "Khaybar," in *Encyclopedia of Jews in the Islamic World* (Brill Online Books and Journals). According to Islamic tradition, the Jews of Khaybar were expelled from Arabia in 642 by Umar, the second caliph.

[15] For scholarly analysis about Muhammad's alleged correspondence see K. Öhrnberg, "al-Muḳawḳis," in *Encyclopaedia of Islam* (2nd ed., Brill

Online Books and Journals). The parchment that is said to be an original from Muhammad was discovered in 1850 but has been disproven on historical and paleographical fronts.

[16] For the triumphant return to Mecca see Martin Lings, *Muhammad* (Rochester: Inner Traditions, 1983), 297–303.

[17] On Tabuk see Lings, *Muhammad*, 317–319.

[18] Lings, *Muhammad*, 317. Walter Kaegi's *Heraclius* (Cambridge: Cambridge University Press, 2003) is a standard work. See Greg Peters' review in *Fides et Historia* 36, no. 2 (Summer–Fall 2004), 141–143. Muslim tradition postures Heraclius as a pious leader who realized that Muhammad was the final prophet of God. On this see Nadia Maria El-Cheikh, "Muhammad and Heraclius: A Study in Legitimacy," *Studia Islamica* 89 (1999), 5–21.

[19] Ramadan, *In the Footsteps of the Prophet*, 191–192. Also, Lings mentions the son's death and the prophet's grief (*Muhammad*, 325).

[20] See Reza Aslan, *No god but God* (New York: Random House, 2011), xxv.

[21] Aslan, *No god but God*, 21.

[22] Aslan, *No god but God*, 60.

[23] Aslan, *No god but God*, 110.

[24] For analysis of miracles and Muhammad in relation to the Qur'an, see Denis Gril, "Miracles," *Encyclopaedia of the Qur'ān* (Brill Online Books and Journals).

[25] Muslims often put "SAW" after Muhammad's name as an abbreviation of the three Arabic words used to bless Muhammad. "PBUH" is also used and stands for "peace be upon him" in English. For technical information see Andrew Rippin, "Taṣliya," in *Encyclopaedia of Islam* (2nd ed., Brill Online Books and Journals).

[26] Ibn Ishaq, *The Life of Muhammad*, 81. To avoid tedious documentation we have chosen to reference only the most important quotations from *No god but God*.

[27] Farida Khanam, "Muhammad's Love and Tolerance for Mankind," IslamOnline, March 15, 2006, http://muhammad.islamonline.net/English/His_Example/HisQualities/07.shtml.

[28] Safi-ur-Rahman al-Mubarakpuri, *Ar-Raheeq Al-Makhtum (The Sealed Nectar)* (Al-Furqan, 1979), 492, 499. This work is also available as a free download on the al-Mubarakpuri website.

[29] Omid Safi, *Memories of Muhammad* (New York: HarperOne, 2009), 42.

[30] Safi, *Memories of Muhammad*, 45.

[31] Safi, *Memories of Muhammad*, 287. For primary material see http://www.dalail.co.uk/home.htm.

[32] Islamic blogs contain extensive argumentation about the superiority of Muhammad to all humans and affirmation that Allah created the worlds for Muhammad. See http://www.sunnah.org/aqida/THE_PROPHETIC_TITLE.htm#_ftn2 and http://salafiaqeedah.blogspot.ca/2011/02/whole-universe-was-created-for.html. The most famous Qur'anic verse used to argue this point is 21:107: "We have not sent you except as a mercy to the worlds."

[33] See Robert Gleave, "Personal Piety," in *The Cambridge Companion to Muhammad*, ed. Jonathan E. Brockopp (Cambridge: Cambridge University Press, 2010), 103–122. This work contains several other chapters that survey the influence of Muhammad in major areas of social and political life. In addition, Carl Ernst devotes a chapter to analysis of some of the highest views of the prophet in Sufi Islam.

[34] For a survey of changing Western views of Muhammad see John Tolan, "European Accounts of Muhammad's Life," in *The Cambridge Companion to Muhammad*, ed. Jonathan E. Brockopp (Cambridge: Cambridge University Press, 2010), 226–250. Amir Hussain's chapter, "Images of Muhammad in literature, art and music," in *The Cambridge Companion to Muhammad*, ed. Jonathan E. Brockopp (Cambridge: Cambridge University Press, 2010), 274–292, is very important. Kecia Ali, *The Lives of Muhammad* (Cambridge: Harvard University Press, 2014), is significant as well since it is comprehensive historically but also deals with contemporary perspectives. See the interview with Ali by Joseph Preville and Julie Poucher Harbin at Juan Cole's Informed Consent (October 23, 2014).

[35] Alphonse de LaMartaine's remark is quoted widely on the Internet by various Muslim sites. For example see http://www.ummah.com/forum/archive/index.php/t-209911.html.

[36] Hans Küng, *Christianity and the World Religions* (New York: Doubleday, 1986), 24–28. Küng expanded his treatment of Muhammad in his recent masterpiece *Islam: Past, Present, & Future* (Oxford: Oneworld, 2007), 91–124.

[37] For a sympathetic portrait of Guillaume, an English scholar, see Sidney Smith's obituary notice in the *Bulletin of the School of Oriental and African*

*Studies* 29, no. 2 (University of London, 1966), 478–481. Guillaume calls Muhammad "one of the great figures of history" whose "ability as a statesman faced with problems of extraordinary complexity is truly amazing." See A. Guillaume, *Islam*, 2nd ed. (Harmondsworth: Penguin, 1956), 23.

[38] On Watt (1897–2006) see the obituary notice in *The Guardian*, November 14, 2006. Watt wrote three biographical works, but the third, *Muhammad: Prophet and Statesman* (1961), is an abridgement of the first two, *Muhammad at Mecca* (1953) and *Muhammad at Medina* (1961).

[39] Karen Armstrong has gained prominence as the most popular Western writer sympathetic to Muhammad. See her *Muhammad: A Biography of the Prophet* (London: Phoenix Press, 2001), which contains an introduction written just after 9/11. She has been critiqued as careless on matters of historical acumen. See Hugh Fitzgerald, "Karen Armstrong: The Coherence of Her Incoherence," in *New English Review* (April 2005), and also note Robert Spencer's critique of Armstrong at his www.jihadwatch.org. He is replying to her critique of his book *The Truth about Muhammad*. See K. Armstrong, "Balancing the Prophet," *Financial Times*, April 27, 2007.

[40] S. H. Pasha is given as the author in the ICNA pamphlet and on various websites. One YouTube video follows Sasha's text but adds a different tribute at the end, saying of Muhammad, "he is our honorable master, teacher, role-model, father figure, and most beloved creation of Allah, the final prophet and messenger." See http://www.youtube.com/watch?v=FF4n6ExEwTI.

[41] Safi, *Memories of Muhammad*, 2.

# Chapter 7–How Reliable Is the Historical Record about Muhammad?

[1] The difficulty in finding Muhammad in the Qur'an is noted even by Western scholars sympathetic to the wider Islamic world. Thus, Angelika Neuwirth, one of the most influential modern scholars of the Qur'an, notes in the *Journal of Qur'anic Studies* 14, no. 1, 34: "it is true that in order to understand the Qur'an we ought not to rely on the details of Muhammad's life, about which after all we know very little (see Crone), and which in its traditional shape is the product of later communal imagination." See Neuwirth's review of *The Qur'an and its Biblical Subtext* in *The Journal of Qur'anic Studies* 14, no. 1, 34, 134.

2 Tom Holland, *In the Shadow of the Sword* (London: Little, Brown, 2012), 29, notes, "allusions to the life of the Prophet within the holy text were so opaque as to verge on the impenetrable." Glen Bowersock (the famous historian of late antiquity) wrote a very critical review in *The Guardian* (May 4, 2012), and Holland was given space for a response (May 7, 2014). Gerald Hawting, a highly regarded specialist in Islamic Studies, wrote a letter to *The Guardian* defending Holland.

3 Michael Cook, *The Koran: A Very Short Introduction* (New York: Oxford University Press, 2000), 135. Cook is using an older but still used title for the Qur'an.

4 Aslan also shows a deep appreciation for W. M. Watt's biographies of Muhammad. Aslan does not interact with scholars who are critical of Watt's rather naïve adopting of Islamic tradition as historical in relation to Muhammad. For critique of Watt see William M. Brinner in *Middle East Journal* 44, no. 4 (Autumn 1990), 734–735. Christopher Melchert notes that Watt treats Muslim sources of the seventh century "blithely." See Melchert's comments in his review of a festschrift for Michael Cook in the *Journal of Islamic Studies* 25, no. 2 (2014), 216.

5 Wim Raven, "Sira," in *Encyclopaedia of Islam* (2nd ed. Brill Online Books and Journals) and "Sira and the Qur'an," *Encyclopaedia of the Qur'ān* (Brill Online Books and Journals).

6 For the limitations of the maghazi material historically, see Martin Hinds, "al-Maghāzī," in *Encyclopaedia of Islam* (2nd ed., Brill Online Books and Journals). Some scholars, notably W. M. Watt, place a high value on the maghazi literature as useful for a biography of Muhammad, but such estimation is largely a matter of trust, given the time between Muhammad's death and the fully developed maghazi material. Muhammad Qasim Zaman refers to the sira and maghazi materials as historical "only with reservations." See "Maghazi and Muhaddithun: Reconsidering the Treatment of 'Historical' Materials in Early Collections of Hadith," *International Journal of Middle East Studies* 28 (1996): 1– 8, especially 1.

7 While G. H. A. Juynboll, "Ḥadīth and the Qur'ān," in *Encyclopaedia of the Qur'ān* (Brill Online Books and Journals), is not totally skeptical about the hadith, he does note that Western investigators believe that the chain of transmission about traditions, known as *isnads*, "are better left alone, inasmuch as not only a good number—as is generally admitted—but, conceivably, *all* of them may be forged, and that there

is no foolproof method of telling which one is sound and which one is not." Juynboll's doubts are of particular significance since he is one of the leading Western scholars to argue for a greater appreciation of hadith transmission. Readers should note that the references to al-Bukhari are given in different and confusing ways on the Internet. Every reference to a hadith by him has been checked to ensure items are not taken out of context.

[8] Scholars have debated whether there is a chronological order to sira, maghazi and hadith material. Sean W. Anthony, "Crime and Punishment in Early Medina," in *Analyzing Muslim Traditions*, eds. Harald Motzki, Nicolet Boekhoff-van der Voort and Sean Anthony (Leiden: Brill, 2010), 390, states, "these genres do not appear in a chronologically evolving chain of genres but, rather, evolve contemporaneously and dialectically with one another."

[9] His tafsir is also famous for his comment that the prophet at one point contemplated suicide. He also gives credence to the view that Muhammad for a brief time authorized the worship of three idols, in the famous incident of the "satanic verses." See "al-Ṭabarī" in *Encyclopaedia of Islam* (2nd ed. Brill Online Books and Journals).

[10] "Ḥadīth," *Encyclopaedia of Islam* (2nd ed., Brill Online Books and Journals). Harald Motzki, "The Collection of the Qur'ān: A Reconsideration of Western Views in Light of Recent Methodological Developments," in *Der Islam* 78 (2001), 1–34, has argued for a more positive view about hadith transmission in relation to reports about the collection of the Qur'an. He still recognizes, "we cannot be sure that things really happened as is reported in the traditions" (31). See also Harald Motzki, Nicolet Boekhoff-van der Voort, and Sean Anthony (eds.), *Analyzing Muslim Traditions* (Leiden: Brill, 2010). Motzki does not believe that the hadiths are largely authentic (234).

[11] Holland, *In the Shadow of the Sword*, 36, quoting an article by Joseph Schacht, a famous German scholar of Islamic law.

[12] Fazlur Rahman, *Islamic Methodology in History* (Islamabad: Islamic Research Institute, 1965), 70–71. Though Rahman denies that the hadith in general are "strictly historical" or "verbally speaking" they "go back to the Prophet," he argues, "its spirit certainly does," 80. His less than total adherence to traditional Islamic views on this and other matters led to charges of heresy against him while he was teaching in Pakistan.

[13] Holland, *In the Shadow of the Sword*, 39.

[14] Robert Hoyland, *Seeing Islam as Others Saw It* (Princeton: Darwin Press, 1997).

[15] Michael G. Marony reviews Hoyland's work positively in the *International Journal of Middle East Studies* 31, no. 3 (August 1999), 452–453.

[16] Patricia Crone and Michael Cook, *Hagarism: The Making of the Islamic World* (Cambridge: Cambridge University Press, 1977).

[17] Crone was the recipient of the 2013 Levi Della Vida medal for excellence in Islamic studies from UCLA.

[18] See Peter Brown, "Understanding Islam," in *The New York Review of Books* (February 22, 1979).

[19] We are not saying that Brown was uncritical of Crone and Cook. He complains about the "truculent and offhand manner" in which they present their assertions and notes "the infuriatingly cerebral and nonhistorical tone." Regardless, Aslan's treatment of Crone leaves the reader uninformed of her importance and acumen in the study of Islam.

[20] Aslan, *No god but God*, 27–28.

[21] For the 2011 update of his *No god but God* Aslan should have consulted Crone's popular article "What do we actually know about Muhammad?" He would have seen clearly that Crone is not totally skeptical of Islamic tradition. See her June 10, 2008, posting at www.opendemocracy.net. Of course, Crone showed her belief in Muhammad's existence and acceptance of some traditional Islamic views long before Aslan's first edition of *No god but God*. See, for example, Patricia Crone, "Serjeant and Meccan Trade," in *Arabica* 39, Fasc. 2 (July 1992), 216–240.

[22] Aslan, *No god but God*, 28.

[23] See R. Strothmann, "Ṣanʿāʾ," in *Encyclopaedia of Islam* (1st ed., Brill Online Books and Journals) and G. R. Smith, "Ṣanʿāʾ," in *Encyclopaedia of Islam* (2nd ed., Brill Online Books and Journals). Aslan would do well to read Crone's conclusions about rigorous historical work in "Serjeant and Meccan Trade." She writes, "a great many Muslim scholars still cannot believe that Western scholars study the rise of Islam for purely historical reasons" and notes that it is hard for scholars to study traditional Islamic views "without being affected by the reverence with which the supposed facts are presented." She laments that some Western scholars of Islam "frequently sound like Muslims, usually of the Sunni

variety, not only in the sense that they accept Sunni information, but also in that [they] revere it in a manner incompatible with the question mark to which they have in principle committed themselves. This is a compliment to the strength of Sunnism, but it does not do the modern study of its origins and development any good" (239).

24 The possibility that the earliest Muslims prayed towards Petra, Jordan, is the argument of Dan Gibson in *Qur'anic Geography* (Independent Scholars Press, 2011). See www.nabataea.net for details.

25 Robert Hoyland, *In God's Path* (New York: Oxford, 2014), Kindle ed., location 639.

26 Michael Bonner, *Jihad in Islamic History* (Princeton: Princeton University Press, 2006), 39.

27 Patricia Crone, Michael Cook and Martin Hinds, *God's Caliph* (Cambridge: Cambridge University Press, 1986), 24.

28 See Fred Donner, *Muhammad and the Believers* (Cambridge: Harvard/Belnap, 2010). Suleiman Mourad also notes the formative influence of Abd al-Malik in the shaping of Islam. See his recent interview in "Riddles of the Book," in *New Left Review* 86 (March–April 2014). Holland, *In the Shadow of the Sword* (379–391), makes much of the significance of Abd al-Malik as well.

29 Robert Spencer, *Did Muhammad Exist?* (Wilmington: ISI, 2012), 59. Spencer makes no claim to originality but builds on both older and newer critics of traditional Islamic claims in relation to historicity and Muhammad. For a sample of such writers see Ibn Warraq (ed.), *The Quest for the Historical Muhammad* (Amherst: Prometheus, 2000).

30 Jonathan A. C. Brown, *Misquoting Muhammad* (Oxford: Oneworld, 2014), electronic edition. It is ironic that Brown is skeptical on the crucial point of Muhammad and historicity given that Brown is mentioned as a new breed of Islamic scholar who shows that orientalism has died. On this latter point see HRH Prince Ghazi bin Muhammad, "The End of Orientalism in Islamic Studies," in *The Muslim 500 2014/15*, ed. S. Abdallah Schleifer (Amman: The Royal Islamic Strategic Studies Centre, 2014). The prince lists various scholars like Bell, Lewis, Cook and Crone and then states that their books and those of "their intellectual heirs" should be "transferred from the Islamic Studies shelves to the historical fiction shelves" (203).

# Chapter 8–Is Muhammad the Greatest Moral and Spiritual Model?

[1] For an example of the impact of traditional reports about Muhammad, see Nabeel Qureshi, *Seeking Allah, Finding Jesus* (Grand Rapids: Zondervan, 2014).

[2] Note Michael Lecker, "Zayd b. Ḥāritha," *Encyclopaedia of Islam* (2nd ed., Brill Online Books and Journals).

[3] William Muir wrote in his famous biography *The Life of Mahomet* 3 (London: Smith, Elder & Co., 1861), 231, "Our only matter of wonder is, that the Revelations of Mahomet continued after this to be regarded by his people as inspired communications from the Almighty, when they were so palpably formed to secure his own objects, and pander even to his evil desires."

[4] There is another, more current, controversy connected to Zayd. This has to do with the suggestion of David Powers, *Muhammad Is Not the Father of Any of Your Men* (Philadelphia: University of Pennsylvania Press, 2009), that Muhammad's ruling against adopted sons as true heirs was part of a larger scheme to ensure that Muhammad was the final prophet. Powers argues that the early text of the Qur'an was changed to make this binding. Walid Saleh, *Comparative Islamic Studies* 6.1–2 (2010), 251–264, believes that Powers' work is proof that "Revisionism in Islamic Studies has finally become a farce" (251).

[5] On Muhammad and polygamy see James Arlandson's work at http://www.answering-islam.org/Authors/Arlandson/women_polygamy.htm.

[6] See Madeline C. Zilfi, "Slavery: Ottoman Empire," in *Encyclopedia of Women & Islamic Cultures* (Brill Online Books and Journals).

[7] For one source on Africa see Humphrey J. Fisher, *Slavery in the History of Muslim Black Africa* (London: Hurst, 2001 and New York University Press, 2001). Fisher's work is especially important because of its argumentation on the causes of slavery in relation to African demographics. His work also contains illuminating commentary on the travel reports about modern slavery by various writers, most notably the German physician Gustav Nachtigal (1834–1885).

[8] For data on Islam and slavery related to India see, for example, K. S. Lai, *Muslim Slave System in Medieval India* (New Delhi, 1994). On Southeast Asia, note Anthony Reid, "Slavery: East Asia and Southeast Asia," in

*Encyclopedia of Women & Islamic Cultures* (Brill Online Books and Journals). The BBC entry on slavery in Islam notes that "the legality of slavery in Islam, together with the example of the Prophet Muhammad, who himself bought, sold, captured, and owned slaves, may explain why slavery persisted until the 19th century in many places (and later still in some countries). The impetus for the abolition of slavery came largely from colonial powers, although some Muslim thinkers argued strongly for abolition." See http://www.bbc.co.uk/religion/religions/islam/history/slavery_1.shtml.

[9] S. Moninul Haq (trans.), *Ibn Sa'd's Kitab al-Tabaqat al-Kabir [Book of the Major Classes]* (Idara Islamiyat-e-Diniyat: Islamic Book Service, 2009), 151.

[10] The advocacy of slavery throughout Church history is also depressing, of course. We take some hope from Paul's liberating dictum in Galatians 3:28, but this verse had little impact in the slave trades of later centuries. See the depressing narratives in Forrest G. Wood, *The Arrogance of Faith* (New York: Knopf, 1990). Thankfully, Christian slaves recognized the difference between a fallen Church and the Kingdom of God. This was expressed in one couplet by Harriot Jacobs: "Ole Satan's church is here below; Up to God's free church I hope to go" (from Wood, *The Arrogance of Faith*, 157).

[11] Tariq Ramadan, *In the Footsteps of the Prophet: Lessons from the Life of Muhammad* (Oxford: Oxford University Press, 2007), 25. Ramadan fails to face the ways in which slavery complicates his case for the Prophet's greatness. Ramadan asserts that the prophet urged that slaves be treated well; however, the prophet could have commanded the abolition of slavery.

[12] C. E. Bosworth writes that al-Tabari "is most famous as the supreme universal historian and Ḳurʾān commentator of the first three or four centuries of Islam." See "al-Ṭabarī," in *Encyclopedia of Islam* (2nd ed., Brill Online Books and Journals). For a detailed history see Michael Fishbein (trans.), *History of al-Tabari* 1–40, ed. Ehsan Yarshater (Albany: State University of New York Press, 1989–2007). The first volume, which contains a lengthy biography, notes, "Tabari's fame was such that no biographer in subsequent centuries who touched on Tabari's age and fields of scholarly activities could afford not to mention him" (1:9).

[13] See Watt, "ʿĀʾisha Bint Abī Bakr," in *Encyclopaedia of Islam* (2nd ed., Brill Online Books and Journals).

[14] Aslan, *No god but God*, 64–65, states that consummation happened after Aisha reached puberty, but he does not say when that was: "And while

Muhammad's union with a nine-year-old girl may be shocking to our modern sensibilities, his betrothal to Aisha was just that: a *betrothal*."

[15] Robert Spencer, *The Truth about Muhammad* (Washington: Regnery, 2006), 171.

[16] For the *Globe and Mail* series see http://www.theglobeandmail.com/static/world/behindtheveil/index.html.

[17] See Robert F. Worth, "Tiny Voices Defy Child Marriage in Yemen," *New York Times*, June 29, 2008.

[18] For analysis on torture and the blindness of the U.S. administration about the "war on terror" see Mark Danner, *Stripping Bare the Body* (New York: Nation, 2009). Charles Simic has an important analysis of *Stripping Bare the Body* in *The New York Review of Books* (February 11, 2010). George Packer gave the book and Danner an ambivalent response in *The New York Times Book Review* (October 15, 2009), which led to a testy exchange in the letters section (November 4, 2009) and further spats elsewhere. For Danner's work since *Stripping Bare the Body* was published, go to www.markdanner.com, and see his regular articles in *The New York Review of Books*. For appreciation on Danner's 2004 book on *Torture and Truth*, see Lawrence D. Freedman's comments in *Foreign Affairs* 84, no. 1 (Jan–Feb. 2005), 183–184.

[19] Fishbein (trans.), *History of al-Tabari* 8, 122.

[20] Fishbein (trans.), *History of al-Tabari* 8, 96. Ibn Ishaq, *Life of Muhammad*, 980, states that she was killed "cruelly" but gives no detail.

[21] Sir William Muir, *Life of Mahomet* 4 (1854), 13, one of the famous Western biographers of Muhammad, claims that the prophet was "an accomplice in the ferocious act." Muir names her Omm Kirfa.

[22] Thanks to Janet Clark, dean of Tyndale Seminary in Toronto, and Blair Clark, Director-at-Large, Canadian Baptist Ministries, for their help with translation of the Indonesian material.

[23] "US condemns Sudan over Christian woman's death penalty," Yahoo News, June 12, 2014.

[24] The Wikipedia entry on *The Satanic Verses* and the fatwa is extensive. See also Daniel Pipes, *The Rushdie Affair* (Piscataway: Transaction Books, 1990).

[25] See F. Griffel, "Apostasy," in *Encyclopedia of Islam* (3rd ed., Brill Online Books and Journals). Griffel also studies two particular Muslim jurists in "Toleration and exclusion. Al-Shāfiʿī and al-Ghazālī on the treatment of

apostates," in *Bulletin of the School of Oriental and African Studies* 64 (2001), 339–354. See as well chapter 4 in Yohanan Friedmann, *Tolerance and Coercion in Islam* (Cambridge 2003). Friedmann's work is reviewed carefully by Elizabeth Sartain in *International Journal for the Study of Modern Islam* 45, 1 (2005), 159–162.

[26] See Wael Hallaq, "Apostasy," in *Encyclopaedia of the Qur'ān* (Brill Online Books and Journals). Hallaq makes the important point that the so-called *ridda* or apostasy wars (AD 632–634) that followed Muhammad's death were not always about apostates, since some of the tribes that were attacked by Muslims were never Muslims themselves. He also notes that a couple of hadith mention various forms capital punishment could take, including beheading, crucifixion or banishment, but that burning someone to death was not acceptable. That is said to be God's punishment.

[27] Droge translation. Pickthall gives the same rendering. A. J. Arberry has "No compulsion is there in religion" while Yusuf Ali has "Let there be no compulsion in religion."

## Chapter 9–How Do Muslims View the Qur'an?

[1] Hans Küng, *Islam: Past, Present & Future* (Oxford: Oneworld, 2007), 62.

[2] Tariq Ramadan, *In the Footsteps of the Prophet: Lessons from the Life of Muhammad* (Oxford: Oxford University Press, 2007), 41.

[3] For these rules and others see Ahmad ibn Naqib al-Misri, *Reliance of the Traveller* (Beltsville: Amana, 1994, rev. ed.). Al-Misri (1302–1367) was a highly regarded shariah scholar of the Shafi'i school.

[4] Omid Safi, *Memories of Muhammad* (New York: HarperCollins, 2009), notes the presence of images of Muhammad in various Islamic circles through the centuries and includes some beautiful images.

[5] For examples of calligraphy from across the centuries see http://darmuseum.org.kw/dai/wp-content/uploads/2013/05/Verses-from-Quran-Brochure.pdf. Francois Deroche contends that an art form related to the Qur'an was developing in the early Umayyad period. See an interview with him at http://iqsaweb.wordpress.com/tag/francois-deroche/.

[6] On the importance of memory and recitation see A. T. Welch, "al-Ḳur'ān," in *Encyclopaedia of Islam* (2nd ed., Brill Online Books and Journals).

[7] For detailed discussion of the Qur'an's self-referencing see A. J. Droge's introduction in his new translation and Mustansir Mir, "Names of the Qur'ān," in *Encyclopaedia of the Qur'ān*.

[8] See Abbas and Masuma Jaffer, *Quranic Sciences* (London: ICAS Press, 2009), 75.

[9] For scholarly entries see William A. Graham, "Fātiḥa," in *Encyclopedia of the Qur'ān* and Ida Zilio-Grandi "al-Fātiḥa," in *Encyclopedia of Islam* (3rd ed., Brill Online Books and Journals).

[10] For a well-known introduction to the Qur'an by a Muslim scholar, see Farid Esack, *The Qur'an* (Oxford: Oneworld, 2002).

[11] See Ahmad Dallal, "Science and the Qur'ān," in *Encyclopedia of the Qur'ān*.

[12] Note the comments by A. J. Droge, *The Qur'an*, in all of the surahs where these strange letters are found.

[13] For detail on the *shahada* and the Qur'an see Andrew Rippin, "Witness to Faith," in *Encyclopaedia of the Qur'ān* (Brill Online Books and Journals).

[14] Consult the separate entries on the pillars in *Encyclopaedia of the Qur'ān* (Brill Online Books and Journals), and for ritual details see the extensive rules on prayer in Nuh Ha Mim Keller (ed., trans.), *Reliance of the Traveller: A Classic Manual of Islamic Sacred Law* (rev. ed., Beltsville: Amana Publishers, 1997), 101–243.

[15] On Shia Islam see W. Madelung, "Shīʿa," *Encylopaedia of Islam* (2nd ed., Brill Online Books and Journals), Andrew Rippin, *Muslims* (London: Routledge, 2001), 113–126, Küng, *Islam: Past, Present & Future*, 194–201, and Marshall Hodgson, *The Venture of Islam* 1 (Chicago: University Of Chicago Press, 1977), 372–384. For information on contemporary Shia realities see Vali Nasr, *The Shia Revival* (New York: W.W. Norton, 2007). Lesley Hazleton, *After the Prophet* (New York: Doubleday, 2009), has been critiqued for being somewhat careless about her historical reading. See Joseph A. Kechichian, "After the Prophet: The Epic Story of the Shia-Sunni Split in Islam (review)" *The Middle East Journal* 64, 2 (2010), 320–321.

[16] For detail on the hadith about the 72 virgins, note the relevant section with appendix in Jonathan A. C. Brown, *Misquoting Muhammad* (Oxford: Oneworld, 2014). For data on sexual rewards in paradise see Maher Jarrar, "Houris," and Wim Raven, "Martyrs," in *Encyclopaedia of the Qur'ān* (Brill Online Books and Journals). The hadith are sometimes explicit about both the sexual potency of Muhammad in his earthly life and virility among Muslims in the afterlife.

[17] See Brannon Wheeler, *Prophets in the Quran* (New York: Continuum, 2002), for analysis of Muslim exegesis relating to prophets in Muslim Scripture.

[18] Aliza Shnizer, "Sacrality and Collection," in *The Blackwell Companion to the Qur'an*, ed. Andrew Rippin (Oxford: Blackwell, 2008), 160–163, discusses the way that Muslims sought to harmonize accounts that the Qur'an was revealed all at once and in stages from 610–632.

[19] Ramadan, one of the most famous Muslim intellectuals, writes in *In the Footsteps of the Prophet*, 36, "Every year, during the month of Ramadan, the Prophet would recite to the Angel Gabriel all that he had received of the Qur'an so far in the order the angel had indicated. Thus was effected a regular verification of the contents and form of the Book that was slowly being constituted over a period of 23 years."

[20] McAuliffe (ed.), *The Cambridge Companion to the Qur'an*, 149.

[21] For an excellent website that provides detail on every Arabic word in the Qur'an, see the Quranic Arabic Corpus at http://corpus.quran.com/.

[22] See Christopher Melchert and Asma Afsaruddin, "Reciters of the Qur'ān," in *Encyclopedia of the Qur'ān* (Brill Online Books and Journals).

[23] For up-to-date scholarship on the Qur'an see the reports of the International Qur'anic Studies Association at http://iqsaweb.wordpress.com/.

## Chapter 10–Is the Qur'an God's Infallible Word?

[1] For a specialized study on early Muslim views about alleged Christian and Jewish changes to Scripture, see Gordon Nickel, *Narratives of Tampering in the Earliest Commentaries on the Qur'an* (Leiden: Brill, 2010).

[2] The orthodox view has been challenged by various Western scholars, including Arthur Jeffery, John Wansbrough, John Burton, Angelika Neuwirth, Günter Lüling, Andrew Rippin, Gerd-R. Puin, H. C. Graf von Bothmer, Patricia Crone, Christoph Luxenberg (a pseudonym) and Gerald Hawting, among many others. A few Muslim scholars have adopted non-traditional views of the Qur'an, most notably Nasr Abu Zaid, Mohammed Arkoun and Taha Hussein. The dissenting views against the orthodox Muslim view were the subject of Toby Lester's controversial article "What Is the Koran?" in *The Atlantic* (January 1999).

[3] Etan Kohlberg and Mohammad Ali Amir-Moezzi, *Revelation and Falsification* (Leiden: Brill, 2009), 2. This work is a critical introduction and translation of al-Sayyari's book against Sunni orthodoxy on the transmission of the Qur'an. Al-Sayyari is one of the earliest Shia writers on the topic. He lived in the mid-900s.

[4] See Frederik Leehmuis, in "Codices of the Qur'ān," in *Encyclopedia of the Qur'ān* (Brill Online Books and Journals).

[5] Keith Small, email correspondence, April 22, 2014.

[6] Fred Donner, in Gabriel Said Reynolds (ed.), *The Qur'an in its Historical Context* (London: Routledge, 2008), 42. John Wansbrough held a highly skeptical view of any traditional Muslim view of the Qur'an's origin and preservation. He also held to a late date for codification of the Qur'an. On Wansbrough see Donner's discussion, 41f. For an appreciation of Wansbrough see Carlos A. Segovia, "John Wansbrough and the Problem of Islamic Origins in Recent Scholarship: A Farewell to the Traditional Account," in *The Coming of the Comforter*, eds. Basile Lourié and Carlos A. Segovia (Piscataway: Gorgias Press, 2012), xix-xviii.

[7] Small, *Textual Criticism*, 168.

[8] Harald Motzki, "Muṣḥaf," in *Encyclopedia of the Qur'ān* (Brill Online Books and Journals).

[9] For a mild critique of Wansbrough see Kohlberg and Amir-Moezzi, *Revelation and Falsification* (Leiden: Brill, 2009), 11–12. They also have a very sober critique of the traditional Sunni view of the compilation of the Qur'an (13–23) combined with a focus on Shia objections to the notion of a faithful Uthmanic Qur'an (24f). For an example of evidence of an early codex of the Qur'an, see Behnam Sadeghi and Uwe Bermann, "The Codex of a Companion of the Prophet and the Qur'an of the Prophet," in *Arabica* 57 (2010), 343–436. The authors date both levels of the palimpsest under discussion to the seventh century with the lower writing to the first half of the century. They also note that the lower text of the Qur'an does not belong to the Uthmanic tradition.

[10] For data on the difficulties created as the oral recitation of the Qur'an gave way to a written text, see James A. Bellamy, "Textual Criticism of the Qur'ān," in *Encyclopaedia of the Qur'ān* (Brill Online Books and Journals). A. J. Droge argues in the preface to his new translation of the Qur'an that the oral transmission of the text has been overstated.

[11] Traditional Muslims will also have to deal with variants in Qur'an inscriptions on early Muslim coinage. On this, for example, see the discussion about copper coins in Iran that date to 702–703 in Luke Treadwell, "Qur'anic Inscriptions on the Coins of the ahl al-bayt from the Second to Fourth Century AH," in *Journal of Qur'anic Studies* 14, no. 2 (2012), 47–71.

[12] Ibn Ishaq, *The Life of Muhammad*, trans. Alfred Guillaume (Oxford: Ameena Saiyid, 2004), 145.

[13] See Shahab Ahmed, "Satanic Verses," in *Encyclopedia of the Qur'ān* (Brill Online Books and Journals). F. E. Peters and William Montgomery Watt are two of many Western scholars who accept the incident. Peters, *Muhammad and the Origins of Islam* (Albany: State University of New York Press, 1994), 160–161, writes, "it is impossible to imagine a Muslim inventing such an inauspicious tale."

[14] For the latest work on the oral composition of the Qur'an see Andrew Bannister, *An Oral-Formulaic Study of the Qur'an* (New York: Lexington, 2014).

[15] See John Renard, "Khaḍir/Khiḍr," in *Encyclopaedia of the Qur'an* (Brill Online Books and Journals), and "Khidr, al-" in *The Oxford Dictionary of Islam* (Brill Online Books and Journals). Sufi Muslims sometimes look to al-Khidr for transmission of spiritual authority. See "Silsilah," in *The Oxford Encyclopedia of the Islamic World* (Oxford Online Books and Journals).

[16] Kevin Van Bladel, "The Alexander Legend in the Qur'an 18:83–102," in *The Qur'an in its Historical Context*, ed. Gabriel Reynolds (New York: Routledge, 2008), 175–203.

[17] Van Bladel, "The Alexander Legend in the Qur'an 18:83–102," 182. The Alexander Legend advances a Christian vision for the Last Days, while the Qur'an avoids, as one would expect, a traditional Christian eschatology.

[18] See Grossfeld, *The Targum Sheni to the Book of Esther* (New York: Sepher-Hermon Press, 1994). Since the dating is uncertain, the details on the borrowing issue will have to wait for future scholarship to settle. For more on the Targum see Jacob Lassner, *Demonizing the Queen of Sheba* (Chicago: University of Chicago Press, 1993), and "Bilqīs" [the common Muslim name for the Queen of Sheba], in *Encyclopedia of the Qur'ān* (Brill Online Books and Journals).

[19] The Mishnah is dated about 200 C.E. See Jacob Neusner, "Rabbinic Judaism, Formative Canon of, II: The Halakhic Documents," in *Encyclopaedia of Judaism* (Brill Online Books and Journals). Neusner's translation of the passage includes a specific reference to Israelites, but Gilbert S. Rosenthal, "The Strange Tale of a Familiar Text," in *The Journal of the Academy for Jewish Religion* 3, no. 1 (2007), 57–65, argues that the earliest manuscripts of the Mishnah have the universalistic reading. Pre-Islamic Jewish materials also

mention a raven in connection to the killing of Abel, as does the Qur'an in the context of surah 5:32.

[20] For discussion of sources for Qur'anic material see James White, *What Every Christian Should Know about the Qur'an* (Bloomington: Bethany, 2013). A primary reference to the story of Abraham, idols and the rescue from fire can be seen in Genesis Rabba in Samuel Rapaport, *Tales and Maxims from the Midrash* (New York: E. Dutton, 1907). Reuven Firestone notes that the Qur'anic material on Abraham destroying the idols "has no biblical parallel but is well-known in Jewish exegetical literature," in "Abraham," in *Encyclopaedia of the Qur'ān* (Brill Online Books and Journals).

[21] See the comments by Suleiman Mourad, "Riddles of the Book," in *New Left Review* 86 (March-April 2014). Firestone makes the same point.

[22] Droge translation. He mentions that Ovid has Jupiter punishing some sinful islanders by turning them into apes. See Droge, notes on 7:164.

[23] Uri Rubin mentions the references about apes and pigs in "Jews and Judaism," in *Encyclopedia of the Qur'ān* (Brill Online Books and Journals).

[24] For documentation on modern use of apes and pigs towards Jews see http://www. jewishvirtuallibrary.org/jsource/History/memrireport.html and http://answering-islam.org/Authors/Arlandson/jew_apes.htm and Andrew G. Bostom, *The Legacy of Islamic Anti-Semitism* (Buffalo: Prometheus, 2008).

[25] Ibn Ishaq, *The Life of Muhammad*, 380. The slander against the Jewish men was given just before 600 to 900 of them were beheaded under Muhammad's watch. As noted elsewhere, Reza Aslan has an extensive apologia on the treatment of the Jewish tribe in *No god but God*. For the perspective of a Jewish writer on Muhammad and Islam, see Martin Gilbert, *In Ishmael's House* (Toronto: McClelland & Stewart, 2010). See also Martin Kramer (ed.), *The Jewish Discovery of Islam* (Tel Aviv: Moshe Dayan Center for Middle Eastern and African Studies, 1999). Kramer's introduction is at http://www.martinkramer.org/sandbox/reader/archives/the-jewish-discovery-of-islam/.

[26] The troubling lack of clarity in the Qur'an is noted in the comic strip *Jesus and Mo* where the barmaid asks, "Are there no editors in heaven?" See www.jesusandmo.net/.

[27] Noldeke also wrote, "Muhammad, in short, is not in any sense a master of style." Quoted in Robert Spencer, *Did Muhammad Exist?* (Wilmington: ISI Books, 2012), 150–151.

[28] Gibbon and Carlyle, quoted in Robert Spencer, *The Complete Infidel's Guide to the Koran* (Washington: Regnery, 2009), 17.

[29] See www.answering-islam.org/Quran/Contra/perspicuity_letters.html.

[30] See http://www.answering-islam.org/Quran/Contra/.

[31] See http://quranbiblecomparison.weebly.com/ for data on contrasts.

## Chapter 11–Does the Qur'an Get Jesus Right?

[1] For information about the life of Muhammad see Ibn Ishaq, *The Life of Muhammad* (trans. A. Guillaume; Oxford: Ameena Saiyid, 2004), written c. 767.

[2] For additional discussion, consult R. Dunkerley, *Beyond the Gospels: An Investigation into the Information on the Life of Christ to be Found outside the Gospels* (Baltimore: Penguin Books, 1957), 145–54; F. F. Bruce, *Jesus and Christian Origins Outside the New Testament* (Grand Rapids: Eerdmans, 1974), 167–86; G. Parrinder, *Jesus in the Qur'an* (New York: Oxford University Press, 1977); N. Robinson, *Christ in Islam and Christianity* (Albany: SUNY Press, 1991); S. A. Mourad, "On the Qur'anic Stories about Mary and Jesus," *Bulletin of the Royal Institute for Inter-Faith Studies* 1.2 (1999), 13–24.

[3] The pronunciation *'Īsā* is not as far removed from the Anglicized pronunciation "Jesus" as one might think. In the Greek writings of the New Testament and other early Christian literature, the name Jesus is *Iesous*. In Latin it is usually rendered *Iesu*. The letter *i* originally had a consonantal value, because the Hebrew name underlying the Greek form is *Yeshuah*, itself a shortened form of *Yehoshuah*, from which we get the well-known Old Testament name Joshua. The shortened Hebrew form *Yeshuah* in the time of Jesus and later was sometimes shortened to *Yeshu*. But the Qur'an's distinctive *'Īsā* form probably does not directly derive from either the Hebrew *Yeshu*, which was common in the rabbinic literature in the time Muhammad wrote, or from the Latin *Iesu*. It may derive from the name Esau, which in Hebrew would be vocalized as *'Esa* or *'Isa*. Some scholars theorize that Jewish scholars taught this pronunciation to Muhammad (which he accepted in good faith), not knowing that Esau (vilified in rabbinic tradition) was the brother of Jacob. Not all scholars accept this explanation.

[4] Jesus is given many names and titles in the Qur'an. He is called "the Messiah" (*al-Masīh*), "prophet" (*nabī*), "messenger" (*rasūl*), "son of

Mary" (*Ibn Maryam*), "Jesus son of Mary" (*'Īsā ibn Maryam*), and various combinations of these titles along with complimentary adjectives and descriptive phrases (e.g., "blessed" [*mubārak*], "worthy of esteem" [*wadjīh*], and the like). The sobriquets "son of Mary" and "Jesus son of Mary" occur some 50 times.

5 For a comprehensive discussion see L. Gardet, "Allāh," in *Encyclopaedia of Islam* (2nd ed., Brill Online Books and Journals). Surah 2:136 teaches that Jesus received revelation from Allah. Most Arab Christians regularly use Allah as their word for God, though some Christians, Arab or otherwise, argue for a distinction between God and Allah. Some Muslims want to ban Christians from using the word Allah altogether. In June 2014, Malaysia's Supreme Court upheld a ban against non-Muslims using the word.

6 For scholarly discussion see S. A. Mourad, "On the Qur'anic Stories about Mary and Jesus," *Bulletin of the Royal Institute for Inter-Faith Studies* 1.2 (1999), 13–24.

7 "Imran" is derived from Amram, probably the Amram of Numbers 26:58–59, who is the father of Aaron, Moses and Miriam. Evidently Muhammad has confused this Miriam (the sister of Moses), with Mary (whose name in Hebrew would also have been pronounced Miriam) the mother of Jesus.

8 This name is provided in the incipit of the Bodmer V manuscript, which dates to the late third or early fourth century. *Arabic Gospel of the Infancy* draws upon *Protevangelium of James*, *Infancy Gospel of Thomas* and Tatian's harmony of the New Testament Gospels, known as the *Diatessaron*.

9 The *Protevangelium of James* also teaches that the "brothers and sisters" of Jesus (see Mark 6:3), were only step-brothers and step-sisters, children born to Joseph, the husband of Mary, from a previous marriage. Some Christian Fathers, like Jerome, argued that the "brothers and sisters" of Jesus were actually cousins, for Joseph himself, like Mary, was a virgin.

10 For the Greek text of *Protevangelium of James*, a new translation and an introduction, see B. D. Ehrman and Z. Plese, *The Apocryphal Gospels: Texts and Translations* (Oxford: Oxford University Press, 2011), 31–71.

11 See A. G. Bannister, *An Oral-Formulaic Study of the Qur'an* (Lanham and New York: Lexington Books, 2014), 30. Bannister believes that one finds in the Qur'an evidence of "repeated, formulaic phrases," which

facilitate composition and live performance. It would also facilitate memorization. Bannister speaks of "a pool in which stories could cross-fertilize and influence one another" (7). Bannister also cites R. Firestone, *Journeys in Holy Lands* (Albany: State University of New York Press, 1990), 18–19, 56–158.

[12] J. A. Williams, *Islam* (New York: Washington Square Press, 1963), 18.

[13] See P. Hayek, *Le Christ de l'Islam: textes présentés, traduits et annotés* (Paris: Éditions du Seuil, 1959), 65.

[14] *Arabic Infancy Gospel* 1 reads, "He has said that Jesus spoke, and, indeed, when he was lying in his cradle said to Mary his mother: 'I am Jesus, the Son of God, the Logos, whom you have brought forth, as the angel Gabriel announced to you; and my Father has sent me for the salvation of the world'" (translation based on A. Walker, "The Arabic Gospel of the Infancy of the Saviour," in A. Roberts and J. Donaldson [eds.], *The Ante-Nicene Fathers: Translations of the Fathers down to AD 325* [10 vols., Edinburgh: T & T Clark, 1867–73], 8:405).

[15] Translation from Ehrman and Plese, *The Apocryphal Gospels*, 15.

[16] See in surah 3:3, where Muhammad says, "he (Allah), revealed the Law and the Gospel beforetime," the reference is to the Law of Moses and to the Gospel, that is, the sacred text of the Jews and the sacred text(s), of the Christians.

[17] Translation from Ehrman and Plese, *The Apocryphal Gospels*, 11. *Infancy Gospel of Thomas* originated in Greek and came to be translated in several languages. It is preserved in whole or in part in a number of languages, including Syriac, a language spoken in the Middle East in late antiquity and in the medieval period (and is still spoken). A simpler version of the story is found in *Arabic Infancy Gospel* 36.

[18] For discussion of the *Arabic Infancy Gospel* see J. K. Elliott, *The Apocryphal New Testament: A Collection of Apocryphal Christian Literature in an English Translation based on M. R. James* (Oxford: Clarendon Press, 1993), 100–107.

[19] The *Toledot Yeshu* is extant in dozens of medieval manuscripts. Most of its contents come from the Talmud and other rabbinic sources, though in some cases distinctive traditions of the *Toledot Yeshu* may have flowed into the Talmud. Peter Schäfer of Princeton University and a number of colleagues have transcribed about one hundred manuscripts and are preparing a critical text, which hopefully will soon be published. For now, one may wish to see

P. S. Alexander, "Jesus and His Mother in the Jewish Anti-Gospel (the Toledod Yeshu)," in C. Clivaz, et al. (eds.), *Infancy Gospels: Stories and Identities* (Tübingen: Mohr Siebeck, 2011), 588–616; P. Piovanelli, "The Toledot Yeshu and Christian Apocryphal Literature: The Formative Years," in P. Schäfer (ed.), *Toledot Yeshu ("The Life Story of Jesus"), Revisited: A Princeton Conference* (Tübingen: Mohr Siebeck, 2011), 89–100.

[20] The story is recounted in the Tosefta ("supplement"), an early fourth-century collection of legal tradition that augments the older Mishnah. The passage cited above is found in *t. Hullin* 2.22–23. For learned discussion of Jesus in the rabbinic literature, including the ben Pantera sobriquet, see P. Schäfer, *Jesus in the Talmud* (Princeton: Princeton University Press, 2007), especially 15–24.

[21] Elsewhere Celsus claims that Mary "was driven out by her husband, who was a carpenter by trade, when she was convicted of adultery" and that "the carpenter hated her and expelled her" (Origen, *Against Celsus*, 1.28, 39).

[22] The history of the charge against Jesus of practicing black magic will be treated further in chapter 12.

[23] There is a great deal of irony in the Gospel of John, some of it touching on the question of Jesus' origin. The question of his paternity is part of that discussion. For the evangelist, the answer is clear: The father of Jesus is God himself.

[24] The word "fornication" (Greek: *porneia*) clearly implies sexual intercourse outside of marriage.

[25] See R. E. Brown, *The Gospel according to John* (2 vols., Garden City: Doubleday, 1966–70), 1:357.

[26] See P. S. Alexander, "Toledot Yeshu in the Context of Jewish-Muslim Debate," 137–58.

[27] For further discussion of how indebted the Qur'an is to the Jewish and Christian biblical tradition, see A. Geiger, "What did Muhammad borrow from Judaism?" (orig. pub., 1898), in I. Warraq (ed.), *The Origins of the Koran* (New York: Prometheus Books, 1998), 165–226; William St. Clair-Tisdall, "The Sources of Islam" (orig. pub., 1901), in I. Warraq (ed.), *The Origins of the Koran* (New York: Prometheus Books, 1998), 227–91; C. C. Torrey, "The Jewish Foundations of Islam" (orig. pub., 1933), in I. Warraq (ed.), *The Origins of the Koran* (New York: Prometheus Books, 1998), 293–348; J. Wansbrough, *Quranic Studies* (Oxford: Oxford University Press, 1977; repr. New York: Prometheus, 2004).

# Chapter 12–Does the Qur'an Get the Death of Jesus Right?

[1] See P. Schäfer, *Jesus in the Talmud* (Princeton: Princeton University Press, 2007), 63–74. For other passages in which the rabbis accuse Jesus of practicing magic see *t. Shabbat* 11.15; *b. Shabbat* 104b; *b. Sanhedrin* 107b; *b. Sota* 47a. The miracles of Jesus, including healing and exorcism, were viewed as works of black magic, which in turn implied a pact with Satan, something of which Jesus was accused during his ministry (see Mark 3:22), and not just later after the death of Jesus in the context of polemic between church and synagogue. For further discussion see G. N. Stanton, "Jesus of Narareth: A Magician and a False Prophet Who Deceived God's People?" in J. B. Green and M. Turner (eds.), *Jesus of Nazareth: Lord and Christ: Essays on the Historical Jesus and New Testament Christology* (Grand Rapids: Eerdmans, 1994), 164–80.

[2] For learned discussion of this debate see S. A. Mourad, "Does the Qur'an Deny or Assert Jesus' Crucifixion and Death?" in G. S. Reynolds (ed.), *The Qur'an in Its Historical Context: New Perspectives on the Qur'an* 2 (London: Routledge, 2011), 349–57; G. S. Reynolds, "The Muslim Jesus: Dead or Alive?" *Bulletin of the School of Oriental and African Studies* 72 (2009), 237–58; S. A. Mourad, "Jesus in the Qur'an and Other Early Islamic Texts," in J. H. Charlesworth, B. Rhea and P. Pokorny (eds.), *Jesus Research: New Methodologies and Perceptions—The Second Princeton-Prague Symposium on Jesus Research, Princeton 2007* (Grand Rapids: Eerdmans, 2014), 753–65. Both Mourad and Reynolds argue that the view held by almost all Muslims—that Jesus did not die on the cross—is incorrect. We find their arguments plausible (they appeal to surah 3:55: "O Jesus, I am causing you to die"; 19.33: "the day I die"), but in the end we side with the majority. Surah 4:157–58 does not deny the death of Jesus; it denies that Jesus was crucified and that the Jews can take credit for killing him. We find the coherence with the teaching of Basilides compelling and fully in support of the long-held majority view.

[3] Technically this is correct, of course. The *Jews* did not kill Jesus; the *Romans* did, but they did so on the basis of the charges brought against him by the Jewish rulers (see Mark 14:43–15:15). But this is not the point the Qur'an is making. *Arabic Infancy Gospel* 35 states that it was the Jews (not Roman executioners) who pierced the side of Jesus with a lance.

[4] The meaning of this rare terminology is quite obscure and has occasioned scholarly discussion. In a recent study, Rick Oakes has argued that *shubbiha*

*lahum* should be translated as Allah "made them uncertain." See W. R. Oakes, "Toward a Contextual, Inter-Textual and Linguistic Translation of the Hapax Legomenon Term *shubbiha lahum* that is Found in Sūrat al-Nisā' 4 āya 157," in H. Darir, A. Zahid, and M. Y. Elidrissi (eds.), *Qur'anic Narratives and the Challenges of Translation* (Jordan: Modern Books' World, 2014), 146–68. Oakes suggests that the point is that God has made the Jewish boast of having killed Jesus very uncertain. For further discussion of Islamic tradition that may have a bearing on belief regarding the crucifixion of Jesus, see W. R. Oakes, "Ibn Wāṣil (D. 697/1298), Explains the Meaning of a Dream of Al-'Awrīs (D. 569/1174), about the Crucifixion of Jesus," *Islamochristiana* 39 (2013), 143–60.

5  For translation and discussion see F. F. Bruce, *Jesus and Christian Origins Outside the New Testament* (Grand Rapids: Eerdmans, 1974), 178–81.

6  The name Ahmad is from the same root as Muhammad. Qur'anic scholars believe that the reference to Ahmad in surah 61:6 is to Muhammad. The idea that Jesus foretold a successor may have been inspired by John 14:16, 26 and 16:7, where he spoke of the coming of a Paraclete, or Comforter.

7  See L. Ragg and L. Ragg, *The Gospel of Barnabas* (Oxford: Clarendon Press, 1907). Lonsdale and Laura Ragg's translation is based on the Italian manuscript housed in Vienna. See Ragg and Ragg, xiv. The manuscript itself probably dates to the late 16th century, while the text itself suggests a composition date in the 14th or 15th century. For recent scholarly discussion of the *Gospel of Barnabas* see J. Joosten, "The *Gospel of Barnabas* and the Diatessaron," *Harvard Theological Review* 95 (2002), 73–96; A. den Hollander, "The Gospel of Barnabas, the Diatessaron, and Method," *Vigiliae Christianae* 61 (2007), 1–20; J. Joosten, "The Date and Provenance of the *Gospel of Barnabas*," *Journal of Theological Studies* 61 (2010), 200–15.

8  For a review of the early evidence relating to the death of Jesus see C. A. Evans and N. T. Wright, *Jesus, the Final Days* (London: SPCK, 2008; Louisville: Westminster John Knox Press, 2009), 3–38. See also J. T. Carrol, J. B. Green, R. E. Van Voorst, J. Marcus, and D. Senior, *The Death of Jesus in Early Christianity* (Peabody: Hendrickson, 1995), 165–81. J. D. Crossan rightly remarks, "That he [Jesus] was crucified is as sure as anything historical can ever be" (*Jesus: A Revolutionary Biography* [San Francisco: HarperCollins, 1994], 145).

9  See J. D. G. Dunn, *Jesus Remembered* (Grand Rapids: Eerdmans, 2003), 855. Professor Dunn states, "This tradition, we can be entirely confident,

*was formulated within months of Jesus' death"* (the author's emphasis).

[10] For a learned and persuasive argument for this view see J. P. Meier, "Jesus in Josephus: A Modest Proposal," *Catholic Biblical Quarterly* 52 (1990), 76–103.

[11] See S. Pines, *An Arabic Version of the Testimonium Flavianum and its Implications* (Jerusalem: Israel Academy of Sciences and Humanities, 1971), 16. See also E. Bammel, "A New Variant Form of the Testimonium Flavianum," *Expository Times* 85 (1973–74), 145–47.

[12] See R. E. Van Voorst, *Jesus Outside the New Testament: An Introduction to the Ancient Evidence* (Grand Rapids and Cambridge: Eerdmans, 2000), 54. Although some scholars have argued that bar Serapion refers to the capture of Jerusalem in AD 70, Van Voorst (56) plausibly suggests that Mar bar Serapion wrote his letter in the second century, probably not long after the Romans defeated the Jewish rebel Simon ben Kosiba, known as Bar Kokhba, "son of the star," in AD 135. After that, the Jewish kingdom was truly taken away and Israel ceased to exist as a nation.

[13] See Van Voorst, *Jesus Outside the New Testament*, 39–53. Van Voorst provides an excellent, up-to-date critical discussion of the value of the testimony of Tacitus.

[14] For learned discussion of Trypho's treatise and its use by Justin Martyr see T. J. Horner, *"Listening to Trypho": Justin Martyr's Dialogue Reconsidered* (Leuven: Peeters, 2001). Horner concludes that Justin Martyr made use of a real text composed by a Jew, in which he raised objections against Christianity.

[15] For further comment see Van Voorst, *Jesus Outside the New Testament*, 58–64.

[16] For discussion of Celsus and his opinions about Christianity, see R. L. Wilken, *The Christians as the Romans Saw Them* (2nd ed., New Haven and London: Yale University Press, 2003), 94–125.

[17] Fragments of Porphyry's *Against the Christians* have been preserved in the *Apocriticus* by Macarius Magnes, a fourth century Christian. For discussion of Porphyry see Wilken, *The Christians as the Romans Saw Them*, 126–63.

[18] Apart from Basilides and a few Gnostic writings, whose denial of the death of Jesus is driven by a larger agendum, one that claims that Jesus was not physical but only appeared to be so.

[19] Reza Aslan, *Zealot: The Life and Times of Jesus of Nazareth* (New York: Random House, 2013), 78–79, 124, 158–59, 172–75, 178. Aslan

repeatedly states that Jesus was crucified. Aslan, however, is not a historian. He is a professor of creative writing at the University of California at Riverside. He is not an expert in the study of the historical Jesus, but he has earned a Ph.D. in the sociology of religion.

[20] Todd Lawson, *The Crucifixion and the Qur'an* (Oxford: Oneworld, 2009), is an important study that seeks to argue that Islamic tradition is somewhat nuanced in the denial of the crucifixion. For review of Lawson see Mustafa Shah in *Journal of Qur'anic Studies* 12 (1–2), 191–203. Shah is impressed by Lawson's work but believes that the Islamic tradition of denial of the crucifixion is much stronger than Lawson implies.

## Chapter 13–Does Islamic Tradition Get Jesus Right?

[1] The translation comes from S. A. Mourad, "Jesus in the Qur'an and Other Early Islamic Texts," in J. H. Charlesworth, B. Rhea and P. Pokorny (eds.), *Jesus Research: New Methodologies and Perceptions—The Second Princeton-Prague Symposium on Jesus Research, Princeton 2007* (Grand Rapids: Eerdmans, 2014), 753–65, especially 760. For a fuller discussion of this tradition see S. A. Mourad, "A Twelfth Century Muslim Biography of Jesus," *Islam and Christian-Muslim Relations* 7 (1996), 39–45.

[2] The translation comes from Mourad, "Jesus in the Qur'an and Other Early Islamic Texts," 761.

[3] One may wonder if the saying was in part inspired by the story of Samson and Delilah, in which the woman attempts to bind the Hebrew champion with cords and robes (see Judges 16:9, 11).

[4] In many places wine is mentioned as a good thing (e.g., Ps 104:15). There is no indication that Jesus abstained from wine or regarded it a "key to evil."

[5] Paul teaches Christians to take care, lest their freedom to eat and drink cause weaker brothers and sisters to stumble, which on occasion might mean not eating meat or not drinking wine (Romans 14:21). Otherwise, there is nothing wrong in eating meat and drinking wine.

[6] The translation comes from Mourad, "Jesus in the Qur'an and Other Early Islamic Texts," 761.

[7] It reads, "Live in Christ and you will acquire treasure in heaven" (*Teaching of Silvanus* [Nag Hammadi Codex VII, 4, 88.15–17]).

[8] It reads, "For where the mind is, there is the treasure" (*Gospel of Mary* [Berlin Gnostic Codex 8502, 1, 10.15–16]). The Gnostic orientation is

seen in replacing "heart" with "mind," thus placing the emphasis on knowledge rather than on loyalty.

[9] The translation comes from Mourad, "Jesus in the Qur'an and Other Early Islamic Texts," 761.

[10] From 'Abd al-Jabbar, *Book of the Signs of Muhammad's Prophecy.* Translation is from Marvin W. Meyer, *The Unknown Sayings of Jesus* (San Francisco: HarperCollins, 1998), 144 (no. 183).

[11] The Talmud says a "certain philosopher" (probably a Christian is meant) is approached and asked a question, in hopes of tripping him up: "I desire that a share be given me in my (deceased) father's estate." The philosopher replies, "Divide."

[12] From al-Jabbar, *Book of the Signs of Muhammad's Prophecy.* Translation is from Meyer, *The Unknown Sayings of Jesus,* 145 (no. 184).

[13] From Abu Hamid al-Ghazzali, *Revival of the Religious Sciences* 1.8. Translation is from Meyer, *The Unknown Sayings of Jesus,* 146 (no. 186).

[14] P. Oxy abbreviates papyri documents from the ancient Egyptian city Oxyrhynchus. The three Greek fragments of the *Gospel of Thomas* date to the third century AD.

[15] From al-Ghazzali, *Revival of the Religious Sciences* 1.49. Translation is from Meyer, *The Unknown Sayings of Jesus,* 148 (no. 188).

[16] "The Pharisees and the scribes have taken the keys of knowledge; they themselves have hidden them. Neither have they entered; nor have they allowed those who are in the process of entering to enter" (*Gos. Thom.* §39, according to P.Oxy. 655). In *Gospel of Thomas* §102 we find a version of one of Aesop's well known fables: "Woe to the Pharisees, for they are like a dog sleeping in the manger of oxen, for neither does he eat nor does he let the oxen eat."

[17] The three sayings are from al-Ghazzali, *Revival of the Religious Sciences,* 3.48.8; 3.140.10; and 3.149.5, respectively. Translations and discussion will be found in F. F. Bruce, *Jesus and Christian Origins Outside the New Testament* (Grand Rapids: Eerdmans, 1974), 184. For the third saying see Meyer, *The Unknown Sayings of Jesus,* 154 (no. 197).

[18] The inscription is on a mosque at Fatehpur, Sikri, India (erected in 1601). Translation is from Meyer, *The Unknown Sayings of Jesus,* 156 (no. 200). See also the comments in J. Jeremias, *Unknown Sayings of Jesus* (London: SPCK, 1957), 99–10; and Bruce, *Jesus and Christian Origins Outside the New Testament,* 130.

[19] Abdallah ibn Omar al-Baidawi (d. c. 1286). Cited by Marvin Meyer, *The Unknown Sayings of Jesus*, 178n200.

[20] It has been suggested that it reflects Jesus' instruction to his disciples, sent out as apostles, not to spend too much time in any one village or any one house (Mark 6:10: "Where you enter a house, stay there until you leave the place"). The early Church took this instruction very seriously (see *Didache* 11:4–5; 12:2: "If the one who comes is merely passing through, assist him as much as you can. But he must not stay with you for more than two or, if necessary, three days").

[21] For brief discussion of this rabbinic saying see Jeremias, *Unknown Sayings of Jesus*, 100.

[22] Christian Syrian language and tradition is in evidence throughout the Qur'an. For studies of the influence of Christian Syrian tradition see S. Griffith, "Syriacisms in the Arabic Qur'ān: Who were those who said 'Allah is third of three,'" in M. Bar-Asher, S. Hopkins, S. Stroumsa, and B. Chiesa (eds.), *A Word Fitly Spoken: Studies in Medieval Exegeses of the Hebrew Bible and the Qur'ān* (Jerusalem: The Ben-Zvi Institute, 2007), 83–110; "The Gospel, the Qur'ān, and the Presentation of Jesus in al-Ya'qubi's Tarikh," in *Bible and Qur'ān: Essays in Scriptural Intertextuality*, ed. J. Reeves (Leiden; Boston: Brill, 2004), 133–60; and "Christian Lore and the Arabic Qur'ān: The 'Companions of the Cave' in Sūrat al-Kahf and in Syriac Christian Tradition," in G. S. Reynolds (ed.), *New Perspectives on the Qur'ān* (The Qur'ān in Its Historical Context 2; London; New York: Routledge, 2011), 109–38; G. Reynolds, *The Qur'ān and its Biblical Subtext* (New York; London: Routledge, 2012); and E. I. El-Badawi, *The Qur'ān and the Aramaic Gospel Traditions* (London and New York: Routledge Press, 2014). For studies of the influence of Syrian language in the Qur'an see A. Mingana, "Syriac Influence on the Style of the Kur'ān," *Bulletin of The John Rylands Library* 2 (1927), 77–98; and E. I. El-Badawi, "The Impact of Aramaic (especially Syriac), on the Qur'ān," *Religion Compass* 8 (2014), 220–28.

[23] On asceticism in the *Gospel of Thomas* see R. Uro, "Is *Thomas* an Encratite Gospel?" in R. Uro (ed.), *Thomas at the Crossroads: Essays on the Gospel of Thomas* (Edinburgh: T & T Clark, 1998), 140–62. Uro recognizes Encratite tendencies in *Thomas* but thinks the original compiler, though ascetic in tendencies, was probably not himself an Encratite.

[24] From personal communication (21 July 2014). The Council of Nicea took place in AD 325 and the Council of Chalcedon took place in AD 451.

## Chapter 14–Does Islam Liberate Women?

[1] Reza Aslan, *No god but God* (New York: Random House, 2011), 57. Aslan points out that it is difficult to know exactly what kind of identity Muhammad's community had in the early years in Medina. Given this, it is hard to know how he and other Muslims can be so confident that Medina was a model society. Further, given the wars and deadly schisms in the immediate aftermath of Muhammad's death, Muslims should give more serious thought to what kind of community was built by the prophet.

[2] Aslan, *No god but God*, 58.

[3] Aslan, *No god but God*, 60.

[4] For these various items see Aslan, *No god but God*, 60–61.

[5] Aslan, *No god but God*, 74.

[6] This is from Jamal Badawi's widely printed essay "Women in Islam." You can see it at many Islamic sites, including http://fair.org.au/women-islam/.

[7] Aslan, *No god but God*, 64.

[8] Aslan, *No god but God*, 72, writes, "the image of the Muslim woman as indubitably oppressed and degraded by Islam not only persists but is being conceived of almost wholly through the singular symbol of the veil." Aslan argues that the veil is a supposed affront to Enlightenment ideals (73).

[9] See Aslan, *No god but God*, 65–66 and 73–74.

[10] Aslan might be confused here because of uncritical reliance on Leila Ahmed's careless use of the Qur'an in regards to veiling in her famous *Women and Gender in Islam* (New Haven: Yale University Press, 1992). For careful analysis of the Qur'anic data consult Mona Siddiqui, "Veil," in *Encyclopaedia of the Qur'ān*, and Anne Sofie Roald, *Women in Islam* (London: Routledge, 2001), 254–294. Though Roald misspells Ahmed as Ahmad, she offers some important corrections to Ahmed and Fatima Mernissi, another famous Muslim feminist.

[11] Roald has a careful and nuanced discussion of the Sunni schools of law and also the *Salafist* tradition that claims to rely largely on the Qur'an alone.

[12] Rahela Nayebzadah, "Representations: The Veiled Muslim Woman: North America," in *Encyclopedia of Women & Islamic Cultures* (Brill Online Books and Journals).

[13] Aslan, *No god but God*, 67.

[14] Aslan, *No god but God*, 69.

[15] Aslan, *No god but God*, 70.

[16] Fakhry and Ali are critiqued in Khaleel Mohammed, "Assessing English translations of the Qur'ān," *The Middle East Quarterly* 12, no. 2 (Spring 2005), 58–71.

[17] See the endorsement of Arberry (1905–1969, longtime professor of Arabic at Cambridge) in Khaleel Mohammed, "Assessing English translations of the Qur'ān," *The Middle East Quarterly* 12, no. 2 (Spring 2005), 58–71.

[18] On the technical issues related to the Arabic terms see Elsaid Badawi and Muhammad Abdel Haleem (eds.), *Dictionary of Qur'anic Usage* (Brill Online Books and Journals). The entry "ḍ–r–b" translates 4:34 as "reason with them, keep apart from them in bed and hit them." Also see the linguistic information in the Quranic Arabic Corpus (http://corpus.quran.com), led by Kais Dukes and a team at the University of Leeds.

[19] Aslan mentions Bakhtiar's work but does not quote it.

[20] Bakhtiar's translation in 4:34 of "go away" came as a result of consulting Edward William Lane's *An Arabic-English Lexicon*. See Neil MacFarquhar, "New Translation Prompts Debate on Islamic Verse," in *The New York Times* (March 25, 2007).

[21] See Amina Wadud al-Muhsin, "Qur'an and Woman," in *Liberal Islam: A Sourcebook*, ed. Charles Kurzman (Oxford: Oxford University Press, 1998), for such an attempt.

[22] Abu Dawud, "Book of Marriage," 2146. Note also al-Bukhari 7, 62:132, where the Muslim is told to "not beat his wives like he would a slave." The immediate occasion for surah 4:34 is noted by various Muslim scholars. See, for example, al-Wahidi, *Asbab al-Nuzul*, trans. Mokrane Guezzou (Louisville: Fons Vitae, 2006). Al-Wahidi (d. 1075) was a major Qur'an commentator.

[23] The quotations from David Cook are from an email he sent to Professor Beverley on August 29, 2014.

[24] Ayesha S. Chaudhry, *Domestic Violence and the Islamic Tradition* (New York: Oxford, 2013).

[25] Chaudhry, *Domestic Violence and the Islamic Tradition*, 3.

[26] Chaudhry, *Domestic Violence and the Islamic Tradition*, 8. Of course, the pre-colonial reading is adopted by some contemporary writers without

blush. Abdul-latif Mushtahiri writes, "If admonishing and sexual deser-
tion fail to bring forth results and the woman is of a cold and stubborn
type, the Quran bestows on man the right to straighten her out by way of
punishment and beating, provided he does not break her bones nor shed
blood. Many a wife belongs to this querulous type and requires this sort
of punishment to bring her to her senses!" (*You Ask and Islam Answers*,
94, quoted at http://www.answering-islam.org/BehindVeil/btv3.html).

[27] See her extended discussion (10–20). Her honesty in facing tough issues
is also shown in "I Wanted One Thing and God Wanted Another," in
*Journal of Religious Ethics* 39, no. 3 (September 2011), 416–439.

[28] Chaudhry and Aslan would do well to ponder the 1996 Sokal hoax, the
clever ploy done by scientist Alan Sokal to show the limits of postmod-
ernism. Sokal wrote deliberate nonsense in fashionable jargon, and it
was accepted in a scholarly journal. See Alan Sokal, *Intellectual
Impostures* (New York: Picador, 1998), and *Beyond the Sokal Hoax*
(Oxford: Oxford University Press, 2008). The debate about Sokal has
gone on for years. See
http://www.physics.nyu.edu/faculty/sokal/index.html#reviews.

[29] Calls to abolish female circumcision are being increasingly joined to
attempts to ban male circumcision. On these matters see
http://www.historyofcircumcision.net/ and David L. Gollaher,
*Circumcision: A History of the World's Most Controversial Surgery*
(New York: Basic Books, 2000).

[30] See details in the fact sheet at www.who.int. Mona Eltahawy has an op-
ed on "Fighting Female Genital Mutilation" in *The New York Times*
(November 16, 2014). Also, see her brave and explosive work
*Headscarves and Hymens: Why the Middle East Needs a Sexual
Revolution* (New York: Farrar, Stratus and Giroux, 2015).

[31] For scholarly discussion of the Qur'an, hadith and schools of law related
to circumcision, see "Khafḍ" [Arabic term], in *Encyclopaedia of Islam*
(2nd ed., Brill Online Books and Journals), and Frederick Mathewson
Denny, "Circumcision," in *Encyclopaedia of the Qur'ān* (Brill Online
Books and Journals).

[32] Muslim websites refer readers to *Time's* coverage on the topic of female
circumcision. See, for example, the February 6, 2014, report where Andrew
Katz and Meeri Koutaniemi, a Finnish photographer, document the ritual in
a Kenyan village. The World Muslim Congress posts graphic photos from

Danish Ahmad Khan from India. Khan started a campaign in 2011 to gather signatures to ask Dr. Syedna Muhammad Burhanuddin, then head of the Bohra Muslims, to abolish the practice. (Burhanuddin died in 2014, and his son Mufaddal Saifuddin now heads the movement.) Ironically, the World Muslim Congress site includes a long, technical article by Afroz Ali that approves a very limited female circumcision only for adults as Islamic.

[33] Aslan, *No god but God*, 71. Aslan's remark about God's stewardship of the Qur'an in terms of its contextualization is a rather strange statement to make of a text that is eternal.

[34] Aslan, *No god but God*, 71.

[35] Ruth Roded, "Women and the Qur'ān" in *Encyclopaedia of the Qur'ān* (Brill Online Books and Journals).

[36] Temporary marriages or *mut'a* were allowed by Muhammad, according to both Sunni and Shia scholars. The second caliph, Umar, prohibited the practice, and it is not allowed in the four Sunni schools of law. For information on *mut'a* see Shahla Haeri, "Temporary Marriage," in *Encyclopaedia of the Qur'ān* (Brill Online Books and Journals), and *Law of Desire* (Syracuse: Syracuse University Press, 1989).

[37] See Phyllis Chesler, "Worldwide Trends in Honor Killings," *The Middle East Quarterly* 17 (Spring 2010), no. 2, 3–11. For statistics see http://wikiislam.net/wiki/Honor_Killing_Index.

[38] See Jennifer Zobair, "Muslim American Women Are the New Normal," at www.altmuslimah.com.

[39] For information about the work of WISE and their profiles of 100 extraordinary Muslim women see http://www.wisemuslimwomen.org/.

[40] The World Economic Forum has produced the Gender Gap Index since 2006. The 2013 report is available at http://www.weforum.org/reports/global-gender-gap-report-2013.

[41] See www.themuslim500.com.

[42] See www.karamah.org.

[43] See Farah El-Sharif, "My First Hajj," at http://www.altmuslimah.com/b/mca/4996.

[44] See www.irshadmanji.com.

## Chapter 15–Is Islam a Religion of Peace?

[1] See Gilles Kepel and Jean-Pierre (eds.), *Al Qaeda in its own Words* (Cambridge: Belknap, 2008), 55. In an interview with *Time* (January 11,

1999), bin Laden told the famous Pakistan journalist Rahimullah Yusufzai, "Fighting is a part of our religion and our Shari'a. Those who love God and his Prophet and this religion cannot deny that. Whoever denies even a minor tenet of our religion commits the gravest sin in Islam." See http://content.time.com/time/world/article/0,8599,2054517,00.html.

[2] Reza Aslan, *No god but God* (New York: Random House, 2011), 83. Aslan also does not give significant attention to the fact that Muhammad broke the Arab custom that no warring take place during sacred times of the year.

[3] For the importance of the raids see Khalil Athamina, "Badr," in *Encylopaedia of Islam* (3rd ed., Brill Online Books and Journals).

[4] Aslan also overplays the reticence of Muhammad for battle unless attacked. If the prophet did not want war, he could have avoided raiding the Meccan caravans in the first place. It was also more than defensive that the prophet plugged the wells nearest the Meccan army before the battle of Badr began. For details see Athamina, "Badr," and Ibn Ishaq, *The Life of Muhammad*, trans. A. Guillaume (Oxford: Ameena Saiyid, 2004).

[5] Aslan quotes one author who says that Badr was "hardly more than a brawl." This is difficult to reconcile with the body count and the monumental importance attached to the victory by Muslims then and ever since. For the battle details and the significance of Badr, see Athamina, "Badr," John Nawas, "Badr" *Encylopaedia of the Qur'an* (Brill Online Books and Journals), Ali Bahramian and Rahim Gholami, "Badr" *Encyclopaedia Islamica* (Brill Online Books and Journals), and Homayra Zaid, "Battle of Badr" in *The Oxford Encyclopedia of the Islamic World* (Oxford Reference online). Muslim exegetes link over 30 separate verses in the Qur'an with the battle.

[6] For Aslan's apologetic on Muhammad and the Jews see *No god but God*, 90–102. Rizwi Faizer notes that the execution of the Jewish men is not linked to any Qur'anic passage in either Ibn Ishaq's history of the killings or Waqidi's military accounts in his *Maghazi*. See Faizer, "Expeditions and Battles," in *Encyclopaedia of Qur'ān* (Brill Online Books and Journals).

[7] See al-Bukhari 1, 4:234.

[8] For reference on Duma see William Montgomery Watt, *Muhammad at Medina* (Oxford: Clarendon, 1956), 115.

[9] Watt, *Muhammad at Medina*, 116.

[10] In relation to Muhammad and the sword, Pope Benedict XVI created enormous controversy by his remarks at Regensburg on September 12, 2006.

The pontiff quoted words from Byzantine emperor Manuel II Paleologus: "Show me just what Mohammed brought that was new, and there you will find things only evil and inhuman, such as his command to spread by the sword the faith he preached." Benedict later said that the quotation did not represent his personal views. His speech is available at www.vatican.va.

[11] Marshall Hodgson, *The Venture of Islam* 1 (Chicago: University of Chicago Press, 1977), 186.

[12] Hans Küng, *Islam: Past, Present & Future* (Oxford: Oneworld, 2007), 120.

[13] Aisha was possibly sarcastic when she noted "Truly thy Lord makes haste to do thy bidding" in relation to Allah's will coinciding with Muhammad's wishes. This remark was supposedly made in the context of God informing the prophet that he did not have to obey the protocols set for visiting his wives in a particular order. See Tor Andrae, *Mohammed: The Man and His Faith* (New York: Routledge, 2008, original 1936), 154. The hadith is found in al-Bukhari 6, 60:311.

[14] Ella Landau-Tasseron, "Jihād," in *Encyclopaedia of the Qur'ān* (Brill Online Books and Journals). The confusing nature of the Qur'an on jihad is also noted in E. Tyan, "Djihād," in *Encyclopaedia of Islam* (2nd ed., Brill Online Books and Journals), and Michael Bonner, *Jihad in Islamic History* (Princeton University Press, 2006), 20.

[15] Aslan, *No god but God*, 82.

[16] David Cook, *Understanding Jihad* (Berkeley: University of California Press, 2005), 46. Cook points out how major interpreters of Islam like John Esposito stress the greater jihad at the expense of accuracy (39–44). Cook also critiques the popular theory that Sufi Muslims are pacifists in relation to military jihad. Cook's stress in his book is on accuracy in historical judgments about jihad in relation to classical Islamic law and the teachings of the giant Muslim jurists and exegetes.

[17] See, for example, William Montgomery Watt, "Islamic conceptions of the *holy war*," in T. Murphy (ed.), *The Holy War* (Columbus: Ohio State University Press, 1976), 141–56, and Reuven Firestone, *Jihad: The Origin of Holy War in Islam* (Oxford University Press, 1999). Firestone notes the varied emphases in the Qur'an on attitudes to war, which he argues is based on the corresponding ambivalence in the earliest Muslim community of Medina. Firestone recognizes, of course, that the more militant stance won out. See Paul Cobb's appreciative review in *Journal of Near Eastern Studies* 62, no. 3 (July 2003),

222–223. For important critical comments note Rudolph Peters' review in *International Journal of Middle East Studies* 34, no. 4 (November 2002), 738–740, and Abdulaziz Sachedina in *The Journal of Religion* 81, part 3 (2001), 506–507.

[18] Here is Michael Lecker's translation: "This is a compact from Muḥammad the prophet, between the Muʾminūn and Muslimūn of the Quraysh and Yathrib and those who join them as clients, attach themselves to them, and fight the **holy** war with them" (emphasis added). See Lecker, "Constitution of Medina," in *Encylopaedia of Islam* (3rd ed., Brill Online Books and Journals).

[19] A. J. Droge translation. The translation of Yusuf Ali uses the term "pagans," while the Sahih International version uses "polytheists."

[20] Aslan, *No god but God*, 86.

[21] Aslan does not give enough attention to the uncomfortable fact that the sword verses were said by classical Muslim exegetes to abrogate or trump the earlier and more peaceful teachings of the Qur'an. On this score, Aslan also offers a sentimental defense of the Qur'an's bewildering chronology and the way abrogation is used to ease the chaos in the Qur'an order, structure and style. After mentioning abrogation, Aslan, *No god but God*, 171, claims that what the ordering of the Qur'an "most clearly indicates is that God was rearing the Ummah like a loving parent, instructing it in stages and making alterations when necessary, from the first Revelation in 610 to the last in 632." On the sword verses and abrogation, see Ella Landau-Tasseron, "Jihād." Her entry on jihad ends by noting its sanctity in relation to warfare.

[22] Rashad Ali and Hannah Stuart argue in their work *A Guide to Refuting Jihadism* (London: Henry Jackson Society, 2014) that Islamic terrorists have misunderstood classical Islamic jihad. Their detailed critique is available on the Henry Jackson Society site (http://henryjacksonsociety.org/wp-content/uploads/2014/02/Refuting-Jihadism.you pdf). For an update by the authors see their report at the Hudson Institute (http://www.hudson.org/research/10459–refuting-jihadism-can-jihad-be-reclaimed-).

[23] Here are President Bush's words on September 20, 2001: "I also want to speak tonight directly to Muslims throughout the world. We respect your faith. It's practiced freely by many millions of Americans, and by millions more in countries that America counts as friends. Its teachings are

good and peaceful, and those who commit evil in the name of Allah blaspheme the name of Allah. The terrorists are traitors to their own faith, trying, in effect, to hijack Islam itself. The enemy of America is not our many Muslim friends; it is not our many Arab friends. Our enemy is a radical network of terrorists, and every government that supports them." See his whole speech at http://georgewbush-white-house.archives.gov/news/releases/2001/09/20010920–8.html.

[24] As a case in point, surah 5:33 states, "The penalty (for), those who wage war (against), God and His messenger, and who strive in fomenting corruption on the earth, is that they be killed or crucified, or their hands and feet on opposite sides be cut off, or they be banished from the earth."

[25] Aslan, *No god but God*, 85.

[26] Points 2 and 3 are from Aslan, *No god but God*, 81.

[27] On the ridda wars see Michael Lecker, "al-Ridda," in *Encyclopaedia of Islam* (2nd ed., Brill Online Books and Journals).

[28] See Yohanan Friedmann, "Dhimma," in *Encyclopaedia of Islam* (3rd ed., Brill Online Books and Journals), and Fred Astren, "Dhimma," in *Encyclopedia of Jews in the Islamic World* (Brill Online Books and Journals). For critique of dhimmitude see Bat Ye'or, *Islam and Dhimmitude* (Madison: Farleigh Dickinson University Press, 2001), and Mark Durie, *The Third Choice* (Deror Books, 2010). Both Bat Ye'or and Durie are critiqued as too polemical. On Ye'or see Robert Irwin in *Middle Eastern Studies* 38, no. 4 (Oct. 2002), 213–215.

[29] Patricia Crone, "Among the Believers," *Tablet* (August 10, 2010), reviewing Donner, *Muhammad and the Believers* (Cambridge: Harvard/Belnap Press, 2010). Other scholars have shared Crone's negativity towards Donner's bold work. See, for example, the lengthy critique by Jack Tannous in *Expositions* 5.2 (2011), 126–141. Tannous argues that Donner's book is "radically revisionist" but historically implausible. Christian C. Sahner raises some concerns in his review in the *Times Literary Supplement* (July 1, 2011). Robert Hoyland suggests that Donner has "apologetic aims" in his book, ones that "are out of place in works of history." See Hoyland's new work *In God's Path* (New York: Oxford University Press, 2015), Kindle ed., 1071–1072.

[30] Hoyland, *In God's Path*, 1065, shares Crone's view that the goal of the conquests, through violence and other means, was not to force conversion, since there was deep interest in gaining booty from non-Muslims.

[31] Aslan, *No god but God*, 95: "Pagans and polytheists, however, were often given a choice between conversion and death." The Muslim conquests of the polytheistic Hindus of India involved some of the greatest massacres in human history. See Will and Ariel Durant, *Our Oriental Heritage* (New York: Simon & Schuster, 1963), chapter 16, section 6. J. Burton-Page, "Hind" [ancient word for India], in *Encyclopaedia of Islam* (2nd ed., Brill Online Books and Journals), mentions that in 1389, Delhi "was given up to pillage, plunder and wholesale massacre."

[32] He references Bernard Lewis, Max Weber and Samuel Huntington in the lead to his complaints about stereotypes (80).

[33] In her *Tablet* article, Crone refers to Donner's earlier work *The Early Muslim Conquests* (Princeton: Princeton University Press, 1981). Crone gave this a mixed response in *American Historical Review* 88, no. 2 (April 1983), 440–442. See also Donald Little's review in *Muslim World* 75, no. 1 (January 1, 1985), 47–48 and Ira Lapidus in *Journal of the American Oriental Society* 103, no. 2 (April–June 1983), 448–449.

[34] The parallels between just war and the Islamic understanding of jihad are made in Bonner, *Jihad in Islamic History*, 4–6.

[35] This statement was made in *Al-Hayat* (the London based Arabic newspaper), on November 5, 2001, and is reproduced in Kanan Makiya and Hassan Mneimneh, "Manual for a Raid," *The New York Review of Books* (January 17, 2002).

[36] The open letter is available at http://lettertobaghdadi.com/ and reprinted in S. Abdallah Schleifer (ed.), *The Muslim 500 2014/15* (Amman: The Royal Islamic Strategic Studies Centre, 2014), 173–197. The scholars also wrote, "Jihad without legitimate cause, legitimate goals, legitimate purpose, legitimate methodology and legitimate intention is not jihad at all, but rather, warmongering and criminality."

[37] Aslan, *No god but God*, 80.

[38] Roy Mottahedeh and Ridwan al-Sayyied trace the division to Muhammad al-Nafs az-Zakiyah in the first half of the 8th century in *The Crusades from the Perspective of Byzantium and the Muslim World*, eds. Angeliki E. Laiou and Roy Mottahedeh, (Washington: Dumbarton Oaks, 2001), 28. They note that Fred Donner places the division in the late 8th century. Mottahedeh and al-Sayyied also point to a third abode in ongoing Muslim history, that of "the realm of treaty relations (Dar al-Ahd)."

[39] For Ibn Taymiyya's interpretive views on the Qur'an see Walid Saleh, "Ibn Taymiyya and the Rise of Radical Hermeneutics," in *Ibn Taymiya and His Times*, eds. Shahab Ahmed and Yossef Rapport (Oxford: Oxford University Press, 2010).

[40] See H. Loust, "Ibn Taymiyya," in *Encylopaedia of Islam* (2nd ed., Brill Online Books and Journals). Ibn Taymiyya's influence on the Wahhabi is also mentioned in Esther Peskes and W. Ende, "Wahhābiyya," in *Encylopaedia of Islam* (2nd ed., Brill Online Books and Journals) and in Milton Viorst's evocative work *In the Shadow of the Prophet* (Cambridge: Westview, 2001), 215–216. Timothy Winter (also known as Shaykh Abdal Hakim Murad) notes Ibn Taymiyya's influence on Sayyid Qutb via Rashid Rida. See his "Bombing without Moonlight" at www.masud.co.uk.

[41] According to Bonner, *Jihad in Islamic History*, Ibn Taymiyya was no moderate in his day, since he adopted the use of jihad against those he regarded as heretics and against corrupt Islamic regimes. Bonner also notes his influence on later radicals. See Bonner, *Jihad in Islamic History*, 143–144, 161–162. Suleiman Mourad makes the same point about Ibn Taymiyya's influence on radical Muslims. See interview in "Riddles of the Book," *New Left Review* 86 (March–April 2014). Also, note a similar view in Cook, *Understanding Jihad*, 66. In William McCants, *Militant Ideology Atlas: Executive Report of November 2006* (West Point: Combating Terrorism Center, 2006), 7, 15, Ibn Taymiyya is listed as the most quoted pre-Modern Islamic figure by modern jihadists. In balance, Ibn Taymiyya abandoned some of his extreme views near the end of his life (see S. Abdallah Schleifer [ed.], *The Muslim 500*, 11.)

[42] Thomas Madden, *First Things* (June–July 2005), review of Thomas Asbridge's *The First Crusade* (Oxford: Oxford University Press, 2004).

[43] Christopher Tyerman, *God's War* (Cambridge: Belnap/Harvard, 2006). As one would expect, Tyerman notes that financers of the Crusades and the soldiers involved hoped for recovery of costs through land and booty (85–86). Aslan's note about the silk route may be his sarcastic use of older and discarded theories that sought to explain the Crusades mainly through economic interests.

[44] In relation to polemics about the Crusades, it is noteworthy that Tyerman condemns both those who "configure the past as comfortingly different from the present day" and those who hold "the past as a mirror to the

present" (xiv). At the end of his staggering detail on the Crusades, Tyerman writes "the internal, personal decision to follow the cross, to inflict harm on others at great personal risk, at the cost of enormous privations, at the service of a consuming cause, cannot be explained, excused or dismissed either as a virtue or sin. Rather, its very contradictions spelt its humanity" (922).

[45] See the testimony in C. R. N. Routh, *They Saw It Happen in Europe 1450–1600* (Oxford: Basil Blackwell, 1965). Miroslav Volf quotes a different brutal eyewitness report in his theological work *Allah: A Christian Response* (San Francisco: HarperOne, 2011), 41–42.

[46] Saladin, quoted in Efraim Karsh, *Islamic Imperialism* (New Haven: Yale University Press, 2006), 83. See D. S. Richards, "Saladin," in *Encyclopedia of Islam* (2nd ed., Brill Online Books and Journals).

[47] It must be noted that Saladin is sometimes pictured inaccurately as a gentle warrior, as in Sir Walter Scott's *The Talisman*. See Ibn Warraq, *Sir Walter Scott's Crusades and Other Fantasies* (Nashville: New English Review Press, 2013). For radical Islamic emphasis on Muhammad see, for example, the posts at defenderofthelands.blogspot.ca or the contents of *Dabiq*, the magazine of the Islamic State first published in July 2014 in various languages, including English.

[48] For an example of the multiplex dynamics involved in state and political power plays on all sides of a colonialist drama, see Scott Anderson, *Lawrence in Arabia* (New York: Random House, 2013).

[49] See Barry Rubin and Wolfgang Schwanitz, *Nazis, Islamists, and the Making of the Modern Middle East* (New Haven: Yale University Press, 2014). Also, note Schwanitz's defense of their book in *Tablet* (March 6, 2014). See the moving memoir by Judith Mendelsohn Rood, "Shoah/Nakbah: Offerings of Memory and History," in *History (1933–1948): What We Choose to Remember*, eds. Margaret Monahan Hogan and James M. Lies (Portland, University of Portland, 2011), 411–448.

[50] See Louis Fishman's opinion piece on Turkey's anti-Semitism in *Haaretz* (July 23, 2014).

[51] See Robert Fisk, *The Great War for Civilisation* (New York: Knopf, 2005). For a critique of Fisk's massive tome see Efraim Karsh, *Commentary* 121, no. 2 (February 2006), 63–66. Like Fisk, Thomas Friedman, the famous *New York Times* columnist, can be powerful in his

critique of all sides in the Middle East. This was shown as early as his *From Beirut to Jerusalem* (New York: Farrar Straus Giroux, 1989).

[52] See Reza Aslan, "The Christian Exodus," *Foreign Affairs* (September 11, 2013). For further analysis see Tom Holland, "Persecution of Christians in the Middle East Is a Crime against Humanity," *The Guardian* (December 22, 2013), and Ronald S. Lauder, "Who Will Stand up for the Christians?" *The New York Times* (August 19, 2014). Also note Raymond Ibrahim, *Crucified Again* (Washington: Regnery, 2013), and Michael Coren, *Hatred: Islam's War on Christianity* (Toronto: Signal, 2014).

[53] Aslan, *No god but God*, 173.

[54] Mustafa Akyol, *Islam without Extremes* (New York: Norton, 2011). While admiring his desire for a liberal Islam, Suleiman A. Mourad, "Real Reform?" in *First Things* (January 2012), chides Akyol's unwarranted adulation of Turkey and careless reading of Islamic history. For a Canadian voice pushing for moderate Islam see Tarek Fatah, *Chasing a Mirage* (Mississauga: John Wiley, 2008).

[55] See Kanan Makiya, *Republic of Fear* (Berkeley and San Francisco: University of California Press, 1998), and *Cruelty and Silence* (New York: W. W. Norton, 1993). While the need for self-criticism in America or every other nation and among all people, religious or otherwise, is an obvious necessity, its absence makes unbearable reading in hindsight. See Brian Urquhart, "A Cautionary Tale," *The New York Review of Books* (June 10, 2004), where he reviews Bob Woodward's famous *Plan of Attack*. After Woodward quotes George W. Bush that he had no doubts over starting the Iraq War, Urquhart comments, "No doubt at all. Perhaps that is one of the most dangerous problems facing the US." For other material about lack of self-criticism see Thomas Ricks, *Fiasco* (New York: Penguin, 2006).

[56] Kanan Makiya in *The Observer* (October 7, 2011). Makiya's appeals for self-criticism in the Muslim world stand regardless of whether or not he is insufficiently self-critical about the second Gulf war. He was one of the most powerful voices in support of the U.S. invasion of Iraq. He told President George W. Bush that the American troops "will be greeted with sweets and flowers in the first months." He watched the fall of Baghdad on TV on April 9, 2003, with Bush in the Oval Office. "It was a wonderful moment. I think that the liberation of Iraq is a great historic

achievement of the United States, and I think that it will go down in history as such. I am very proud to have been in that room on that day." See the interview with Sam Spector, *The Middle East Quarterly* 12, no. 2 (Spring 2005). For analysis of Makiya see Dexter Filkins, "Regrets Only?" *The New York Times Magazine* (October 7, 2007), Tara McKelvey, "Interventionism's Last Hold-Out" *The American Prospect* (May 14, 2007), and the Radio Open Source interview with Makiya at http://radioopensource.org/he-got-it-wrong-alas-kanan-makiya/.

[57] For interpretation on the Islamic State see Patrick Cockburn, *The Jihadis Return* (New York: OR Books, 2014), and the writings of Aymenn Jawad Al-Tamimi at www.aymennjawad.org, Daveed Gartenstein-Ross at www.defenddemocracy.org, Jonathan Spyer at www.jonathanspyer.com, Charles Lister at the Brookings Doha Centre, Thomas Joscelyn at *The Long War Journal* and Jessica T. Mathews in *The New York Review of Books*. Mathews is president of the Carnegie Endowment.

[58] Adulation of jihad is now ubiquitous. The Islamic State leader called for "volcanoes of jihad" in a November 13, 2014, speech. A former justice minister of Pakistan wrote, "The most glorious word in the vocabulary of Islam is jihad." See quotation in Laurent Murawiec, *The Mind of Jihad* (Cambridge: Cambridge University Press, 2008), 321. He meant the jihad of violence. For important data on terrorism see the *Global Terrorism Index* from the Institute for Economics & Peace (at www.start.umd.edu/gtd/ and www.visionofhumanity.org, for example) though note critique of some methodological issues at Global Research (www.globalresearch.ca). For analysis of terrorism in Pakistan and Afghanistan see Ahmed Rashid at www.ahmedrashid.com and his *Descent into Chaos* (New York: Viking, 2008) and *Taliban* (New Haven: Yale University Press, 2010, second edition).

## Chapter 16–Easter Truths, Muslim Realities and Common Hope

[1] For scholars who defend the historicity of the resurrection of Jesus we recommend N. T. Wright, *The Resurrection of the Son of God* (Minneapolis: Fortress, 2003), Gary Habermas and Michael Licona, *The Case for the Resurrection of Jesus* (Grand Rapids: Kregel, 2004), Michael Licona, *The Resurrection of Jesus* (Downers Grove: InterVarsity, 2010) and Stephen T. Davis, *Risen Indeed* (Grand Rapids: Eerdmans, 1993), among others.

[2] For examples of Christian scholars who face difficult issues see William J. Webb, *Slaves, Women and Homosexuals: Exploring the Hermeneutics of Cultural Analysis* (Downers Grove: InterVarsity, 2001), and Paul Copan, *Is God a Moral Monster?* (Grand Rapids: Baker, 2011). In addition, John Kessler works with difficult topics in his magisterial *Old Testament Theology* (Waco: Baylor University Press, 2013).

[3] We commend the writings of C. S. Lewis and Ravi Zacharias for readers interested in popular intellectual defense of Christianity. On a more philosophical level, consult works by Alvin Plantinga, Richard Swinburne and William Lane Craig. Those who want to explore the relationship of Christian faith and science can turn to Alister McGrath, Robin Collins, John Lennox, Bruce Gordon, Francis Collins and John Polkinghorne. Francis J. Beckwith is a great resource on moral and political issues in the light of Christian teaching.

[4] The Qur'an has a distorted understanding of the Christian doctrine of the Trinity. See the material at www.answering-islam.org/Trinity/index.html.

[5] Kenneth Cragg provides an eloquent argument for witness to the Jesus of the New Testament in his work *The Call of the Minaret* (Maryknoll: Orbis, 1985). He writes this of the connection between the Cross and Easter: "The resurrection is not an arbitrary finale to a situation that otherwise would have been different. It is the intrinsic victory of Christ as crucified and of the cross as Christ bore it, a victory that seals human redemption and opens the door of eternal life…. To bypass the cross is to remain unaware of Easter. The garden where there was an empty tomb is not reached save by way of the garden of the agony" (275).

[6] For a dramatic conversion that illustrates these realities see Mosab Hassan Yousef, *Son of Hamas* (Carol Stream: Tyndale House, 2010). For other conversion stories see http://answering-islam.org/Testimonies/index.html.

[7] For an example of Reza Aslan's dogmatic dismissal of miracles, see *Zealot: The Life and Times of Jesus of Nazareth* (New York: Random House, 2013), 104, where he writes, "To be clear, there is no evidence to support any particular miraculous action by Jesus."

[8] See Reza Aslan, *No god but God* (New York: Random House, 2011), 159. Aslan also fails to see the contradiction between his skepticism about miracles and his belief in God as creator, given the dazzling realities of the universe as proof of an intelligent miraculous designer.

[9] Aslan, *Zealot*, 176

[10] Aslan, *Zealot*, 177.

[11] For critique of Hume see, for example, C. S. Lewis, *Miracles* (London: Collins, rev. ed. 1960), Richard Swinburne, *The Concept of Miracle* (New York: Macmillan, 1970), Francis Beckwith, *David Hume's Argument Against Miracles* (Lanham: University Press of America, 1989), Robert Larmer, *Questions of Miracle* (Montreal: McGill-Queen's University Press, 1996), Douglas Geivett and Gary Habermas (eds.), *In Defense of Miracles* (Downers Grove: InterVarsity, 1997), Craig S. Keener, *Miracles: The Credibility of the New Testament Accounts* (2 vols., Grand Rapids: Baker Academic, 2011), and, most significantly, John Earman, *Hume's Abject Failure* (New York: Oxford University Press, 2000). Also, look for Timothy McGrew's critique of Hume in a forthcoming volume in honor of Alvin Plantinga to be edited by Trent Dougherty and Jerry Walls.

[12] See David Baggett (ed.), *Did the Resurrection Happen?* (Downers Grove: InterVarsity, 2009). This work consists of the transcript of a conversation/debate between Gary Habermas and Flew, with a review essay on the topic by Baggett. Professor Beverley was a student and then friend of Antony Flew and knew firsthand his openness to the possibility of the resurrection of Jesus as historical.

[13] Aslan, *Zealot*, 174–175.

[14] One can see the ideological alternatives on the Israel-Palestinian conflict in the opposing views of Efraim Karsh in his *Palestine Betrayed* and *Fabricating Israeli History* versus Ilan Pappe's *The Ethnic Cleansing of Palestine*. The same divide is illustrated in the website perspective of Eli Hertz at www.mythsandfacts.org/ versus Juan Cole at www.juancole.com.

[15] See, for example, Rory Stewart, "Afghanistan: A Shocking Indictment," *The New York Review of Books* (November 6, 2014). As well, note Carlotta Gall's *The Wrong Enemy* (New York: Houghton Mifflin Harcourt, 2014) and Ahmed Rashid's review "Pakistan: Worse than We Knew," in *The New York Review of Books* (June 5, 2014).

[16] See the open letter and related material at www.acommonword.com. Some Christian leaders at Yale (Harold Attridge, Miroslav Volf, Joseph Cumming and Emilie Townes) gave the open letter a warm reception through publication in *The New York Times* (November 18, 2007) of

"Loving God and Neighbor Together" (see http://faith.yale.edu/common-word/common-word-christian-response). Various evangelical Christians have been critical of the Yale response, for example, John Piper and Al Mohler. However, both of them expressed their concerns in the context of appreciation for dialogue with Muslims that was created by the Common Word project. For further information see Miroslav Volf, Ghazi bin Muhammad and Melissa Yarrington (eds.), *A Common Word* (Grand Rapids: Eerdmans, 2009). Our appreciation for *A Common Word* is not without concern about some of its content. For various critiques from Sam Solomon and others see the extensive material at http://www.answering-islam.org/Letters/common_word.htm.

[17] See Khaled Abou El Fadl, *The Great Theft* (New York: HarperCollins, 2005).

[18] Haroon Sidiqqi, *Being Muslim* (Toronto: Groundwood, 2006). Karim H. Karim should be noted as well. He is a very influential and erudite Muslim leader based at Carleton University in Ottawa, Canada. See, for example, his "Clash of Ignorance" article in *Globe Media Journal* 5, no. 1 (2012): 7–27.

[19] See http://www.canadiancouncilofimams.com/canadian-council-of-imams-declaration/. The declaration includes this statement: "We believe in peaceful coexistence, dialogue, bridge building, and cooperation among all faiths and people for the common good of humanity."

[20] H. R. H. Prince Ghazi bin Muhammad, *Love in the Holy Quran* (Chicago: Kazi Publications, 2011). The Prince, the main author behind *The Common Word*, has received great endorsements for his book from high-ranking Christian leaders and scholars.

[21] See the profile on Seyyed Hossein Nasr at http://www.nasrfoundation.org/bios.html.

[22] See www.pluralism.ca for an example of the Aga Khan's work.

[23] *Christianity Today* magazine has several reports on the Reconciliation Walk. See, for example, Thomas Dixon, "Jerusalem: Reconciliation Walk Reaches Pinnacle" (September 6, 1999). See interview with Lynn Green at http://www.charlesstrohmer.com/writings/interviews/lynn-green-muslims-christians/. The YWAM YouTube channel has a three-part report from Lynn Green. Also Cathy Nobles is interviewed at http://vimeopro.com/highwaysolutions/contemporarytv/video/86543123.

[24] For data on Rick Love see www.ricklove.net and www.peace-cata-lyst.net/about.

[25] See the Grace and Truth affirmation at www.30-days.net/reveal/wp-content/uploads/pdf/grace_and_truth_affirmation.pdf.

[26] Joseph Cumming's work is available at www.josephcumming.com.

[27] See Carl Medearis, *Muslims, Christians, and Jesus* (Minneapolis: Bethany, 2008), and Ted Dekker and Carl Medearis, *Tea with Hezbollah* (New York: Doubleday Religion, 2010).

[28] See Norman Geisler and Abdul Saleeb, *Answering Islam*, 2nd ed. (Grand Rapids: Baker, 2002). Christine Schirrmacher is at the Islamic Studies Institute in Bonn but also works with the International Institute for Religious Freedom. Dudley Woodberry is an emeritus professor at Fuller Seminary and editor of *Muslims and Christians on the Emmaus Road* (Monrovia: MARC Publications, 1989). Lamin Sanneh's *The Crown and the Turban* (Boulder: Westview Press, 1996) is significant for his analysis of Islam in Africa.

[29] Lamin Sanneh, *Whose Religion is Christianity?* (Grand Rapids: Eerdmans, 2003), and *Christianity Today* interview: www.christianitytoday.com/ct/2003/october/35.112.html.

[30] For data on Jay Smith see http://www.apologetics-central.com/leaderjaysmith.htm#Misc, and for Robert Spencer's site visit www.jihadwatch.org.

[31] On the overuse of the Islamophobic charge see Douglas Murray, *Islamophilia* (Kindle edition, 2013).

[32] Paul Moses captures the amazing story in his book *The Saint and the Sultan* (New York: Doubleday, 2009).

[33] Readers are encouraged to note the combination of optimism and realism in Hans Küng's *Islam* (Oxford: Oneworld, 2007). The great theologian critiques Judaism, Islam and Christianity for their weaknesses but wants to build on their strong ethical agreements, since there will be "no peace among the nations without peace among the religions" (661).

# Appendix 1–Reza Aslan's *Zealot*: Wrong at Many Points

[1] For current, mainstream perspectives on New Testament scholarship consult P. Achtemeier, J. B. Green and M. M. Thompson (eds.), *Introducing the New Testament: Its Literature and Theology* (Grand Rapids: Eerdmans, 2001), or R. E. Brown, *An Introduction to the New Testament* (New York: Doubleday, 1997).

[2] E. P. Sanders, *The Historical Figure of Jesus* (London and New York: Penguin, 1993), 100.

[3] See A. Runesson, D. D. Binder, and B. Olsson, *The Ancient Synagogue from its Origins to 200 CE: A Source Book* (Leiden: Brill, 2010); C. A. Evans, *Jesus and His World: The Archaeological Evidence* (London: SPCK; Louisville: Westminster John Knox Press, 2012), 38–58.

[4] R. E. Brown, *The Birth of the Messiah: A Commentary on the Infancy Narratives in the Gospels of Matthew and Luke* (Garden City: Doubleday, 1977; updated ed., New York: Doubleday, 1993).

[5] Some reviewers have charged Aslan with exaggerating his credentials. We can see why they do. See Allan Nadler's review in *Jewish Review of Books* (http://jewishreviewofbooks.com/articles/449/reza-aslan-what-jesus-wasnt/), as well as Dale Martin's review in *The New York Times* (http://www.nytimes.com/2013/08/06/books/reza-aslans-zealot-the-life-and-times-of-jesus-of-nazareth.html?pagewanted=2&_r=4). Aslan claims he invested "two decades of rigorous academic research into the origins of Christianity" (xix–xx) and wrote *Zealot* "based on [his] two decades of scholarly research into the New Testament and early Christian history" (*Zealot: The Life and Times of Jesus of Nazareth* [New York: Random House, 2013], xx). This may impress the general public, but it does not impress qualified scholars in the field, especially given the sloppiness and errors in *Zealot*.

Aslan's name does not appear in the University of Innsbruck's databank of scholarly publications and authors, which suggests that he probably has not published in any academic, peer-reviewed journals and reference works related to New Testament and Christian origins. In 2009, Aslan received his PhD in sociology from the University of California in Santa Barbara. The title of his dissertation is "Global Jihadism as a Transnational Social Movement: A Theoretical Framework." He is associate professor in the Creative Writing program at the University of California in Riverside. *Zealot* might better be viewed in part as a piece of creative writing, not a serious piece of learned scholarship.

Aslan's *Zealot* has been given sustained and devastating critique by scholars of the New Testament, whether evangelical or mainline Christian, Jewish or otherwise. Several academics have rebuked Random House for allowing such an inept book to be published. This should indicate to Aslan that there are very troubling aspects to his scholarship. As well, we suggest that his status as a scholar is muted by his intemperate and vulgar language in social media.

## Appendix 2–Was Jesus Married to Mary Magdalene?

[1] Some scholars assign much later dates. Scholars tend to think *The History of Joseph and Aseneth* was originally in Greek, probably by a Jew living in Egypt. The text may have been glossed in a few places by later Christian scribes, though that is debated.

[2] J. H. Charlesworth (ed.), *The Old Testament Pseudepigrapha* (2 vols., New York: Doubleday, 1983–85). *The History of Joseph and Aseneth* appears in volume 2.

## Appendix 6–The Islamic State and *The Atlantic*

[1] Graeme Wood clarified his position in an interview with Sam Harris (see www.samharris.org/blog) and in a follow-up online piece for *The Atlantic* (February 24, 2015). Bernard Haykel defended himself in an interview with Jack Jenkins at www.thinkprogress.com and clarified his argument in conversation with Anderson Cooper on CNN. While Haykel is the one scholar of Islam quoted by Wood, other scholars (like David Cook at Rice University) were consulted.

[2] Patrick Cockburn, *The Jihadis Return* (New York: OR Books, 2014), is noted in chapter 15, endnote 57, along with other resources on the Islamic State. In addition, for other sources (of varying quality) see Daniel Byman, *Al Qaeda, the Islamic State and the Global Jihadist Movement* (New York: Oxford University Press, 2015); Charles Lister, *The Islamic State* (Washington: Brookings, 2015); Loretta Napoleoni, *The Islamist Phoenix* (New York: Seven Stories Press, 2014); Robert Spencer, *The Complete Infidel's Guide to ISIS* (Washington: Regnery, 2015); Erick Stakelbeck, *Isis Exposed* (Washington: Regnery, 2015); Jessica Stern and J. M. Berger, *ISIS: The State of Terror* (New York: HarperCollins, 2015); and Michael Weiss and Hassan Hassan, *ISIS: Inside the Army of Terror* (New York: Regan Arts, 2015). Also, note Dexter Filkins, "In Extremists' Iraq Rise, America's Legacy," *The New Yorker* (June 11, 2014); Shadi Hamid, "The Roots of the Islamic State's Appeal," *The Atlantic* (October 31, 2014); and Sarah Birke,

"How ISIS Rules," *The New York Review of Books* (December 9, 2014). Rukmini Callimachi, Michelle Shephard and Bridget Moreng are important sources as well on the Islamic State. See Callimachi's coverage, for example, of Boko Haram's allegiance to the Islamic State in *The New York Times* (March 7, 2015). Shephard is the author of *Decade of Fear* (Madeira Park: Douglas & McIntyre, 2011) and the *Toronto Star*'s national security reporter. Moreng is a threat analyst at Valens Global, a new security firm founded by Daveed Gartenstein-Ross, a leading terrorism expert.

[3] For extensive interaction with Wood and Haykel, see the online analysis by, among others, Hamza Yusuf, Murtaza Hussain, Shadi Hamid, Robert Wright (in *The New Yorker*), Hamid Dabashi, Eamon Murphy, J. M. Berger and Andrew Anderson. The latter argued that the Islamic State owes its ideology more to the 13th century than the 7th century. Caner K. Dagli wrote an online response on *The Atlantic* site. Dagli, Adis Duderija, Kecia Ali, Anver Emon, Walid Saleh and many other academics wrote extensive comments about the Wood article on the American Academy of Religion email distribution list on Islam. In parallel, French academics are currently involved in extensive debate over Michel Houellebecq's novel *Soumission*. On this, see Mark Lilla, "Slouching Toward Mecca," *The New York Review of Books* (April 3, 2015), online.

[4] For recent concerns about America's reach, see, for example, David Cole, "Must Counterterrorism Cancel Democracy?," *The New York Review of Books* (January 8, 2015), and the interview with Noam Chomsky at *Salon* (February 16, 2015).

[5] President Obama received major criticism for his comments about the Crusades when he addressed the National Prayer Breakfast on February 5, 2015. His remarks about the Crusades were minimal and in a context where non-Christian evils were mentioned. Of most importance, he gave significant push for freedom of religion and freedom of speech around the world. What complicates appreciation for democracy and freedom, of course, is the fact that democratic means can be used to pursue ultimately illiberal ends. On this, see Shadi Hamid, *Temptations of Power* (New York: Oxford University Press, 2014).

[6] For analysis of American failure in Iraq, see, for example, Jon Lee Anderson, "What the War in Iraq Wrought," *The New Yorker* (January

15, 2014); Dexter Filkins, "What We Left Behind," *The New Yorker* (April 28, 2014); and Ali Khedery, "Why we stuck with Maliki and lost Iraq," *Washington Post* (July 13, 2014).

[7] A largely negative verdict on Islam, the view of this book, in no way demands adoption of baseless claims like Islam is totally wrong or all Muslims are terrorists, etc. We hope that our critics do not dismiss our serious work with allegations that we are Islamophobic, an all too common and often careless reaction to strong critics of Islam. While some critics are careless, most legitimately focus on huge issues like lack of freedom in many Islamic countries, rigidity in Islamic law, abuse of women in some Islamic traditions, anti-Jewish and anti-Christian bias and persecution, negativities in the traditional portrait of Muhammad and troubling issues in the Qur'an. On the latter, see Bahis Sedq (a pseudonym), *The Quran Speaks* (Indianapolis: Dog Ear Publishing, 2013). Regardless of legitimate worries about Islamic law among critics of Islam, it is imperative that experts on shariah law be consulted since it is a vast and complex field. On this, see, for example, the works of Mashood Baderin (London), Anver Emon (Toronto), Wael Hallaq (Columbia) and Faisal Kutty (Valparaiso).

[8] Aslan has critiqued Maher on various issues related to Islam. Aslan had a very testy exchange on CNN with Alisyn Camerota and Don Lemon, on September 29, 2014, about Maher. While Aslan deserves credit for apologizing for one of his remarks to Camerota, he constantly hurts his credibility by overstatement and non sequiturs. In that interview he called Saudi Arabia the "closest ally" of America (closer than Canada or Israel or the UK!) and opined that "women are absolutely 100 percent equal to men" in Indonesia. The Gender Gap Index places Indonesia in 97th place out of 142 countries.

[9] For appreciation of the article and use of it to critique Islam in a general sense, see online comments by Rush Limbaugh, Glenn Beck and Robert Spencer. Roger Cohen, an op-ed columnist for *The New York Times*, wrote about "Islam and the West at War" just after the controversy erupted over Graeme Wood's piece. Cohen's op-ed (February 16, 2015) was critiqued in a piece by Robert Wright in *The New Yorker* ("The Clash of Civilizations that Isn't" in the February 25, 2015, issue).

[10] In relation to Islam, a more open version from the Islamic past is celebrated by Gerard Russell, author of *Heirs to Forgotten Kingdoms:*

*Journeys into the Disappearing Religions of the Middle East* (New York: Basic Books, 2014), in an interview with Graeme Wood for *The Boston Globe* (November 16, 2014, online). Hans Küng in his *Islam: Past, Present & Future* (Oxford: Oneworld, 2007) commends the Islam of Spain in the 10th and 11th centuries without overstating the freedoms offered to Jews and Christians (376f.). This more moderate Islam is also commended as historical Islam by Zachary Karabell in his work *Peace Be Upon You* (New York: Vintage, 2009) and by Fareed Zakaria, one of the most famous Muslim American public figures. On a more skeptical note, Ayaan Hirsi Ali, the famous ex-Muslim dissident, has called for a reformation in Islam that leads to a more humane version of the religion. See her "Why Islam Needs a Reformation," *The Wall Street Journal* (March 21, 2015), and *Heretic: Why Islam Needs a Reformation Now* (New York: HarperCollins, 2015). Given her courage in speaking out against major weaknesses in Islam, it is regrettable that Brandeis University withdrew its offer of an honorary degree to her.

[11] While Lewis is not beyond critique, he does not deserve the vitriol he receives on various sites on the Internet. For an example of his balanced and erudite assessment of Islam, note his lecture at the Hebrew University of Jerusalem on "Radical Islam's War against the West" (available at https://www.youtube.com/watch?v=a9RXdovHKtE). The same remarkable felicity in balance combined with erudition is shown in Michael Cook's *Forbidding Wrong in Islam* (Cambridge: Cambridge University Press, 2003) and lecture on "The Appeal of Islamic Fundamentalism" at the British Academy.

[12] It is ironic that those who argue opposite views on whether Islam is a religion of peace often share similar appreciation for democracy, freedom of religion and egalitarian views of women. See, for example, the IQ2 debate with Maajid Nawaz (Quilliam) and Zeba Khan (founder of Muslim-Americans for Obama) versus Ayaan Hirsi Ali and Douglas Murray. While Ali and Murray won the debate, they obviously respect the kind of Islam envisioned by Nawaz and Khan.

# Index of Scripture
# and Ancient Writings

## Old Testament

# Old Testament Apocrypha

# New Testament

# Pseudepigrapha

# Dead Sea Scrolls

# Later Jewish Writers

## Josephus

### Antiquities

| | |
|---|---|
| 4.152 | 71 |
| 5.104 | 71 |
| 17.149–67 | 74 |
| 18.63–64 | 32, 177 |
| 20 | 178 |
| 20.200–201 | 178 |

### Jewish Wars

| | |
|---|---|
| 1.648–55 | 74 |
| 1.653 | 74 |
| 1.654 | 74 |
| 5.193–94 | 73 |
| 6.300–309 | 232 |
| 7.270 | 74 |

## Philo

### Allegorical Interpretation

| | |
|---|---|
| 3.242 | 71 |

### Confusion

| | |
|---|---|
| 57 | 71 |

### Migration

| | |
|---|---|
| 146 | 189 |

### To Gaius

| | |
|---|---|
| 212 | 72 |
| 242 | 72 |

### Unchangeable

| | |
|---|---|
| 159 | 189 |

# Rabbinic Literature

## Mishnah

### 'Abot

| | |
|---|---|
| 4.16 | 189 |

### Tosefta

### Hullin

| | |
|---|---|
| 2.22–23 | 302 |

### Shabbat

| | |
|---|---|
| 11.15 | 303 |

## Talmud (Babli)

### Sanhedrin

| | |
|---|---|
| 43a | 171 |
| 106a | 169 |
| 107b | 303 |

### Shabbat

| | |
|---|---|
| 104b | 303 |
| 116b | 186–87 |

### Sota

| | |
|---|---|
| 47a | 303 |

# Later Christian Writers and Writings

## Justin Martyr

*Dial. with Trypho*

90   179

## Macarius Magnes

*Apocriticus*

2.14–15   180

## Origen

*Against Celsus*

1.28   302
1.32   169
1.38   169
1.39   302
2.34–39   180

## Polycarp

*Philippians*

9:2   185
11:2   185

## Shepherd of Hermas

*Similitudes*

9   59

*Visions*

3   59

# Greek and Roman Writers

## Lucian

*Peregrinus*

§11   180
§13   180

## Pliny the Younger

*Letters*

10.96   35

## Tacitus

*Annals*

15.44   35, 179

# Other Writers and Literature

# CASTLE QUAY BOOKS
## www.castlequaybooks.com

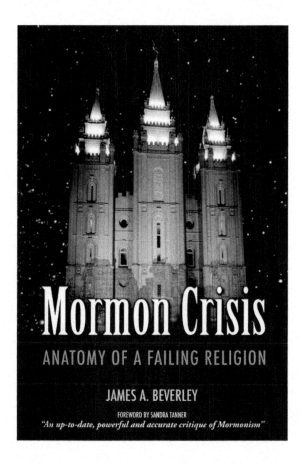

# Mormon Crisis
## ANATOMY OF A FAILING RELIGION

### JAMES A. BEVERLEY

FOREWORD BY SANDRA TANNER

*"An up-to-date, powerful and accurate critique of Mormonism"*

In *Mormon Crisis*, Dr. Jim Beverley deals with major issues about Joseph Smith, the first LDS prophet. He provides a sustained critique of Mormon Scripture, examines flaws in the LDS understanding of church leadership, and probes unique doctrines and practices, including the secret temple ceremonies. This book offers a serious indictment of the LDS belief system and presents a way out of the current crisis facing one of America's most famous and controversial religions.

ISBN 978-1-927355-32-9

CPSIA information can be obtained
at www.ICGtesting.com
Printed in the USA
LVOW01s2121040716

495098LV00011B/158/P